REFERENCE
SOURCES
FOR SMALL AND
MEDIUM-SIZED
LIBRARIES

REFERENCE SOURCES
FOR SMALL AND MEDIUM-SIZED
LIBRARIES

EIGHTH EDITION

JACK O'GORMAN, EDITOR

AN IMPRINT OF THE
AMERICAN LIBRARY ASSOCIATION
CHICAGO • 2014

© 2014 by the American Library Association

Printed in the United States of America

18 17 16 15 14   5 4 3 2 1

Extensive effort has gone into ensuring the reliability of the information in this book; however, the publisher makes no warranty, express or implied, with respect to the material contained herein.

ISBNs: 978-0-8389-1212-6 (paper); 978-0-8389-1975-0 (PDF); 978-0-8389-1976-7 (ePub); 978-0-8389-1977-4 (Kindle). For more information on digital formats, visit the ALA Store at alastore.ala.org and select eEditions.

Library of Congress Cataloging-in-Publication Data
Reference sources for small and medium-sized libraries / Jack O'Gorman, editor. — Eighth Edition.
    pages cm
  Includes bibliographical references and index.
    ISBN 978-0-8389-1212-6 (acid-free paper)   1. Reference books—Bibliography.   2. Small libraries—United States—Book lists.   I. O'Gorman, Jack.
   Z1035.1.A47 2014
   011'.02—dc23
                                     2013049993

Cover design by Kimberly Thornton. Image ©Shutterstock, Inc.

Text design in the Berkeley and Helvetica typefaces. Composition by Scribe, Inc.

♾ This paper meets the requirements of ANSI/NISO Z39.48-1992 (Permanence of Paper).

CONTENTS

9 *Science and Technology*   *99*

PREFACE

I would like to welcome you to the eighth edition of *Reference Sources for Small and Medium-Sized Libraries*. Many of the experienced team who were involved with the seventh edition have returned for this one. Additionally, other subject experts have joined us to present a guide to reference sources for libraries.

Forty years ago, the preface to the second edition stated, "This edition is a product of its own time." Once again, the focus is on new reference sources published since the last edition (in 2008) and reference titles that have retained their relevance. A few classic titles that are now out of print have also been included. Most of the titles are intended for a North American readership. In keeping with tradition, chapters, except for the first, have been organized more or less according to the Dewey Decimal Classification (DDC) system. Brief DDC and Library of Congress (LC) call numbers are included to help subject selectors with recommended titles in their areas. Online resources do not have call numbers. As always, inclusion in this guide constitutes a firm recommendation for acquisition or retention of a title in the reference or circulating areas of your library, or as part of your online public access catalog (OPAC).

Size

The size of the library remains an important criterion for inclusion. This guide, as its title suggests, is designed to be particularly relevant to smaller and medium-sized libraries. According to the staff of the ALA Library, the criteria for public libraries based on population served are as follows:

> Fewer than 10,000 = very small
> 10,000 to 24, 999 = small
> 25,000 to 99,999 = medium
> 100,000 to 499,999 = large
> More than 500,000 = very large

Libraries that fall into the first three categories are the main audience for this guide.

Cost

Cost, always an important factor in selection, is indicated in this guide by the following shorthand:

Free	Free
$	Less than $100
$$	$100–499
$$$	$500–$1,000
$$$$	More than $1000
CP$	Contact publisher for price
OP	Out of print

This edition lists an impressive number of electronic resources available at no cost. I suggest to librarians to include some or all of the free resources described in this guide in their OPAC. Two examples of particularly helpful resources are the Directory of Open Access Journals and the *Encyclopedia of Life*.

Format

Electronic reference sources have evolved significantly in the last five years. In fact, the reader can now assume that many if not most of the titles in this guide are available in electronic form. Beginning with the fifth edition, ISBNs (and, for series, ISSNs) were listed along with titles. But with the proliferation of formats and versions, each one typically having its own identifier, it was decided not to include them in this edition. Today's librarians and library science students have the tools to find resources given basic bibliographic information. They also should be able to decide which e-book vendor best suits their library.

Meanwhile, printed reference collections are getting smaller. My own library's collection has shrunk by about half in the last five years. Keeping up with electronic versions of reference titles as they become available can be challenging for a reference librarian. The library's OPAC, then, assumes a more central role, and it is discussed at length in a new section on library search tools at the end of chapter 1.

What's New?

About 40 percent of the content is new to this edition. Some of the chapters have reorganized headings to better match a more modern and consistent way of organizing sources. The relatively short biography chapter has been merged into chapter 1. All content was checked for continued relevancy, and most of the annotations were updated.

Alongside the continued growth of electronic sources, a significant change since the last edition is the increase in consolidated reference resources. An example of this is Oxford Music Online. These consolidated sources are great for smaller libraries if they can afford the price. If not, some of the titles may be available in either electronic or print form as stand-alone products or as subsets of the larger collection. This guide, which lists nearly a dozen such options for Oxford Music Online alone, has been designed to help small and medium-sized libraries maximize their buying power by making the right choices.

Acknowledgments

I am impressed with the depth of subject knowledge of the contributors and with the quality of their recommendations. I am also pleased with the number of new titles corralled for this edition. I would like to thank the contributors for their hard work on this project. I would also like to thank Thomas Weitzel from the University of Dayton for his advice during the editing of this work. And I would like to thank J. Michael Jeffers and Jenni Fry at ALA. All the contributors to this edition were great; we had fun in the process of writing this book. I would also like to give my wife, Kathy, a very special thanks for all her love and support while I compiled this edition. I'm proud to see it come together and I hope that you enjoy the results.

General Reference

JACK O'GORMAN, BARBARA M. BIBEL,
AND CAROLYN M. MULAC

This chapter stands out from the other chapters in this book. Whereas chapters 2–19 are arranged by subject, this one is a general reference resource guide. It includes almanacs, bibliographies, and guides to the literature, biographical sources (formerly a stand-alone chapter), general-purpose databases, and Internet search sites. Library search tools such as discovery layers are also described here. The Internet continues to have a huge impact on reference services. Some of that influence is via search interfaces like Oxford Reference or general databases like Academic Search Complete. It can also be seen with Internet sources that go beyond the library, like Google Search or Facebook. This chapter hopes to guide reference librarians by describing these changes.

Almanacs and Fact Books

1   Canadian almanac and directory.
Grey House, Canada. Annual. CP$
971.00   AY414
This is the source for all things Canadian. It includes business and government information, maps and charts, traditional almanac features such as a perpetual calendar and weights and measures, and listings for associations.

2   CQ researcher. CQ Press. Weekly. CP$
CQ Researcher offers comprehensive, original reporting and analysis of the major issues in the world. Weekly reports on topics such as the changing demographics of the Unites States and vanishing biodiversity in the world provide information on all sides of the issue. The researcher also covers U.S. elections and the proceedings of Congress. The print issues include an annual bound volume. This is an essential resource for academic, school, and larger public libraries.

3   Guinness world records. Guinness
World Records. Annual. $
032   AG243
This is a guide to the world's superlatives, both natural and human. It commemorates the tallest, shortest, biggest, smallest, and so on, with charts, graphs, and color photographs. It has a detailed index.

**4   Statistical abstract of the United
States.** U.S. Census Bureau, U.S.
Government Printing Office, 1878–2012.
Annual. $
317.3   HA202
The 2012 issue of this indispensable resource is the last one published by the Government Printing

Office and the Census Bureau. ProQuest and Bernan will continue to publish it online and in print, respectively. Contact the new publishers for pricing information. The *Statistical Abstract* contains a wealth of information about all aspects of life in the United States as well as a section on international statistics. Since all tables cite their sources, libraries may want to retain the last edition as a finding aid to other government statistical resources. The volume is arranged by subject area and contains a detailed index.

5 **The world almanac and book of facts.** World Almanac. Annual. $

317   AY67

Containing a wealth of statistical material, this title is an excellent ready reference. It includes information for current and preceding years, astronomical information, and quick facts about major events, states and countries, and associations and societies. The publisher offers free "bonus content" at www .worldalmanac.com.

Bibliographies and Guides

Readers' Advisory

6 **Book lust: Recommended reading for every mood, moment, and reason.** Nancy Pearl. 287p. Sasquatch Books, 2003. $

011   Z1035

More book lust: Recommended reading for every mood, moment, and reason. Nancy Pearl. 286p. Sasquatch Books, 2005. $

011   Z1035

Book crush: For kids and teens: Recommended reading for every mood, moment, and interest. Nancy Pearl. 288p. Sasquatch Books, 2007. $

028.5   Z1037

Book lust to go: Recommended reading for travelers, vagabonds, and dreamers. Nancy Pearl. 301p. Sasquatch Books, 2010. $

011.6   Z6004

The author of these titles is the well-known readers' advisory librarian Nancy Pearl. They can be fun for patrons looking for something to read and for librarians wishing to expand their reading interests. Chapters are by categories, which can be whimsical. There is a title index for serious folk, but everybody else can enjoy browsing through "Chick Lit," "Dreaming of Africa," "Here Be Dragons," or "Zero: This Will Mean Nothing to You." Recommendations come in the text or in lists. The second title, *More Book Lust*, is, according to the author, more of a companion than a sequel and consists of titles that the author had to leave out of the first volume along with suggestions from librarians, readers, and friends. Some categories include "Other People's Shoes," "Gone Fishin'," and "Fractured Fairy Tales." *Book Crush* includes titles recommended for kids and teen readers, and *Book Lust to Go* recommends titles for both armchair travelers and adventurers.

7 **Great books for girls: More than 600 books to inspire today's girls and tomorrow's women.** Rev. ed. Kathleen Odean. 420p. Ballantine, 2002. $

028.1   Z1037

Mary Pipher, author of *Reviving Ophelia*, states about this title: "I recommend it for all those who want girls to grow up strong, free, bold, and kind." The revised edition includes 294 new books and more than 600 total books portraying girls in a positive light. The author draws on her experience as a children's librarian to find stories of girls and women "who face the world with courage, either from the first or after overcoming their fears." The chapters include picture books and storybooks, folktales, books for beginning readers, books for middle readers, books for older readers, and poetry. Entries contain author, title, illustrator, publishing information, age range, and annotation. If titles were Newbery or Caldecott winners, this is mentioned in the annotation. Magazines and websites for girls are included along with author and title indexes.

8 **1001 children's books you must read before you grow up.** Julia Eccleshare. 960p. Universe, 2009. $

011.62   Z1037

This source is a guide to recommended children's literature. Arranged by age group, each entry includes a colorful graphic from the book, bibliographic information, and a summary of the work. It is highly browsable and includes many classics of children's literature. Great to help young readers find books to read, and for adults to remember the classics of their youth.

9   Quick and popular reads for teens.
Pam Spencer Holley. 228p. American Library Association, 2009. $
028.5   Z1037
The Young Adult Library Services Association has a long history of readers' advisory for teenage readers. This book comes from the Quick Picks for Reluctant Readers and Popular Paperbacks for Young Adult programs. Its purpose is to provide librarians and others interested in teen literature with "quick and popular" titles. This title will be useful in libraries serving teen readers.

10   Serving boys through readers' advisory. Michael Sullivan. 152p. American Library Association, 2010. $
028.5   Z1039
This guide by a children's librarian and teachers helps librarians reach boys as readers. It includes lists of great authors for boys and has more than 500 books to recommend. There is a chapter called "If your first thought is . . ." Instead of recommending *Old Yeller*, it suggests *Rescue Josh McGuire* by Ben Mikaelsen. This guide can help you help boys become successful readers.
See also **"Children's Literature," in chapter 17.**

Reference Guides

11   Guide to reference. 12th ed. Robert Kieft, ed. American Library Association, 2008. www.guidetoreference.com. CP$
011   Z1035
Since its publication in 1902, *Guide to Reference Books* has become the standard resource for reference sources and is used to answer users' questions, train staff, educate library science students, create local bibliographic materials, and develop collections. *Guide to Reference* is the first online edition and the first to incorporate Internet sources. It is organized by academic disciplines and contains new categories such as "Interdisciplinary Fields," "The Web as Reference Tool," and "Online

General Reference Libraries." Content and internal category organization were significantly revised for this edition to reflect new sources and changes in publishing and information-seeking behavior. The interface affords multiple browse and search functions and interactive features.

12   Introduction to reference work. 8th ed. William A. Katz. 2v. McGraw-Hill, 2002. $
025.5   Z711
Frequently used as a text, this title has the beginning or inexperienced reference librarian as its audience. Volume 1 deals with basic information sources and is arranged by form of materials. Volume 2 covers reference sources, processes, evaluation, and techniques, including online reference. It addresses not only printed sources but electronic ones, where the reference librarian acts as a "key professional information expert."

13   Magazines for libraries. 20th ed. Cheryl LaGuardia, ed. Bill Katz, creator. 898p. ProQuest, 2012. $$$
This annual title is an important selection tool with an annotated listing of journals recommended by subject specialists. It can help libraries determine which periodicals or databases they should subscribe to. Entries are listed alphabetically by title within subject categories and include information about intended audience and publication details— for instance, where the journal is indexed and whether it is peer reviewed. About 5,500 annotations of recommended journals for public and academic libraries are listed. The introduction includes a discussion of library journal trends, including the end of the "big deal" and progress with discovery tools. Available electronically, but this source is still viable in print.

14   The Oxford guide to library research. 3rd ed. Thomas Mann. 293p. Oxford, 2005. $
025.5   Z710
The third edition of this title presents what research libraries can offer that the Internet cannot. The author has a PhD and is a former private investigator. He has also worked as a reference librarian at the Library of Congress Reading Room. The audience is readers who need to know about modern research methods. It could be an excellent text for

library science students or for university research-methodology classes. It focuses on books and other resources available to large research libraries and has a structure around nine methods of subject searching: controlled-vocabulary searching, subject-classified book stacks, keyword searching, citation searching, related-record searching, subject bibliographies, Boolean searching, using the subject expertise of people, and type-of-literature searching. It also covers encyclopedias, indexes to journal articles, review articles, published bibliographies, search limiters, finding materials in other libraries, reference sources, and special subjects and formats. Interestingly, there is an appendix on wisdom.

15 Resources for college libraries.
American Library Association and R. R. Bowker, 2007. www.RCLweb.net. CP$
This source presents a core collection for undergraduate libraries, including recommended reference titles and web resources. It is organized into broadly defined subject areas such as humanities, languages and literature, history, social sciences and professional studies, science and technology, and interdisciplinary and area studies. Entries indicate if they have previously appeared in *Books for College Libraries* or *Choice*. The print version of the 2007 edition is also available. For the electronic edition, pricing is based on FTE enrollment.

Reference Review Journals

16 Choice reviews online. American Library Association. www.cro2.org. CP$
This resource, required for all academic libraries, is also valuable to medium-sized and larger public libraries. Each issue includes reviews of a sizable number of reference sources appropriate for the undergraduate library. The reviews are brief, critical, comparative, and signed. Each May issue features "Outstanding Academic Books and Nonbook Materials." *Choice Reviews Online* supports advanced searching and includes My Monthly Reviews and My Lists features. Users can browse, e-mail, print, and download any reviews, bibliographic essays, forthcoming title lists, or outstanding title lists.

17 Library journal. Library Journal, 1976–. $$
020   Z671

This journal is useful even in the smallest library. A good part of each issue is devoted to current events in libraries and book reviews, including reference books. The reviews are brief, signed, timely, and critical. Online databases are frequently discussed in articles and columns, and the use of technology in libraries is a focus of the journal.

18 Reference and user services quarterly.
Reference and User Services Association, 1997–. $
025.5   Z671
The "Sources" section of this journal contains reviews of databases, reference books, and professional reading. The reviews are critical, comparative, and written by practicing librarians or educators. Useful for the evaluation and selection of reference sources and to keep up with topics in reference.

19 Reference services review: RSR.
Pierian Press, 1973–. $$
011   Z1035
This journal is a timely acquisition for medium-sized to larger reference departments. Rather than isolated reviews of just-published books, *RSR* provides a generous number of review essays, most focusing on a particular subject or type of reference source. Whether the articles are literature surveys, comparative reviews, core collections, or examinations of databases, they are highly informative and cover a broad range of issues and sources important to reference services.

20 School library journal. Reed Business Information, 1961–. $$
027.8   Z675
One of the standard selection tools for libraries serving children and young adults. Approximately half of each issue is devoted to reviews, including audiovisual materials, computer software, and about 3,000 books each year. Because so few reference sources are published for young people, however, most of these reviews are for circulating books. Of particular interest to reference librarians is the annual "Reference Books Roundup" in the May issue.

21 Voice of youth advocates. E. L. Kurdyla Publishing, 1978–. $
027.62   Z718

This journal is an essential purchase for libraries serving young adults. It contains up-to-date features about teen activities and practical articles about dealing with teens in the library. In addition to news, comments, and features, *VOYA* is also useful for its reviews and collection development articles. The journal examines a variety of materials, including reference sources. The reviews are usually two to three paragraphs long and evaluate the sources in light of their value and appeal to young adults.

Biography

22 **American national biography online.** American Council of Learned Societies and Oxford. www.anb.org. CP$

Oxford University Press and the American Council of Learned Societies published the *ANB* in 1999 as both a print and electronic resource. Includes 19,000 biographies of women and men from colonial times to the present. Entries are for deceased individuals only and include bibliography, cross-references, and some photos. The online version includes the *Oxford Companion to United States History* and links to the *Oxford Dictionary of National Biography*.

23 **Biography and genealogy master index.** Gale Cengage. www.gale.com. CP$

Originally a print product, this source functions very well as a subscription database. Searchable by multiple entry points, including name, dates, portrait, and source. More than 15 million biographies are included from ninety sources.

24 **Biography in context.** Gale Cengage. www.gale.com. CP$

More than 600,000 biographies drawn from nearly 200 Gale reference titles are available in this rich subscription database. Tip sheets, video tutorials, free lesson plans, and downloadable apps are available.

25 **Biography source.** EBSCO. www.ebsco host.com/us-high-schools/biography -collection-complete. CP$

This database, which debuted in 2013, includes more than 600,000 biographies and obituaries

drawn from a variety of titles, including *Notable American Women*, the *Cambridge Dictionary of American Biography*, and *Current Biography*.

26 **The Cambridge biographical encyclopedia.** 2nd ed. David Crystal. 1179p. Cambridge, 1998. OP
920   CT103

Although currently out of print, this is one title to retain. Its 16,000 entries are cross-referenced and include pronunciation guides. Some 150 pages of lists, of popes, kings, Nobel Prize winners, and the like, are useful for ready reference.

27 **Current biography illustrated.** EBSCO. www.ebscohost.com/academic/ current-biography-illustrated. CP$

A searchable database comprising of the content of the printed *Current Biography* magazine, first published in 1955 by H. W. Wilson. Includes more than 25,000 articles and obituaries and more than 19,500 images. Also available in print through Salem Press (www.salempress.com).
Encyclopedia of women in today's world, see **292.**

28 **Encyclopedia of world biography.** 2nd ed. Gale Cengage, 1998–. $$$$
920   CT103

A well-known biographical reference source with thousands of biographies of world leaders. Entries include portrait, biography, and bibliography. Entrants were chosen "for their contributions to human culture and society [and] reputations that stand the test of time." Although older, this resource is useful for biographies of historical individuals.

29 **Marquis who's who on the web.** Marquis Who's Who. www. marquiswhoswho.com. CP$

The site includes 1.5 million entries of persons who have been listed in any Marquis publication since 1985. This comprehensive resource, which includes the birth and death dates, background, education, and career of its biographees, is updated daily.

30 **The Nobel Prize.** Nobel Media. www .nobelprize.org. Free

The official Nobel Prize website lists all the winners of each prize and includes their biographies and acceptance speeches as well as general information about the prizes and how the winners are selected.

31 Oxford dictionary of national biography. Oxford. www.oxforddnb .com. CP$

Contains 58,326 biographies and 10,972 portraits of people who "shaped the history of the British Isles and beyond." This means that George Washington is included, but the point of view is quite different. The entries include cross-references and bibliographies. The bibliography feature will search local library catalogs.

Databases and Indexes

32 Academic search premier. EBSCO. www.ebscohost.com/academic/academic -search-premier. CP$
InfoTrac. Cengage Learning. http://info trac.thomsonlearning.com. CP$
ProQuest 5000. ProQuest. www.pro quest.com/en-US/catalogs/databases/ detail/pq_5000.shtml. CP$

Every library needs a general-purpose database. The ones that come to mind are EBSCO's Academic Search Premier, Gale Cengage's InfoTrac, and ProQuest 5000. Librarians should evaluate these options according to coverage, indexing, interface, ease of use, and limiters. Access should be to PDF full text, and the preferred database should be OpenURL link enabled. The database that a library chooses is up to the library and its consortium. Reference librarians should be very familiar with their multipurpose database and its functionality.

Directories

33 American library directory: A classified list of libraries in the United States and Canada, with personnel and statistical data. Information Today, 1923–. $$
021   Z731

This directory includes U.S. and Canadian public, academic, and special libraries arranged by state or province, city, and institution. Entries include name and address of school, key personnel, and library holdings. Income expenditures, e-mail addresses, subject specialties, automation, publications, and a code for type of library are also included. Additional sections include listings of networks and consortia; library schools; library systems; libraries for the blind, deaf, and disabled; state and provincial public library agencies; the interlibrary loan code; and armed forces libraries overseas. Includes an organizational and personnel index.

Annual register of grant support: A directory of funding sources, **see 310.**

34 Directories in print. 2v. Gale, 1989–. $$$
300   Z5771

Describes and indexes 16,000 directories of all kinds, arranged in twenty-six broad subject categories. A detailed subject index and thesaurus has more than 4,700 terms and cross-references. Entries give title, subtitle, publisher's address, telephone number, description of contents, arrangement, coverage, frequency, usual month of publication, pages, indexes, price, editor's name, and ISBN, GPO, or other pertinent numbers. Volume 1 covers descriptive listings; volume 2 contains the subject and title and keyword indexes. Includes supplements as they appear. Available in electronic format as part of Gale's Ready Reference Shelf.

35 Encyclopedia of associations. Frederick G. Ruffner, Margaret Fisk, and Gale Research Company. 5v. Gale, 1961–. $$$
060   AS22

Contains essential information on more than 22,000 national membership organizations representing numerous business, social, educational, religious, fraternal, ethnic, and vocational interests. Convention and meeting dates and locations and titles of organizations' directories and publications are included in the entries. There are also international and regional volumes. Volume 1 covers the Great Lakes states; volume 2, Northeastern states; volume 3, Southern and Middle Atlantic states; volume 4, South Central and Great Plains states; and volume 5, the Western states. Libraries should subscribe to the national and at least their regional directory. Available online as part of the Gale Directory Library.

36 The Foundation directory. Foundation Center, 1960–. CP$
061   AS911

The Foundation Center publishes *The Foundation Directory*, *Foundation Grants to Individuals*, and *Directory of Corporate Giving*. These guides offer information about grants and grant makers as well as companies with philanthropic programs. The online directory is updated weekly. The website also includes news, blogs, webinars, tutorials, live chat, and a mobile app. Libraries may apply to become affiliate collections and receive these products at a lower price. The directories are arranged by state with four indexes: state and city; donors, trustees, and administrators; foundation name; and fields of interest. Contact the publisher for pricing and affiliation arrangements.

37 Gale directory of publications and broadcast media. 5v. Gale, 1990–. $$$
302.23   Z6951

This is a geographical listing of newspapers, magazines, radio stations, and other publications in the United States and abroad. The first two volumes include the United States and Canada. Volume 3 contains the indexes, while volume 4 has regional market indexes. Volume 5 includes international coverage. Indexes include a subject index, agricultural publications, foreign-language publications, fraternal publications, magazines, newspapers, trade and professional publications, and a master index. Newsletters and directories are excluded. Defunct organizations are removed from entries and listed in the index as ceased or unable to locate. Entries include title, publisher contact information, e-mail address, description, subtitle, date founded, frequency, circulation, online availability, ad rates, and editors. Great for finding local newspapers and radio stations. It is also part of the Gale Directory Library.

38 International directory of little magazines and small presses. Dustbooks, 1974–. www.dustbooks.com. $
070.5   Z6944

This directory is now online and includes *The International Directory of Little Magazines and*

Small Presses, *The Directory of Poetry Publishers*, *The Directory of Small Press/Magazine Editors and Publishers*, and *The Small Press Record of Books in Print*. It is a great resource for aspiring authors and librarians who support them.

39 Ulrich's periodicals directory. 4v. Bowker/ProQuest, 1932–. $$$$

Provides directory information on more than 220,000 regular and irregular serials worldwide. Entries include information about where the titles are indexed and whether they are peer reviewed. The directory also includes a list of titles that have ceased publication and a list of publications that are available online. Also available online.

Postal Directories

40 Canada Post. Canada Post Corporation. www.canadapost.ca. Free

This is the official site for Canada Post. It offers information about postal codes, calculating postage rates, finding a post office, or filing a change of address. The site is available in English and French.

41 Correos de México. www.sepomex.gob .mx. Free

The Mexican Postal Service website provides information about postal codes and rates, stamp collecting, package tracking, money orders, and international mail. The site is in Spanish, but parts of it are also available in English.

42 United States Postal Service. USPS. www.usps.com. Free

The U.S. Postal service site provides a zip code directory, information about postal rates and regulations, and a post office look-up tool. Customers with accounts may also arrange for a pickup, print shipping labels, track packages, and buy stamps online.

Electronic Reference Sources

43 ABC-CLIO ebook collection. ABC-CLIO. http://ebooks.abc-clio.com. CP$

According to their website, this collection includes "7,000 encyclopedias, dictionaries, handbooks, and guides from ABC-CLIO, Greenwood Press, Libraries Unlimited, and Praeger." The interface is user-friendly, with many features, including bookmarks, user profiles, and unlimited simultaneous users. It includes a citation formatter for MLA, APA, Chicago, and Harvard styles. It also has a dictionary link to the fourth edition of the *American Heritage College Dictionary*. The OPAC can function as a portal to multiple e-book interfaces that will return the content users are seeking. Public, academic, and school libraries can use this interface for the books from ABC-CLIO and its partners.

44   Credo reference. Credo Reference. http://corp.credoreference.com. CP$

Credo Reference is an online subscription reference service with more than 3.5 million entries from 11,300 reference titles. Its focus is on ready-reference content, and it includes subject dictionaries, biographical data, statistics, quotations, and more. Subscribers can customize pages with library logos and links, create user guides, and generate usage statistics. All the reference titles included are automatically updated and cross-referenced across titles, publishers, and topics.

45   Gale virtual reference library. Gale. www.gale.com/gvrl/. CP$

This interface makes available thousands of reference titles from Gale Cengage and twenty other publishers. Content will depend on what titles your library purchases. Results can be ranked by relevance, document title, publication title, or publication date. A single title or multiple titles can be searched simultaneously. Articles, with photos, are presented in web format, and a citation and URL are included. This interface has continued to mature and develop since the last edition of *Reference Sources for Small and Medium-Sized Libraries*. For example, searches can be performed and content can be automatically translated in fourteen languages, including Chinese. Articles can be downloaded in MP3 format or can be read aloud. Access can be via the library's OPAC or directly through the Gale Virtual Reference Library. Includes a search tab for *Merriam-Webster's Collegiate Dictionary*. This reliable interface is the platform by which much reference content can be made available.

46   LibGuides. Springshare. http://spring share.com/libguides. CP$

LibGuides are today's version of the pathfinders that academic and public librarians have long created. With LibGuides you can create research portals, library instruction modules, course guides, book club pages, and other kinds of customized content geared to meet the reference needs of your patrons. Examples of publicly accessible guides can be found at LibGuides Community (http://libguides.com/community.php), which indexes sites by title, author, institution, and so forth. There is also a special website, Best of LibGuides (http://bestof.libguides.com), where Springshare features a selection of LibGuides created by its clients.

47   Oxford reference. Oxford. www.oxford reference.com. CP$

According to its promotional literature, this product "brings together 2 million-plus entries into a single cross-searchable resource." It includes Oxford Quick Reference, with about 125 dictionaries, and Oxford Reference Library, with about 180 Oxford University Press titles. These titles can be purchased by institutions on a title-by-title basis. Content includes timelines and illustrations, and the interface has a library widget for searching within a browser. Individual entries include full text and illustrations if available. More on this topic and related content is available from the side navigation bars. Content can be printed and saved, and cited in APA, MLA, or Chicago format. It can also be shared via social media. A reference librarian can use this resource for quick definitions from multiple disciplines or for longer encyclopedia articles.

48   Reference universe. Paratext. http:// reference.paratext.com. CP$

This product searches the article titles and indexes of electronic and print encyclopedias, giving librarians and researchers access to content that is not available via the OPAC. Searching is by either keyword or browsing, with the option to show nonlocal results. Advanced searching is also available. Electronic collections searched by Reference Universe include ABC-CLIO eBooks, Credo Reference, Oxford Reference, and Gale Virtual Reference Library. Titles are linked to the library catalog for quick access. Titles owned or leased by the subscribing library are linked to at the title and article level, allowing the library to more fully utilize its existing reference collection.

49   SAGE knowledge platform. SAGE. www.sagepub.com/knowledge.sp. CP$
According to the publisher, this interface is a "social sciences digital library for students, researchers, and faculty." Includes more than 2,500 titles, covering a wide range of SAGE reference content. It can be used as the interface for electronic access to SAGE encyclopedias and guides.

50   Sharpe online reference. www.sharpe -online.com. CP$
This is an electronic interface for reference works published by M. E. Sharpe. Features include an image gallery, primary source archives, web links, and teacher resources. Content can be e-mailed, printed, or bookmarked.

Encyclopedias

Print

51   The World Book encyclopedia. 22v. World Book. Annual. $$$
031   AE5
This is the only remaining print encyclopedia published in the United States. It is appropriate for elementary grades through high school and for general use in the home. Reference librarians rely on it, too. Thousands of signed articles with numerous cross-references, lots of color illustrations and maps, and an index and research guide make it easy for users to find current information on the social sciences, arts, humanities, and physical and life sciences.

Electronic

52   Encyclopedia Britannica. Britannica. www.britannica.com. CP$
The last print edition of this venerable resource appeared in 2010. It is now available only online, with versions suitable for school, public, and academic libraries, as well as versions

in French, Spanish, Japanese, Korean, and simplified Chinese. The site includes a dictionary, audio and video material, access to periodical articles and e-books, and an atlas. It is updated biweekly with selected content updated daily. The site provides limited free access. Individual subscriptions with full access are about $70 per year. Institutional subscribers should contact publisher for pricing.

53   Grolier online. Scholastic. www.grolier .com. CP$
Grolier Online offers access to *The New Book of Knowledge*, *The Grolier Multimedia Encyclopedia*, *Encyclopedia Americana*, and *Nueva Enciclopedia Cumbre*, as well as other sources for students. It includes a world newspaper feature, an atlas, a dictionary, and access to periodical articles and websites. There are separate interfaces for elementary school, middle school, high school/adult, and librarian/educator users.

54   Wikipedia. Wikimedia Foundation. www.wikipedia.org. Free
This free encyclopedia is available online in many languages. Although there has been an increase in oversight, there is still no editorial or authority control. Anyone may contribute an article or edit an existing entry. Content must be "verifiable," without copyright restrictions, and cannot consist of original research. The articles are mostly unsigned. There is lots of good information on arcane subjects, but users should be careful and verify what they find with another reliable source.

55   World Book online. World Book. www .worldbookonline.com. CP$
World Book Online offers authoritative content covering the arts, humanities, sciences and technologies, along with a selection of e-books, periodical articles, and web links. There are audio and video files, maps, an atlas, and a dictionary as well. A variety of interfaces provide options for children, middle and high school students, adults and college students, and those with learning disabilities. There are also French- and Spanish-language versions. The encyclopedia now has a mobile app, too. *World Book Online* is the electronic equivalent of the *World Book Encyclopedia*.

Internet Sources

56 **Alibris.** Alibris. www.alibris.com. Free
Alibris is a website dedicated to the sale of books, movies, and music. It also acts as a middleman for out-of-print and older in-print titles and titles unavailable via other channels. When you search for a title in its huge inventory, you see the available copies, their prices, and a ranking of the reliability of the seller. Alibris for Libraries (http://library.alibris.com) offers collection development support, consolidated shipping, and other features such as wish lists and book fetch.

57 **Amazon.com.** Amazon.com. www
.amazon.com. Free
Amazon.com began as an Internet-based bookstore but has expanded into numerous other retail areas. It is particularly useful for verifying titles and determining their availability. In addition to offering titles currently in print, Amazon.com also functions as a middleman for the sale of used books from third-party vendors. The editorial reviews (from *Library Journal*, *Booklist*, and *Publishers Weekly*) and "search inside this book" feature are also quite helpful.

58 **Bing.** Microsoft. www.bing.com. Free
Bing is the second most popular Internet search engine. Yahoo! Search also uses Bing for its searching. Bing comes as the default search engine on Microsoft Internet Explorer and for Microsoft mobile devices. It has a simple search interface with colorful graphics and links to Outlook.com and Bing Maps. Ties to Internet searching on Facebook give Bing a strong social connection.

59 **Books in print.** R. R. Bowker, 1948–.
www.booksinprint.com/bip/. CP$
This large web-based bibliographic database contains more than 20 million records of print, out-of-print, and forthcoming titles (books, e-books, audiobooks, and videos). It provides full-text reviews and tables of contents as well as contact information for publishers, distributors, and wholesalers. Searching is easy and includes such special features as "The Complete Connection," where you can search for similar titles and also explore titles by topic, genre, setting,

character, location, and time frame. Although there are two subscription levels available, small libraries or those with very limited budgets may opt to use other Internet-based book resources.

60 **Directory of open access journals.**
Infrastructure Services for Open Access.
www.doaj.org. Free
According to its site, the Directory of Open Access Journals (DOAJ), founded in 2003 at Lund University in Sweden, "aims to be comprehensive and cover all open access scientific and scholarly journals that use an appropriate quality control system, and it will not be limited to particular languages or subject area." A link to the Budapest Open Access Initiative (www.budapestopenaccessinitiative.org), an international organization that supports the publication and creation of open access scientific and scholarly journals, explains the concept of open access. Basically, open access journals are journals that make their content freely available on the Internet, with the consent of the copyright holder. Journals listed in DOAJ are peer reviewed, and publishers are required to make the editorial boards of these journals transparent. DOAJ catalogs its resources on the level of journal title and encourages journals to supply article metadata to make its content searchable. As of 2013, there were nearly 10,000 journals listed in DOAJ. This free, online resource can supplement a library's subscriptions and make more articles available to readers. Libraries should also take a look at the Directory of Open Access Books (www.doabooks.org). As of 2013 it included just more than 1,500 titles, but it may continue to grow.

61 **The extreme searcher's Internet handbook: A guide for the serious searcher.** 3rd ed. Randolph Hock. 339p. CyberAge Books, 2010. $
025.04   ZA4230
Okay, so a printed book about Internet searching is a little bit anachronistic, but this guide can get the casual searcher up to speed and searching like an information scientist. It contains chapters on searching basics, portals, specialized directories, search engines, mailing lists, and creating an Internet reference shelf. Sights and sounds, news, online shopping, and Internet publishing and netiquette round out this source.

62   Facebook. Facebook. facebook.com. Free
Facebook has become a phenomenon on the Internet. But how would you use it in reference? One use is to find people, but librarians will want patrons to do their own searching. Your patrons can log in to it to find long-lost classmates, old neighbors, or friends. Other sites that are useful to find people are AnyWho, Switchboard, and Yahoo! People Search. Facebook can also be used to find out about events, through a program sponsor's Facebook page. As the demographic for Facebook ages and becomes more corporate, younger users may move on to alternative services such as Pinterest or Path.

63   Google search. Google. www.google.com.
  Free
Google is not a search engine. It is an advertising company that provides search results and a suite of technology products. According to Google's annual report of January 19, 2012, 96 percent of its revenue for 2011 was from its sale of ads. And in spite of its phenomenal growth and number one ranking among Internet sites, many users have voiced concerns about Google's policies related to privacy, copyright, and censorship. Nonetheless, "google" has become synonymous with search. Google Search incorporates dozens of features, including results for weather and sports, units and currency conversion, a dictionary, maps, flight status, movie times, and package tracking. Google uses Boolean logic to limit searches and includes a number of advanced options—for example, to search a specific domain such as census.gov.

Everybody uses Google Search, but what can librarians add to the mix? How can they use it better, and how can they help users understand what they find? At the very least, librarians should learn how to incorporate advanced search terms and other advanced features to help their clientele go beyond ordinary keyword searching. And it is part of a librarian's role to help users to critically evaluate information. Librarians can teach patrons to consider a source's authority, content, point of view, and other factors in evaluating content.

In addition to Google Search, there are many other useful products from Google. They include Google Earth, Google Books, Google Scholar, Google Images, and YouTube. Google Scholar is OpenURL link enabled and thus allows users to see which libraries subscribe to materials found in a search. Libraries should configure their browsers to allow this feature. YouTube has many useful how-to videos. Google Chrome is a web browser. Google Goggles is imaging software, and Google Wallet is an application for using a cell phone to make purchases. Google Patent is developed in partnership with the United States Patent and Trademark Office. Google is also developing Google literacy lesson plans. Google.org is the philanthropic branch of the company. There is even an interactive Google PAC-MAN Doodle (www.google.com/pacman).

With its many features and products, it seems as if Google has begun to realize the dream Vannevar Bush described in his article "As We May Think" (*Atlantic*, July 1945). Even so, users of this product should remember one of Ronald Reagan's favorite adages, "Trust, but verify."

**64   The Internet: A historical
  encyclopedia.** Hilary W. Poole et al. 3v.
  ABC-CLIO, 2005. $$
  004.67   TK5105.875
The three volumes of this source contain biographies, a chronology, and essays on issues related to the Internet and its history. Forty-four leaders are chronicled in the biography section; most are still living and working in their fields. Sample topics include content filtering, the digital divide, and spam. The index is done volume by volume. Because this resource is appropriate for high school, college, and general readers, it will be useful.

65   Twitter. Twitter. https://twitter.com. Free
Perhaps this annotation should be only 140 characters, the length of a Twitter post, or tweet. Twitter is useful for what is happening right now. It has millions of users updating and posting in real time. It can also be monitored by library staff to see what users are saying about the library. As more students use Twitter, librarians can expect to see reference questions tweeted. This technology will be an opportunity for libraries to reach a different patron base.

66   Tumblr. Yahoo! www.tumblr.com. Free
Founded in 2007 by David Karp, Tumblr is a social networking website and microblogging platform where you can "follow the world's creators." According to the site, you can "post text, photos, quotes, links, music, and videos from your browser,

phone, desktop, email or wherever you happen to be." With more than 100 million blogs and 50 billion posts, you and your patrons are sure to find something of interest.

67   Wolfram|Alpha. Wolfram Research. www.wolframalpha.com. Free

Rather than calling itself a search engine, this site calls itself a computational knowledge engine. It can be very useful for scientific and mathematical communication, but use it with caution for other topics. What this site does well is computation and quick lookups. If you'd like to know what time the dawn was on a particular day, or what time it is in Hawaii right now, this is a great site. You can determine if a number is prime, or look up the Reynolds number. The word usage pattern is very nice, as are the crossword puzzle clues. Two other examples: finding a CAS Registry Number or converting a color from RGB scale to hexadecimal. If the system does not understand your query, the answer is less good. Wolfram|Alpha Pro is available on a subscription basis. Apps for mobile devices are also available, for a small fee. A criticism of this product is that it tends to cite itself as a source. In September 2012, O'Gorman queried it about the population of the Earth. It gave a 2009 estimate, but failed to cite a source (other than itself). A handy site for helping patrons at the reference desk, as long as its limitations are understood.

68   WorldCat. OCLC (Online Computer Library Center). www.worldcat.org. Free

OCLC's WorldCat is "the world's largest network of library content and services" and offers access to more than one billion items in 10,000 libraries worldwide. Users may search for books, music, videos, and digital items and find a library nearby or around the world that owns them. The World-Cat database can be accessed directly or through a local participating library's website. There is now a mobile app (http://worldcatmobile.org) for searching on the go.

69   Yahoo! Yahoo! www.yahoo.com. Free

Begun by two graduate students at Stanford University, Yahoo! was originally based on the Gopher directory at the University of Michigan Library. Yahoo! is a popular e-mail, chat, game, news, and entertainment site. It includes search capability for video, audio, news, directory, shopping, and more. Yahoo! Search is a popular feature that now runs on the Bing search platform. Entertainment, news, and directory information are strengths of Yahoo! The site functions as a portal to help users organize and make sense of the web for popular news topics, videos of dogs on trampolines, or whatever the user may be looking for.

See also "**Computer Science,**" **in chapter 9.**

Library Science

70   ALA glossary of library and information science. 4th ed. Michael Levine-Clark and Toni M. Carter, eds. 288p. American Library Association, 2012. $

020.3   Z1006

Librarianship has its own technical vocabulary, and library science students and seasoned practitioners alike often need a little help in deciphering acronyms and arcane expressions. This concise guide has been updated to include the latest terms in technology and the current processes and systems in use today.

71   Copyright law for librarians and educators. 3rd ed. Kenneth D. Crews. 208p. American Library Association, 2012. $

346.73   KF2995

Copyright law has never been an easy subject to grasp, and with the advent of digital information, it is harder than ever to stay informed about current developments in this area. Crews explains the basics of copyright, rights of ownership, and fair use and discusses the Digital Millennium Copyright Act and its interpretation. Provides useful checklists related to fair use, the TEACH Act and distance education, and making copies for preservation or replacement or for private study, as well as a model letter for permission requests. Also available as an e-book or in a print/e-book bundle.

72   Encyclopedia of library and information sciences. 3rd ed. 5742p. Taylor and Francis, CRC Press, 2010. $$$$

020   Z1006

A comprehensive treatment of the field available electronically as well as in print. Signed articles address archives, information systems, bibliography, records management, knowledge management, informatics, museum studies, and much more. The online subscription offers citation tracking and alerts as well as HTML and PDF format options. This title may be an optional choice for smaller libraries or those on a tight budget.

73   Fundamentals of managing reference collections. Carol A. Singer. 184p. American Library Association, 2012. $
025.2   Z711

Part of the ALA Fundamentals series, this practical guide for any size reference collection covers best practices for collection management, including selection, weeding, staffing, licenses, polices, and more. The reference collection development policy template that appears as an appendix is available at www.alaeditions.org/files/Singer_Reference -Collection-Development-Policy-Template.docx. Also available as an e-book or in a print/e-book bundle.

74   Fundamentals of reference. Carolyn M. Mulac. 131p. American Library Association, 2012. $
025.5   Z711

The newest volume in the ALA Fundamentals series provides a concise yet thorough overview of reference services in the contemporary library. The author covers the major sources that a reference collection should have, the reference interview, telephone and online service, and service to children and young adults. She also discusses reference service for specialized subjects such as law, business, and medicine, reference policies and standards, and the evaluation of reference service. All libraries should have a copy.

75   Library and book trade almanac. 57th ed. Dave Bogart, ed. 850p. Information Today, 2012. $$
020   Z731

Originally published by R. R. Bowker in 1962, this work continues to provide statistical and directory information "of broad interest to the library and publishing worlds." A variety of special reports address the issues and developments of the preceding year. Includes lists of notable books and the ever-useful entry on how to obtain an ISBN. This title was formerly *The Bowker Annual.*

76   Managing the small college library. Rachel Applegate. 349p. Libraries Unlimited, 2010. $
025.1   Z675

Specifically addressing the needs of small or community college libraries, this book offers librarians in those types of institutions "information on every important managerial function specific to their facilities." The key responsibilities of a small college library director are addressed through real-life examples and illustrated in organizational reference charts and discussed in depth. Includes a bibliography for further reading.

77   Practical strategies for library managers. Joan Giesecke. 102p. American Library Association, 2001. $
025.1   Z678

Career advice for library managers from an experienced librarian, author, and management expert. Mentoring, decision making, planning, managing, team building, and other necessary skills are covered in this useful guidebook.

78   Reference and information services: An introduction. 4th ed. Richard E. Bopp and Linda C. Smith, eds. 743p. Libraries Unlimited, 2011. $
025.5   Z711

The latest edition of a popular library science textbook has been thoroughly revised and updated. New contributors add the wisdom of their experience as reference teachers and practitioners. Part 1, "Concepts and Processes," covers new methods and ideas in reference service. Part 2, "Information Sources and Their Use," discusses print and nonprint resources. Includes a companion website.

79   Reference and information services: An introduction. 3rd ed. Kay Ann Cassell and Uma Hiremath. 528p. Neal-Schuman, 2013. $
025.5   Z711

The best introductory reference textbook available (known as *Reference and Information Services in the 21st Century* in previous editions), this book addresses everything from the fundamental concepts of reference service to reference sources, services, management, assessment, collection development, reference 2.0, and the future of information services. A companion website will be updated biannually. Available as an e-book or as a print/e-book bundle.

80 Small public library management.
Jane Pearlmutter and Paul Nelson. 152p. American Library Association, 2012. $
025.1   Z675
This concise handbook offers practical advice on topics including budgeting, personnel, collection management, facilities, services, programs, and much more. Checklists, tips, and "tales from the field" provide a wealth of useful information for the small public library manager.

81 Small public library survival guide: Thriving on less. Herbert B. Landau. 168p. American Library Association, 2008. $
025.1   Z678.6
In this hands-on guide aimed at the small public library faced with funding cuts, Landau provides a variety of successful techniques, practical tools, and tested strategies for generating resources, including funding and marketing programs. Includes samples of press releases, survey questions, and other useful tools.
See also "Bibliographies and Guides," in chapter 1.

Library Search Tools

82 Discovery layer tools.
A discovery layer tool is a search interface designed to make your content more findable. It can be integrated into your existing OPAC. Your library either has a discovery layer product already or is in negotiation for one, perhaps via its consortium. Libraries have lots of content buried in lots of categories. How can the user get to that information? And what role does reference play, and where do the IT folks take over? Reference should have input in picking out the interface. When it arrives, reference librarians should kick the tires, learn about it, and learn what it does and does not do. You will be

instructing users on how to use it. Here are some of your options:

> **BiblioCommons.** www.bibliocommons. com
> **EBSCO Discovery Service.** www.ebsco host.com/discovery
> **Ex Libris Primo.** www.exlibrisgroup .com/category/PrimoOverview
> **Innovative Interfaces Encore.** www.iii .com/products/
> **OCLC WorldCat Local.** www.oclc.org/ worldcat-local.en.html
> **Oracle Endeca.** www.oracle.com
> **Project Blacklight.** http://projectblack light.org
> **Scriblio.** http://scriblio.net
> **Serials Solutions AquaBrowser.** www.serialssolutions.com/en/services/ aquabrowser
> **Serials Solutions Summon.** www.serials solutions.com/en/services/summon
> **SirsiDynix Enterprise.** www.sirsidynix .com/enterprise
> **The Social OPAC.** http://thesocialopac.net
> **VTLS Visualizer.** www.vtls.com/ products/visualizer
> **VuFind.** http://vufind.org

It is beyond the scope of this title to recommend which discovery layer your library should subscribe to. If you do not already have one, reference librarians should participate in the process of its selection. You can find out what other libraries are using at the Library Technology Guides website (see www.librarytechnology.org/discovery.pl).

83 Online public access catalog.
The online public access catalog, or OPAC, is probably the most important reference source in at the reference librarian's toolbox. There are many successful library OPAC developers, including Ex Libris, Innovative Interfaces, OCLC, SirsiDynix, VTLS, and others. These are the same companies that develop discovery layer tools, which can enhance the search capabilities of your existing OPAC. The OPAC is an essential portal. It is a guide to your library's holdings, both print and electronic, including monographs, serials, and everything else. Reference librarians should know

all the ins and outs of their OPAC. They should know how to tell if a book is in remote storage or if a journal is available electronically. With printed reference collections getting smaller, and more reference sources available electronically, the OPAC becomes even more important as an access tool for reference resources.

84 OpenURL link resolver.

This is another important library technology that reference librarians need to be aware of. An OpenURL link resolver takes users from a citation in one database to the full text of the corresponding resource, usually in another database. The results are only as good as the metadata, so if there is an error, a reference librarian needs to understand how the link resolver works and how to follow it to the resource that contains the requested article. With the vast amount of data available, it is also incumbent upon reference librarians to assist cataloging or IT staff when they encounter errors. OpenURL link resolvers are available from EBSCO, Ex Libris, Innovative Interfaces, OCLC, Ovid, Serials Solutions, SirsiDynix, Swets, and other companies. Homegrown link resolvers such as OhioLINK's OLinks are also viable options.

2 Philosophy, Religion, and Ethics

BARBARA M. BIBEL

There are few general reference sources in philosophy, so librarians continue to rely on classics such as *The Encyclopedia of Philosophy*. Sources on religion, however, are abundant. New ones appear daily. As our population becomes increasingly diverse, our collections should reflect changing interests. Sources on Asian religions, Islam, and nontraditional religions and movements should join the Judeo-Christian materials on the shelves. Some sources on mythology, superstition, and folklore are included in this chapter because they reflect the ancient social traditions that are the basis of Western culture.

Philosophy

Databases and Indexes

85   Philosopher's index. Philosopher's Information Center, 1967–. CP$

This is the principal index in the field, covering philosophy and the philosophy of other academic disciplines. It has an author index with abstracts as well as subject and book review indexes. Also available through EBSCO and Ovid.

Dictionaries and Encyclopedias

86   Cambridge dictionary of philosophy.
2nd ed. Robert Audi, ed. 1039p.
Cambridge, 1999. $
103   B41

Compiled by an international team of 436 scholars, this edition has 400 new entries with 50 covering contemporary philosophers. The definitions are clear and thorough and cover non-Western philosophy, applied ethics, and the philosophy of the mind as well as traditional philosophical subjects.

87   Encyclopedia of classical philosophy.
Donald J. Zeyl, ed. 630p. Fitzroy
Dearborn, 1997. $$
180.3   B163

The only current encyclopedia devoted to classical philosophy, this covers the teachings, schools, and philosophers of ancient Greece and Rome.

88   Encyclopedia of philosophy. 2nd ed.
Donald Borchert, ed. 10v. Gale, 2005.
$$$$
103   B51

First published in 1967, this classic is the first stop for research in philosophy. The second edition contains material from an international group of scholars. It has more than 2,100 articles, including more than 450 that are new, and 1,000 biographies

16

of major philosophers. It covers both Western and non-Western thought.

89 Masterpieces of world philosophy. Frank N. Magill, ed. 704p. HarperCollins, 1991. $

100 B75

Magill has written critical essays on 100 influential philosophical works. He summarizes the major ideas in the text and provides historical background and an overview of the relevant literature on the topic.

90 New dictionary of the history of ideas. Maryanne Cline, ed. 6v. Gale, 2005. $$$$

903 CB9

The first *Dictionary of the History of Ideas* was published in 1973–74 and "became a landmark of scholarship on European thought." That edition is now available online through the University of Virginia Library (http://xtf.lib.virginia.edu/xtf/view?docId=DicHist/uvaBook/tei/DicHist1.xml). The *New Dictionary of the History of Ideas* is a new work of scholarship that expands coverage into North America, Africa, Asia, Latin America, and the Middle East. This source is "designed to introduce a general audience to the main ideas and movements of global cultural history from antiquity to the twenty-first century."

91 The new encyclopedia of unbelief. Tom Flynn, ed. 809p. Prometheus Books, 2007. $$

211 BL2705

This is a comprehensive reference work covering the history, beliefs, and thought of those who choose to live without religion: atheists, skeptics, agnostics, and secular humanists. An international group of more than 200 scholars wrote more than 500 entries covering topics such as sexuality, intelligent design, and morality.

92 Routledge encyclopedia of philosophy. Edward Craig, ed. 10v. Routledge, 1998. $$$$

103 B51

The shorter Routledge encyclopedia of philosophy. Edward Craig, ed. 1077p. Routledge, 2005. $

103 B51

This is one of the standard reference sources in philosophy. More than 2,000 entries cover the philosophy of the mind, philosophy of science, applied ethics, non-Western philosophies, and contemporary thought. The shorter version is a single volume containing the full text of the most important articles and condensed versions of the others in a single volume. The online version (www.rep.routledge.com) is a new edition with more than 150 new articles, revisions, and updates of others as well as links to philosophy websites.

93 World philosophers and their works. John K. Roth, ed. 3v. Salem Press, 2000. $$

109 B104

Here, 285 alphabetical entries cover 226 of the world's greatest philosophers and five significant ancient works of undetermined authorship. Articles contain a biography of the author or a discussion of the context and possible authorship, an overview of the work, and a bibliography. Subject and title indexes and a chronological list of philosophers and works will help students find what they need.

Biographical Sources

94 Biographical dictionary of twentieth-century philosophers. Stuart Brown, ed. 968p. Routledge, 2002. $

109 B4

With more than 1,000 entries, this dictionary provides essential, difficult-to-obtain information on twentieth-century philosophers from all over the world. Entries include biographical highlights, major publications, secondary literature, and key concepts.

Religion

General Sources

DATABASES AND INDEXES

95 ATLA religion database. American Theological Library Association. www.atla.com/products/catalog/pages/rdb-db.aspx. CP$

This database indexes journal articles, essays, and book reviews from more than 1,500 journals covering all aspects of religion. It is available online and updated quarterly. The journals represent all major religions and denominations, and the scope is international.

DICTIONARIES AND ENCYCLOPEDIAS

96   Encyclopedia of angels. 2nd ed. Rosemary Ellen Guiley. 416p. Facts on File, 2004. $
202   BL477

An overview of angels that includes their origins, natures, functions, and manifestations. The second edition includes 600 new entries, many revisions, and new images. Entries include Abraham, dreams and visions, Joan of Arc, and Gnosticism. This is a definitive source on the subject.

97   Encyclopedia of religion. 2nd ed. Lindsay Jones, ed. 15v. Macmillan Reference USA, 2004. $$$$
200.3   BL31

Mircea Eliade's classic work was published in 1987. The second edition includes almost all of the 2,750 entries from the original, updated, as well as approximately 600 new ones. An international team of scholars collaborated to preserve Eliade's cross-cultural approach while emphasizing religion's unique role in individual cultures.

98   Religions of the world: A comprehensive encyclopedia of beliefs and practices. J. Gordon Melton and Martin Baumann, eds. 6v. ABC-CLIO, 2010. $$$
203   BL 31

This encyclopedia covers the world's religions, emphasizing practices, cultures, and customs rather than scriptures. It includes small but newsworthy sects such as the Branch Davidians and the Muslim Brotherhood. It provides coverage of the world's contemporary religious scene.

99   Religious celebrations: An encyclopedia of holidays, festivals, solemn observances, and spiritual commemorations. J. Gordon Melton, ed. 2v. ABC-CLIO, 2011. $$
203.6   BL590

This encyclopedia offers alphabetical entries covering more than 800 celebratory occasions from the world's many religions. It includes information about religious calendars and explanations of the significance of each occasion. All entries include references. Features a 67-page index, extensive cross-referencing, and the occasional black-and-white photograph.

Bible

ATLASES

100   HarperCollins atlas of Bible history. James B. Pritchard. 192p. HarperOne, 2008. $
220.9   G2230

Pritchard was an eminent biblical archeologist. He supplements maps with photographs of archeological findings and art, giving users context.

101   Interdisciplinary atlas of the Bible: Scripture, history, geography, archeology, and theology. Giacomo Perego. 124p. St. Paul's/Alba House, 1999. $
220.9   G2230

This basic atlas not only includes maps but also discusses the history and archeology of the corresponding areas as well as relevant quotes from biblical texts.

COMMENTARIES

102   International Bible commentary. William R. Farmer et al., eds. 1986p. Liturgical Press, 2005. $
220.7   BS511.2

This title is a Catholic Bible commentary with bibliographical references and an index. Scholars from all over the world have contributed to this multicultural interpretation of scripture.

103   New interpreter's Bible. Leander E. Keck et al. 12v. plus index. Abingdon, 1994–2004. $$$
220.9   BS491.2

The *New Interpreter's Bible* provides authoritative exposition and exegesis of the Bible using both the New Revised Standard Version and the New

International Version as base texts. Also available on CD-ROM.

104 The new Jerome Bible commentary.
3rd ed. Raymond E. Brown et al., eds.
1475p. Prentice Hall, 1999. $
220.7 BS491.2

A single-volume Catholic commentary that offers line-by-line explanation as well as thorough topical articles on hermeneutics, canonicity, the Old Testament, and biblical theology. There are also articles on Gnosticism, Jesus, and the early church.

CONCORDANCES

105 New Strong's exhaustive concordance of the Bible. Rev. ed. James Strong.
1968p. Thomas Nelson, 2010. $
220.5 BS425

A classic source since 1894, the latest edition of Strong's concordance features expanded word studies so that readers can better understand the Hebrew, Greek, and Chaldee words used in the Bible. The concordance is based on the King James Version. There is also a 2005 publication, *New Strong's Concise Concordance of the Bible.*

DATABASES AND INDEXES

106 New Testament abstracts. Weston Jesuit School of Theology, 1956–. $
220.05 BS410
Old Testament abstracts. Catholic Bible Association of America, 1978–. $
220 BS410

Taken together, these two sources provide abstracts of articles and books from 350 Jewish, Catholic, and Protestant periodicals. These databases are good for studying either the Old Testament or New Testament of the Bible. Abstracts are in English. These resources are also available via EBSCO.

DICTIONARIES AND ENCYCLOPEDIAS

107 Anchor Bible dictionary. David Noel Freedman. 6v. Doubleday, 1992. $$
220.3 BS440

Nearly 1,000 scholars with various religious affiliations participated in creating this comprehensive six-volume set. It contains 6,280 entries with

bibliographies and serves as a companion to the Anchor Bible Commentaries series. This scholarly, well-written source is an important text in Biblical scholarship.

108 HarperCollins Bible dictionary.
3rd ed. Mark Allen Powell. 1168p.
HarperOne, 2011. $
220.3 BS440

This revision of a favorite source is a nonsectarian scholarly work based on the Revised Standard Version. It includes an outline of each book in the Bible and all of the important names, places, and topics. Major articles cover recent archaeological findings and explain the variety and significance of the many versions of the Bible. It has a color map section, black-and-white photographs, an index, and cross-references.

109 Mercer dictionary of the Bible. Watson E. Mills et al., eds. 973p. Mercer, 2004. $
220.3 BS44

A balanced dictionary of current biblical scholarship containing 1,450 signed articles. Feminist thought is included where appropriate.

110 The new interpreter's dictionary of the Bible. Katharine Doob Sakenfeld, ed.
5v. Abingdon, 2006–2009. $$
220.3 BS440

This dictionary has articles on 7,100 topics, including persons, places, things, and theological concepts. It is based on the New Revised Standard Version and written by more than 800 scholars from forty countries and from a variety of perspectives.

111 Zondervan encyclopedia of the Bible.
Rev. ed. Moisés Silva and Merrill Chapin Tenney, eds. 5v. Zondervan, 2009. $$
220.3 BS440

The new edition of this source features more than 7,500 articles from 238 international contributors. It has both color and black-and-white illustrations and thirty-two pages of maps. Articles cover a wide spectrum of biblical topics.

HANDBOOKS

112 The complete book of who's who in the Bible. Philip W. Comfort and

Walter A. Elwell. 656p. Tyndale House, 2005. $

220.9   BS570

This title provides a complete list of all of the people in the Bible, with information about their lives. It contains biographies from both the Old Testament and New Testament.

113 Oxford companion to the Bible. Bruce M. Metzger and Michael D. Coogan, eds. 874p. Oxford, 1993. $

220.3   BS440

This concise handbook offers criticism and historical background on the full range of questions surrounding the Bible and its content. It has maps, a bibliography, and an index.

Religion in the United States

114 American religions: An illustrated history. J. Gordon Melton. 316p. ABC-CLIO, 2000. $

200.97   BL2525

This book looks at the development of religion in America from the early tribal religions to the diversity of the twenty-first century.

115 Encyclopedia of American religious history. 3rd ed. Edward L. Queen II et al. 3v. Facts on File, 2009. $$

200.97   BL2525

This encyclopedia examines the people, religions, and social movements that played important roles in American history. The articles are signed and have brief bibliographies.

116 The encyclopedia of Native American religions. Rev. ed. Arlene B. Hirschfelder and Paulette Fairbanks Molin. 390p. Facts on File, 2000. $

299.7   E98

The 1,200 alphabetical entries in this work describe the practices, ceremonies, sacred places, myths, and principal figures associated with Native American religions. The work also examines the impact of missionaries and contact with Europeans and Americans and their effects on these traditions.

Religions

GENERAL SOURCES

117 How to be a perfect stranger: The essential religious etiquette handbook. 5th ed. Stuart M. Matlins and Arthur J. Magida, eds. 432p. Skylight Paths, 2010. $

291.38   BJ2010

This book seeks to address questions you may have when "invited to a wedding, funeral or other religious service of a friend, relative or coworker whose faith is different from our own. . . . What will happen? What do I do? What do I wear? What do I say? What should I avoid doing, wearing, and saying? Is it okay to use a video camera? How long will it last? What are their basic beliefs? Will there be a reception? Will there be food? Should I bring a gift? When is it okay to leave?" A religious glossary, calendar of holidays and festivals, and a summary of proper forms of address for religious leaders are included. Unfortunately, there is no index.

118 Introduction to the world's major religions. Emily Taitz et al. 6v. Greenwood, 2005. $$

200   BL80

Each of these six volumes covers one of the world's major religions: Judaism, Confucianism and Taoism, Buddhism, Christianity, Islam, and Hinduism. They offer good overviews of the history, texts and major tenets, branches, practice worldwide, rituals and holidays, and major figures. They have glossaries, bibliographies, and indexes.

ASIAN RELIGIONS

119 Buddhism. 3rd ed. Madhu Bazaz Wangu. 128p. Facts on File, 2006. $

294.3   BQ4032

This concise encyclopedia gives users the history and development of Buddhism and information on the three major schools of thought, its philosophy, and its precepts.

120   The complete idiot's guide to Taoism.
Brandon Toropov and Chad Hansen.
336p. Alpha, 2002. $
299.5   BL1920
Taoism is a philosophical and religious tradition that developed in China. It has no one god or founding prophet and states that each person must follow his or her own path to the Tao. This book examines the tradition and its influence on the world's cultures.

121   Encyclopedia of Hinduism. Constance
Jones and James D. Ryan. 512p. Facts on
File, 2007.
294.50   BL1105
This encyclopedia provides a good overview of the Hindu religion, history, scripture, practices, gods and goddesses, and culture.

122   An introduction to Confucianism.
Xinzhong Yao. 361p. Cambridge, 2000. $
299.5   BL1852
Confucianism is a system of ethical behavior and social responsibility that evolved into one of the world's great spiritual traditions. This encyclopedia presents the basic tenets of Confucian thought, its evolution in response to Chinese history, and its relevance in the modern world.

123   Shinto. 3rd ed. Paula R. Hartz. 144p.
Chelsea House, 2009. $
299.5   BL2220
Shinto is an ancient Japanese tradition, and it is deeply ingrained in Japanese culture. This book explains the rituals, traditions, and values and their role in contemporary society.

124   Sikhism: An introduction. Nikky-
Guninder Kaur Singh. 272p. I. B. Tauris,
2011. $
294.6   BL2018
Sikhism is one of the world's newest religions, founded in India only 500 years ago. Sikhs believe in the Ultimate Reality, a formless force that is above all things and yet present in them. They reject distinctions based on social class and race. This concise volume explains the beliefs and practices as well as the political problems facing Sikhs in India and the struggles of Sikhs living in the West.

CHRISTIANITY

Dictionaries and Encyclopedias

**125   Blackwell encyclopedia of modern
Christian thought.** Alister E. McGrath,
ed. 720p. Blackwell, 1995. $
230.09   BR95
This source presents the views of the most eminent theologians of the eighteenth through the twentieth centuries on the key issues of the times.

126   Encyclopedia of early Christianity.
2nd ed. Everett Ferguson, Frederick W.
Norris, and Michael P. McHugh, eds. 2v.
Garland, 1997. $$
270.1   BR162.2
More than 150 scholars collaborated to create 1,200 entries covering the early church from the life of Jesus to the seventh century. The scholarly but accessible presentation makes this an important part of the reference collection.

127   Encyclopedia of Protestantism. J. Gordon
Melton. 628p. Facts on File, 2005. $$
280   BX4811.3
More than 600 alphabetical entries cover people, places, theological issues, and historical and modern views of Protestant movements. The introduction provides a definition of Protestantism and a historical outline of the Reformation.

128   Mormonism for dummies. Jana Riess
and Christopher Kimball Bigelow. 384p.
Wiley, 2005. $
289.3   BX8653.3
Two Mormons explain how the Church of Jesus Christ of the Latter-day Saints differs from other Christian churches. They cover the history, beliefs, and rituals as well as the debates over race, polygamy, and the status of women.

129   New Catholic encyclopedia. 2nd ed.
Berard Marthaler, OFM Conv., ed. 15v.
plus supplements. Gale, 2003. $$$$
282   BX841
The first new edition of this monumental work in more than thirty years is the product of more than

200 contributors under the auspices of the Catholic University of America. A total of 12,000 entries are completely revised and updated to reflect the new (1983) Code of Canon Law. There are hundreds of new articles, including biographies of contemporary religious figures and coverage of controversial issues such as gender and reproduction. Supplemental volumes (2009–2013) update the text. A jubilee volume covers the years of John Paul II.

130   New international dictionary of Pentecostal and charismatic movements. Stanley M. Burgess and Eduard M. van der Maas, eds. 1328p. Zondervan, 2002. $
270.8   BR1644
This dictionary has 1,000 entries and 500 photographs that provide information on Pentecostal and charismatic movements in sixty countries around the world. Bibliographies and indexes to people, places, and subjects provide easy access to the content.

131   New Westminster dictionary of liturgy and worship. 1st American ed. Paul F. Bradshaw. 493p. Westminster John Knox Press, 2003. $
264   BV173
This work presents an ecumenical approach to the liturgies of the various Christian sects. It covers revisions made by the Catholic and Protestant churches as well as historical background.

132   Oxford dictionary of the Christian Church. 3rd ed. F. L. Crosby and E. A. Livingstone, eds. 1840p. Oxford, 2005. $$
270.03   BR95
More than 6,000 alphabetical entries cover Christian history, beliefs, practices, traditions, and people. An authoritative one-volume work, this edition is not a major revision: some changes were made to accommodate an electronic version, some new articles were added, and bibliographies were updated.

133   Oxford history of Christian worship. Geoffrey Wainwright and Karen B. Westerfield Tucker, eds. 960p.

Oxford, 2005. $
264   BV15
This is a comprehensive and authoritative treatment of the history of the origins and development of Christian worship. It looks at Catholic, Orthodox, Protestant, and Pentecostal practices in all parts of the world.

Directories, Yearbooks, and Almanacs

134   Catholic almanac. Matthew Bunson. Our Sunday Visitor, 1904–. Annual. $
282   BX845
This annual compendium of facts about the Catholic Church includes a chronological summary of the year's events from the Vatican, the United States, and the world as well as handbook information on Catholic topics. It is well edited and indexed.

135   Official Catholic directory. National Register Staff. P. J. Kenedy & Sons, 1817–. Annual. $$
282   BX845
This directory provides current information about churches, clergy, schools, hospitals, and other institutions in each diocese of the United States. It also contains statistics, a pilgrimage guide, and information about the Catholic Church worldwide.

136   A place for God: A guide to spiritual retreats and retreat centers. Timothy K. Jones. 480p. Doubleday, 2000. $
647.94   BV5068
This is a guide to 250 retreat centers, mostly Catholic, in the United States. It is organized by states and includes information on the type of accommodations and nearby sites of interest.

137   Yearbook of American and Canadian churches. Eileen W. Lindner. National Council of Churches, 1973–. Annual. $
This source includes directory, statistical, and historical information about religious and ecumenical organizations, service agencies, churches, educational institutions, and depositories of religious

materials. It also has lists of religious periodicals. Also available online.

Biographical Sources

138 Butler's lives of the saints. Alban Butler; Paul Burns, ed. 640p. 12v. Liturgical Press, 2005. $
282.09   BX4654.3

This concise and updated version of Butler's work offers one saint per day per month through the calendar year. They are selected from the new full edition, published 1995–2000, in twelve volumes.

139 Dictionary of saints. Rev. ed. John J. Delaney. 720p. Doubleday, 2005. $
282.09   BX4655.8

This compendium of 5,000 saints has been revised to include those newly canonized and beatified. It includes listings of feast days, patron saints, and saint's symbols.

140 Encyclopedia of saints. Rosemary Ellen Guiley. 432p. Facts on File, 2001. $
282.09   BX4655.8

The 400 entries in this encyclopedia describe the lives of saints within a social and historical context. Detailed appendixes provide information on patron saints by topic, a calendar of feast days, beatified and canonized popes, and an explanation of the canonization process. There are also glossaries of heresies and terms.

141 Oxford dictionary of popes. Rev. ed. J. N. D. Kelley and Michael Walsh. 368p. Oxford, 2006. $
282.09   BX955.25

The new edition of this work is current with coverage of John Paul II's life and an entry for Benedict XVI. It is arranged chronologically with an alphabetical index.

ISLAM

142 The American Muslim. The American Muslim. www.theamericanmuslim.org. Free

According to its website, the American Muslim strives to "provide an open forum for the discussion of ideas and issues of concern to Muslims in America" and to "provide a forum for and encourage intercommunity dialogue particularly on divisive issues, and to encourage interfaith dialogue to find common ground for cooperation on issues of mutual concern." It also seeks to "help people of faith (Muslims, Christians, and Jews) who share our concern for dialogue, peaceful resolution of problems to find each other so that we can work together" and "provide a balanced, moderate, alternative voice focusing on the spiritual dimension of Islam rather than the more often heard voice of extreme political Islamism."

143 A concise encyclopedia of Islam. Gordon Newby. 256p. Oneworld, 2002. $
297.03   BP40

This illustrated guide to Islamic tradition contains more than 1,000 entries covering people, places, events, beliefs, and rituals. It includes the different branches within Islam: Sunni, Shia, and Sufi. A chronology, a bibliography, and a list of the ninety-nine divine names complete the work.

144 Encyclopedia of Islam and the Muslim world. Richard C. Martin, ed. 2v. Gale, 2004. $$
909   BP40

This two-volume set has 500 entries by 500 international scholars. It includes a glossary of common Arabic and Islamic terms as well as photographs, drawings, and charts.

145 The Holy Qur'an. Alawi D. Kayal; M. H. Shakar, trans. 10v. Kegan Paul International, 2002. $
297   BP109

With high interest in Islam, libraries of all sizes should have a Qur'an. This edition is a good choice. The bilingual text in English and Arabic is the accepted way to publish the Qur'an. The multivolume format is handy.

146 New encyclopedia of Islam. 3rd ed. Cyril Glassé. 720p. Rowman & Littlefield, 2008. $
297.03   BP40

The new edition of this encyclopedia has more than 1,400 entries, including new ones covering contemporary issues such as the Taliban. It also contains a chronology covering the entire history of Islam.

JUDAISM

147 American Jewish year book. Springer, 2011–. Annual. $
296   E184
This almanac has information about Jewish life and culture, including population statistics, directories of Jewish organizations and periodicals, a religious calendar, necrology, and coverage of international Jewish politics, communities, and periodicals. The American Jewish Committee published it from 1899 to 2008. Springer took over its publication in 2011. The archives are available for free online at http://ajcarchives.org.

148 Biblical literacy: The most important people, events, and ideas of the Hebrew Bible. Joseph Telushkin. 656p. Morrow, 1997. $
221.6   BS1140.2
Rabbi Telushkin acts as a guide for a tour of the Hebrew Bible, pointing out the important people, places, and ideas within the text.

149 The book of Jewish values: A day-by-day guide to ethical living. Joseph Telushkin. 544p. Crown/Harmony/Bell Tower, 2000. $
296.3   BJ1285
This book offers advice based on Jewish sacred texts or living an ethical life in a morally complex world.

150 A code of Jewish ethics. Joseph Telushkin. 2v. Harmony, 2006–2009. $
296.3   BJ1285.2
Rabbi Telushkin's major treatise on Jewish ethics uses scripture and rabbinic commentary to explain conduct in personal life. The first volume is titled *You Shall be Holy*. The second volume, *Love Your Neighbor as Yourself*, deals with interpersonal issues and family, friends, and community.

151 Dictionary of Jewish lore and legend. Alan Unterman. 216p. Thames &

Hudson, 1997. $
296   BM50
This illuminated volume explains the colorful characters and legends in Jewish folklore and the traditions on which they are based. Both Ashkenazic and Sephardic lore are included. Also includes information on mystical movements, customs, festivals, and home life.

152 Encyclopedia Judaica. Fred Skolnik and Michael Berenbaum, eds. 22v. Gale, 2006. $$$$
This classic resource has been thoroughly revised and updated. The new edition has 22,000 signed articles by American, Israeli, and European scholars, including 2,500 new entries dealing with gender issues and Jewish life in New World geographic areas. It also has more than 600 maps, charts, and other illustrations.

153 The essential Kabbalah: The heart of Jewish mysticism. Daniel C. Matt. 240p. HarperCollins, 1996. $
296.1   BM525
An eminent Kabbalah scholar has created an anthology in translation of the principal Jewish mystical texts.

154 The essential Talmud. Adin Steinsaltz. 304p. Jason Aronson, 1992. $
296.1   BM503.5
One of the greatest living teachers of Talmud offers an introduction to this Jewish text, describing its structure and the methods used to study it.

155 Etz Hayim: Torah and commentary. David L. Lieber, ed. 1560p. Jewish Publication Society, 2001. $
222   BS1223
The Torah: A modern commentary. Rev. ed. W. Gunther Plaut and David E. Stein. 1604p. Union for Reform Judaism, 2004. $
222   BS1225.53
These two Torahs with commentary present the first five books of the Hebrew Bible divided into weekly readings along with commentary from scholars. Written and edited by a group of Conservative rabbis affiliated with the Jewish Theological Seminary, *Etz Hayim* is a Torah

commentary from a Conservative point of view. It is divided into the weekly Torah portions and contains the Haftarah portions and cantillation markings. *The Torah: A Modern Commentary* is from the Reform movement. It includes the weekly Torah portion, Haftarah portions, and commentary on the text.

156 How to run a traditional Jewish household. Blu Greenberg. 520p. Simon & Schuster, 1985. $

296.74   BM700

This concise guide to Jewish living provides clear explanations of the dietary laws, family purity laws, and traditions and holidays, and how they are integrated into home life.

157 Jewish traditions: A JPS guide. Ronald L. Eisenberg. 806p. Jewish Publication Society, 2008. $

296.4   BM50

This is a comprehensive guide to Jewish life and culture. It explains life-cycle events, the Sabbath and festivals, the synagogue and prayers, and such miscellaneous topics as food, animals, plants, and magic and superstition.

158 Jewish women in America: An historical encyclopedia. Paula E. Hyman and Deborah Dash Moore, eds. 2v. Routledge, 1997. $$

Sponsored by the American Jewish Historical Society, this award-winning work contains authoritative entries on more than 800 women as well as 110 topical entries on organizations, movements, vocations, culture, and so forth. Spanning the years 1654 to 1997, these volumes include more than 500 photographs and an extensive bibliography. A masterful reference source.

159 JPS Hebrew–English Tanakh: Standard edition. 2040p. Jewish Publication Society, 1999. $

221.44   BS895

The Jewish study Bible: Jewish Publication Society Tanakh translation. Adele Berlin, Marc Zvi Brettler, and Michael Fishbane, eds. 2818p. Oxford, 2003. $

220.447   BS895

The *JPS Hebrew–English Tanakh* contains the complete Hebrew text based on the Leningrad Codex side-by-side with an English translation based on modern biblical scholarship. *The Jewish Study Bible* uses that translation along with introductions and extensive commentary by eminent scholars to help readers understand the text.

160 Oxford dictionary of the Jewish religion. 2nd ed. Adele Berlin, ed. 960p. Oxford, 2011. $$

296   BM50

This one-volume work serves as a reference to the various facets of Jewish religion and its teachings. The new edition includes recent developments such as the formation of gay and lesbian synagogues and the growth of baby-naming ceremonies for girls. With its focus on religion rather than culture, it provides an excellent scholarly reference work for the library and the home. All entries have bibliographic citations.

161 Seasons of our joy: A modern guide to the Jewish holidays. Arthur Waskow. 288p. Jewish Publication Society, 2012. $

296.4   BM690

This guide explains the Jewish festivals and traditions associated with them. It discusses the theological basis of the holidays and offers appropriate readings and recipes for holiday foods.

OTHER LIVING RELIGIONS

162 Baha'i faith: A guide for the perplexed. Robert H. Stockman. 224p. Continuum, 2012. $

297.93   BP365

Although it is among the youngest religions, it now has six million members worldwide. This book explores the history, beliefs, and practices of the Baha'i faith.

163 The complete idiot's guide to Wicca and witchcraft. 3rd ed. Denise Zimmerman and Katherine Gleason; rev. with Miria Liguana. 384p. Alpha, 2006. $

299   BF1566

This book clarifies the principles, underlying beliefs, and practices of Wicca. It includes information about festivals and group rituals as well as information for home practitioners. *See also* **"The Occult," in chapter 3.**

164 Encyclopedia of cults, sects, and new religions. 2nd ed. James R. Lewis, ed. 775p. Prometheus Books, 2001. $$
200.3   BL2525
This book has 1,000 entries covering a wide range of historically significant and obscure religious groups. The entries are brief and objective.

165 Encyclopedia of new religious movements. Peter Clarke, ed. 800p. Routledge, 2005. $$
200.90   BL31; BL98
This encyclopedia covers new religious movements all over the world. Entries cover people, movements, concepts, and ideologies as well as topics such as exit counseling.

166 New age encyclopedia: A mind-body-spirit reference guide. Rev. ed. Belinda Whitworth. 268p. Career Press, 2003. $
299   BP605
This source provides an overview of New Age beliefs and practices, including various bodywork techniques, numerology, and spirit guides. It also has a directory of addresses for organizations and websites.

167 Oxford handbook of new religious movements. James R. Lewis. 576p. Oxford, 2008. $
200.90   BP603
This is an interdisciplinary look at new religious movements. It discusses issues such as conversion, brainwashing, and millennialism and examines Satanism, UFO religions, and neopaganism.

168 The Rastafarians. 20th ed. Leonard E. Barrett Sr. 328p. Beacon Press, 1997. $
299   BL2532
This is a classic study of the culture, religion, history, ideology, and influence of the Rastafarians.

169 Santería: The religion. Migene González-Wippler. 384p. Llewellyn, 2002. $
299.67   BL2532

The author presents the gods, beliefs, practices, herbs, and sacrifices that are part of the Santería religion. The book includes photographs and interviews with Santería leaders.

170 Voodoo in Haiti. Alfred Métraux. Schocken Books, 1972. $
133.4   BL2490
This older title is a classic study that explains the origins of Voodoo and its rites and traditions.

171 Zoroastrianism: An introduction. Jenny Rose. 328p. I. B. Tauris, 2011. $
295   BL1572
Zoroastrianism is one of the world's oldest monotheistic religions. This book traces its history and explains its beliefs. It also looks at Zoroastrian communities in the world today.

MYTHOLOGY

172 Dictionary of classical mythology. Pierre Grimal; Stephen Kershaw, ed.; A. R. Maxwell-Hyslop, trans. 480p. Penguin, 1992. $
292.1   BL715
The first English translation of a French classic, this is a superb guide, with thirty-four pages of genealogical tables to clarify relationships.

173 Encyclopedia of Greek and Roman mythology. Luke Roman and Monica Roman. 561p. Facts on File, 2010. $
292   BL715
This encyclopedia has 365 alphabetical entries covering Greek and Roman gods and heroes, mythical creatures, and great works of literature inspired by them. There are black-and-white illustrations, a bibliography, and an index.

174 Facts on File encyclopedia of world mythology and legend. 3rd ed. Anthony S. Mercatante and James R. Dow. 2v. Facts on File, 2008. $$
291.1   BL303
This thoroughly revised and updated edition covers more than 3,000 myths and legends from around the world, both ancient and modern. It has 400 illustrations, a bibliography, and extensive cross-referencing.

175   Oxford companion to world mythology. David Leeming. 512p. Oxford, 2009. $

201.3   BL312

The author explores the role of mythology in history and examines all aspects of the world's major mythological traditions. The work is illustrated and has appendixes with family trees of the major pantheons; equivalency charts for the major gods of Greece, Rome, Babylon, and Sumer; an extensive bibliography; and an index.

176   Tree of souls: The mythology of Judaism. Howard Schwartz. 704p. Oxford, 2007. $

296.1   BM530

The first anthology of Jewish mythology has nearly 700 Jewish myths gathered from the Bible, the Talmud and Midrash, Kabbalistic literature, and pseudographia as well as medieval and Hasidic lore.

Ethics

177   Bioethics Research Library at Georgetown University. http://bioethics.georgetown.edu. Free

This is a major center for bioethics research. The website contains periodical articles and special collections dealing with Islamic ethics, Jewish ethics, and genetics and ethics, as well as papers from the U.S. Bioethics Commission.

178   Encyclopedia of applied ethics. 2nd ed. Ruth Chadwick, ed. 4v. Academic Press, 2012. $$$$

170.3   BJ63

The second edition of this award-winning resource updates material from the earlier work and adds new material about topics that are now ethical issues, including reality TV, electronic surveillance, and obesity. All entries are signed and have a brief glossary, a bibliography, and selected web links.

Encyclopedia of bioethics, see **641.**

179   Encyclopedia of ethics. 2nd ed. Lawrence C. Becker and Charlotte B. Becker, eds. 3v. Routledge, 2001. $$$

170.3   BJ63

The editors of this edition worked with 325 scholars to update all of the articles and add 150 new ones. New entries include fiduciary relationships, the Holocaust, gay ethics, bad faith, and political correctness.

180   Ethics. Rev. ed. John K. Roth, ed. 3v. ✓ Salem Press, 2004. $$

170.3   BJ63

This edition has 1,007 essays, 200 of which are new. The main emphasis is applied ethics, and it has a student focus rather than a scholarly one. It covers people, concepts, cultures, and works. It has an annotated list of organizations with web addresses, a biographical directory of people mentioned, and a timeline of primary works of moral and ethical philosophy.

181   Medicine, health, and bioethics: Essential primary sources. K. Lee Lerner and Brenda Wilmoth Lerner, eds. 513p. Gale, 2006. $$

174.2   R724

This book contains 175 primary documents dealing with health, medicine, and bioethics. An introduction to each document provides historical context and information about its significance. Information about the author and resources for further research are included.

182   The Westminster dictionary of ✓ Christian ethics. Rev. ed. James F. Childress and John Macquarrie, eds. 700p. Westminster John Knox Press, 1986. $

241   BJ1199

Scholars from many backgrounds contributed to this ecumenical work addressing ethical questions relevant to philosophy and theology.

Psychology and Psychiatry

3

SARAH BARBARA WATSTEIN

Mental health, including psychology and psychiatry, is the focus of this chapter, which also includes a small section devoted to the occult. Today, interest in psychological topics is shared by researchers, educators, clinicians, students, and consumers. Topics such as aging, autism, marriage and divorce, and posttraumatic stress disorder are on people's minds. Many of these individuals also seek information about reimbursement, relationships with managed care companies, and Medicare and Medicaid. Without a doubt, consumers are just one population seeking information related to psychological issues that affect their daily physical and emotional well-being. It is safe to say that today, appreciation of psychology's and psychiatry's complementary roles in advancing both societal and individual health is widespread.

This interest will be served by sources that are comprehensive in scope as well as sources devoted to specific topics in the field. These include sources in all categories, from databases to dictionaries, encyclopedias, handbooks, style manuals, web-based portals, and more. And they include sources written for a broad and diverse readership of students, specialists, and nonspecialists. Undergraduate and graduate students, alongside professionals—psychologists, psychiatrists, residents, neurologists, nurses, social workers, counselors, lawyers, claims reviewers—and lay readers with an interest in mental health issues alike, will be well served by the many sources cited in this chapter.

Psychology sources are presented first, followed by psychiatry and, finally, sources pertaining to the occult. The Dewey Decimal Classification system assigns Parapsychology and Occultism within the main class for Philosophy and Psychology. It is for this reason that we include the occult in this chapter.

Psychology

Databases and Indexes

183 Mental measurements yearbook with tests in print. Buros Institute. http://buros.org. CP$
Mental Measurements Yearbook with Tests in Print, from the Buros Institute, contains the most recent

descriptive information and critical reviews of new and revised tests from the Buros Institute's ninth and more recent yearbooks. It offers evaluations of the latest assessments in education, psychology, business, law, health care, counseling, and management. In addition to test reviews, descriptions of the purpose, target population, administration, scores, price, author, and publisher for all listed tests are provided. Reviews are written by highly qualified professionals with expertise in a range of disciplines. Beginning in 2010, the database provides a comprehensive record that combines the full-text reviews with the citations from the print publications *Mental Measurements Yearbook* and *Tests in Print*. The database is updated every six months to ensure timely access to current information.

184 MICROMEDEX. Truven Health
Analytics. www.micromedex.com. CP$
Considered one of the most authoritative resources available, this database provides access to a suite of evidence-based drug information resources, including *DRUGDEX, POISINDEX, Martindale: The Extra Pharmacopoeia, Index Nominum,* and *Physicians' Desk Reference.*

185 PEP Archive. Psychoanalytic Electronic
Publishing. www.p-e-p.org. CP$
A fully searchable digital archive of classic psychoanalytic texts, the PEP Archive is the most authoritative source of peer-reviewed scholarly and scientific articles from the field of psychoanalysis. Produced by Psychoanalytic Electronic Publishing, the database offers the full text for more than fifty principal psychoanalytic journals and 100 classic psychoanalytic books dating as far back as 1920. The materials encompass thousands of articles, book chapters, book reviews, letters, and commentaries as well as thousands of figures and illustrations. Besides psychology and psychiatry, students and professionals researching anthropology, linguistics, nursing, physiology, neurosciences, and women's studies will find this source indispensable. Co-owned by the American Psychoanalytic Association and the British Institute of Psychoanalysis, the PEP archive represents the PEP's mission in action—"to further psychoanalytic scholarship, research and outreach through the promotion of its literature."

**186 Psychology and behavioral sciences
collection.** EBSCO. www.ebscohost
.com/academic/psychology-behavioral
-sciences-collection. CP$
This database indexes more than 450 journals in psychology and the behavioral sciences, with coverage going back to the 1930s. The database was introduced by EBSCO in the early 2000s. It is a subject database with full-text access, and it uses the standard EBSCO interface. It does not have PsycINFO's extensive coverage, but it is useful for undergraduate psychology students.

187 PsycINFO. American Psychological
Association. www.apa.org/pubs/data
bases/psycinfo/. CP$
The preeminent database from the American Psychological Association (APA), PsycINFO contains more than 3.5 million records for sources related to the behavioral sciences and mental health. U.S. and international books, book chapters, and dissertations are covered along with peer-reviewed journals. With resources dating back to the seventeenth century, PsycINFO is especially well suited as a discovery and linking tool for scholarly research in a number of disciplines. Coverage includes related disciplines such as medicine, law, social work, neuroscience, business, nursing, forensics, engineering, and more. Features include grant and sponsorship data, a tests and measures field to help locate specific tests, indexing for "first posting" records that yields access to earliest publication of journal articles, and publication history to track submission, acceptance, and publication dates.

Authoritative and comprehensive, APA databases provide myriad gateways for students, scholars, professionals, and practitioners in the behavioral sciences. Core resources include

> PsycARTICLES, "a robust database offering complete access to the full text of more than 90 landmark journals in behavioral science" (www.apa.org/pubs/databases/psycarticles/).
> PsycBOOKS, "a full-text database that provides electronic access to thousands of scholarly and professional titles published by APA, including recent titles in psychological and behavioral science,

plus a substantial back file of classic and historic works" (www.apa.org/pubs/data bases/psycbooks/).

PsycCRITIQUES, "a full-text database with tens of thousands of incisive book and film reviews from 1956 to present. It provides users with insight on publications from a psychological perspective allowing them to choose relevant reading material, to select appropriate course materials, and more" (www.apa.org/pubs/databases/psyccritiques/).

PsycTESTS, "a research database that provides access to psychological tests, measures, scales, surveys, and other assessments as well as descriptive information about the test and its development and administration" (www.apa.org/pubs/databases/psyctests/index.aspx).

PsycTHERAPY, "a database containing more than 300 videos featuring therapy demonstrations showing clinicians working with individuals, couples, and families" (www.apa.org/pubs/databases/psyc therapy/index.aspx).

Users may also want to consider PsycEXTRA, "a unique database that combines bibliographic records with full-text professional and lay-audience literature such as legal testimony and amicus briefs, reports, conference materials, popular magazines, factsheets, grants, and web materials" (www.apa.org/pubs/databases/psycextra/).

PubMed, *see* **681.**

Dictionaries

188 APA dictionary of psychology. Gary R. VandenBos, ed. American Psychological Association, 2007. $
150.3   BF31
Containing approximately 25,000 terms and definitions in psychology and mental health, this resource "includes coverage of concepts, processes, and therapies across all the major subdisciplines of psychology." Aimed at students and mental health, medical, and legal professionals. Most entries are short, averaging about forty words, but some are longer and explore an important topic in depth.

The four appendixes include headwords listed biographically, institutionally, by tests and assessments, and by psychotherapeutic approach. Academic and public libraries will find this source useful.

189 The counseling dictionary: Concise definitions of frequently used terms.
3rd ed. Samuel T. Gladding. 197p. Pearson, 2011. $
361   BF637
Serving both experienced and novice counselors, the third edition of this work presents "over 3000 of the most frequently used terms in the field of counseling." It includes 400 new terms in this edition. Includes as an appendix a timeline of important events in counseling. Also includes as appendixes a list of the movers and shakers who have helped define the counseling profession and a list of national resources that will help seasoned and junior professionals alike. Includes cross-references.

190 Dictionary of biological psychology.
Philip Winn, ed. 857p. Routledge, 2001. $$
612.8   QP360
The focus of this work is the field of biological psychology, that branch of psychology that studies the biological foundations of behavior, emotions, and mental processes. Terminology from a variety of nonpsychological sources, such as clinical medicine, psychiatry, and neuroscience, as well as specialist areas of psychology, such as ethology, learning theory, and psychophysics, is drawn together in this first-of-its-kind volume. Readers, researchers, and practitioners interested in understanding both the physical properties of the terms included as well as their behavioral significance will not be disappointed.

191 Dictionary of psychological testing, assessment, and treatment. 2nd ed. Ian Stuart-Hamilton. 285p. Jessica Kingsley, 2007. $
150.28   BF176
The second edition of this work contains about a 10 percent revision from the first edition. More than 3,000 terms commonly encountered in psychology and testing are defined. To avoid overlap with the

Mental Measurements Yearbook and similar sources, tests are given brief coverage. Cross-references are in italics. Undergraduate and postgraduate students as well as practitioners of psychology and associated fields seeking a guide to tests, experimental methods and analyses, and therapies will find this resource useful.

192 A dictionary of psychology. 3rd ed. Andrew M. Colman. 882p. Oxford, 2009. $

150   BF31

Weighing in with more than 11,000 entries, the third edition of this classic is distinguished by coverage of both the more widely used terms as well as the technical terminology of neuroanatomy, neurophysiology, psychopharmacology, and statistics not always covered in previous psychological dictionaries. Also included is the basic vocabulary of psychoanalysis. Providing clear and concise definitions, entries include parts of speech, numbered senses, synonyms, alternate forms, and cross-references. Etymological or word origin information is provided for many terms. Birth and death dates are noted for the individuals behind eponymous terms. Added value is provided by two appendixes—a twenty-page "Phobias and Phobic Stimuli" lists phobias by their technical names, and appendix 2 includes definitions for more than 700 abbreviations and symbols. This dictionary is essential for students, teachers, and professionals of psychology and the related fields of psychoanalysis, psychiatry, criminology, neurosciences, and statistics.

193 Dictionary of psychopathology. Henry Kellerman. 278p. Columbia, 2009. $

616.89   RC437

Psychopathology is the study of the origin, development, and manifestations of mental or behavioral disorders. This dictionary is intended for students and practicing professionals in the allied mental health fields. It includes more than 2,000 definitions of psychopathological terms. Terminology is from *DSM-IV* but includes some previous *DSM* terms, historical terms, and terms outside of traditional classifications.

194 The SAGE glossary of the social and behavioral sciences. Larry E. Sullivan,

ed. 577p. SAGE, 2009. $$

300.3   H41

This resource combines terminology from nine separate social and behavioral sciences, including communication, economics, geography, media and politics, psychology, public administration, sociology, and education. Entries range from 50 to 425 words. If a term has different meanings in different disciplines, this is noted in the entry. This glossary is intended to serve users with definitions that are in between a short dictionary entry and a longer subject encyclopedia treatment of a concept.

Encyclopedias

195 The concise Corsini encyclopedia of psychology and behavioral science. 3rd ed. W. Edward Craighead and Charles B. Nemeroff, eds. 1112p. Wiley, 2004. $$

150   BF31

The name Corsini has long been associated with essential, solid, and important reference works in psychology and behavioral science. No exception, this work serves as a reference companion for both students and professionals in the field. It is also accessible to general readers. Craighead and Nemeroff have chosen more than 500 entries from the full *Corsini Encyclopedia of Psychology and Behavioral Science* for coverage. For smaller and medium-sized libraries, the *Concise Corsini* should suffice. *The continuum complete international encyclopedia of sexuality*, **see 290.**

196 Encyclopedia of behavior modification and cognitive behavior therapy. Michel Hersen, ed. 3v. SAGE, 2005. $$$

616.89   RC489

This three-volume work provides comprehensive treatment of behavior modification, including history, biography, theory, and application for both child and adult populations in a variety of settings. The editors bring together relevant aspects of behavior modification, cognitive behavior therapy, and behavior therapy. Entries include a description of the intervention strategy, its research basis, population, compilations, case illustrations, and suggested readings. The editors have tried to be jargon-free and to define specialized terminology. Biographies are included. This work will benefit general readers, students, and mental health practitioners.

197 Encyclopedia of child behavior and development. Sam Goldstein and Jack A. Naglieri, eds. 1591p. Springer, 2010. $$$

This specialized encyclopedia covers child development and behavior. Entries are in alphabetical order and address major conceptual areas in the field. Its distinguished editors, editorial board, and contributors have created a reference source that students, researchers, and child development professionals will find useful.

198 Encyclopedia of clinical neuropsychology. Jeffrey S. Kreutzer, John DeLuca, and Bruce Caplan, eds. 4v. Springer, 2011. $$$$
616.8   RC343.4

Neuropsychological disorders such as traumatic brain injury, stroke and other vascular impairments, epilepsy and nonepileptic seizure disorders, and dementia are covered in this encyclopedia. Students and adult readers interested in the diagnosis, evaluation, and rehabilitation of persons with neuropsychological disorders will find this work to be a useful starting point.

199 Encyclopedia of cognitive behavior therapy. Arthur Freeman, ed. 451p. Springer, 2005. $$
616.89   RC489

A form of psychotherapy that seeks to modify behavior by manipulating the environment to change the patient's response, cognitive behavior therapy (CBT) is an approach characterized by diversity. This authoritative volume covers common disorders and conditions, essential components of treatment, treatment methods, applications of CBT with specific populations, and emerging problems. Comprehensive in scope, this work will appeal to a wide spectrum of readers, students, practitioners, patients, and educators.

200 Encyclopedia of counseling. Frederick T. L. Leong, ed. 4v. SAGE, 2008. $$$
158   BF636

The intended audience for this work is counselors, social workers, psychiatric nurses, psychologists and psychiatrists, and students learning about counseling as a field. In four volumes, it contains 600 entries exploring key theories, models, techniques, challenges, and contemporary issues in counseling. Each volume contains a reader's guide and a cross-referencing system to allow the reader to move between the entries. Contents include *Changes and Challenges for Counseling in the 21st Century* (v. 1), *Personal and Emotional Counseling* (v. 2), *Cross-Cultural Counseling* (v. 3), and *Career Counseling* (v. 4).

201 Encyclopedia of group processes and intergroup relations. John M. Levine and Michael A. Hogg, eds. 2v. SAGE, 2009. $$
302   HM716

With approximately 300 alphabetically arranged entries, this work covers concepts ranging from conformity to diversity and from small group interaction to intergroup relations on a global scale. The work serves several populations well, especially undergraduate students seeking to understand the complexities that define intra- and intergroup behavior. Graduate students and faculty will find the encyclopedia adequately explores the many facets of group processes and intergroup relations, providing timely, thorough, and accessible introductions, complete with references for further readings, to core topics. General adult readers with little or no behavioral science background will also find the entries easy to read.

202 Encyclopedia of human relationships. Harry T. Reis and Susan Sprecher, eds. 3v. SAGE, 2009. $$
302   HM1106

Written with both practitioners of "relationship science" and nonacademics in mind, this source discusses all sorts of human relationships, from birth, love, and marriage to death. Entries have an alphabetical arrangement, with longer entries containing about 3,000 words, medium entries about 2,000 words, and shorter entries about 1,000 words. Users may also refer to the reader's guide, which organizes the work into substantive themes such as cognitive processes in relationships and types of relationships. Cross-references allow the reader to move between entries.

203 Encyclopedia of interpersonal violence. Claire M. Renzetti and Jeffrey L. Edleson, eds. 2v. SAGE, 2008. $$
303   HM1121

The landscape of interpersonal violence is the subject of this set, which contains more than 500 entries on the different forms of interpersonal violence, their incidence and prevalence, theoretical explanations, public-policy initiatives, and prevention and intervention strategies. This encyclopedia helps students and the general public understand various aspects of interpersonal violence as well as providing a quick reference for professionals. Readers interested in public service to end interpersonal violence will also find this a helpful resource. Alphabetically arranged entries include cross-references to related entries as well as suggested readings for further information. Also included is information about organizations and agencies, legislation, research methods and data-collection instruments, and theories and theoretical perspectives. Appendixes provide information on current data sets, regional and national organizations specializing in various dimensions of interpersonal violence, and relevant websites.

204 The encyclopedia of phobias, fears, and anxieties. 3rd ed. Ronald M. Doctor, Ada P. Kahn, and Christine A. Adamec. 572p. Facts on File, 2008. $
616.85   RC535

The third edition of this work continues to explore the workings of phobias, fears and anxieties. The editors have attempted to be inclusive in their coverage of recognized psychological disorders. In addition to phobias that are psychosocial in origin, they have included ones with sociocultural origins. Although this title would be useful for mental health professionals, the primary audience is the general reader who is looking for information about these phenomena. About 2,000 entries include a description of the disorder and common treatments. Some self-test and self-help suggestions for phobia sufferers are included. There is also an appendix with a resource directory.

205 Encyclopedia of psychological assessment. Rocío Fernández-Ballesteros, ed. 2v. SAGE, 2003. $$
150   BF39

Comprehensive coverage of the discipline of psychological assessment is provided in this set. Each of the work's 235 entries, organized alphabetically and covering a variety of fields, includes a general conceptual and methodological overview, a section on relevant assessment devices, cross-references to related concepts, and a list of references. Classifying entries into nine general categories, a reader's guide assists readers in locating entries on related topics. Readers seeking up-to-date coverage of all areas of psychology will need to supplement this work with more current sources. Nonetheless, it remains a breakthrough resource.

206 Encyclopedia of psychology. Alan E. Kazdin, ed. 8v. Oxford, 2000. $$$
150   BF31

This work continues to be the definitive source of information, reference, and research on every area of psychological theory, research, and application. Organized alphabetically, the articles range from 500 to 7,000 words in length and include 400 biographies. As the publisher states, it includes "an extensive system of cross-references and blind entries facilitate research from article to article and clarify links within the field." A comprehensive index provides many additional points of access across areas of interest and fields of study. A variety of readers will continue to be well served by this source, a joint effort of the American Psychological Association and Oxford University Press.

207 Encyclopedia of psychology and religion. David A. Leeming, Kathryn Madden, and Stanton Marlan, eds. 2v. Springer, 2010. $$$
200.1   BL53

The preface to this interdisciplinary encyclopedia says that it covers "religion, psychology, psychology and religion, and psychology of religion." Entries are intended help the reader delve deeper into the topics without providing definitive answers. Ancient and modern religious belief systems are included, such as Christianity, Judaism, Islam, and ancient Celtic, Germanic, and Native American religions. Some articles cover the same topic from more than one point of view. Entries are extensively cross-referenced.

208   Encyclopedia of psychopharmacology.
Ian P. Stolerman. 2v. Springer, 2010. $$$
615.78   RM315

Interest in the actions of drugs and their effects on mood, sensation, thinking, and behavior (i.e., contemporary psychopharmacology), appears to know no bounds. Here, readers will find substantial essays on individual drugs and groups of drugs and descriptions of fundamental psychological and biological processes affected by psychoactive drugs, alongside basic methodological or technical descriptions.

209   The encyclopedia of schizophrenia and other psychotic disorders. 3rd ed. Richard Noll. 409p. Facts on File, 2007. $
616.89   RC514

The latest edition of this encyclopedia has been revised and expanded to reflect the latest scientific and scholarly research. Biologically related schizophrenic disorders, genetics, antipsychotic drug treatments, and pathophysiology are a few of the topics explored in the more than 600 entries. Appendixes list diagnostic criteria for schizophrenia and information for pertinent organizations. Clear language makes this volume equally suitable for use by patients, scholars, and general readers.

210   Encyclopedia of stress. 2nd ed. George Fink, ed. 4v. Elsevier/Academic, 2007. $$$
616.9   BF575

This comprehensive and cross-disciplinary survey of all aspects of stress research and medicine updates the 2000 work of the same title. The second edition is more than warranted by advances in the years since the first edition in our understanding of stress psychology and biology, the different types of stress, and stress management. Readers interested in topics as wide ranging as genetics and genomics to diurnal, seasonal, and ultradian rhythms will not be disappointed.

211   The encyclopedia of stress and stress-related diseases. 2nd ed. Ada P. Kahn. 438p. Facts on File, 2006. $
616.9   QP82.2

The second edition of *The Encyclopedia of Stress and Stress-Related Diseases* differs little in format from the first. Entries are listed alphabetically. At the end of longer entries are cross-references, bibliographic listings, and, where appropriate, organizations to contact for further information. New entries for stressors relating to technology, the workplace, aging, fear, social situations, and crime have been added. The appendix and index have been expanded to include the new topics. General readers and professionals working in related fields will appreciate this concise encyclopedic gateway to anxiety diseases.

212   Gale encyclopedia of mental disorders. Ellen Thackery, ed. 2v. Gale, 2002. $$
616.89   RC437

Including both traditional and alternative therapies, this resource provides a good overview of mental illness, psychotherapy, and other treatments. Four hundred signed, alphabetical entries make up the set. The entries cover disorders, diagnostic procedures and techniques, therapies, medicines and herbs, and related topics. Entries for disorders include a definition, description, causes and symptoms, demographics, diagnosis, treatments, prognosis, and prevention. Those for medications contain the definition, purpose, description, recommended dosage, precautions, side effects, and interactions. Entries for herbs and supplements have a leaf icon next to the heading. All entries have a resource list of print and electronic sources and organizations to contact. One hundred black-and-white photographs and charts illustrate the text. A color photo gallery repeated in both volumes has enhanced versions of some of the photographs. There are ample cross-references, making it easy to locate drugs, which are entered by generic name. Boxes with definitions of key terms help readers understand the material. A full glossary is at the end of volume 2. Users will find a symptom list here also.

Handbooks and Manuals

213   Comprehensive handbook of psychological assessment. Michel Hersen, ed. 4v. Wiley, 2003. $$$
150.28   BF176

This four-volume reference is a guide to major types of psychological assessment. The introduction to volume 1 helps orient readers to the source. Each volume covers an area of assessment. Volume titles include *Intellectual and Neuropsychological Assessment* (v. 1), *Personality Assessment* (v. 2), *Behavioral Assessment* (v. 3), and *Industrial and Organizational Assessment* (v. 4). The subject encyclopedia coverage is intended for graduate students or professionals in the field.

214 Diagnostic and statistical manual of mental disorders: DSM-IV-TR. 4th ed., text rev. 943p. American Psychiatric Association, 2000. $$
    616.89   RC455.2

Psychiatric diagnoses are categorized by this guide. Better known as the *DSM-IV*, the manual is published by the American Psychiatric Association and covers all mental health disorders for both children and adults. It lists known causes of these disorders, statistics in terms of gender, age at onset, and prognosis as well as some research concerning optimal treatment approaches. Mental health professionals use this manual when working with patients in order to better understand their illness and potential treatment and to help third-party payers (e.g., insurance) understand the needs of the patient. The book is typically considered the bible for any clinical and counseling psychologists as well as other professionals who make psychiatric diagnoses in the United States and many other countries. The *DSM-5* was published in spring 2013.

215 Handbook of psychology. Irving B. Weiner, ed. 12v. Wiley, 2003. $$
    150   BF121

This exhaustively researched work fills a visible gap in the literature of psychology by providing a cross-disciplined approach that allows scholars and practitioners to keep abreast of the state of scholarship. Volume 1 offers a history of the field while volume 2 covers research methods. The remaining volumes are divided into five areas of study (3–7) and applications (8–12). Psychologists, practitioners, researchers, and students are well served by the twelve volumes of the *Handbook of Psychology*. Professionals and also adjunct fields like medicine and sociology will also be well served by this classic. The online version features a dynamic table of contents and subject index, advanced search

options, hyperlinked cross-references, and customizable viewing options.

216 The Oxford companion to consciousness. Tim Bayne, Axel Cleeremans, and Patrick Wilken, eds. 672p. Oxford, 2009. $
    153   BF311

Ambitious in scope, and including more than 250 entries, *The Oxford Companion to Consciousness* merits its reputation as the most complete authoritative survey of the rapidly expanding interdisciplinary field of consciousness studies. Both fundamental knowledge as well as more recent advances in this rapidly evolving domain are covered. Beginning students seeking a map of current work on consciousness as well as seasoned researchers will find this authoritative reference to be invaluable.

217 The Oxford companion to the mind. 2nd ed. Richard L. Gregory, ed. 1004p. Oxford, 2004. $
    128   BF31

The long-awaited second edition of a classic, this work provides the reader with discussions of concepts like language, memory, and intelligence, side by side with definitions. Added value is provided by three "mini symposia" on consciousness, brain scanning, and artificial intelligence. As with its predecessor, this work is cultural as well as scientific in its approach, and it offers authoritative descriptions and analysis. Weighing in at 1,001 A–Z entries ranging from brief statements to substantial essays on major topics, this book introduces the reader to how philosophers, physiologists, psychologists, and psychiatrists differ in their understanding of what the mind is and how it works.

Style Manuals

218 APA style. www.apastyle.org. Free

On this site, visitors will find tutorials, FAQs, and other resources to help improve their writing, master APA style, and learn the conventions of scholarly publishing. Links to information about references and formatting provide quick answers to popular queries.

219 Publication manual of the American Psychological Association. 6th ed. 272p. American Psychological Association, 2009. $

808   BF76.6

APA style has been adapted by many disciplines and is used by writers around the world. *The Publication Manual of the American Psychological Association* continues to enjoy the status of being the preeminent resource for the preparation and submission of manuscripts for publication in the behavioral and social sciences. The rules of APA style, detailed in this manual, offer sound guidance for writing with simplicity, power, and concision. The sixth edition boasts three changes: it has been updated to acknowledge and incorporate advances in computer technology; it has been reorganized and streamlined for ease of use; and its focus has been broadened to include readers in the behavioral and social sciences.

Tests, Measurements, and Questionnaires

220   Health and psychosocial instruments (HaPI). Behavioral Measurement Database Services, 2000–. CP$

Provides information on measurement instruments (including tests, questionnaires, interview schedules, rating scales, vignettes/scenarios, etc.) in the fields of health and psychosocial sciences. Information about a measurement instrument comes from studies that use that instrument. The full text of instruments is not, however, included in the database.

Mental measurements yearbook with tests in print, see **183**.

PsycTESTS; *see* PsycINFO, **187**.

Websites

221   Alexander Street Press counseling. Alexander Street Press. http://alexander street.com/about/about-us/alexander -street-press-counseling/. CP$

This collection contains more than 2,000 hours of video with more than 84,000 pages of text. Other single-title videos are available for purchase or as streaming video. As the website states: "The full suite of counseling materials features therapy session videos and transcripts, client narratives,

interviews, presentations, and more to support teaching and research in counseling and related disciplines."

222   American Psychological Association. American Psychological Association. www.apa.org. Free

The official website of the American Psychological Association (APA), a scientific and professional organization representing psychology in the United States. As the world's largest association of psychologists, APA's membership extends to researchers, educators, clinicians, consultants, and students. The site is an excellent jumping-off point to information about the organization, psychology topics, news and events, research, education, careers, and more.

223   Association for Psychological Science. Association for Psychological Science. www.psychologicalscience.org. Free

The Association for Psychological Science was previously known as the American Psychological Society. Its mission is to "to promote, protect, and advance the interests of scientifically oriented psychology in research, application, teaching, and the improvement of human welfare." This free site will be of interest to students, mental health professionals, and general readers.

224   Counseling and psychotherapy transcripts, client narratives, and reference works. Alexander Street Press. http://alexanderstreet.com/products/ counseling-and-psychotherapy -transcripts-client-narratives-and -reference-works. CP$

A searchable collection containing actual transcripts of therapy and counseling sessions and first-person narratives illuminating the experience of mental illness and its treatment, as well as reference works to contextualize the unique primary material.

225   National Institutes of Health. National Institutes of Health. www.nih.gov. Free

The National Institutes of Health (NIH), a part of the U.S. Department of Health and Human Services, is the nation's medical research agency. Of NIH's twenty-seven institutes and centers, those with relevance for psychology and related disciplines include the National Cancer Institute; National Heart, Lung, and Blood Institute; National Institute on Aging; National Institute on Alcohol Abuse and Alcoholism; National Institute of Child Health and Human Development; National Institute on Drug Abuse; National Institute of Mental Health; National Institute of Neurological Disorders and Stroke; and the Office of Behavioral and Social Sciences Research.

226 National Science Foundation. National Science Foundation. www.nsf.gov. Free

The National Science Foundation (NSF) is an independent agency of the federal government. It was created in 1950 to support scientific and technology-related research. According to its website, NSF is responsible for about 20 percent of basic research in U.S. universities.

227 U.S. Department of Health and Human Services. U.S. Department of Health and Human Services. www.hhs. gov. Free

The Department of Health and Human Services (HHS) is a U.S. government agency that works to ensure the safety of food, react to public health emergencies, and to cure and prevent illnesses. Agencies within the HHS include the Centers for Disease Control and Prevention (CDC), the Food and Drug Administration (FDA), the National Institutes of Health (NIH), and the Substance Abuse and Mental Health Services Administration.

Psychiatry

Dictionaries

228 Campbell's psychiatric dictionary. 9th ed. Robert J. Campbell. 1051p. Oxford, 2009. $

  616.89   RC437

This work has continued to grow and keep pace with the changes in psychiatry and neurosciences. The ninth edition has significantly increased in size from the previous edition. In addition to historical terms from psychoanalysis, this edition includes progress in brain chemistry, neuroscience, cognition, and neurodegenerative diseases. Mental health professionals, students, and general readers interested in the terminology of psychiatry will find

this source useful. Appendix includes abbreviations and acronyms. Libraries that own the eighth edition will want to replace it with the ninth.

Handbooks and Manuals

229 American Psychiatric Association practice guidelines for the treatment of psychiatric disorders: Compendium 2006. 1600p. American Psychiatric Association. $

  616.89   RC480

Quick reference to the American Psychiatric Association practice guidelines for the treatment of psychiatric disorders: Compendium 2006. 297p. American Psychiatric Association, 2006. $

  616.89   RC480

Contains thirteen practice guidelines developed by the American Psychiatric Association. Each guideline has also been published in the *American Journal of Psychiatry*. The guidelines are presented in *DSM-IV* order. Includes "watches" for guidelines that have been revised—for example, treatment of panic disorders and bipolar disorders. There is also a quick reference guide for each guideline. Practitioners may want to refer to the American Psychiatric Association's website (www.psych.org) for both continuing education information and updated information on the guidelines.

Diagnostic and statistical manual of mental disorders: DSM-IV-TR, see **214.**

230 Kaplan and Sadock's comprehensive textbook of psychiatry. 9th ed. Benjamin J. Sadock, Virginia A. Sadock, and Pedro Ruiz, eds. 2v. Wolters Kluwer Health/Lippincott Williams & Wilkins, 2009. $$

Arguably the gold standard when it comes to the teaching and practice of psychiatry, the "CTP" is an extremely comprehensive and up-to-date text. Psychiatry and mental health are explored from all angles, with especial attention to psychiatry's historical roots; biological, psychological, and social determinants; medications; and subspecialties. Practitioners, trainees, and students are the primary audience, although others will benefit from this enduring text.

Websites

231 American Psychiatric Association.
www.psychiatry.org. Free
Founded in 1844, the American Psychiatric Association is the world's largest psychiatric organization. Information about APA and psychiatry, mental health, advocacy, publications, practice, and more can be found on this website.

232 PsychiatryOnline. American Psychiatric
Publishing. http://psychiatryonline.org.
Free
This web-based research portal provides online access to major print reference materials and journals in the area of psychiatry. Included are the *DSM Library*, featuring the popular *Diagnostic and Statistical Manual of Mental Disorders—DSM-5*, and the *American Journal of Psychiatry*. Diverse audiences will appreciate this landing page for lifelong learning in psychiatry. This site is free to search, but users may have to use the library's OPAC to determine if journal articles are available.

The Occult

Dictionaries

**233 The dictionary of demons: Names of
the damned.** Michelle Belanger. 362p.
Llewellyn, 2010. $
133.4   BF1503
This is not a "how to" of grimoiric magic, but rather a dictionary of the names of demons from occult and metaphysical author Michelle Belanger. It includes the titles and ranks and hierarchy for about 1,500 names. Also included are entries on the most frequently consulted sourcebooks and impact articles to put the demons in the context of Western European traditions. There is an index of associated powers.

**234 The Watkins dictionary of magic:
Over 3,000 entries on the world of
magical formulas, secret symbols,
and the occult.** Nevill Drury. 328p.
Watkins, 2005. $
133.43   BF1588

This dictionary seeks to define terms around a magical worldview. It includes "Wicca, western ceremonial magic, alchemy, astrology, Gnosticism, Kabbalah, Rosicrucianism, Tarot, shamanism, voodoo, Macumba, and Santería." It also incorporates Enochian angelic magic, Goetia, and Thelemic and Ordo Templi Orientis (O.T.O.) cosmologies. The editor admits a sympathy toward a magic approach.

Encyclopedias

**235 The encyclopedia of demons and
demonology.** Rosemary Ellen Guiley.
302p. Checkmark Books, 2009. $
133.4   BF1503
The editor of this title also edited *The Encyclopedia of Angels*, *The Encyclopedia of Ghosts and Sprits*, and other supernatural titles. This title focuses on the role of demons in folklore and religion. It covers topics like exorcism, magic, witchcraft, and djinns or genii. Longer entries include further readings, and some entries include illustrations or photos. Checkmark Books is an imprint of Infobase Publishing, which also publishes Facts on File titles.

236 The new encyclopedia of the occult.
John Michael Greer. 555p. Llewellyn,
2003. $
133   BF1407
This work is written by an occult practitioner, a self-identified Druid, Freemason, geomancer, Cabalistic ceremonial magician, and ordained minister "with roots in traditional Louisiana hoodoo." The encyclopedia endeavors to present a scholarly account of the occult, principally from Europe and North America. It includes alchemy, astrology, divination, palmistry, Golden Dawn, Rosicrucianism, Wicca, Theosophy, and information about modern pagans. Biographical entries are included, but not of living people.

Handbooks and Manuals

**237 The complete magician's tables:
The most complete set of magic,
Kabbalistic, angelic, astrologic,
alchemic, demonic, geomantic,
grimoire, gematria, I Ching, tarot,
planetary, pagan pantheon, plant,**

perfume, emblem, and character correspondences in more than 777 tables. 2nd ed. Stephen Skinner. 448p. Llewellyn, 2006. $

133.4   BF1611

The subtitle of this work describes some of the coverage found within. It includes the standard correspondences found in Aleister Crowley's *Liber 777*. It also includes tables from tarot, geomancy, Olympic Spirits, Mithraic grades, and several grimoires. Chapters include astrology, gematria and isopsephy, pagan pantheons, Kabbalah, magic, both Middle Eastern and Eastern polytheism, Western symbolism, and timelines. Appendixes include a bibliography and full list of columns. Public libraries may wish to have this book on hand for the curious and scholarly pagan.

Websites

238   The Alchemy Website. Adam McLean. www.alchemywebsite.com/index.html. Free

From the home page of this complex and extensive website: "457 megabytes currently online of information on alchemy in all its facets. Divided into over 2500 sections and providing tens of thousands of pages of text, over 3000 images, over 300 complete alchemical texts, extensive bibliographical material on the printed books and manuscripts, numerous articles, introductory and general reference material on alchemy." Readers seeking full-length alchemical texts will be well served.

239   Flesko: Esoterics and occult. RentabiliSense S.L. www.flesko.co.uk/ directory/other/astro_esotericism/ esoterics-occult.php. Free

A free directory to sites on esoterics and the occult. Though the focus of the site is the United Kingdom and Ireland, there are a number of U.S. sites listed as well.

240   PaganSpace. PaganSpace.net and Alexandrian Archives. www.paganspace .net. Free

This website purports to be the social network for the occult community.

241   Twilit grotto: Archives of Western esoterica. Joseph H. Peterson. www .esotericarchives.com. Free

This website offers another database of occult texts. Includes a timeline of esoterica and a collection of links.

Social Sciences and Sociology

DREW ALFGREN AND KATHRYN SULLIVAN

Given the broad nature of the social sciences, it is no surprise that the number of reference works available in this area is vast. Sources that attempt to summarize the entire field cannot do justice to all of the new research being generated by the disciplines under review. All libraries, but especially those with limited budgets, are encouraged to build their collections with a disciplinary focus that will be most useful for the programs supported by their institutions.

The titles selected for this chapter include entries from the last edition along with many new works published since then. No titles were retained that are no longer in print; while some older material may still have great value, the emphasis here is on highlighting the wealth of new work and, in particular, the international scholarship now occurring in the social sciences. The titles selected may be available in print or online, and no attempt has been made to differentiate between formats.

Social Sciences (General Sources)

Databases

242   SocINDEX with full text. EBSCO. www.ebscohost.com/academic/socindex -with-full-text. CP$

The social sciences include so much, and topics are often so inter- or multidisciplinary, that finding a single database that fulfills all research needs is difficult. EBSCO's SocINDEX with Full Text is the most comprehensive of the social science databases available, providing indexing of the journal literature back to the beginning of the twentieth century and full text of more than 800 books and 16,000-plus conference papers. Added value comes from more than 25,000 author profiles giving contact information, publishing information, and areas of interest. A subject thesaurus, EBSCO's search limiters, and citation statistics make advanced searching more accessible for students and faculty alike. While not inexpensive, the scope and depth of the literature indexed and the amount of full text available make this a good choice for purchase.

Dictionaries and Encyclopedias

243   International encyclopedia of the social sciences. 2nd ed. William A.

Darity, ed. 9v. Macmillan Reference USA, 2008. $$$$

| 300 | H40 |

The second edition of the *International Encyclopedia of the Social Sciences* covers developments in social science fields that have emerged and matured since the publication of the first edition in 1968 (reprinted in 1979). This edition includes nearly 3,000 new articles and biographies on an array of multidisciplinary topics. This is a core resource for students in sociology, political science, economics, anthropology, psychology, policy studies, and related fields. Content is appropriate for a variety of user groups, including high school and college students, researchers, and lay readers.

244 The SAGE encyclopedia of social science research methods. Michael S. Lewis-Beck, Alan Bryman, and Tim Futing Liao, eds. 3v. SAGE, 2004. $$$$

| 300 | H62 |

This three-volume reference covers topics that are essential for users across the social sciences field, including anthropology, communications, education, psychology, sociology, and so forth. Although the material is important for social science students, the entries are written in ordinary English, which makes them accessible to general readers who do not have advanced knowledge of the methods. The encyclopedia includes more than 900 alphabetically arranged entries, which can be divided into two types. The first are short entries that are merely definitions that provide the reader a quick explanation of a methodological term. The second type of entry is in-depth essays of varying lengths, which include references and cross-references for additional reading. Each volume includes the same comprehensive bibliography as the appendix, and volume 3 contains an index of subjects and names.

245 Social issues in America: An encyclopedia. James Ciment, ed. 8v. M. E. Sharpe, 2006. $$

| 361.973 | HN57 |

Designed for the general reader, this eight-volume encyclopedia provides access to information on a wide range of social issues existing in the United States. Examples of topics include academic freedom, consumer debt, homeland security, medical malpractice, stem cell research, and terrorism. Entries are approximately ten pages each and are arranged alphabetically. They include an overview of the topic, a chronology of events related to the topic, bibliographic references including websites, a glossary of important terms, and excerpts from important documents related to the topic. Tables and graphics accompany many of the entries. Each volume includes a topic finder, which lists articles under fourteen broad topics. A cross-reference index listing related topics is also available near the beginning of each volume. Volume 8 is an extensive index to the entire collection.

African Americans

246 The African American almanac. 11th ed. Alan Hedblad, ed. 1500p. Gale, 2011. $$

| 305 | E185 |

Published every three years, this large one-volume reference (formerly titled *The Negro Almanac*) contains a wealth of information on African American history, society, and culture. Topics covered include Africa and the black diaspora, film and television, population, religion, science and technology, sports, and more. Content includes chronologies, primary source documents, legislation, speeches, biographical profiles, and essays. A general bibliography, with references arranged by chapter, supports further research. A more affordable though much less extensive publication is *African American Almanac: 400 Years of Triumph, Courage, and Excellence*, by Lean'tin Bracks.

247 African American national biography. ✓ Henry Louis Gates Jr. and Evelyn Brooks Higginbotham, eds. 8v. Oxford, 2008. $$$$

| 920 | E185.96 |

With more than 4,000 entries, *African American National Biography* is the most comprehensive resource of its kind. An online component to this resource allows for the addition of new entries over time. The scope is broad. Entries cover African American politicians, scientists, athletes, educators, musicians, businessmen and women, artists, and more. Unlike the *Dictionary of National Biography*, this resource includes living and deceased subjects. Signed entries range in length from one page to three or more. References for further reading are included.

See also "Biography," in chapter 1.

248 Africana: The encyclopedia of the African and African American experience. 2nd ed. Kwame Anthony Appiah and Henry Louis Gates Jr., eds. 5v. Oxford, 2005. $$

960   DT14

The initial edition of this reference work (published in 1999) was inspired by W. E. B. DuBois's vision to publish a black *Encyclopedia Britannica*. Now in its second edition, this five-volume set includes more than 4,000 entries on individuals, events, places, ethnic groups, organizations, movements, and countries. Alphabetically arranged entries include cross-references and a bibliography, along with colorful images, maps, charts, and tables. Volume 1 includes a selected chronology of importation events in African and African American history. Volume 5 contains a topical outline of selected entries under such broad topics as abolitionism and political and social movements. Also included are a bibliography and a comprehensive index.

Encyclopedia of African American education, **see 442.**

249 Encyclopedia of African American history, 1896 to the present: From the age of segregation to the twenty-first century. Paul Finkelman, ed. 5v. Oxford, 2009. $$$

973   E185

This collection, along with the earlier Oxford publication *Encyclopedia of African American History, 1619–1895: From the Colonial Period to the Age of Frederick Douglass* (2006), sets out to illustrate two African American histories: an internal history that charts how black communities in the United States developed over time, and an external history that shows how the interaction of blacks and whites has shaped the larger national history. Signed essays, which range in length from two pages to more than ten, include cross-references and a short list of references for further reading. Contributors have written in clear, nontechnical language. A thematic outline guides readers to all articles that relate to one another.

250 Milestone documents in African American history: Exploring the essential primary sources. Paul Finkelman, ed. 4v. Schlager, 2010. $$

305.89   E184.6

This reference combines full-text primary sources with in-depth expert analysis. The 125 entries cover nearly 400 years of African American history—from the time of the arrival of blacks in North America to the Senate apology for slavery in 2009. Documents, reprinted as they originally appeared, include letters and personal narratives, laws and legal cases, proclamations, petitions, and speeches. The set is organized chronologically. Each entry is divided into two sections: analysis and document text. Analysis includes an overview of the primary source, context that places the document in its historical framework, and a timeline of relevant events. Each entry also provides a brief biographical profile of the author, information about the intended audience, and an explanation of its historical impact. Further readings and a glossary of terms further enhance each entry. This is a unique and highly recommended resource.

Aging

251 Encyclopedia of aging. David J. Ekerdt, ed. 4v. Macmillan, 2002. $$$

305.26   HQ1064

Although a little older, this award-winning set is a standard reference source in the field. More than 400 alphabetically arranged entries are individually signed and cover a broad range of topics surrounding aging, including medical, psychological, sociological, public policy, and biological subjects. The authors aim "to present advanced ideas about aging at an accessible level." Extensive cross-references and bibliographies enhance the entries. A content outline explains the encyclopedia's approach to aging and allows the reader to see related content grouped by broad theme. This source covers the field with great scope and authority.

252 The encyclopedia of elder care: The comprehensive resource on geriatric and social care. 2nd ed. Elizabeth A. Capezuti, Eugenia L. Siegler, and Mathy D. Mezey, eds. 860p. Springer, 2008. $$

362.1   RC954

With more than 300 signed articles, this encyclopedia is designed to provide quick reference for elder-care concerns in four areas: society, community, caregiving, and the individual. Clinical topic coverage includes broad overviews of diagnosis, treatment, and disease management. With its multidisciplinary approach, this resource is useful for students and professionals in a range of health professions, including social work, nursing, medicine, psychology, and gerontology. Entries attempt to provide concise introductions rather than in-depth coverage of individual topics. Indexing and cross-referencing encourage exploration of related topics, while extensive references provide readers with additional sources of information.

253 Encyclopedia of gerontology. 2nd ed.
James Birren, ed. 2v. Academic Press,
2007. $$$
618.97   RC952.5

This extensive resource is intended for both research professionals and students. Coverage includes five major areas: the biology of aging, the psychology of aging, aging and the social sciences, health sciences, and the humanities of aging. Articles are lengthy as they are intended to provide comprehensive overviews of a given area. Topics are broad and discipline related, such as memory and retirement. Each article contains a glossary of terms and a list of primary and secondary sources, both recent and seminal. Glossary definitions are in the context of its use within that particular article. Extensive cross-referencing allows for the easy exploration of related topics.

Anthropology

**254 Biographical dictionary of social and
cultural anthropology.** Vered Amit, ed.
613p. Routledge, 2004. $$
301.09   GN20

This one-volume work presents biographical information on some 600 individuals whose work has contributed to the shaping of social and cultural anthropology, particularly as it developed in the United States and Britain. Influential individuals from physical anthropology and archaeology are also included, and there is a distinctly international aspect to the work as many of the scholars included

trained outside the United States and United Kingdom before relocating there. Each entry includes date and place of birth, education and field work locales, and a short list of key publications. Entries are alphabetical but indexes by interests, institutions, and concepts make searching for experts in specialties or specific areas simpler. The work is useful for researchers beginning a literature review or seeking information on historical aspects or trends in various aspects of the field.

255 Encyclopedia of anthropology.
H. James Birx, ed. 5v. SAGE, 2006. $$$
301.03   GN11

Described as the first comprehensive international encyclopedia of anthropology, this five-volume work includes contributions from more than 250 international authors with entries on subjects and issues in geology, paleontology, biology, evolution, sociology, psychology, and numerous other areas relevant to the study of anthropology as well as entries on theory, methodology, and fieldwork and biographies of important figures in the history and development of the discipline. Written for the general reader or undergraduate, entries are clear and informative, with suggested further readings. Cross-references, a reader's guide by subject, and a detailed index help users find appropriate entries. Color illustrations add to the overall appeal of the work, and a master bibliography at the end of the final volume is useful for continued research.

**256 Routledge encyclopedia of social
and cultural anthropology.** 2nd ed.
Alan Barnard and Jonathan Spencer, eds.
855p. Routledge, 2010. $$
306.03   GN307

This second edition of this encyclopedia includes some 275 main entries, 300 short biographical entries, and more than 600 definitions in the glossary, all in a one-volume work. The editors describe their book as a "map which will help [readers] find their way around the anthropological landscape." Main entries are of sufficient length to provide clarity and include extensive references; cross-references are highlighted in bold text. Entries from the first edition were reviewed and updated; added entries highlight the emergence of new sub-disciplines: medical anthropology, gay and lesbian anthropology, and transnational anthropologies that are outgrowths of traditional work, to name only a few. An analytical table of contents and a detailed index are very helpful.

257 21st century anthropology: A reference handbook. H. James Birx, ed. 2v. SAGE, 2010. $$

301   GN25

James Birx, editor of the five-volume *Encyclopedia of Anthropology* (2006), also edits this two-volume work on anthropology in the new century. Exceptionally useful as a state-of-the-discipline survey, this handbook reviews current research topics being investigated by anthropologists and related scholars in science and philosophy. Its 102 essays are divided into fifteen areas of interest, from biological anthropology, archaeology, and sociocultural anthropology through methodology, temporal frameworks, and theories. Essays are clearly written and scholarly but should be accessible for almost all readers. Each is signed and includes extensive references and further readings. Given the scope of the discipline, this is a remarkably coherent work that should be of worth to researchers looking for either specific information or a general sense of what is going on in a particular area.

Archaeology

258 Concise Oxford dictionary of archaeology. 2nd ed. Timothy Darvil, ed. 547p. Oxford, 2008. $

930.1   CC70

This one-volume reference, now in its second edition, contains more than 4,000 brief definitions of archaeological terms. Each term is coded by type, such as artifact, biographical, legal, slang, and so forth. A quick reference section includes lists of principal international conventions concerning historical sites and artifacts, stratigraphic subdivisions of different periods in different regions, a timeline of cultural phases in the Americas, and list of Egyptian and Roman rulers. For students or general readers in need of definitions or clarification of time periods, dynasties, and the like, this is a very useful work.

259 Encyclopedia of archaeology. Deborah M. Pearsall, ed. 3v. Elsevier, 2008. $$$

930.1   CC70

Containing articles by more than 260 international archaeologists, this three-volume encyclopedia "showcase[s] archaeological knowledge at the beginning of the twenty-first century." A four-part structure highlights archaeology as a discipline, the practice of archaeology, global and regional topics and issues, and archaeology in the everyday world. Although clearly aimed at new students of the discipline, the articles are scholarly and current enough to be useful to advanced researchers as well. Each entry has a glossary of terms listed before the text, and many are illustrated with photographs, maps, or graphics; cross-references and references are numerous and detailed. Volume 3 ends with an extensive subject index.

260 Encyclopedia of archaeology. Tim Murray, ed. 5v. ABC-CLIO, 2001. $$
Milestones in archaeology: A chronological encyclopedia. Tim Murray, ed. 639p. ABC-CLIO, 2007. $

930.1   CC100

These two works, both edited by Tim Murray, offer different perspectives on the history and development of archaeology. The five-volume encyclopedia will be more useful for libraries supporting undergraduate programs or engaged general readers needing more detailed resources. The three volumes of history and discoveries and two of biography cover the who, what, and where of archaeology clearly and sufficiently for beginning research. Entries have extensive references for continuing research. For libraries with smaller programs or those looking for supplementary material, *Milestones* is a chronologically arranged analysis of the development of archaeological theory and practice through its discoveries, establishment of institutions, and publications. The content is presented in three sections: pre-1800, nineteenth century, and twentieth century and beyond. Each section contains an introductory essay providing context and then the individual entries. The essays have extensive bibliographies, and entries have citations and references. The *Encyclopedia of Archaeology* is particularly useful for identifying primary sources as well as being a useful survey of the discipline.

261 The Oxford handbook of archaeology. Barry Cunliffe, Chris Gosden, and Rosemary A. Joyce, eds. 1161p. Oxford, 2009. $$

930.1   CC65

With submissions written by thirty-five specialists from the various fields of archaeology, this handbook could very well serve as a textbook for a course on the subject but works equally well as a reference for researchers in search of information on specific topics. Presented in seven sections are papers on the history of the field, tools and practices, the discovery of early humans, and the origins of societies and early states. The final section is on current issues and debates. Written specifically for the nonspecialist, the entries are clear, factual, illustrated when necessary, and fully cited. Advanced researchers will find new material here and the bibliographies useful for additional sources. This work will not replace a good encyclopedia for detail, but it is an excellent survey of the history and current state of the discipline.

262 The Oxford handbook of public archaeology. Robin Skeates, Carol McDavid, and John Carman, eds. 727p. Oxford, 2012. $$

930.1   CC135

Public archaeology is an emerging specialty of the discipline that draws on elements of traditional archaeology, cultural resource management, heritage and museum studies, and related social sciences. The *Handbook* contains thirty-four papers that provide an overview of the field; arranged in four sections, the essays address histories of public archaeology, researching public archaeology, managing public archaeological resources, and working at archaeology with the public. Apart from a few textbooks and a growing amount of journal literature, this is the first work to offer a summary of the current state of affairs and the directions future research could take. Not for beginners, but of significant value to more advanced researchers interested in the field.

Asian Americans

263 Asian American chronology: ✓ **Chronologies of the American mosaic.**

Xiaojian Zhao. 147p. Greenwood, 2009. $

973   E184.A75

This resource presents a record of key events in Asian American history, chronicling developments from the eighteenth century to the present day. Events are categorized into broad subject categories, such as civil rights and protests, crime, languages, population, science and scientists, trade, and treaties, allowing the reader to easily view the development of these areas over time. Entries for each year present developments in each relevant category. A glossary of terminology and a bibliography of sources for further reading are included. This resource is appropriate for the general reader.

264 Encyclopedia of Asian American folklore and folklife. Jonathan H. X. Lee and Kathleen M. Nadeau, eds. 3v. ABC-CLIO, 2011. $$

398.2   GR111

With more than 600 entries, this source documents the origins, spread, and transformations of Asian American folklore and folklife. As a resource, this encyclopedia surveys the histories, people, and cultures of many Asian American ethnic and cultural groups, including those that have previously been underrepresented in the literature, such as Tibetan Americans. Thematic essays on topics such as religion and folk music are arranged under ethnic and cultural group headings. Introductory and lead essays run between 1,500 and 3,000 words, while minor essays run up to 1,000 words. Also included are a general introductory essay that details disciplinary theories and methods in the study of folklore and folklife, an extensive bibliography, and an appendix of Asian American folktales. This resource is highly recommended for academic and larger public libraries.

265 Encyclopedia of Asian American issues today. Edith Wen-Chu Chen and Grace J. Yoo, eds. 2v. Greenwood, 2010. $$

305.89   E184

The first major reference work of its kind, this resource focuses on the entire experience of contemporary Asian Americans in the United States. Topics range from those confronting the Asian American community as a whole to specific ethnic identities within the Asian American community.

Examples include Chinese and Japanese Americans and newer communities such as Hmong Americans. This encyclopedia includes 110 entries that are thematically arranged into broad subjects including education, health, politics, economy and work, identity, family, immigration, law, and more. Each thematic section has a helpful introduction that provides context for the entries within that section. Each essay includes a list of resources for further reading. This encyclopedia is a useful information resource for college and university students, educators, social workers, and lay readers.

Criminology

266 Crime in the United States. Federal Bureau of Investigation. www.fbi.gov/about-us/cjis/ucr. Free
364.97   HV364
This annual online publication (printed publication ceased in 2004) contains Federal Bureau of Investigation (FBI) data on the volume and rate of crime offenses for the nation, the states, and individual agencies. Additionally, arrest, clearance, and law enforcement employee data are included. As of late 2012, *Crime in the United States* was available online back to 1995, and an additional *Uniform Crime Reporting* data tool provided some data access back to 1960. The website links to other useful annual publications put out by the FBI, including *Hate Crime Statistics* and *Law Enforcement Officers Killed and Assaulted.*

267 Criminology: The key concepts. Martin O'Brien and Majid Yar. 219p. Routledge, 2008. $$
364   HV6025
This work is particularly well suited for undergraduate researchers studying criminology and related fields, as it acts as both a reference resource and a study guide. Entries are concise and were selected to address the areas, concepts, and theories that students most usually deal with in their studies. Longer entries introduce readers to key theories. Shorter, descriptive entries deal with particular forms of crime and key concepts used in criminological research and theory, along with key issues, institutions, and politics that figure into social and political

response to crime. Entries contain cross-references and a brief list of references for further reading.

268 Encyclopedia of capital punishment in the United States. 2nd ed. Louis J. Palmer Jr. 623p. McFarland, 2008. $
364.66   HV8694
The second edition of this work reflects the many changes in capital punishment laws and policies in the last ten years. It provides a comprehensive resource of information on the legal, social, and political history and the status of capital punishment. It contains entries for almost all capital punishment opinions issued by the Supreme Court through 2006. Additionally, it contains entries describing the status of capital punishment in the nations of the world, information about organizations lobbying for or against capital punishment, and the impact of capital punishment on particular groups, such as African Americans, among other things. It is intended for both academic researchers and lay readers.

269 Encyclopedia of criminological theory. Francis T. Cullen and Pamela Wilcox, eds. 2v. SAGE, 2010. $$$
364.01   HV6017
This source strives to fill a void in the literature—one comprehensive compendium of theories of crime, both past and present. The introduction, in addition to providing suggested use of the resource, provides a brief overview of the development of criminology theory. A reader's guide divides alphabetical entries into twenty-one schools of criminological thought. Additionally, a timeline presents top theoretical contributions to the field across the history of criminology. These two resources provide readers with much needed context. Signed entries are often multiple pages long and provide cross-references and references for further reading. This resource is particularly useful for upper-level undergraduate and graduate students studying criminology and related fields.

270 Encyclopedia of criminology. Richard A. Wright and J. Mitchell Miller, eds. 3v. Routledge, 2005. $$$
364.03   HV6017
The more than 525 entries of this three-volume work provide a comprehensive overview of the

pivotal concepts, measure, theories, and practices that comprise criminology and criminal justice. While the focus of this resource is on criminology and the criminal justice system in the United States, extensive coverage of other nations' justice systems is provided. A thematic list of entries arranges them by broad topic, such as criminal law and victimization. Signed essays are enhanced by numerous graphics and charts and include cross-references and suggested sources for further reading.

271   The Oxford handbook of criminology.
5th ed. Mike Maguire, Rod Morgan, and Robert Reiner, eds. 1029p. Oxford, 2012. $
364   HV6025

The fifth edition of this source has been substantially revised and updated to give further voice to areas such as youth crime and justice, terrorism and counterterrorism, community sanctions, and state crime and human rights. This handbook is thematically arranged to cover history and theory, social constructions of crime and crime control, dimensions of crime, forms of crime, and reactions to crime. In order to provide a comprehensive view of each topic, individual essays bring together relevant theory, recent research, policy, and current debates. Essays include substantial reference lists for further reading. Appropriate for undergraduate and graduate students in criminology and related disciplines.

272   The SAGE encyclopedia of terrorism.
2nd ed. Gus Martin, ed. 720p. SAGE, 2011. $$
303.6   HV6431

This resource presents a comprehensive picture of the global terrorist environment in the post-9/11 era, including terrorist-related events, groups, individuals, methods, and activities. The second edition provides new insight into such timely issues as economics and terrorism, international relations and terrorism, and religious perspectives. In addition to an alphabetical arrangement of entries, a reader's guide arranges them into broad topic areas, such as counterterrorism and groups. Signed entries are cross-referenced and contain references for further reading. A number of useful appendixes are found, including a world map highlighting locations of terrorist activities and a chronology of terrorist attacks in the United States and on U.S. interests abroad.

Death and Dying

273   The encyclopedia of death and dying.
Dana K. Cassell, Robert C. Salinas, and Peter S. Winn. 369p. Facts on File, 2005. $
306.9   HQ1073

This encyclopedia contains more than 500 articles explaining the medical, social, religious, and legal concepts surrounding death and dying. Entries present clear, concise definitions of terms and, in many cases, a bibliography for further reading. There are also some interesting inclusions in the appendixes, including a table with odds of dying from various injuries and a sample "Advanced Care Plan" document, a checklist for funeral preplanning, and a list of organization and web resources. A comprehensive index and bibliography are also included.

274   Encyclopedia of death and the human experience. Clifton D. Bryant and Dennis L. Peck, eds. 1160p. SAGE, 2009. $$
306.90   HQ1073

Covering approximately 330 death-related issues, concepts, perspectives, and theories, the *Encyclopedia of Death and the Human Experience* attempts to organize, define, and clarify this growing and multidisciplinary field. A reader's guide that arranges entries by broad concept, such as causes of death, assists the reader in locating entries on related topics. Special focus is given to the cultural artifacts and social institutions and practices that constitute human experience. Contributors from all over world provide an international, cross-cultural perspective. Signed entries range in size from a few paragraphs to many pages. Cross-references and references for further reading enhance the source.

275   Handbook of death and dying. Clifton D. Bryant, ed. 2v. SAGE, 2003. $$
306.9   HQ1073

This two-volume work presents 103 essays on various topics related to thanatology, the study of death and dying. The first volume, *The Presence of Death*, contains articles on confronting death, the fear of death, euthanasia, and the dying process. Volume 2 is entitled *The Response to Death* and includes entries about death ceremonies, body disposition, the bereavement process, and the legalities of death. Articles are individually signed and include bibliographic references for further reading. A comprehensive index is available.

Ethnic Studies

276 Encyclopedia of race, ethnicity, and society. Richard T. Schaefer, ed. 3v. SAGE, 2008. $$$

305.80   HT1521

With nearly 600 entries, this encyclopedia broadly explores the complex topic of race and ethnicity in society. Coverage includes the issues of ability status, age, class, gender, and sexual orientation. More than 120 essays cover specific ethnic, nationality, tribal, and racial groups in the United States, while an additional 100 essays look at race and ethnicity in countries and regions outside of the United States. Individual entries range in length from 500 to 6,000 words, accompanied by more than 200 visuals. A reader's guide arranges individual entries around broad subject headings, allowing the reader to discover other relevant information. Entries include cross-references and further readings and websites for more information. More than 375 experts from fourteen countries contributed to this encyclopedia. Contributors come from a large variety of academic backgrounds, adding to the multidisciplinary scope of this work.

277 Encyclopedia of the world's minorities. Carl Skutsch, ed.; Martin Ryle, consulting ed. 3v. Routledge, 2005. $$$

305.8   GN495

This three-volume reference contains 562 essays divided into four main categories: topic entries, nation entries, minority-group entries, and biographical entries. Topic entries cover broad ideas, concepts, and concerns surrounding minority issues (e.g., affirmative action and racism). One hundred and seventy-three nation entries describe historical background, social conditions, and current situations for each location. Group entries explain the history and current situation of more than 250 minority groups. The final category of entries contains biographies of significant persons within minority communities. Group and nation

entries include information about location, language, population, and religion. Entries range in length from 1,000 to 5,000 words and include references for further reading. A comprehensive index is available.

278 Multicultural America: An encyclopedia of the newest Americans. Ronald H. Bayor, ed. 4v. Greenwood, 2011. $$

305.80   E184

This resource was designed to provide a comprehensive narrative of immigrants arriving to the United States following the 1965 Immigration and Nationality Act. Though statistics are provided, the encyclopedia emphasizes history, identity, and culture. The essays, ranging in length from 10,000 to 20,000 words, include fifty country entries. Entries are divided into background, causes and waves of migration, demographic profiles, adjustment and adaptation, integration and impact, second and later generations, and issues in relations between the United States and the country of origin. Also included are relevant statistical tables, a glossary of pertinent words, notable immigrants, and an annotated further-readings list for each essay. A lengthy introduction and a chronology of immigration provide context. This is a unique and useful resource for academic libraries.

279 Race relations in the United States: A chronology, 1896–2005. Paul D. Buchanan. 211p. McFarland, 2005. $

305.8   E184

Starting with the *Plessy v. Ferguson* decision in 1896, this book recounts the chronology of more than 200 significant events affecting race relations in the United States, up to 2005. Entries are arranged chronologically, and a bibliography and index are included.

280 Racial and ethnic diversity: Asians, blacks, Hispanics, Native Americans, and whites. 6th ed. Cheryl Russell. 707p. New Strategist, 2009. $

305.80   E184

This one-volume reference presents various statistics related to the many racial and ethnic groups in the United States. The sixth edition includes a chapter on attitudes by race and Hispanic origin, based on data from the General Social Survey. In addition to detailed estimates and projections of the population by race and Hispanic origin, socio-economic data such as household spending and wealth data are also included. Population projections to 2025 are in this edition, as well as tables on college enrollment and retirement plan participation. Content is broken into sections based on major racial and ethnic groups (American Indians, Asians, blacks, Hispanics, and non-Hispanic whites). A sixth section provides comparative information for the total population.

Family, Marriage, and Divorce

281 Battleground: The family. 2nd ed.
Kimberly P. Brackett, ed. 2v. Greenwood,
2009. $$

306.8   HQ515

This work contains some 80 entries on issues and problems related to the modern family. The topics covered are diverse, from the usual (abortion, child abuse) to the unexpected (pet death, deadbeat parents). Entries are several pages in length and include an overview of pertinent research, current perspectives, and directions for possible future research. Cross-references and references for further reading are provided, and volume 2 includes a comprehensive bibliography. A reader's guide at the beginning of each volume organizes entries by topic. Entries are written for the general reader or beginning student, and the work should be considered as a good starting point for research.

**282 The family in America: An
encyclopedia.** Joseph M. Hawes and
Elizabeth F. Shores, eds. 2v. ABC-CLIO,
2001. $$

306.8   HQ536

This two-volume set is the final title in the American Family series from ABC-CLIO, which includes encyclopedias on parenthood, infancy, boyhood, girlhood, and adolescence in America. This title offers a reference work that includes scholarship on all aspects of the family from many different disciplines; there are historical essays, biographies, policy analyses, and cultural and ethnic studies. The range of topics is expansive and comprehensive. Essays are concise.

283 Handbook of world families. 2nd ed.
Bert N. Adams and Jan Trost, eds. 649p.
SAGE, 2005. $$

306.8   HQ515

Edited by two of the leading scholars in the field of family studies, this one-volume handbook examines families from around the globe. Contributions from international experts from the twenty-five countries included offer analysis of family life as they have both lived and studied it. Intended as a comparative work, each section includes information on set topics ranging from mate selection through fertility, marriage/divorce, aging, and death. Examination of family, institutions, family policy, and unique or interesting variations highlight both general trends and the range of diversity in family life. The writing is clear without muting the distinctive style of the various authors, and each chapter has a substantial bibliography useful for further research.

**284 International encyclopedia of
marriage and the family.** 2nd ed. James
J. Ponzetti Jr., ed. 4v. Macmillan, 2003.
$$$

306.8   HQ9

This four-volume work serves as a reference for the diverse marriage and family lifestyles throughout the world. Coverage includes information from fifty different countries on marriage and family-related issues. Entries on birth control and wedding rings give an idea of the scope of topics covered. Entries are brief to moderate in length (2–6 pages), well cited, cross-referenced, and indexed.

285 Marriage and divorce. American
Psychological Association. www.apa.org/
topics/divorce/. Free

The American Psychological Association offers free professional information on topics of interest. The Marriage and Divorce page is a good example of what is on offer: a short descriptive entry from the *Encyclopedia of Psychology* followed by a series of sections addressing different aspects of the problem, what can be done, and how to find help. Recent news articles on the topic help establish the currency of the information. Related topics, readings, and resources are listed in the sidebar. A valuable resource for a discipline where reference resources can be costly.

286   Marriage customs of the world: From henna to honeymoons. George Monger. 327p. ABC-CLIO, 2004. $

392.5   GT2690

This interesting reference explores the many marriage customs of various cultures and religions throughout the world, highlighting both the similarities and differences. There are approximately 200 alphabetically arranged entries that examine such expected topics as arranged marriage and polygyny as well as some truly strange customs, such as marriage to a tree. Entries include cross-references and a bibliography, with some pictures included as well. A comprehensive index is also available.

Gender and Sexuality Studies

287   American masculinities: A historical encyclopedia. Bret E. Carroll, ed. 652p. SAGE, 2003. $$

305.31   HQ1090.3

As one of the earlier encyclopedias of men's studies, this single-volume work illustrates the scope that gender studies has achieved in the three decades since such studies were started. Multidisciplinary in approach, it includes more than 250 entries on individuals, organizations, events, political and social issues, and concepts and theories that help define the context for "masculinity." Entries can be as brief as half a column to several pages in length, with occasional illustrations. All entries are signed, with bibliographies, suggestions for further reading, and cross-references. A consolidated bibliography arranged by subject and a comprehensive index complete the volume.

288   American men: Who they are and how they live. 3rd ed. New Strategist, eds. 344p. New Strategist, 2008. $

305   HQ1090.3

289   American women: Who they are and how they live. 4th ed. New Strategist, eds. 360p. New Strategist, 2008. $

305.4   HQ1421

These complementary volumes are now in their respective third (men) and fourth (women) editions. While many of the demographics offered come from government or institutional sources (e.g., the American Community Survey and the University of Chicago's General Social Survey), the tables presented are not reprints; the New Strategist editors have reviewed the data to highlight emerging trends and characteristics not seen in other publications. Both volumes follow the same format: ten chapters providing statistics on topics from attitudes and education to wealth. Each chapter has a brief summary of the data and the conclusions to be drawn; each also has a glossary of terms, index, and list of tables. Whether used singly or for comparison, these works offer valuable insights into the lives of American men and women.

290   The Continuum complete international encyclopedia of sexuality. Robert T. Francoeur and Raymond J. Noonan, eds. 1419p. Continuum, 2004. $$

306.7   HQ21

This large, one-volume reference includes information on sexual attitudes and behaviors in 60 countries, compiled by more than 270 authorities. Each country's information is presented in a similar format: twelve categories, starting with demographics and a brief historical perspective, basic sexological premises, and religious, ethnic, and gender factors and continuing through such topics as autoerotic behaviors, gender diversity, contraception and abortion, AIDS, and sex research. Statistical tables present data (when available) for most countries, and an extensive list of references and suggested readings ends each entry. The directory of sexological organizations that follows the country entries is no longer current but is still of use in identifying sometimes obscure organizations. A detailed thematic index completes the volume.

291   Encyclopedia of gender and society. Jodi O'Brien, ed. 2v. SAGE, 2009. $$

305.3   HQ1115

As the editor admits, the scope of the project that produced this two-volume work is "immense" and she therefore worked to create an encyclopedia that would give users a "gender lens" on society grounded in significant gender scholarship. The result is impressive; the material focuses on all aspects of gender in social life from the individual to the global. The 450 articles range from art and beauty pageants to popular culture, queer studies, and the women's movement. Entries can be brief to several pages in length, are signed and cross-referenced, and include citations for further readings. A list of entries and a reader's guide begins volume 1, and a comprehensive index completes the set.

292 Encyclopedia of women in today's world. Mary Zeiss Stange, Carol K. Oyster, and Jane Sloan, eds. 4v. SAGE, 2011. $$

305.4   HQ1115

The strength of this work lies in its emphasis on contemporary women's issues. International in scope and comprehensive in the topics covered, it offers a feminist approach to discussing the advances and setbacks of women in the twenty-first century. Historical components of issues are kept to a minimum, with the focus instead on current concerns and debates. For example, there is no entry for "abortion" per se; instead there are entries for access to abortion, international abortion law, late abortion, and ethical issues related to abortion. Entries for countries focus on the legal status of women, basic demographic data, educational opportunities, women's representation in government, and other policy issues. Biographical entries are primarily of living women who have attained prominence in some area of endeavor, be it government, business, politics, or the arts. Entries are cross-referenced and include further readings, and there is a very useful reader's guide at the beginning of the first volume. With two updates planned to the online edition by 2014, this title should continue to offer a solid starting point for research into the current state of the world's women and will be appreciated in both public and academic libraries. *See also* "Biography," in chapter 1.

293 Gender and women's leadership: A reference handbook. Karen O'Connor, ed. 2v. SAGE, 2010. $$

305.42   HQ1233

A combination of biography, history, and theory makes this two-volume work exceptionally useful for students in gender studies, political and policy science, history, and the arts, to name only the major disciplines covered. Each chapter contains up to a dozen full-length papers on various facets of women and leadership: Part 1 is on feminist

theories of leadership, part 2 is on the history of women in public leadership roles. Subsequent chapters treat women as leaders in social movements, business, and the arts, women leaders outside the United States, and so on. The papers are scholarly and well cited but clearly written with undergraduates in mind. Arguments and conclusions are clearly presented and each ends with a summary and future directions for research. This is a superior collection and should remain useful for years to come.

294 International encyclopedia of men and masculinities. Michael Flood, Judith Kegan Gardiner, Bob Pease, and Keith Pringle, eds. 744p. Routledge, 2007. $$

305.3   HQ1090

Intended as a "key reference guide" to theoretical and empirical research about men and masculinity studies around the world, this encyclopedia helps establish the scope and diversity of the literature on the topic. The thematic list of entries that begins the volume starts with "lifecourse" and progresses through such categories as practices, theory, key concepts, cultural formations, histories, masculinity politics, and working with men and boys. Topics range from the historical to the theoretical (no biographies) and can sometimes be quite dense. Entries in this one-volume work are necessarily concise (400–2,250 words) but do have substantial bibliographies and cross-references, and there is a detailed index. This is probably not the work to give to lower-level undergraduates, but it will be very worthwhile for more advanced researchers.

295 Men and masculinities: A social, cultural, and historical encyclopedia. Michael S. Kimmel and Amy Aronson, eds. 2v. ABC-CLIO, 2004. $$

305.3   HQ1090

In comparison to the *International Encyclopedia of Men and Masculinities*, this two-volume encyclopedia has an equally broad focus but will have more popular appeal. It includes biographical and popular culture material not found in the other source, and though the entries are scholarly, there is less of an emphasis on theory and more explication. Entries are indexed and include bibliographies and cross-references with some illustrations.

296 **The Oxford encyclopedia of women in world history.** Bonnie G Smith, ed. 4v. Oxford, 2008. $$$

305.4   HQ1121

With entries submitted by more than 900 scholars from more than fifty countries, this four-volume work achieves its stated objective: "to survey the history of women in the world." The content includes biographical, geographic, and historical entries; individual biographies tend to be briefer (1–2 pages), while historical and topical entries can be quite extensive (more than twenty pages); all have bibliographies and cross-references. Related topics are arranged as subentries under main headwords for continuity, and there is a detailed topical outline and index. A chronology of more than 100 pages, arranged by period and region, follows the introduction in the first volume. The content is scholarly but written for a general audience and very readable. Although slightly more expensive than other titles in this section, this set is worth the cost.

Folklore and Folklife

297 **A companion to folklore.** Regina F. Bendix and Galit Hasan-Rokem, eds. 660p. Wiley-Blackwell, 2012. $$

398.2   GR45

Edited by two of the world's preeminent folklorists, this volume includes scholarship from all over the world on all aspects of folklore. It is divided into four parts, each with an introductory essay by the editors followed by the topical entries. In "Concepts and Phenomena," the essays are mainly theoretical; "Locations" essays consist of folklore scholarship from a number of countries or regions. In "Reflection," the essays deal with how folklore is incorporated in other areas such as literature or law. "Practice" essays deal with applied folklore. The work is intended for both introductory and advanced readers; all essays draw on contemporary scholarship and have extensive references for further research.

298 **The Greenwood encyclopedia of world folklore and folklife.** William M. Clements, ed. 4v. Greenwood, 2006. $$

398   GR35

Intended for all audiences, this four-volume work contains more than 200 entries on folklore worldwide written by an international team of folklorists. Volume 1 starts with thirty-nine short essays on processes, tools, social and intellectual movements, and concepts basic to an understanding of folklore. Entries for geographical areas follow a standard format: geography and history, religion and ritual, oral traditions, the arts, challenges to the modern world, and a list of folklore studies of the region. Entries are often illustrated with photographs, maps, or drawings, and all have references. Volume 4 contains a glossary of key terms and each volume has a complete index.

Hispanic Americans

299 **The borderlands: An encyclopedia of culture and politics on the U.S.-Mexico divide.** Andrew Grant Wood, ed. 322p. Greenwood, 2008. $

972/.1003   F786

This encyclopedia covers a broad range of topics and figures related to the extensive borderlands between the United States and Mexico. Geared toward undergraduate students and the general public, this reference is designed to provide an introduction to the history, culture, lifestyle, and politics of the U.S.-Mexican border. It contains 151 signed entries, with topics ranging from art, cuisine, and the environment to sports, slavery, tourism, and more. Entries range from short paragraphs to multiple pages and include a list of references for further reading. The arrangement is alphabetical, but a list of entries by topic allows the reader to quickly see related entries. A three-page chronology of events assists in providing context.

300 **Celebrating Latino folklore: An encyclopedia of cultural traditions.** María Herrera-Sobek, ed. 3v. ABC-CLIO, 2012. $$

305.86   E184

Celebrating Latino Folklore is the first encyclopedia in publication to focus on the folklore of the Latino people of the United States. Of the 318 entries, shorter essays, ranging in length from 500 to 1,500 words, include minor topics such as maize and alabados. Longer essays (3,500–8,000 words) cover important and extensive folk topics, folk tales, and people. A wide range of folklore genres are addressed, including folk narrative, folk speech, folk religion, folk dance, and folk songs. Entries are signed and include a list of references for further reading. A "Guide to Related Topics" arranges individual entries into broad subject areas, providing readers with an easy way to see related topics. Most appropriate for students and lay readers.

301 **The Oxford encyclopedia of Latinos and Latinas in the United States.** Suzanne Oboler and Deena J. González, eds. 4v. Oxford, 2005. $$$
973   E184

This four-volume reference contains more than 900 articles on topics related to the often overlooked historical, intellectual, social, artistic, and political experiences of Latinos and Latinas in the United States. Entries are arranged alphabetically and include cross-references and bibliographic references. More than 400 illustrations, charts, and maps are included throughout the resource. Volume 4 includes a topical outline of entries in fourteen broad categories, such as society, education, places, and biographies. Topics include court cases, specific states, geographic regions (e.g., East Los Angeles), organizations, individuals, and so forth. A nearly 200-page index completes the set.

Native Americans

302 **Encyclopedia of Native American history.** Peter C. Mancall, ed. 3v. Facts on File, 2011. $$
970.00   E77

This resource provides a comprehensive look at the individuals, events, and ideas that have shaped Native American history. Covering the period from the first human settlements in the Americas to the present day, it provides in-depth information about tribes, customs, events, leaders, government, religion, dress, and dwellings. Signed entries range in length from a paragraph to multiple pages, and references for further reading are included. Numerous black-and-white images and in-color maps enhance the content. With its readable, concise language, this resource is particularly

useful for high school students, college students, and laypeople.

303 **Encyclopedia of native tribes of North America.** 3rd ed. Michael Johnson; color plates by Richard Hook. 320p. Firefly, 2007. $
970   E76.2

In addition to providing a thorough history of more than 400 separately identifiable peoples native to North America, this resource includes a comprehensive classification of native languages. Hundreds of color illustrations and photos enrich the work, demonstrating tribal dress, art, crafts, and daily life, both past and present. Entries are arranged by cultural and geographical area (e.g., "Northwest Coast"). The third edition of this publication is greatly expanded and better organized than the previous edition. The unique and extensive collection of images and very reasonable cost make this an excellent addition to all types of libraries.

LGBT Studies

304 **Encyclopedia of lesbian and gay histories and cultures.** Bonnie Zimmerman and George Haggerty, eds. 2v. Garland, 2000. $$
306.76   HQ75

Although no longer unique for its equal treatment of gay and lesbian issues, this two-volume work (v. 1, lesbian histories; v. 2, gay histories) remains valuable for the broad scope of topics covered. A subject guide at the start of each volume helps identify multiple entries within a given topic. Coverage ranges from surveys of broad topics such as literature, theater, health, and politics to specific entries on prominent individuals and seminal events in gay and lesbian history and culture. Each entry includes cross-references and a bibliography.

305 **Encyclopedia of lesbian, gay, bisexual, and transgender history in America.** Marc Stein, ed. 3v. Scribner/Thomson/ Gale, 2004. $$$
306.76   HQ76.3

This three-volume set contains some 550 articles covering various aspects of lesbian, gay, bisexual, and transgender history and society in America.

Half of the entries are biographical; topical entries cover arts and culture, politics, economics, religion, and geographic locations (e.g., New York City, Mississippi). Volume 1 contains a chronology of LGBT history (through 2003). Volume 3 has a systematic outline of contents and a detailed index. All entries have bibliographies and are often illustrated with black-and-white photographs.

306   The gay and lesbian atlas. Gary
      J. Gates and Jason Ost. 232p. Urban
      Institute, 2004. $
      306.76   HQ76

Using information on same-sex partners collected in the 2000 census, this atlas provides a statistical and demographic overview of gay and lesbian couples in the United States. The early chapters discuss the data and methodologies used and the importance of location patterns in helping to dispel stereotypes. Subsequent chapters present data in tabular formats covering such topics as the top-ten states, cities, and zip codes with gay and lesbian couples; housing and neighborhood characteristics; and other demographic indices. Maps make up the largest portion of the book: each state has a map and data providing information on concentrations of gay/lesbian couples, age and ethnicity profiles, and supportive laws ranking. There are also several national maps and maps for selected cities. A short bibliography and index are included. As the 2000 census was the first in which information on same-sex households was collected, this work serves as a benchmark for ongoing research.

**307   Same-sex marriage: A reference
      handbook.** David E. Newton. 298p.
      ABC-CLIO, 2010. $
      306.84   HQ1033

Following the same format as other titles in the Contemporary World Issues series, this work is a useful introduction to the topic of same-sex marriage. A historical overview of same-sex relationships is followed by an outline of the arguments, both pro and con, as they have developed in Western culture, the United States in particular, and other parts of the world. A chronology and biographical entries of important people in the debate provide additional context. Of particular importance are the sections

on documents and data listing major legislation and court cases, government reports, and statistics. Concluding chapters on organizations both for and against same-sex marriage and resources for further research are equally valuable. A glossary and index are also provided.

**308   Who's who in gay and lesbian
      history: From antiquity to World
      War II.** Robert Aldrich and Garry
      Wotherspoon, eds. 502p. Routledge,
      2001. $
      **Who's who in contemporary gay and
      lesbian history: From World War II
      to the present day.** Robert Aldrich and
      Garry Wotherspoon, eds. 460p. Routledge, 2001. $
      306.76   HQ75.2

These two volumes present biographical information on prominent men and women in gay and lesbian history. Each volume contains approximately 500 individuals included for their impact on gay or lesbian culture, regardless of their personal sexual orientation. Most entries have references for further research. Although the majority of entries are on males from the Western world, the work is a good resource for beginning research.

**309   Routledge international encyclopedia
      of queer culture.** David A. Gerstner, ed.
      720p. Routledge, 2006. $$
      306.76   HQ75.13

As the editor states in the introduction, the aim of this one-volume encyclopedia is to "emphasize international queer cultural production" post-1945. While not intended to be "definitive," it is nevertheless comprehensive in scope, with more than 1,000 cross-referenced entries and three appendixes. Both thematic and alphabetical lists of entries help readers navigate the work. There is an almost equal mix of biographical and topical articles, each signed. Entries tend to be succinct and without bibliographies, although major topics can have longer treatments with extensive bibliographies or suggestions for further reading. When published in 2006, the three appendixes (archives of LGBT research materials, international sex laws, and international political and community organizations) would have been more useful; time and changes in legal and political policy have made the listings less than completely accurate. Nevertheless, the encyclopedia is a major asset for the study of international aspects of the queer community since World War II.

Philanthropy

310 Annual register of grant support: A directory of funding sources. 46th ed. 1145p. Information Today, 2013. Annual. $$

001.44   AS911

For libraries unable to pay a great deal for grant-finding resources, the *Annual Register* is a practical choice from among many competing products. The 2013 edition lists more than 2,700 grant support programs from government, public and private foundations, and a variety of other trusts, associations, and special interest organizations. Each new edition provides contact information, details on who can and cannot apply, deadlines, and other pertinent information in plain language and an easily readable format. There are subject, program, geographic, and personnel indexes to assist in identifying appropriate grants and a very helpful chapter on program planning and proposal writing at the front of each edition.

311 Philanthropy in America: A comprehensive historical encyclopedia. Dwight Burlingame, ed. 3v. ABC-CLIO, 2004. $$

361.7   HV91

Available now only in the online edition, this title remains valuable as one of the rare works offering an overview of the history and development of philanthropy in America. Biographies of philanthropic individuals and profiles of organizations are concise and informative but can also be found elsewhere; the strength of this work is in the entries on the historical concepts and theories on charity, obligation to community, and self-interest that contributed to the evolution of philanthropic giving as it now exists. A set of primary source documents that includes examples from Aristotle to Supreme Court rulings on charitable giving help illustrate primary points. All entries are signed and

have bibliographies, and there is a timeline of key events and a glossary of terms.

Social Work and Social Services

312 Catalog of federal domestic assistance. General Services Administration. www.cfda.gov. Free

338.9   HC110

Available online as a database and as a PDF (print copies are available by request), the catalog provides access and information on federal programs, projects, services, and activities offering assistance or benefits to individuals or groups in the United States and its territories. It currently lists more than 2,100 assistance programs from the Departments of Health and Human Services, Education, Interior, Agriculture, and Housing and Urban Development. Additional resources are listed for new programs available under the Recovery and Reinvestment Act of 2009. A CFDA User Guide is available along with brief descriptions and histories of programs and a current list of regional agency offices.

313 Child abuse sourcebook. 3rd ed. Valarie R. Juntunen, ed. 629p. Omnigraphics, 2013. $

362.7   HV6626.5

Now in its third edition, this source is a comprehensive reference for current information on neglect and all types of abuse of children. Definitions, statistics, guidelines for reporting abuse, legal protections, prevention programs, and support groups are covered. Includes information for parents and adult survivors of child abuse, and several directories provide contact information.

314 Comprehensive handbook of social work and social welfare. Karen M. Sowers and Catherine N. Dulmas, eds. 4v. Wiley, 2008. $$$

361   HV40

Published in four volumes, this handbook is an in-depth introduction to the main areas of the field for students and a reference for working professionals and scholars. Each volume in the set covers a major area: *The Profession of Social Work, Human Behavior in the Social Environment, Social Work Practice,* and *Social Policy and Policy Practice*. Each volume contains from eighteen to twenty-eight essays with author and subject indexes and can be purchased individually. The essays are wide ranging, written by international experts citing both seminal historical work and current research in the field.

315 Encyclopedia of social work. 20th ed. Terry Mizrahi and Larry E. Davis, eds. 4v. Oxford, 2008. $$

361.3   HV12

Now in its twentieth edition, this encyclopedia is considered one of the essential reference works in the field. Published by the National Association of Social Workers and Oxford University Press, this latest edition is more comprehensive in scope, reflecting changes in the social work community nationally and internationally, and in depth, adding significantly more overview entries explaining major framework or content areas. Increased contributions from international scholars add to the diversity of the content. Major topics covered include research methodologies, social policy and social welfare, and practice methods and interventions. There is a new biographical section for individuals who have had a significant impact on the field and an appendix including a chronology of the history of social work and welfare in the United States. All entries are signed and have references and suggestions for further reading and suggested links when appropriate.

316 The national directory of children, youth and families services. 984p. Dorland Health, 2011. Annual. $$

362.7   HV741

Published annually, this title includes state listings of social services, health and mental health services, juvenile justice agencies, educational services, and other resources for assisting children and youth. Part 2 has information about federal agencies and national organizations, grants, and other funding available for programs to assist children. Part 3 is a buyer's guide and resource section.

317 Social workers' desk reference. 2nd ed. Albert R. Roberts, ed. 1312p. Oxford, 2009. $

361.3   HV40

The second edition of this well-received source

continues the format of concise, easy-to-read entries on social work practice and research. Now with 171 authored entries, this work focuses on the increased complexity of social work issues brought about by accelerated global human interaction, the growing scarcity of food and energy, the increased complexity of political and economic transactions, and advances in the fields of human biology and neuroscience. To achieve brevity, entries often employ diagrams and bulleted lists. Social work practices are illustrated by incident overviews with timelines. All entries have references and list the websites of relevant organizations, agencies, or institutions useful for continued research. A detailed glossary of terms and author and subject indexes complete the volume. A practical and useful guide for students and practitioners.

Sociology

Dictionaries and Encyclopedias

318 Blackwell encyclopedia of sociology online. George Ritzer, ed. 11v. Wiley-Blackwell, 2011. $$$$

301.03   HM425

Building on the 2007 print publication, this massive online resource is updated three times a year, providing readers with instant access to up-to-date scholarship in the field. Entries are written and edited by an international team of scholars and teachers. The work includes more than 1,800 entries written in clear, concise terms. Entries, which range from short definitions to extensive explorations of major concepts in the field, are signed and contain extensive cross-references and suggested readings. As in *The Concise Encyclopedia of Sociology*, entries are assigned within a lexicon to at least one broad subject category, and readers are encouraged to scan the entire lexicon in order to select headings and terms of special interest. This resource represents the single most comprehensive collection of sociological knowledge ever compiled.

319 The Cambridge dictionary of sociology. Bryan S. Turner, ed. 688p. Cambridge, 2006. $

301.03   HM425

Many of the more than 600 entries in this resource

are quite lengthy, facilitating the exploration and debate of critical and contested concepts in the field. References are included in-text to allow the reader to get an immediate grasp of key bibliographic sources. A large number of biographies of sociologists, both classical and contemporary, are intermingled with other entries. Entries are written in accessible language to allow for the greatest access for users ranging from scholars to lay readers. Authors were drawn from many countries in order to reflect the cosmopolitism of sociology as a field.

320 The concise encyclopedia of sociology. George Ritzer and J. Michael Ryan, eds. 726p. Wiley-Blackwell, 2011. $$

301.03   HM425

This reference draws largely from the eleven-volume *Blackwell Encyclopedia of Sociology* (2007), though nearly 20 percent of the entries are unique to this work. This book attempts to be more accessible to the average student, scholar, or lay reader, both in terms of conciseness and affordability. In order to assist in organization and ease of access, entries are assigned within a lexicon to at least one broad subject category. Readers are encouraged to scan the entire lexicon in order·to select headings and terms of special interest. Entries are written by an international array of experts in order to provide the work with a global perspective. A timeline of more than 600 pivotal events, figures, and publications provides context.

321 A dictionary of sociology. 3rd ed. rev. John Scott and Gordon Marshall, eds. 816p. Oxford, 2009. $

301   HM425

The revised third edition of *A Dictionary of Sociology* includes carefully scrutinized links to online sources of information in many of its 2,500-plus entries. Entries for this resource have been compiled by an international group of leading experts in sociology. Topic coverage is comprehensive within the field of sociology but also includes terms from related fields such as psychology, economics, anthropology, philosophy, and political science. Cross-references are presented throughout. Biographical entries are intermixed with other terms.

322 The Penguin dictionary of sociology. 5th ed. Nicholas Abercrombie, Stephen Hill, and Bryan S. Turner. 484p. Penguin, 2006. $

301.03   HM17

Authored by three eminent professors in the field, this reference has been updated to reflect key developments in areas such as gender issues and sociobiology and economic sociology and globalization. This user-friendly and affordable dictionary is particularly useful for students of sociology and related fields. Entries are concise yet provide enough context to explain relationships between terms. Entries include statistical data and references. Useful cross-references are provided throughout.

Handbooks

323 The SAGE handbook of sociology. Craig Calhoun, Chris Rojek, and Bryan S. Turner, eds. 590p. SAGE, 2005. $$

301   HM585

This handbook provides a comprehensive overview of the ever-changing field of sociology. While addressing new developments in the field, it provides an authoritative guide to theory and method. Contributions from younger researchers give voice to emerging areas of research. Contributors come from both European and American institutions. Each article contains references for further reading. This handbook is relevant not just for sociologists but for students and researchers across the range of disciplines within the social sciences.

Statistics and Demography

324 American community survey. U.S. Census Bureau, 1993–. www.census.gov/acs/. Free

The American Community Survey is the current instrument for collecting data on the population of the United States. It replaced the census long form as the preferred method for generating the information necessary for economic forecasting and the distribution of federal and state funds. Data are collected on a variety of categories: age, sex, race, income, households, education, veteran status, disabilities, and so forth. There is detailed documentation on using the available data and a growing library of completed surveys (by year or keyword).

325 America's top-rated cities: A statistical handbook. 19th ed. Laura Mars and David Garoogian, eds. 4v. Grey House, 2012. $$
America's top-rated smaller cities: A statistical profile. 9th ed. Laura Mars and David Garoogian, eds. 2v. Grey House, 2012. $$

317.3   HT123

These two works provide statistical profiles for America's top 100 large cities (population greater than 100,000) and top 124 smaller cities (the online version profiles even more), respectively. The data reported in the two differ somewhat, but both provide current statistical snapshots of a city's social, business, economic, demographic, and environmental profile. Entries include background and ranking information, followed by data on transportation, occupations, fastest-growing labor markets, crime, minority-owned business, sports venues, and a wealth of other information of interest to individuals and businesses looking to invest or relocate.

326 Demography: Analysis and synthesis. Graziella Caselli, Jacques Vallin, and Guillaume Wunsch, eds. 4v. Elsevier, 2006. $$$

304.6   HB871

This four-volume set is appropriate for upper-level undergraduates and graduate students, researchers, teachers, and faculty interested in demography, sociology, history, health care, and basically any discipline concerned with the accurate collection and analysis of population information. In the 140 chapters, each with at least one essay, there is an even mix of methodological, theoretical, and practical aspects. Volume 1 addresses population dynamics; volume 2, mortality; volume 3, the history of population and population forecasting; and volume 4, the history of population policy. More than 100 international experts contributed to the work, and it is both comprehensive and thorough. All the essays are heavily illustrated with charts and graphs, are signed, and have references. A detailed index ends each volume.

327 Encyclopedia of the U.S. Census: From the Constitution to the American Community Survey. 2nd ed. Margo J. Anderson, Constance F. Citro, and Joseph J. Salvo, eds. 456p. CQ Press, 2012. $$

304.6   HA37

Understanding the census and the methods used to collect and analyze the data it collects is the objective of this work. Essays focus on the principal concepts, issues, processes, and techniques of census taking along with the policy implications of the data collected. Each of the decennial censuses is discussed along with a snapshot of the nation in that era; both the 2000 and 2010 censuses are included. Other essays focus on the mechanics of the census, the replacement of the long form in 2000 with the American Community Survey (ACS), and the increasing refinement of the data obtained. Each of the signed essays has references and the work is rich with tables and graphs of data illustrating concepts and trends. Appendixes include historical population data, congressional apportionment, and samples of the 2010 short form and the 2010 ACS form. Exceptionally useful for helping to interpret census data and understand its limitations.

328 Historical statistics of the United States: Earliest times to the present. Millennial ed. Richard Sutch and Susan B. Carter, gen. eds. 5v. Cambridge, 2006. $$$

317.3   HA202

Although the price may be off-putting for smaller libraries, this five-volume work is the definitive source for U.S. historical statistics. This is the first comprehensive update since the bicentennial edition and includes the results from the 2000 census. It contains some 37,000 data series in five areas: population, work and welfare, economic structure and performance, economic sectors, and governance and international relations. Straightforward arrangement and excellent indexes make it easy to find and compare time-series data on almost any topic imaginable. This is an essential work for any library supporting research in American history. *Statistical abstract of the United States,* **see 4.**

329 Statistical yearbook. Annuaire statistique. 55th ed. UN Statistics

Division. United Nations Publications, 2012. Annual. $$

310   HA155

The *Statistical Yearbook* is one of the few sources for international statistics on social and economic conditions and activities at the national, regional, and world level. As of 2013, this annual yearbook has more than sixty tables in four sections, the first presenting world and regional summaries and the other three reporting on countries or areas. Topics include population and gender, education, culture and communication, economic activity, financial statistics and labor force, wages and prices, manufacturing, energy, science and technology, and others. Series data are usually from one to ten years. International statistics are notoriously unreliable for areas in conflict or economic distress; the UN produces this data from national sources when available and independent sources reviewed by professionals when not.

Substance Abuse

330   Encyclopedia of addictions. Kathryn H. Hollen. 2v. Greenwood, 2009. $$

616.86   RC563.4

This encyclopedia contains more than 200 entries related to a wide range of addictive behavior, from pathological gambling to dependence on prescription drugs. Entries discuss causes, symptoms, prevalence, treatment, and prevention, as well as associated terms such as compulsion, denial, and withdrawal. An additional 200 entries cross-reference addictive drugs and medications by both their generic and trade names. There are also biographical entries on such pioneers in the field as Benjamin Rush and Bill Wilson. An explanation of the science of addiction, including a description of basic brain anatomy and neurotransmitter function and how the brain's chemical messengers operate to influence feelings and sensation, helps to provide a broad scientific context for addiction. One helpful appendix contains an index of the street names by which many of these substances are known. An additional appendix contains a list of organizations to which readers may apply for assistance or further information. A bibliography of sources appears at the end of the book, and some entries contain references for further reading.

331   The encyclopedia of drug abuse. Esther Gwinnell and Christine A. Adamec. 380p. Facts on File, 2008. $

616.86   RC563.4

Following an extensive introduction on the history of drug abuse, the 200 individual entries of this work cover a variety of drugs, the causes and consequences of abuse, and prevention. Additionally, this work contains information about drug use within particular countries and groups. Entries range in length from a few paragraphs to a few pages and include cross-references where appropriate and a list of references for additional information. A number of helpful appendixes provide a convenient place to browse such things as state mental health agencies and health departments and tables of drug use by race, age, and sex. Though less than exhaustive, this very affordable resource provides an excellent introduction to the subject for students and lay readers.

332   Encyclopedia of drugs, alcohol, and addictive behavior. 3rd ed. Pamela Korsmeyer and Henry R. Kranzler, eds. 4v. Macmillan, 2008. $$$

362.29   HV5804

The third edition of this work is a major revision of the award-winning previous edition. In addition to 133 new articles, 236 have been substantially revised. New entries report on such changes as the evolving coverage of drugs in the media, use of drugs and alcohol in sports and the fashion industry, and the impact of the Internet on drug and alcohol use. In addition, this latest edition expands coverage of the topic outside of the United States. Broadly speaking, this work addresses the medical, social, legal, and political issues related to drug and alcohol use. Entries range from two to four pages in length and include some cross-referencing. A bibliography of additional resources is included in some of the longer essays. This resource is intended primarily for a nonspecialist audience.

Urban Studies

333   Encyclopedia of American urban history. David Goldfield, ed. 2v. SAGE, 2007. $$

307.7   HT123

Urban history is an interdisciplinary field, and the two volumes of this encyclopedia reflect that diversity. The reader's guide lists entries under categories ranging from biographies, cities, and doctrines to education, housing, transportation, and women. Topics range from air pollution and baseball to the Fair Housing Act and yellow journalism. A strong historical element adds entries on individual cities in particular and the evolution of the city and city planning in general. Entries are written for the undergraduate or nonprofessional but are useful for more advanced researchers as well. All entries are signed, with further readings and references. The reader's guide, list of contributors, and detailed index are included in both volumes.

334 Encyclopedia of community: From the village to the virtual world. Karen Christensen and David Levinson, eds. 4v. SAGE, 2003. $$$

307   HM756

This four-volume reference was the first encyclopedia to focus on the concept of community. Included are 500 articles on diverse topics ranging from community case studies and biographies to aspects of religion, politics, human development, urban and suburban life, and virtual communities. Photographs and sidebar information enhance many of the articles. Each volume includes an appendix of subject areas listing related books, journals, organizations, and websites (rather dated now) for additional research. The fourth volume offers additional appendixes on the vital role of libraries in communities and on the community in popular culture plus a master bibliography of community literature. A detailed index completes the set.

335 Encyclopedia of the city. Roger W. Caves, ed. 564p. Routledge, 2005. $$

307.7   HT108.5

This one-volume work is most useful as an entry point or enhanced dictionary for urban studies and related fields. There are more than 500 signed entries, the majority half a page to a page in length, with brief references for further reading. Biographical entries cite key works at the top of the essay, a useful arrangement. As the editor notes in the introduction, "the term 'city' means anything and everything," and the diversity of topics included reflects this view; aspects of history, architecture,

demography, sociology, policy and planning, and many other topics are all included.

336 Encyclopedia of urban studies. Ray Hutchison, ed. 2v. SAGE, 2010. $$

307.7   HT108.5

As urban studies has matured as a discipline, so have the reference materials supporting research in it. This two-volume work is no exception. Ideas treated in other works get the benefit of additional content or analysis from more recent scholarship, and new topics incorporate developments from the twenty-first century. An entry for the ancient Acropolis coexists with one for "Cyburbia," a term for the study of the impact of new technology and social media. The range of topics in the reader's guide is broad and international in scope, reflecting the multidisciplinary nature of the subject. Articles are signed and have extensive references; many are suitable for undergraduate or general researchers, though some are particularly rich in jargon or theory, which makes them less accessible. In addition to the guide in volume 1, there is a list of entries in each volume and an index completes volume 2.

337 Key concepts in urban studies. Mark Gottdiener and Leslie Budd. 2v. SAGE, 2005. $

307.7   HT108.5

Part of the SAGE Key Concepts series, this title is a useful tool for helping new students understand the concepts and terms of urban studies. Entries are concise but not particularly short, written for the newcomer, and include references. Only 183 entries are included but they represent the spectrum of topics covered by the field: Chicago School, immigration, preservation, sustainable urbanization, and urban violence, to name just a few. An updated edition would be useful, but this is still a worthwhile acquisition for very little investment.

Youth and Child Development

338 Encyclopedia of adolescence. B. Bradford Brown and Mitchell J. Prinstein, eds. 3v. Elsevier/Academic, 2011. $$$

305.2   HQ796

More of a handbook than an encyclopedia, this three-volume work contains 125 comprehensive articles on adolescent issues and experiences. Each article begins with a glossary of terms and contains extensive cross-references to other articles and a list of further readings and sources. Volume 1 contains articles on theories and studies of development, including brain and cognitive development, adolescent decision making, puberty, self-esteem, and stages of adolescence. Volume 2 focuses on interpersonal and sociocultural factors such as sibling relations, gender roles, and the influence of media. Volume 3 is on psychopathology and non-normative processes—addiction, attention deficit hyperactivity disorder, autism, eating disorders, and the like. Articles are substantial, averaging seven to ten pages in length, often with illustrative diagrams or tables. Not recommended as a basic text but very useful for upper-level undergraduates and above.

339   Encyclopedia of applied developmental science. Celia B. Fisher and Richard M. Lerner, eds. 2v. SAGE, 2005. $$$

305.2   HQ767.8

This two-volume work is a comprehensive encyclopedia on all aspects of applied developmental science, with equal weight given to topics of childhood and adolescence. Issues of adult development (parenting, family policy, etc.) are included as well. Numerous biographical (and autobiographical) entries on persons important to the development of the field are included. Entries can be long for major topics and overviews, and all have substantial references and suggestions for further reading. Considering the scope of topics covered, students in psychology, sociology, public policy, intercultural studies, and the like will all find this work useful.

340   Encyclopedia of children and childhood: In history and society. Paula S. Fass, ed. 3v. Macmillan, 2004. $$

305.2   HQ767.8

This three-volume resource contains 445 alphabetically arranged entries on various topics and individuals related to childhood, from birth to adolescence. As the title indicates, historical aspects of childhood in various periods, from Ancient Greece and Rome to the present, are incorporated into a number of essays. Volume 3 includes an annotated collection of fifty primary source documents selected by the editors as essential works of the field. All entries are signed, with references and cross-references; many have illustrations. The language is accessible and the work should be useful to both new and more advanced researchers.

341   Youth, education, and sexualities: An international encyclopedia. James T. Sears, ed. 2v. Greenwood, 2005. $$

371.8   LC192.6

While this work could as easily have been listed with the LGBT or education titles, the focus is on youth (adolescence through college age) and particularly LGBT youth, in the context of educational systems. The nearly 250 entries are broad ranging and will be useful to both students and researchers in education, psychology, health, history, and sociology. The international coverage is not particularly strong (large countries have individual entries while small ones do not), but the overview articles (Africa, Asia, etc.) are worthwhile. Entries run from a page to several pages in length, all have references, and cross-references are indicated in the text by boldface. Volume 2 contains a general bibliography, a list of online resources (now somewhat dated), and a detailed index.

See also **"LGBT Studies," in this chapter.**

5 Business and Careers

ERICA COE

The various sources here will be beneficial to students, business professionals, and the general public. This is not intended to stand alone as a core resource guide, but it should provide general guidance for beginning or expanding a collection. Although business has an increasingly international perspective, publications out of the United States and United Kingdom were selected for their ready availability. Book entries are for print sources, but libraries interested in e-books will find that many publishers—including Gale, Greenwood, and Routledge—provide electronic versions as well. Entries include publication information for the most recent edition when available, even if the item is published as a serial.

General Sources

Bibliographies and Guides

342 Basic business library: Core resources and services. 5th ed. Eric Forte and Michael Oppenheim, eds. 240p. Libraries Unlimited, 2012. $
016.027   Z675
Designed for librarians and library students, the completely revised fifth edition begins with an introductory chapter entitled "Core Resources for the Accidental Business Librarian" that includes reviews of key resources and concepts. To supplement the core list, additional chapters cover periodicals, government information, investment, marketing research, start-ups, and in-depth academic research. For smaller and budget-conscious libraries, free resources are also included throughout. The final chapters, on collection development, reference, and future trends, provide practical information for business librarians, especially those new to the field.

343 How to find business information: A guide for business people, investors, and researchers. Lucy Heckman, ed. 218p. Praeger, 2011. $
016.65   HD30
In its first addition, this handbook provides students, researchers, and librarians with annotated lists of common resources for many business fields. Standout chapters cover personal finance and investing and careers and job hunting. Free organizational and commercial websites are integrated throughout each chapter. Appendixes include acronyms and abbreviations, major business libraries, federal government resources, and major stock market and securities exchanges.

344 Strauss's handbook of business information: A guide for librarians,

students, and researchers. 3rd ed. Rita W. Moss and David G. Ernsthausen, eds. 399p. Libraries Unlimited, 2012. $

016.33   HF1010

Librarians and researchers will benefit from the source reviews, concept overviews, and research strategies in this guide, which has been revised to highlight the abundance of free resources now available. It is divided into two parts, with the first covering basic sources in print and online. The second part is divided by specific business fields, with explanations of the specialized concepts and terminology as well as reviews of resources. Appendixes cover acronyms and abbreviations, federal government departments and agencies, federal government corporations and independent agencies, key economic indicators, and selected websites. Indexes are provided for titles and subjects.

Biographical Sources

345   African-American business leaders and entrepreneurs. Rachel Kranz. 322p. Facts on File, 2004. $

338.092   HC102.5

This encyclopedia is still useful for its historical perspective on African American businesspeople from colonial times to 2004. The arrangement is the same as *American Inventors, Entrepreneurs, and Business Visionaries*. This easy-to-read and engaging encyclopedia will be of interest to students, historians, and the general public.

See also "**African Americans,**" **in chapter 4.**

346   American inventors, entrepreneurs, and business visionaries. Rev. ed. Charles W. Carey Jr.; rev. by Ian C. Friedman. 481p. Facts on File, 2011. $

338.09   CT214

Part of the American Biographies series, this revised edition provides more than 300 biographical entries on famous and not-so-famous men and women who illustrate the history of invention and entrepreneurialism in America. The introduction covers how the economy has changed between centuries and the individuals involved in these changes. The A–Z entries include birth and death dates, the subject's role and contributions, and a chronological telling of his or her life. Suggestions

for further reading follow each entry, and a separate bibliography of recommended sources is also included. Entries are classified by invention/business type and year of birth. The index is fairly comprehensive. This easy-to-read and engaging encyclopedia will be of interest to students, historians, and the general public.

Databases and Indexes

347   ABI/Inform. ProQuest. www.proquest .com/en-US/catalogs/databases/detail/ abi_inform.shtml. CP$

Provides articles from major business publications, including newspapers, magazines, journals, and trade publications. Three versions exist to meet the needs of different libraries, and content varies. Easy-to-use search features, some full-text availability, and quality sources.

348   Business insights: Essentials. Gale. www.cengagesites.com/literature/782/gale -business-insights-global-essentials/. CP$

Formerly Business and Company Resource Center, this database provides industry rankings, company profiles, market share data, company histories, live charts, news, and a glossary. Includes information on associations and government offices. Easy-to-use search features, full-text availability, and quality sources.

349   Business source premier. EBSCO. www.ebscohost.com/academic/business -source-premier. CP$

Provides access to articles, company profiles, case studies and reports on industries, market research, and country reports. Articles are from magazines, newspapers, journals, and trade publications. Two other versions exist, Business Source Elite and Business Source Complete. Coverage increases from Elite to Premier to Complete. Easy-to-use search and navigation features, full-text availability, and a large quantity of quality sources. Librarians will have to decide which level of coverage is appropriate for their libraries.

350   Hoover's. Hoover's. www.hoovers.com. CP$

Contains company and industry profiles, executive biographies, news and press releases, and company financials and SEC reports. Three subscription packages are available. The website also includes some free content with limited information on the companies. Easy-to-use, full-text availability, and excellent company information.

Dictionaries and Encyclopedias

351 The American economy: A historical encyclopedia. Rev. ed. Cynthia L. Clark, ed. 2v. ABC-CLIO, 2011. $$
330.97   HC102
Covering American history from colonial times to the present, biographical and topical entries in volume 1 are supplemented by in-depth essays and primary documents in volume 2. Topical entries include court cases, laws, events, and commodities. The essays cover larger concepts like advertising or education with lengthier lists of references. Useful for students and researchers alike.

352 Business: The ultimate resource. 3rd ed. 1605p. A & C Black, 2011. $
658   HD38.15
This "ultimate resource" serves as a practical, multipurpose desk reference for students and businesspeople. The best-practice essays from leading writers provide practical advice and overviews on common issues, while the management "action-lists" provide dos, don'ts and FAQs on business processes. Also included are one-page summaries of the most influential business books, profiles of business thinkers and management giants, and a global dictionary.

353 Cambridge business English dictionary. 980p. Cambridge, 2011. $
330.03   HF1001
This dictionary includes 35,000 terms and is aimed at students, laypeople, and nonnative English speakers. Many terms include phonetics and use examples and category labels. Select terms also include "Focus on Vocabulary" boxes identifying near-synonyms and theme-related terms to assist users with word choice. Extra help pages located in the center of the book cover business communication and writing skills such as interviewing and report writing as well as general topics such as company structure and corporate social

responsibility. Sections at the back cover symbols, countries, regions, continents, world currencies, and major financial centers with their stock exchanges. A free version is available online at http://dictionary .cambridge.org/us/dictionary/business-english/ and includes audio pronunciations.

354 Dictionary of business and economics terms. 5th ed. Jack P. Friedman, ed. 800p. Barron's Educational Series, 2012. $
330.03   HF1001
Aimed at students and laypeople, this revised edition provides concise definitions for 8,000 terms dealing with numerous fields of business. Definitions include cross-references as needed but do not include phonetics. Terms with varying field-dependent definitions are noted with the field and appropriate definition. For example, the term *recovery* includes definitions from economics, finance, and investment. Key legislation, organizations, and associations are also included.

355 Encyclopedia of American business. Rev. ed. W. Davis Folsom and Stacia N. VanDyne, eds. 2v. Facts on File, 2011. $$
338.09   HF1001
Written in an easy-to-understand style, this encyclopedia is geared toward students and others who need a basic understanding of economic issues, concepts, principles, laws, and institutions. This revised edition emphasizes financial markets, instruments, and regulatory authorities. New entries focus on building consumers' understanding of their role and rights in American business. Most entries have further-reading suggestions, and there is a general bibliography at the end. The index is well planned and provides a good starting point for researchers.

Directories

356 Directory of business information resources. 19th ed. 2000p. Grey House, 2013. Annual. $$
016.65   HF54.52
This annual directory provides quick access to the contacts, names, and resources useful for marketers and researchers. Organized by industry, it includes associations, newsletters, magazines and journals, trade shows, directories and databases,

and websites. An alphabetical entry index and a publisher index are included.

357 Headquarters USA: A directory of contact information for headquarters and other central offices of major businesses and organizations in the United States and in Canada. 35th ed. 2800p. Omnigraphics, 2013. Annual. $$

384.6   E154.5

This annual directory provides quick and easy access to contact information for businesses, non-profit organizations, government agencies, professional associations, educational and cultural institutions, and high-profile individuals. Listings are provided alphabetically and by subject. Area and zip code guides are also included. This directory will be useful for all libraries.

Handbooks, Yearbooks, and Almanacs

358 Business rankings annual. 988p. Gale Cengage, 2012. Annual. $$

338.7   HG4050

This annual publication provides students and researchers with lists of companies, products, services, and activities ranked by factors including assets, sales, revenue, production, employees, market value, and more. It is arranged by subject and is international in scope. Data has been compiled from a variety of published sources, and each entry provides the source information, including publication schedule (e.g., annual or semiannual). This makes it easy to search for updated statistics—a useful feature, as many of the results are two to three years old. It also allows libraries to justify purchasing this costly title only every two or three years. The index is fairly comprehensive and provides entry numbers, not page numbers. A separate cumulative index going back to 1989 is provided as part of the set.

359 Business statistics of the United States: Patterns of economic change. 16th ed. Cornelia J. Strawser, ed. 642p. Bernan, 2011. $$

Compiled largely from government sources, this book of statistical tables is an excellent starting point for gathering data on the U.S. economy, industry profiles, historical data, and regional

and state data. The sixteenth edition has been reorganized to include historical data back to 1929 or earlier alongside recent data, rather than splitting these into two sections. Commonly requested data covered here include GDP, household income distribution, consumer income and spending, consumer price indexes, and international comparisons and exchange rates. GDP, personal income, and employment are also provided by region and state. The reader is provided with an introductory section on how to use the data, and each chapter includes notes and definitions. The index is well organized and includes cross-references.

360 Handbook of U.S. labor statistics: Employment, earnings, prices, productivity, and other labor data. 15th ed. Mary Meghan Ryan, ed. 531p. Bernan, 2012. $$

This updated edition provides recent and historical data compiled from the Bureau of Labor Statistics. Chapters cover employment, wages and compensation, productivity and costs, labor force by industry and occupation, price indexes, and consumer expenditures. Also included are chapters on recent trends, including mass layoffs, international comparisons, labor-management relations (including union affiliation and work stoppages), the American Time Use Survey, and occupational health and safety. Highlights, notes, and definitions supplement the statistical tables. The index includes cross-references and is a good entry point for researchers.

Accounting

361 Accounting handbook. 5th ed. Joel G. Siegel and Jae K. Shim. 1046p. Barron's, 2010. $

657   HF5635

This updated edition provides a practical overview of accounting principles and practices and a dictionary of related terms. An overview of financial accounting includes financial statements, reporting requirements, and accounting principles and standards. Additional chapters cover individual income tax preparation and planning, auditing, personal financial planning, accounting for governments and nonprofits, information technology, quantitative methods, international accounting and standards, and forensic accounting. Appendixes cover the Sarbanes-Oxley Act. Entries are clear and include illustrations and examples, making this resource useful for students and business professionals alike.

362   Dictionary of accounting terms. 5th ed. Jae K. Shim and Joel G. Siegel. 523p. Barron's, 2010. $
    657   HF5621

This clear, well-written dictionary provides definitions and illustrative examples for more than 2,500 key terms from all areas of accounting and related business fields. Entries for organizations and associations include brief mission statements. A section with abbreviations follows the dictionary. This dictionary is appropriate for professionals, students, and the general public.

Advertising, Marketing, and Consumer Research

363   The Advertising Age encyclopedia of advertising. John McDonough and Karen Egolf, eds. 3v. Fitzroy Dearborn, 2003. $$
    659.1   HF5803

This comprehensive and fascinating encyclopedia will be useful for a historical look at advertising. Entries include biographies, select countries, theories, methods and mediums, cultural issues, agency histories, and histories of advertisers, brands, and markets. Entries on ad agencies include a brief chronology of key dates, a selective list of clients, and a chronologically arranged descriptive history. Illustrations and further-reading lists accompany many entries. The vast amount of information on advertising makes this work a standard for all collections serving students, business professionals, and historians. The advertising images and related information will also be of interest to the general public. Libraries holding this source should retain it either in the reference or circulating area of the library.

364   American generations series. 4v. New Strategist. $–$$

The increased focus on consumer age groups makes this series a must for libraries serving business professionals, entrepreneurs, and students. The series provides data on trends in education, health, housing, income, labor force, living arrangements, population, spending, and wealth in a user-friendly, easy-to-read format. Titles include *Baby Boom*, *Generation X*, *Older Americans*, and *The Millennials*. Each section begins with highlights of the major trends in that area. These trends, and others, are then discussed further and illustrated with charts and tables of statistical data, primarily from the U.S. Census and other government documents. Available for purchase individually or as a set.

365   American Marketing Association dictionary. www.marketingpower.com/_layouts/Dictionary.aspx. Free

This continuously updated dictionary provides concise definitions with cross-references. This site is useful for students wanting to understand marketing terminology.

366   Consumer series. 11v. New Strategist. $–$$

This eleven-title series provides demographic, spending, and lifestyle data on the U.S. population in a user-friendly and easy-to-read format. Each section begins with highlights of the major trends in that area. These trends, and others, are then discussed further and illustrated with charts and tables of statistical data, primarily from the U.S. Census and other government documents. Appendixes include a brief glossary and bibliography. The indexes in each volume are fairly comprehensive and provide good entry points for researchers looking for specific data. These sources will prove valuable for libraries serving business professionals, entrepreneurs, and students. Titles updated in or after 2010 include

- *American Attitudes: What Americans Think about the Issues That Shape Their Lives*
- *American Generations: Who They Are and How They Live*
- *American Health: Demographics and Spending of Health Care Consumers*
- *American Marketplace: Demographics and Spending Patterns*

- *American Men and Women: Who They Are and How They Live*
- *American Time Use: Who Spends How Long at What*
- *Americans and Their Homes: Demographics of Homeownership*
- *Demographics of the U.S.: Trends and Projections*
- *Racial and Ethnic Diversity*

367   Money series. 4v. New Strategist. $$
This four-volume series provides useful information for anyone examining American spending patterns. *American Buyers: Demographics of Shopping* provides weekly and quarterly buyer statistics by major product and service category. *American Incomes: Demographics of Who Has Money* covers income trends in the following categories: household income, men's income, women's income, discretionary income, wealth, and poverty. *Best Customers: Demographics of Consumer Demand* analyzes household spending on more than 300 products and services, indicating the national average, best customers, and biggest customers (market share) by age, income, household type, race, Hispanic origin, region, and education. *Household Spending: Who Spends How Much on What* serves as a companion to *American Buyers* and provides household and detailed spending statistics organized by major product and service category from unpublished data collected by the Bureau of Labor Statistics' Consumer Expenditure Survey. The indexes are fairly comprehensive and provide a good entry point for researchers looking for specific data. These volumes will prove valuable for libraries serving business professionals, entrepreneurs, and students.

Banking, Finance, and Investment

368   Barrons.com. Barron's. http://online .barrons.com. Free
Provides news, daily analysis, and commentary on the markets, investing ideas, and market data.

369   CNNMoney. Cable News Network. http://money.cnn.com. Free
This service of CNN, *Fortune*, and *Money* includes

news on personal finance, economy, technology, markets, investing, small business, and leadership.

370   Finance and investment handbook.
8th ed. John Downes and Jordan Goodman, eds. 1168p. Barron's, 2010. $
332.678   HG173
This well-written handbook is useful for students and investors alike. The first part covers key personal investment opportunities with an overview, buying/selling/holding information, investment objectives and risk, and tax and economic considerations. Additional sections cover how to read annual and quarterly reports and understanding financial news. A ready-reference section includes information sources, major financial institutions, mutual funds and ETFs (exchange-traded funds), historical data, and publically traded companies. A dictionary of key terms rounds out this affordable handbook.

371   Investopedia. ValueClick. www .investopedia.com. Free
"Investopedia offers an abundance of financial content, from articles, dictionary terms, tutorials and video, to frequently asked questions and exam prep quizzes." Investopedia articles are written by freelance writers around the world with expertise in related areas. The newly introduced Stock Simulator allows users to learn about trading and compete against other virtual traders. Useful for students, businesspeople, and anyone interested in investing or personal finance.

372   Kiplinger.com. The Kiplinger Washington Editors. www.kiplinger.com. Free
"Personal finance advice, business forecasting, investing advice, and financial management tools." From the trusted names behind Kiplinger's magazine, this resource is useful for students, businesspeople, and the general public.

373   The Palgrave Macmillan dictionary of finance, investment, and banking.
Erik Banks. 565p. Palgrave Macmillan, 2010. $
332   HG151
This dictionary provides more than 5,000 clear and concise definitions for commonly used terms in accounting, banking, corporate finance,

investment management, and insurance on an international scope. Colloquialisms, foreign terms, and acronyms are also included, and there is a list of these terms before the introduction. Many definitions include formulas or graphs when relevant. Cross-references are provided to direct readers to related terms. Supplementary sections provide selected references and abbreviations with full title for accounting standards. Useful for anyone needing to understand terminology in these fields.

Careers and Vocational Guidance

374   Occupational outlook handbook. U.S. Department of Labor, Bureau of Labor Statistics. www.bls.gov/oco/. Free

This premier source presents overviews of careers in the fields of management, the professions, service, sales, administration, farming, construction, installation, production, transportation, and the armed forces. Entries include nature of the work, working conditions, education and training requirements, employment statistics and industries, job outlook, earnings, related occupations, and sources of additional information. Browse occupations by pay, education level, projected number of jobs, and growth rate. This is a great source for students and others looking for career information.

375   O*NET OnLine. U.S. Department of Labor, Employment and Training Administration. www.onetonline.org. Free

Explore occupations and connect to other online career information resources. Profiles include tasks, knowledge, skills, abilities, work activities, education, and wages and employment. Browse by industry, career cluster, or the areas within the profile.

Company and Industry

376   Hoover's handbooks. Hoover's. $$
338   HG4057

For those not able to subscribe to the Hoover's database, there is a series of handbooks published annually covering American business, emerging companies, private companies, and world business. Profiles include company overview, history,

executives, locations, products/operations, competitors, and historical financials. Each handbook includes lists ranking companies by various criteria including largest, most profitable or valuable, and fastest-growing. Indexes cover industry, headquarter location, and executives. The series is also available as an indexed set. Useful for all libraries who do not have an equivalent online source for company information.

377   Hoover's masterlist of U.S. companies. 2v. Hoover's, 2012. $$
338.7   HF5035

This two-volume set covers more than 10,000 companies including public companies, large and important private companies, associations, organizations, foundations, universities, government agencies, and major subsidiaries of large corporations. Entries contain contact information, key executives, company type, product and operations overview, basic financials, and employees. Company rankings are provided by sales, employees, sales growth, and market value. Indexes cover industry, headquarters location, and stock exchange symbol. Useful for all libraries who do not have an equivalent online source for company information.

Economics

The American economy: A historical encyclopedia, see 351.

378   Booms and busts: An encyclopedia of economic history from Tulipmania of the 1630s to the global financial crisis of the 21st century. James Ciment, ed. 3v. M. E. Sharpe, 2010. $$

This three-volume encyclopedia provides students and researchers with more than 360 articles detailing the causes, history, and effects of boom-and-bust economic cycles. Introductory sections cover pre-twentieth century, twentieth and twenty-first centuries, and causes and consequences. The well-written and easy-to-read A–Z entries cover economic terms and concepts, people, corporations and institutions, nations and regions, industries, legislation, and events. Entries include cross-references and further readings. A topic finder and comprehensive index provide useful entry points for readers. Additional content includes a chronology, glossary, and selected bibliography. Useful for all libraries.

379   A dictionary of economics. 4th ed. John Black, Nigar Hashimzade, and Gareth Myles. 464p. Oxford, 2012. $
330   HB61

This revised dictionary provides clear, concise definitions of more than 3,400 economic terms and related terms from mathematics, statistics, and personal finance with an international scope. Entries include illustrative graphs and equations as well as cross-references. New entries cover recent economic developments, financial instruments, regulations, and policy responses to the financial crisis. Appendixes include institutional acronyms, Nobel Prize winners, and the Greek alphabet. There is a web page for the dictionary with a list of links from the text. This dictionary will be useful for students and the general public.

Entrepreneurship and Small Business

380   AllBusiness.com. www.allbusiness.com. Free

Provides tools and resources to start, grow, and manage a business, including news, feature articles, blogs, and videos. The business library includes articles from key publications, a glossary, and downloadable forms, checklists, and legal documents.

381   Business plans handbook. 27th ed. Gale, 2013. $$
658.4   HD62.7

This handbook provides actual business plans written by entrepreneurs who are seeking funding for their retail, service, or manufacturing business. Each edition provides unique plans. Appendixes provide a business plan template; two fictional plans; a directory of organizations, agencies, and consultants; a glossary of small business terms; and updated bibliography. The cumulative index covers the entire series. This is an excellent source for libraries serving business students, entrepreneurs, and small business owners.

382   Encyclopedia of small business. 4th ed. 2v. Thomson Gale, 2011. $$$
658.02   HD62.7

This fully revised and expanded edition provides more than 600 in-depth articles and overviews of key topics related to small business. Forty new entries cover emerging topics such as social media, crowdsourcing, socially responsible investment, and sustainable business practices. Illustrations include tables, graphs, and photographs. Entries include further-reading recommendations. This is an excellent source for libraries serving business students, entrepreneurs, and small business owners.

Political Science and Law

6

DONALD ALTSCHILLER

For library users wanting the most up-to-date information on international, national, and local politics or the names of current government officials and political leaders, the Internet has emerged as the essential source. Nevertheless, print literature still serves a vital function in offering a vast range of information on political science and law. Although some books listed here may be out of print (OP), these titles should still be considered when creating a comprehensive reference collection. This chapter includes entries on important print reference volumes and also on the burgeoning web sources now available on these subjects.

Bibliographies and Guides

383 **American foreign relations since 1600: A guide to the literature.** 2nd ed. Robert L. Beisner, ed. 2v. ABC-CLIO, 2003. $$
016.32   E183

Produced under the auspices of the Society for Historians of American Foreign Relations, this massive two-volume work contains 16,000 annotated entries covering books, journal articles, microforms, and some websites. Each entry includes basic bibliographic information and an evaluative annotation; works listed more than once are cross-referenced to the primary citation. This is an invaluable literature guide.
Consumer protection (USA.gov), *see* **766.**

384 **C-SPAN.** National Cable Satellite Corporation. www.c-span.org. Free

Established by the cable industry in 1979 to provide public-service programming, this cable network—an acronym for Cable-Satellite Public Affairs Network—has become a vital resource on American politics and government. The site offers free access to its archives and also live streams a wide range of political and public affairs programming.

385 **Legal information institute.** Cornell University Law School. www.law.cornell.edu. Free

The Cornell Law Library created this site in 1992, attracting widespread use by the general public and legal professionals. Known as the "law-not-com" site, it reportedly has the most links to law resources on the web. Their admirable goal is to "ensure that the law remains free and open to everyone." An essential first stop for library users looking for any type of legal information.

386 **Legal research in a nutshell.** 10th ed. Morris L. Cohen and Kent C. Olson.

499p. West, 2010. $

340   KF240

First published in 1969, this classic research guide has increasingly incorporated electronic sources, but it still devotes considerable coverage to print materials. The first few chapters introduce the major primary and secondary sources; later sections discuss more specialized topics, including administrative law, international law, and legislative history, among many other topics. Several hundred websites are discussed. Compact in size, this work is a superb source for general readers and both law and other students.

387 USA.gov. U.S. General Services Administration, Office of Citizen Services and Innovative Technologies, 2000–. www.usa.gov. Free

"Whatever you want or need from the U.S. government, it's here" is the seemingly boastful yet probably accurate description of this metasite.

Dictionaries and Encyclopedias

388 American conservatism: An encyclopedia. Bruce Frohnen, Jeremy Beer, and Jeffrey O. Nelson. 979p. ISI Books, 2006. $

320.52   JC573

Containing more than 600 entries, this comprehensive encyclopedia surveys the history, personalities, and philosophies of an important ideological movement that has helped transform U.S. politics for the last several decades.

389 The American political dictionary. 11th ed. Jack C. Plano and Milton Greenberg. 702p. Harcourt Brace, 2002. $

320.473   JK9

Arranged alphabetically by broad subject heading (finance and taxation, business and labor, etc.), this work serves as both a dictionary and a study guide. Each entry contains a brief description of the topic and also includes a unique feature—its historical and contemporary "significance." Frequent cross-references and a useful index provide easy access.

390 Black's law dictionary. 9th ed. Bryan A. Garner, ed. 1810p. Thomson/West,

2009. $

340   KF156

Published since 1891, this work is the preeminent reference dictionary on law. Containing more than 25,000 terms, the dictionary also includes thousands of quotations from scholarly works and also pronunciation information. An abridged version, a pocket edition, and an electronic edition are also available.

391 Brewer's politics: A phrase and fable dictionary. Nicholas Comfort. 693p. Cassell, 1993. $

320   JA61

According to the editor, this work "perpetuates the mildly whimsical approach to the selection of entries" in the venerable reference work *Brewer's Dictionary of Phrase and Fable*. Unsurprisingly, this British work devotes much coverage to Great Britain—with the customary delightful wit—but it also contains much political material on the English-speaking Commonwealth countries, the United States, and some other countries. Author Comfort acknowledges that some material and quotations are offensive—reflecting the crude attitudes of some politicians or unsavory political behavior—but he nevertheless disclaims responsibility. Although these selections and the occasional lack of references may compromise the suitability of this work, it is still browsable and fun, with some useful reference material.

392 Encyclopedia of the American left. 2nd ed. Mari Jo Buhle, Paul Buhle, and Dan Georgakas, eds. 1024p. Oxford, 1998. $$

335   HX86

First published in 1990, this one-volume work is the most comprehensive reference encyclopedia—although now dated—on the history and politics of American radicalism since the American Revolution. The book features a wide variety of entries on left-wing activists, organizations, and ideological views. A helpful glossary and an outline of topics provide easy access to the text.

393 Encyclopedia of the United States cabinet. Mark Grossman, ed. 3v. ABC-CLIO, 2000. $$

352.24   E176

Five Nobel Peace Prize winners and ten individuals who later became presidents have served in U.S. cabinets. This three-volume set contains biographies of the hundred individuals who served as cabinet secretaries from the presidencies of George Washington to Bill Clinton. Compiled over eight years by a remarkably diligent editor, this work fills a noticeable literature gap on this vital component of the executive branch. Although this book doesn't cover presidential cabinets since 2000, it still provides much useful historical information.

394   Lend me your ears: Oxford dictionary of political quotations. 4th ed. Antony Jay, ed. 480p. Oxford, 2012. $

320   PN6084

The editor succeeds at his admirable goal: to produce a classic reference work containing the "political quotations [that] are part of the currency of political speeches and writings throughout the English-speaking world." Alphabetically arranged by author, the entries are set in two well-spaced columns. In contrast to the many quotation dictionaries printed in small type, with little space between entries, the appealing hardcover graphic design enhances the readability of this well-researched reference source.

395   Macmillan dictionary of political quotations. Lewis D. Eigen and Jonathan P. Siegel, eds. 785p. Macmillan, 1993. $

082   PN6084

Organized in approximately 100 broad subject headings, this dictionary contains a wide variety of quotations. The topics include campaigns and conventions, freedom and liberty, and foreign policy. Selections were based on "terseness [and] clear statement of an important principle, controversy, humor, surprise," and many other factors. Because a large number of world leaders and political philosophers have been white Christian men, the editors honestly acknowledge an "inevitable" bias in their selections. They also readily declare that there was "no serious attempt to provide balance on issues. If, on a particular issue, one side was more witty, pithy, urbane, and widely published, that is the way it appears in this book." Each entry includes the source reference;

an author and concept index provides easy access to the text.

396   Penguin dictionary of international relations. Graham Evans and Jeffrey Newnham. 623p. Penguin, 1998. $

327   JZ1161

Published soon after the end of the cold war, this paperback contains more than 700 entries covering ideas, organizations, events, and specialized terms. Frequent cross-references help broaden the understanding of each term.

397   Presidential campaigns, slogans, issues, and platforms: The complete encyclopedia. 2nd ed. Robert North Roberts, Scott John Hammond, and Valerie A. Sulfaro. 3v. Greenwood, 2012. $$

324.70   JK524

Originally a one-volume work, the latest edition has enlarged in length to three volumes. The first volume contains entries on issues, trends, strategies, and slogans, among other topics. The next two volumes cover every presidential campaign from 1788–1789 to the 2008 contest. Each entry contains a list of additional resources covering both books and journal articles; black-and-white illustrations help enhance the text. This title is a useful reference source for general readers and high school and undergraduate students.

398   Safire's new political dictionary: The definitive guide to the new language of politics. William Safire. 930p. Random House, 1993. $

320   JK9

William Safire, the late *New York Times* columnist and former speechwriter, produced this outstanding compilation, a culmination of more than a quarter century of writing about the language of politics. According to the author, this political dictionary does not define such common terms about government or governmental offices as, for example, *vice president* or *president*; rather, it offers the etymology of terms and phrases such as *veep, heartbeat away from the presidency*, and *the loneliest job in the world*. A very diligent researcher and witty literary stylist, the author has performed a superb service for librarians and library users in compiling this unique and essential reference work.

Directories

399 Black Americans in Congress, 1870–present. U.S. House of Representatives, Office of the Historian and Office of Art and Archives. http:// baic.house.gov. Free

An official U.S. government website containing a historical survey of African Americans who served in Congress, in addition to biographical profiles of each member, historical data, and educational resources. This well-designed and easily navigable site serves as an outstanding portal for general readers, students, and scholars.

400 Chiefs of state and cabinet members of foreign governments. Central Intelligence Agency. www.cia.gov/library/ publications/world-leaders-1/. Free

Formerly a print directory, this CIA directory "is intended to be used primarily as a reference aid and includes as many governments of the world as is considered practical, some of them not officially recognized by the United States."

401 Congressional directory. U.S. Congress. www.gpo.gov/fdsys/browse/ collection.action?collectionCode=CDIR. Free

The *Congressional Directory* is the official directory of the U.S. Congress, prepared by the Joint Committee on Printing. It presents short biographies of each member of the Senate and House, listed by state or district, and their committee memberships, terms of service, administrative assistants and/or secretaries, and rooms and telephone numbers. It also lists officials of the courts, military establishments, and other federal departments and agencies, including DC government officials, governors of states and territories, foreign diplomats, and members of the press, radio, and television galleries.

402 Federal regulatory directory. 15th ed. CQ Press, 2011. $$

351.025   HC110

Known as *FRED*, this perennial reference work provides listings on more than 100 federal regulatory agencies, brief histories and contact information,

legislative purview, and profiles of regulatory officials.

403 State and local government on the net. www.statelocalgov.net. Free

973.025   Z1123

This metasite provides quick and easy access to a large number of state and local information sources.

404 U.S. courts. Administrative Office of the U.S. Courts. www.uscourts.gov. Free

A metasite providing links to U.S. district and appellate courts. A superb portal for information about the judicial branch of the U.S. government.

405 U.S. Government Printing Office: Keeping America informed. www.gpo .gov/fdsys/search/home.action. Free

The GPO's FDsys (Federal Digital System) provides quick and easy access to official publications from all three branches of the U.S. government. Access is free, including links to fifty different collections of federal government information. An outstanding portal.

406 Washington information directory, 2012–2013. CQ Press, 2012. $$

975.3   F192

Published for more than thirty years, this directory provides contact information for the vast number of government agencies and congressional committees in the nation's capital. Especially helpful are entries on nongovernmental organizations, which are listed alongside government agencies. Flow charts and easy-to-read entries enhance its usefulness. This is a superb source to find the phone numbers, websites, and capsule descriptions of governmental agencies.

Handbooks, Yearbooks, and Almanacs

407 Almanac of American politics, 2012. Michael Barone and Chuck McCutcheon. 1856p. Chicago, 2012. $

328.3   JK1341

This biennial volume contains entries on all 535 members of the current Congress. Arranged alphabetically by state, the entries provide basic biographical information, votes on major issues, ratings by special interest groups, narrative descriptions of their districts, and the political and economic issues influencing local voters. Similar to *Politics in America*, this work is a superb ready-reference source. Also available electronically.

408 The American presidency project.
University of California, Santa Barbara.
www.presidency.ucsb.edu. Free

Established in 1999 as a collaboration between Professors John T. Woolley and Gerhard Peters at the University of California, Santa Barbara, this free online resource includes the papers and documents of U.S. presidents from George Washington to Barack Obama. Continually updated, this superb site includes executive orders, proclamations, press conferences and briefings, Saturday radio addresses, fireside chats, veto messages, signing statements, radio and television correspondents dinners, debates, party convention addresses, party platforms, State of the Union addresses and messages, and inaugural addresses, among many other sources of information.

409 Basic facts about the United Nations.
Rev. ed. United Nations, Department of Public Information, 2011. $

341.23   JX1977

This inexpensive official handbook describes the organization, programs, agencies, and activities of this world body. A superb ready-reference source, this paperback volume contains the full names of all of the UN's constituent agencies in addition to charts and maps.

410 The book of the states 2012.
Council of State Governments. http://knowledgecenter.csg.org/drupal/view-content-type/1502. Free

353.9   JK2403

A unique source covering the legislative, judicial, and executive branches of all fifty states and also providing extensive comparative data and surveys of state legislation. The website offers free access; print copies can be purchased.

411 Congress A to Z. 5th ed. David R. Tarr and Ann O'Connor. 703p. CQ Press,

2008. $$

328.73   JK1021

Part of the *Congressional Quarterly*'s American Government A to Z series, this work describes the structure, operation, and history of the U.S. Congress. Entries range from the "Courts and Congress" to "War Powers." Excellent appendixes include reference material and charts on the Speaker of the House, dates of every session since 1789, and party leadership, among other charts. Also available electronically.

412 Congressional Quarterly's desk reference on American government.
2nd ed. Bruce Wetterau. 344p. CQ Press, 2000. $

320.47   JK274

Similar in format to the *Congressional Quarterly's Desk Reference on the Presidency*, this volume contains more than 600 questions and answers on the executive, legislative, and judicial branches of the U.S. government.

413 Congressional Quarterly's desk reference on the presidency. Bruce Wetterau. 311p. CQ Press, 2000. $

973   JK516

Containing more than 500 questions and answers, this reference source provides a vast range of information on the lives of U.S. presidents and their families and the history of the most powerful position in the world. Frequent cross-references provide easy access to related material. A superb ready-reference source.

414 Elections A to Z. 4th ed. Bob Benenson and David Tarr. 614p. CQ Press, 2012. $$

324.6   JK1976

Complementing *Congress A to Z*, this volume will answer basic questions about U.S. elections and the electoral process. Engagingly written, entries cover a wide variety of topics, including contested elections, the origin of the "whistle stop" campaign appearance, and a delightful section on voter apathy and boredom, aptly titled "ZZZ," for snoozing! Also includes useful charts and reference material.

415 European political facts of the twentieth century. 5th ed. Chris Cook and John Paxton. 493p. Palgrave

Macmillan, 2001. $
320.94   JN12
An excellent compilation covering the changing
political history of Europe, including names and
dates of prime ministers, election statistics, and
short histories of political parties. Also available
electronically via EBSCO.

**416 Factcheck.org: A project of the
    Annenberg Public Policy Center.**
Annenberg Public Policy Center,
University of Pennsylvania. www.fact
check.org. Free
378.04   JK275
A nonpartisan, nonprofit project at the University of Pennsylvania that aims "to reduce the level
of deception and confusion in U.S. politics." The
site monitors the factual accuracy of what is said by
major U.S. political players in the form of TV ads,
debates, speeches, interviews, and news releases.
It offers an invaluable feature called "Viral Spiral,"
which lists false or misleading rumors and a brief
summary of the facts. The statements cited by Fact-
Check.org are frequently reported in the national
media, especially during heated election campaigns.
The website received national attention—and also
evoked much public snickering—in its first year
during the 2004 election debates. Vice President
Cheney erroneously referred to it as "factcheck.
com," which, in fact, was an anti-Bush website.
He meant, of course, to recommend the nonpartisan FactCheck.org. An important resource for the
informed citizen and voter.

417 Federal Election Commission. Federal
    Election Commission. www.fec.gov. Free
Provides updated information about the financing
of federal elections, including information on contributions, contributors, political action committees (PACs), and federal candidates. Users can find
the level of individual contributions to candidates.
Also includes finance laws, court opinions, commission rulings, and much more useful information on federal elections.

418 Freedom in the world. Freedom House.
    www.freedomhouse.org/report/freedom
    -world/freedom-world-2012. Free
Published annually since 1972 by Freedom House,
this comprehensive survey provides ratings and

narrative reports on 195 countries and disputed
territories. The site is frequently quoted in the
media and has become the benchmark for assess-
ing the state of democracy in nations throughout
the world. The *Freedom in the World* data and
reports are available in their entirety on the Freedom House website.

**419 Gay and lesbian Americans and
    political participation: A reference
    handbook.** Raymond A. Smith and
    Donald P. Haider-Markel. 339p. ABC-
    CLIO, 2002. $
305.9   HQ76
Although the gay and lesbian political movement
has made enormous strides since this first reference
book on the topic was published, the title nevertheless offers useful historical information, important documents, a chronology, and an annotated
bibliography.
See also **"LGBT Studies," in chapter 4.**

**420 A historical guide to the U.S.
    government.** George T. Kurian, ed.
    741p. Oxford, 1998. $$
352.3   JK9
This hefty volume surveys the history of federal
agencies, departments, and cabinet posts and
describes their evolution, growth, and occasional
demise. Each alphabetically arranged entry offers a
concise history followed by a bibliography. Compiled by historians and government specialists, this
work is an outstanding ready-reference source for
queries on the history of the U.S. executive branch.
Please note: a couple of new departments were
established since publication.

421 Jews in American politics. L. Sandy
    Maisel et al., eds. 506p. Rowman &
    Littlefield, 2001. $
973   E184
This unique reference source contains both historical analysis and much ready-reference material,
including biographies and interesting facts and
statistics.

**422 The Oxford companion to American
    law.** Kermit L. Hall, ed. 912p. Oxford,
    2002. $
349.73   KF154

Aimed at a diverse audience ranging from general readers to law scholars, this work provides succinct and authoritative entries covering a wide range of legal topics: biographies of law scholars and activists, major constitutional cases, and legal philosophy, to name only some. The contributors—both scholars and practitioners—have produced an easily read work, remarkably devoid of arcane legal jargon.

423 Political handbook of the world, 2012. Tom Lansford, ed. 1834p. SAGE/ CQ Press, 2012. $$

320.9   D860

First published in 1928 by the Council on Foreign Relations, this classic work contains a wealth of information on more than 200 countries and territories, including political parties and organizations, statistics, names of leaders and cabinet members, and extensive essays on recent government political history. There is also a section on regional and international organizations.

424 Politics in America, 2012: 112th Congress. CQ Roll Call Staff; John Bicknell and David Meyers, eds. 1214p. CQ Press, 2011. $$

328.73   JK1012

Similar to the *Almanac of American Politics*, this biennial work provides biographical and political information on every member of Congress, descriptions of the state and congressional districts, and data on campaign contributions and interest group ratings, among other topics.

425 Project vote smart. Project Vote Smart. http://votesmart.org. Free

With goals that are similar to the League of Women Voters, this outstanding nonpartisan site aims to help educate an informed electorate. It provides links to voting records, the stated positions of candidates for public office, and information about minority political parties and campaign finance, among other data.

426 THOMAS. Library of Congress. http:// thomas.loc.gov. Free

Launched in January of 1995 at the inception of the 104th Congress, this marvelous portal has expanded the scope of its offerings to include

the following content: bills and resolutions; activity in Congress; Congressional Record; schedules and calendars; committee information; presidential nominations; treaties; and other government resources. In late 2013, the beta version of Congress.gov states that it eventually will incorporate all of the information in THOMAS.

427 United States government manual. National Archives and Records Administration, Office of the Federal Register. 1974–. Annual. $

351.97   JK421

As the official handbook of the federal government, the *United States Government Manual* provides comprehensive information on the agencies of the legislative, judicial, and executive branches. It also includes information on quasi-official agencies; international organizations in which the United States participates; and boards, commissions, and committees. Also available electronically, at www .gpo.gov/fdsys/browse/collection.action?collection Code=GOVMAN.

428 U.S. Department of State. U.S. Department of State. www.state.gov. Free

This website provides links to foreign policy and trade information, among many other issues involving this cabinet department. Also includes full-text versions of the venerable documentary collection *Foreign Relations of the United States*.

429 Vital statistics on American politics. Harold W. Stanley and Richard G. Niemi. CQ Press, 1988–. Annual. $

324   JK274

This annual volume offers a cornucopia of political and government statistics—on campaign finances, elections, public-opinion polling data, Medicare, foreign aid, civil service, employment, television ownership of presidential debates, and so forth. One needn't be a statistics junkie to enjoy this remarkably eclectic work. One learns, for example, that it took only three months from congressional approval until ratification of the Twenty-Sixth Amendment to the Constitution; the Twenty-Seventh Amendment, however, which sets congressional salaries, took 203 years to enact!

Biographical Sources

430 The almanac of the unelected: Staff of the U.S. Congress. 23rd ed. Suzanne Struglinski and Lisa Friedman, eds. 788p. Bernan, 2011. $$

328   JK1083

A unique source for biographical information on selected House and Senate committee staff. Arranged by committee name, this work offers interesting background material on influential—yet generally unknown—individuals. Available electronically.

431 Biographical directory of the U.S. Congress. House Legislative Resource Center; Senate Historical Office. bioguide.congress.gov. Free

Formerly a print directory, this unique biographical resource was first posted online in November 1998. Besides the extensive biographies, the online database includes bibliographies and a guide to available research collections. You can search for information on members of the U.S. Congress from 1774 to the present day by entering a name, position, state, or party. It is also a good way to get lists (e.g., of Nullifiers, Greenbackers, etc.).

432 Women in Congress. U.S. House of Representatives, Office of the Historian and Office of Art and Archives. http://history.house.gov/Exhibition-and-Publications/WIC/Women-in-Congress/. Free

This site contains biographies of former and current women representatives and senators. It includes bibliographies and some references to manuscript collections. This work complements the *Biographical Directory of the U.S. Congress*.

Education

JOANNA GADSBY

The nature of education continues to evolve, and education reference tools do the same. As education receives more popular and legislative attention, reference publishers are responding with more encyclopedic resources. Subject encyclopedias in education provide a wealth of information in context with the shifting times, and many of these volumes are provided as e-books as well as print books. The periodic, often annual guides to educational institutions and curriculum resources are still important, but they no longer dominate the reference collection. Many of these sources are freely available on the web.

Bibliographies and Guides

433 **Education: A guide to reference and information sources.** 2nd ed. Nancy Patricia O'Brien. 189p. Libraries Unlimited, 2000. $
016.37   LB15
A comprehensive and classic source, this guide concentrates on items published from 1990 to 1998, with older materials included in some circumstances. Most of the older items listed have newer editions published. This bibliography presents almost 500 items, arranged in fourteen categories. Bibliographic

information, price, and short annotations are given. Indexed by author, title, and subject.

Media and Curriculum Materials

434 **Best books for children: Preschool through grade 6.** 9th ed. Catherine Barr and John T. Gillespie. 1901p. Libraries Unlimited, 2010. $
011.62   Z1037
This volume is designed to provide recommended recreational reading as well as to support a typical school curriculum. Coverage is from preschool through grade six. Basic arrangement is by subject, with indexes by author/illustrator, title, and subject/grade level. Entries include publication data, price, and short description. There is also a supplement to the ninth edition. Libraries Unlimited publishes a series of similar titles for different audiences/age groups.
See also "Bibliographies and Guides," in chapter 1.

435 **Educational media and technology yearbook.** Springer, 1985–. Annual. $$
371.3   LB1043
Articles by specialists provide state-of-the-art reviews of recent developments and trends, technology updates, and leadership profiles. A significant portion provides directories of media organizations and associations, graduate programs,

funding sources, and producers, distributors, and publishers.

436 Free teaching aids. Educators Progress Service, 2012. www.freeteachingaids .com. Free

This website provides access to guides for teachers and others in the education field. The guides give source and acquisition information for a wide variety of resources, many from the U.S. government. Topics for the guides include locations for free teaching materials on a wide variety of subjects and for both elementary and secondary students.

437 Special educator's complete guide to 301 diagnostic tests. Roger Pierangelo and George A. Giuliani. 484p. Jossey-Bass, 2006. $

371.9   LC4019

Discusses assessments of intelligence, achievement, language, and spelling as well as physical and psychological assessments. Provides basic information, strengths and weaknesses of each test, and information about the parents' role in assessment and individual education plans.

438 Tests: A comprehensive reference for assessments in psychology, education, and business. 6th ed. Taddy Maddox, ed. 555p. PRO-ED, 2008. $$

150   BF176

"Education Instruments" is the largest section in this book, which gives descriptive annotations for a wide variety of tests. Population, purpose, description, format (including time), scoring, and cost are considered. This volume provides a tremendous amount of information for the price.

Databases and Indexes

439 Education source. EBSCO. www.ebsco host.com/academic/education-source. CP$

Education Source is the flagship EBSCO database for education. It combines both Education Full-Text and Education Research Complete and adds extra content from other publishers. It indexes more than 3,800 educational journals with more than 1,700 full-text titles. Formerly an H. W.

Wilson database, Education Full-Text contains the full text for more than 350 journals dating back to 1996 and indexes more than 770 periodicals going back to 1983. Coverage includes educational tests and more than fifty journals on the topic of special education. Education Research Complete is another EBSCO database covering topics on all levels of education; it provides indexing and abstracts for almost 2,400 journals and full text for more than 1,400 journals, 550 books and monographs, and many conference publications. Complete title lists are available through www.ebscohost.com. Areas covered extend to curriculum instruction, educational specialties, and administration and policy. For libraries that can afford it, Education Source is the recommended database.

440 ERIC. U.S. Department of Education. www.eric.ed.gov. Free

ERIC serves as an index to education journals and to nonjournal documents, many of which are now provided as full text with no fee. This database contains more than 1.4 million records and links to more than 337,000 full-text ERIC documents dating back to 1966. In late 2012, many ERIC documents were removed from the database to check for potential breaches of security. ERIC hoped to have all documents restored to the database in 2013. ERIC is also available via EBSCO.

Dictionaries and Encyclopedias

441 Concise encyclopedia of special education. 2nd ed. Cecil R. Reynolds and Elaine Fletcher-Janzen, eds. 1062p. Wiley, 2004. $$

371. 9   LC4007

Derived from the three-volume *Encyclopedia of Special Education* (Wiley, 2000), this one-volume edition will handily fill the need in smaller libraries. It features assessment instruments, teaching methods, legal issues, and more. Designed to give the reader (educator, administrator, or parent) an overview of the subject, including history and current practice.

442 Encyclopedia of African American education. Kofi Lomotey, ed. 2v. SAGE, 2010. $$

371.829   LC2771

This two-volume set covers a wide range of educational issues related to African Americans. The highly readable entries span topics from historic legal cases to present-day programs. The second volume is mostly made up of the appendix and is primarily dedicated to the *Journal of Negro Education*.

443 Encyclopedia of American education.
3rd ed. Harlow Unger. 3v. Facts on File, 2007. $$
370   LB17
A comprehensive encyclopedia with more than 2,500 articles covering educational trends, people, and terms. Appendixes give a chronology of American education from the first settlement of Jamestown, significant legislation, and an overview of education for the profession. Essential for all education collections.

444 Encyclopedia of educational research.
6th ed. Marvin C. Alkin, ed. 4v. Macmillan, 1992. $$
370   LB15
Sponsored by the American Educational Research Association, this standard source presents a critical synthesis and interpretation of reported research in about 250 articles. Article topics are broad—for example, "attitude measurement" and "motivation." Extensive bibliographies complete each article.

445 The Greenwood dictionary of education. 2nd ed. John W. Collins III and Nancy Patricia O'Brien, eds. 581p. Greenwood, 2011. $$
370   LB15
The first comprehensive dictionary of education in more than twenty-five years is now available as an e-book. This volume presents more than 2,600 terms that focus on contemporary terminology in education as well as words from other disciplines defined within an educational context. An essential purchase.

446 Higher education in the United States: An encyclopedia. James J. F. Forest and Kevin Kinser, eds. 2v. ABC-CLIO, 2002. $$
378.73   LA225
A well-rounded resource on higher education in the United States in approximately 200 articles.

Appendixes include an annotated bibliography of important books about higher education and a timeline of significant events.

447 World education encyclopedia: A survey of educational systems worldwide. 2nd ed. Rebecca Marlow-Ferguson, ed. 3v. Gale/Thomson, 2002. $$
370   LB15
This encyclopedia provides a descriptive survey of 233 worldwide educational systems and is arranged alphabetically. Well-written and easily readable essays cover the history and background of each geographical entity and provide overviews of the educational systems. This set provides an enormous amount of comparative data at a very affordable price.

Directories

448 Accredited institutions of postsecondary education; 2011: Includes candidates for accreditation and accredited programs at other facilities. 1235p. American Council on Education, 2011. $
378.73   L901
Information on accredited degree-granting institutions is readily available, but this volume also includes non-degree-granting institutions, such as cosmetology schools, business schools, and mechanical institutes.

449 American universities and colleges. 19th ed. 2v. Praeger, 2010. $$
378.73   LA226
Arranged alphabetically by state, and then institution, this guide gives basic information, including accreditation, calendar, distinctive educational programs, and characteristics of student body and teaching staff. This two-volume work is an asset to every library and is available as an e-book.

450 Barron's guide to graduate business schools. 15th ed. Eugene Miller and Neuman F. Pollack, eds. 821p. Barron's, 2007. $
650.07   HF1131

This guide provides information on more than 600 institutions in the United States and Canada. Arranged alphabetically by state and indexed by institution. Basic information includes programs, requirements, admissions, costs, library, research and computer facilities, and information on student body and faculty.

451 Barron's guide to law schools. 20th ed. 633p. Barron's, 2012. $
340.07   KF266

This guide provides information on more than 200 law schools in the United States and Canada. Arranged alphabetically by state and indexed by institution.

452 Barron's guide to medical and dental schools. 12th ed. Saul Wischnitzer and Edith Wischnitzer. 739p. Barron's, 2009. $
610   R690

Provides information on medical and dental schools in the United States and Canada and international medical schools with significant numbers of American students. Includes information about admissions requirements, curriculum, and affiliated hospitals. In addition, this volume also provides essays about choosing a medical career, preparing for medical school, and opportunities available for women and minorities.

453 Barron's profiles of American colleges. 30th ed. 1680p. Barron's, 2012. $
378.73   L901

Comprehensive guide, with website subscription, to accredited four-year colleges in the United States. Profiles include data on admission requirements, application deadlines, housing, campus environment, financial aid, extracurricular activities, and other essential information.

454 The college blue book. Macmillan Reference USA. Annual. $$$
378.73   L901

Still the standard, *The College Blue Book* provides data on more than 3,000 two- and four-year institutions in the United States and Canada; 6,500 institutions providing occupational education; more than 4,500 subject areas; and nearly 3,000 distance-learning programs as well as providing background information for this growing field.

455 International handbook of universities. International Association of Universities. Palgrave Macmillan. Annual. $$$
378   L900

Arranged alphabetically by country, this title provides information on international universities with data provided from the IAU/UNESCO Information Centre on Higher Education database. Information includes contacts, areas of study, and statistics for faculty, students, libraries, and other facilities.

456 Peterson's guides. Peterson's. www. petersons.com. $

This website provides substantial information for the student, parent, or educator who is interested in performing a college search. With numerous criteria to search, the website replaces the many guides published by this company for years. The site also contains information about scholarships and financial aid.

Handbooks, Yearbooks, and Almanacs

457 The educator's desk reference (EDR): A sourcebook of educational information and research. 2nd ed. Melvyn N. Freed, Robert K. Hess, and Joseph M. Ryan. 570p. Praeger, 2002. $$
370   LB1028.27

This useful source for the educator and the educational administrator provides a guide to finding additional information for the job, descriptions of useful education websites and journals, a guide to publishing in the education field, and an overview of research.

458 The hows and whys of alternative education: Schools where students thrive. Darlene Leiding. 182p. Rowman & Littlefield, 2008. $
371.04   LC46.4

A guidebook for parents, this volume provides general information about the history of alternative forms of education. Issues covered range from charter schools to distance learning. A useful and unique set of information.

459 The law of schools, students, and teachers in a nutshell. 4th ed. Kern Alexander and M. David Alexander. 593p. West Group, 2009. $

344.73   KF4119.3

Handy synopsis of U.S. law pertaining to education, including references to court cases. Issues discussed include teacher dismissal, educational taxes, and privacy of student records. Highly recommended for all collections.

460 Requirements for certification of teachers, counselors, librarians, administrators for elementary and secondary schools. 76th ed. Elizabeth A. Kaye, ed. 309p. Chicago, 2011. Annual. $

370.11   LB1771.W6

The most current and thorough source for initial certification requirements in the public-education field. Arranged by state and then by category. Also provides addresses of state offices of certification. This helpful guide is available as an e-book.

461 The SAGE handbook of African American education. Linda C. Tillman, ed. 559p. SAGE, 2009. $$

379.89   LC2717

This collection of essays presents a thorough and current look at the history and future of African American education. Well researched and highly readable, articles in this book range in topic from the dissolution of black state teachers' associations in the mid-twentieth century to the possibilities for current and future policy.

Statistical Sources

462 Condition of education. U.S. Department of Education, National Center for Education Statistics, 1975–. Annual. $

370   L112

Annual data on sixty key education indicators that shed light on the condition of education in the United States. Essential for public and academic collections. Online edition and PDF downloads of publications are available at http://nces.ed.gov/programs/coe/.

463 Digest of education statistics. U.S. Department of Education, National Center for Education Statistics, 1975–. Annual. $

370   L11

Essential compilation of educational statistics from the U.S. Department of Education, covering preschool through postgraduate, with some information on libraries and educational technology. Online edition and PDF downloads available at http://nces.ed.gov/programs/digest/.

464 Projections of education statistics to 2020. William J. Hussar. 163p. U.S. Government Printing Office, 2011. $

370.21   LB2846

The National Center for Education Statistics, part of the Institute of Education Science and the U.S. Department of Education, projects statistics to the future. This is an essential tool for educational planning. Also available at nces.ed.gov/pubsearch/pubsinfo.asp?pubid=2011026.

465 State-by-state profiles of community colleges: Trends and statistics. 7th ed. American Association of Community Colleges. 123p. Community College Press, 2007. $

378.15   LB2328

Arranged alphabetically by state, this volume presents basic statistical information about community colleges in that state; demographics, including educational attainment; and workforce information, including highest-paying, fastest-growing, and fastest-declining occupations requiring some college or a community college degree.

8 Words and Languages

MARY ELLEN QUINN

Encyclopedic reference sources focusing on the study of words and languages are still relatively new. On the other hand, stylebooks, desk dictionaries, thesauri, and other practical writers' aids have been around for decades and continue to be in great demand: the supply has been robust, and the best products are continually updated and augmented. Principal or unabridged dictionaries, the result of painstaking and time-consuming scholarship, are few and far between in any language; English is fortunate to have several excellent sources to turn to. Though revised on a less frequent basis than their thematic relatives, they are the sources from which the other products draw their data, and new editions are looked upon as great and significant events. Bilingual foreign-language dictionaries are in a middle ground. The most studied languages—as one might expect—provide the largest market and see the largest number of commercial players. When seeking a small to middle-sized English-based bilingual dictionary for the more popular languages, a visit to the publications lists of Oxford University Press, HarperCollins, or Larousse generally reveals several viable options.

General Sources

Encyclopedias, Companions, and Atlases

466 Atlas of the world's languages. 2nd ed. R. E. Asher and C. J. Moseley, eds. 416p. Routledge, 2007. $$$
402.23   G1046.E3
Covering more than 6,000 languages, this superbly organized source is intended to "map as far as current knowledge allows the location of all living languages no matter how small the number of speakers." Each of the eight sections includes the linguistic history of the region, a hierarchy of language families, and descriptive paragraphs about each language. Statistical tables and maps supplement the main atlas pages, and pie charts indicate languages spoken in urban areas.

467 The Cambridge encyclopedia of the world's ancient languages. Roger D. Woodard, ed. 1162p. Cambridge, 2004. $$
409   P371
Selected as an outstanding reference title by *Choice*, this encyclopedia of ancient languages contains forty-three chapters prepared by thirty-five internationally recognized scholars. Each chapter describes an individual language or language group; its historical relevance; and its script, grammar, phonology, morphology, syntax, and lexicon

and suggests sources for further reading. Indexing by subject, grammar, linguistic law or principle, and language.

468 Compendium of the world's languages. 3rd ed. George L. Campbell and Gareth King. 2v. Routledge, 2013. $$$

403 P371

The second edition of the *Compendium* was designated an outstanding reference title by *Choice*. In the third edition, entries have been thoroughly revised and all cultural and historical notes as well as statistical data have been checked, updated, and in many cases expanded. Entries for several hundred languages, ancient and modern, are arranged alphabetically. Each entry provides information about the language's script, phonology, morphology, and syntax; sample texts are provided as are a glossary and a bibliography.

469 Dictionary of languages: The definitive reference to more than 400 languages. Andrew Dalby. 800p. Columbia, 1998. $

403 P371

This work was designated an outstanding reference source by the American Library Association. Its aim is to categorize and describe the major languages, providing a historical, social, and geopolitical context as well as information about the language's origin, dialects, number of speakers, characteristics, and alphabet. Illustrative specimens include anecdotes and literary quotations. Includes maps, extensive cross-references, glossary, and index.

470 Ethnologue: Languages of the world. 16th ed. M. Paul Lewis, ed. 1248p. SIL International, 2009. $

410 P371

Produced by the Summer Institute of Linguistics, *Ethnologue*'s aim is to catalog "all the languages known to be spoken in the world today." The sixteenth edition includes descriptive entries for 6,909 known living languages, organized by content and country. Entries include name of language, alternate names, estimated population of speakers, region where the language is spoken, dialects, availability of dictionaries, and the linguistic classification. A total of 208 color maps display the location and distribution of languages. A free web version (www.sil.org/ethnologue/) provides the same content as the print in an easily searchable database format.

471 International encyclopedia of linguistics. 2nd ed. William Frawley, ed. 4v. Oxford, 2003. $$$

410.3 P29

This second edition, appearing ten years after the first, highly acclaimed original, was designated an outstanding title by *Choice*. Arranged alphabetically, the entries range from broad topical articles such as "Sociolinguistics" and specific concepts such as cognitive grammar to descriptions of individual languages and biographical essays. With contributions from 600 scholars, this work is authoritative, easy to use, accessible, up-to-date, well illustrated, and expertly indexed.

English Language

Dictionaries

DATABASES AND INDEXES

472 Oxford dictionaries pro. Oxford. www .oxforddictionaries.com. $$

Billed as the largest language research program in the world, this subscription database weaves a number of Oxford publications on the English language into one interface for its 350,000 definitions, 600,000 synonyms, and more than 1.9 million sample sentences. Almost everything that appears on the screen is linked to something else. Audio pronunciations are available. The database also offers writing, grammar, and spelling guidance; crossword puzzle and word game solvers; and more. The focus is on current English, in contrast with the historical approach of the *Oxford English Dictionary*, which is not available on this site.

DESK DICTIONARIES

473 The American Heritage dictionary of the English language. 5th ed. 2112p. Houghton Mifflin Harcourt, 2011. $

423 PE1628

The most practical and comprehensive of the desk dictionaries, the *American Heritage* contains more than 200,000 entries. Its bright, clear, easy-to-read definitions; numerous illustrations along the sidebars; and extensive illustrative quotations make this one of the most pragmatic tools in the collection. Entries for words, abbreviations, biographical names, and geographic names are interfiled. The fifth edition adds 10,000 new words and 4,000 full-color illustrations and is an excellent selection for the home or the ready-reference collection.

474   Concise Oxford English dictionary.
12th ed. Angus Stevenson and Maurice Waite, eds. 1728p. Oxford, 2011. $
423   PE1628

The centennial edition contains more than 240,000 words, phrases, and definitions, providing "snapshot" coverage of contemporary English from around the world. Its focus on international English, its currency, and its descriptive approach make it an excellent complement to major American English desk dictionaries. The accompanying CD-ROM includes 50,000 spoken audio pronunciations plus twelve months of access to Oxford Dictionaries Online.

475   New Oxford American dictionary. 3rd ed. Angus Stevenson and Christine A. Lindberg, eds. 2096p. Oxford, 2010. $
423   PE1628

First published in 2001, this is the most pragmatic American English dictionary on the market. Its distinguishing feature is that it provides the most common meaning of each of its 350,000 entry words first. By linking meaning to modern usage norms, it precludes the confusion that exhaustive multiple meanings often engender. The dictionary provides definitions for more than 12,000 proper names and incorporates several handy features, including a history of the language, a grammar usage guide, a punctuation guide, presidents of the United States, the Constitution and Declaration of Independence, chemical elements, weights and measures, and so forth. Purchase includes six months of free access to Oxford Dictionaries Online.

476   Shorter Oxford English dictionary on historical principles. 6th ed. 2v. Oxford, 2007. $$
423   PE1625

Part abridgement of the *OED* and part entirely new work, this dictionary brings the scholarship and authority of the *OED* to the general reader and smaller library. Some 300,000 words are described, defined, and explicated. It prefers British pronunciation and usage but remains international in scope, listing words from all parts of the English-speaking world, including South Africa, Australia, and the Caribbean. Like the *OED* it traces every word back to the first documented use and makes extensive use of quotation to illustrate meaning. It is the most literate and scholarly of the desk dictionaries. The accompanying CD-ROM includes the full text of both volumes.

Encyclopedias

477   The Cambridge encyclopedia of the English language. 2nd ed. David Crystal. 506p. Cambridge, 2003. $
420   PE1072

Crystal is a widely published authority on language. This work is divided into twenty-five chapters covering the history of the English language, vocabulary, grammar, spoken and written English, usage, learning English, and English online. The attractive layout and generous use of illustrative materials, including photographs, maps, graphs, and diagrams, enhance its readability and appeal for the generalist as well as for students who are beginning their study of languages and linguistics and wish a general overview of the primary discoveries and issues. Appendixes include a glossary of terms, a key to symbols and abbreviations, and references. The bibliography is extensive and there are indexes for names, items, and topics.

Principal English-Language Dictionaries

478   Dictionary.com. www.dictionary.com. Free

This popular online dictionary is fine for quick lookups. It offers many features a standard print dictionary doesn't provide—translations, audio pronunciations, games, quizzes, ads (which can be turned off with a login and a small monthly fee), and much more. The definitions themselves are drawn from a variety of sources, ranging from *Collins English Dictionary* and *Stedman's Medical Dictionary* to the *Online Etymology Dictionary*.

479 Oxford English dictionary. 2nd ed. J. A. Simpson and E. S. C. Weiner, eds. 20v. Oxford, 1989. $$$
Oxford English dictionary: Additions series. J. A. Simpson, E. S. C. Weiner, and Michael Proffitt, eds. 3v. Oxford, 1993–1997. $$

423   PE1625

This source is the preeminent dictionary of the English language. A complete revision of the monumental dictionary first published in 1933, the second edition integrates the text of the first edition published in twelve volumes, the four-volume supplement (1972–1986), and approximately 5,000 new words or new senses of existing words. This edition contains general revisions and presents an alphabetical list of words in the English vocabulary from the time of Chaucer to the present day, with all the relevant facts concerning their form, history, pronunciation, and etymology. Also valuable for the 2,400,000 quotations that explain the definitions and provide examples of usage over time. Spellings are British, with American spellings listed as variants. The volumes in the *Additions* series offer definitions of approximately 3,000 new words each, incorporating illustrative quotations from around the world. Large libraries will want to retain the print edition because of its iconic status, but for small and medium-sized libraries the online edition will suffice. Smaller libraries may consider the *Shorter Oxford English Dictionary on Historical Principles*.

480 Oxford English dictionary online.
Oxford. www.oed.com. $$$

The *Oxford English Dictionary Online* (*OED Online*) is, by everyone's estimation, a triumphant success. Comprehensive and up-to-date, this online version of the greatest language reference work ever compiled includes the contents of the earlier editions and the *Additions* series and adds new entries and revises older ones at a rate of some 5,000 per year. It is easy to search and a wonderful tool for exploring the richness of English words, their meanings, their usage, their pronunciation, their etymology, and their spellings. The 3 million quotations are

searchable by year as well as by author or source. Tracing the meaning and usage history of more than 600,000 English-language words, the *OED Online* is an inexhaustible treasure. The *OED* is currently undergoing a comprehensive revision with the aim of producing a third edition, and revised and new entries are being issued online.

481 Random House Webster's unabridged dictionary. 2nd ed. 2256p. Random House, 2005. $

423   PE1625

The smallest and youngest of the unabridged dictionaries, this revised second edition of a dictionary originally published in 1966 keeps the work up-to-date. The second edition contains many new entries and new definitions, bringing the total number of entries to more than 315,000. Adhering to a descriptive approach, *Random House* emphasizes words in current use, including new scientific and technical terms, idiomatic phrases, slang and colloquialisms, and proper names. Stylistic labels employ such restrictive tags as "slang," "offensive," "vulgar," and "informal," and the most frequently used meaning is given first. Many entries also note the date of a word's first appearance in the language. Features include extensive biographical and geographical entries as well as numerous black-and-white illustrations. Although not as comprehensive as *Webster's Third*, this is an easy-to-use and authoritative unabridged dictionary for contemporary English.

482 Webster's third new international dictionary of the English language. Rev. ed. Philip Babcock Gove. 2662p. Merriam-Webster, 2002. $$

423   PE1625

The largest and most prestigious dictionary published in the United States, *Webster's Third* was first published in 1961, covering English language in use since 1755. An addendum of new words is added to each subsequent printing (e.g., eight pages of new words appeared in the 1966 printing, sixteen pages in 1971, thirty-eight in 1976, forty-eight in 1981, fifty-six in 1988, and so on). *Webster's Third* excludes biographical and geographical names and is much less prescriptive regarding usage than *Webster's Second*. Clear, accurate definitions are given in historical order.

Outstanding for its numerous illustrative quotations, impeccable authority, and etymologies, *Webster's Third* is regarded as the most reliable, comprehensive one-volume unabridged dictionary. Libraries owning *Webster's Second* will want to retain it for its prescriptive usage labels and biographical and geographical names. The online version, *Merriam-Webster Unabridged*, incorporates entries from other Merriam-Webster dictionaries and adds audio pronunciations for some 100,000 words as well as additional quotations and extensive cross-references.

Regional Dictionaries

483   Dictionary of American regional English. Frederick G. Cassidy and Joan Houston Hall, eds. 6v. Harvard, 1985–2013. $$$

427   PE2813

In the works since the 1960s, the *Dictionary of American Regional English* (*DARE*) has made it to its sixth and last volume. The content, documenting words, phrases, and pronunciations that vary across the United States, is based on extensive fieldwork data plus citations from a vast collection of printed materials that provide a history for each headword. Entries include regional pronunciations, variant forms, some etymologies, and regional and social distributions of the words and phrases. *Volume I: A–C* was published in 1985. *Volume II: D–H* followed in 1991, *Volume III: I–O* was published in 1996, and *Volume IV: P-Sk* appeared in 2002. *Volume V: Sl–Z*, which includes the bibliography, and *Volume VI*, the index, were finally available in 2012. This title won the Dartmouth Medal for 2013.

Abbreviations and Acronyms

484   Abbreviations dictionary. 10th ed. Dean Stahl, Karen Kerchelich, and Ralph De Sola. 1529p. CRC Press, 2001. $$

423.1   PE1693

This edition of a standard reference work now boasts 300,000 entries, including abbreviations, acronyms, contractions, geographical equivalents, initials, nicknames, short forms, signs, symbols, and lists of specialized terms. Entries are arranged alphabetically and numerically. Also included are lengthy lists of items frequently abbreviated or standing for something else, such as airlines, airports, eponyms, birthstones, nicknames, signs and symbols, and winds and rains of the world. Although there is some overlap with the *Acronyms, Initialisms, and Abbreviations Dictionary*, larger ready-reference collections will want both.

485   Acronyms, initialisms, and abbreviations dictionary: A guide to acronyms, abbreviations. contractions, alphabetic symbols, and similar condensed appellations. 46th ed. 4v. Gale, 2012. $$$$

423.1   P365

Now in its forty-sixth edition and contained in four hefty volumes, this standard Gale annual expands 800,000 entries—acronyms, initialisms, abbreviations, and similar contractions—so that their full context is apparent. Entries are arranged alphabetically and often provide descriptive information, such as language source or sponsoring organization. With the growing sophistication of Internet searching and the advent of such free tools as Acronym Finder (www.acronymfinder.com), an annual purchase is no longer requisite.

Crossword Puzzle Dictionaries

486   American Heritage crossword puzzle dictionary. 885p. Houghton Mifflin, 2003. $

793.73   GV1507

Based on the *Chambers Concise Crossword Dictionary*, this iteration offers 230,000 puzzle answers intended to serve both classic and modern crossword puzzle styles. It includes 15,000 proper names and arranges all entries alphabetically by subject. This edition includes numerous reference lists such as poets, countries, and capital cities.

487   The million word crossword dictionary. Stanley Newman and Daniel Stark. 1268p. HarperCollins, 2004. $

793.73   GV1507

Claiming to be the first all-new crossword puzzle dictionary in twenty years, this source offers more than 1,000,000 answers to 250,000 clues. Included are 3,000 literary works, 5,000 film titles, 20,000 famous people; lists of Oscar winners, Nobel laureates, popes, auto makes; and more than 75,000 fill-in-the-blank clues. This is probably the most complete crossword dictionary on the market.

488 Random House Webster's crossword puzzle dictionary. 4th ed. Stephen Elliot. 870p. Random House, 2006. $
793.73   GV1507

The fourth edition of this standard crossword puzzle dictionary features 700,000 clues and answers and includes thousands of new words from pop culture. All answer words are grouped by their number of letters for easy review. This is the most recently published of the three dictionaries noted here.

Etymology and Word and Phrase Origins

489 Chambers dictionary of etymology. Robert K. Barnhart and Sol Steinmetz, eds. 1284p. Chambers, 1999. $
422   PE1580

Originally published in 1988 as the *Barnhart Dictionary of Etymology*, this dictionary focuses on words used in contemporary American English and words of American origin and incorporates current American scholarship. Entries give spelling variations, pronunciation for difficult words, part of speech, definition, and information on word origins. Written for a wide audience, this is a very attractive, readable work suited for most library users.

490 The Facts on File encyclopedia of word and phrase origins. 4th ed. Robert Hendrickson. 948p. Facts on File, 2008. $
422   PE1689

This popular, highly readable, often humorous, comprehensive etymological dictionary covers more than 15,000 words and phrases. Entries range from one line to about a page in length. It includes an alphabetical index and numerous *see* and *see also* references, and authoritative sources are cited. Written in a nonacademic style, this work will appeal to the general reader curious about the origins of words or expressions used in everyday speech.

491 Oxford dictionary of English etymology. C. T. Onions et al., eds. 1024p. Oxford, 1966. $
422   PE1580

This authoritative work by one of the giants of English lexicography is in its fifth printing. Tracing the history of common English words back to their roots, this etymological dictionary provides the pronunciation, definition, century of origin, and first recording of more than 38,000 English words. It is the most complete and reliable of the etymological dictionaries.

492 Oxford dictionary of word origins. 2nd ed. Julia Creswell, ed. 512p. Oxford, 2010. $
422.03   PE1580

Describing the origins and development of more than 3,000 words and phrases, this dictionary relates the stories behind many of the most curious terms and expressions in the English language. Organized A–Z, the entries include first known use along with examples that illustrate the many facets of the particular word or phrase. Also featured are almost twenty special panels that cover expressions common in English but drawn from other languages.

Foreign Words and Phrases

493 The Facts on File dictionary of foreign words and phrases. 2nd ed. Martin H. Manser. 496p. Facts on File, 2008. $
422   PE1670

This delightful dictionary defines and describes some 4,500 foreign words and phrases, from *Abacus* to *Zombie*. Entries include everyday expressions, technical terms, and familiar phrases. For each word or phrase, information on the pronunciation in American English, language of origin, and original meaning is provided. Sample quotations illustrate contemporary usage of the word or phrase. An index by language of origin helps one to visualize the variety, richness, and scope of foreign expressions naturalized into modern English usage.

494 The Oxford dictionary of foreign words and phrases. 2nd ed. Andrew

Delahunty, ed. 432p. Oxford, 2010. $

422.4   PE1582

This dictionary aims to provide a comprehensive record and explanation of foreign expressions currently used by speakers of the English language. Included are more than 6,000 foreign words and phrases from forty different languages. Each entry defines the word or phrase, indicates common pronunciation, provides examples of usage, and indicates its language of origin. Changes in meaning are traced over time. An appendix provides a listing by language and century of origin of all words included.

Handbooks

495 The writer's market. F & W
Publications, 1922–. $

808   PN161

This source contains very useful information for aspiring and established authors. For instance, it lists fifty literary agents and sample rates for advertising, copywriting, and public relations. Chapters include interviews, the business of writing, literary agents, book publishers, Canadian and international book publishers, small presses, consumer magazines, trade journals, contests and awards, a glossary, and indexes. Each listing includes name and address of the publication or company, its editorial needs, and its rate of payment.

Idioms and Usage Dictionaries

**496 American Heritage dictionary of
idioms.** 2nd ed. Christine Ammer. 512p.
Houghton Mifflin, 2013. $

423.1   PE2839

This authoritative dictionary includes more than 10,000 figures of speech, phrases, clichés, and colloquialisms; entries are listed alphabetically in boldface. For each entry there is a clear definition, an example of use, and an indication of historical origin. Variant definitions are numbered and ordered by frequency of use.

**497 The Cambridge guide to English
usage.** Pam Peters. 608p. Cambridge,
2004. $

423.1   PE1464

This work does not aim to target a particular language community but rather to address the broad international population of English speakers. Drawing on the latest research, it offers two kinds of entries: specific words and phrases and general topics on language and writing. The 4,000 short entries are arranged in A–Z format and provide authoritative information on spelling, punctuation, grammar, and style. The longer entries offer analytical discussions of contemporary grammar, speech, and language rules. For those interested in the precise and effective use of the English language, this is a superb source.

**498 Columbia guide to standard
American English.** Kenneth G. Wilson.
482p. Columbia, 1993. $

428.0097   PE2835

This is a superb addition to our English-language usage tools. Wilson, without being overly prescriptive, still advocates linguistic good manners. He presents 6,500 entries, primarily American expressions, explaining appropriate uses, pointing out some of the finer nuances between words (e.g., *naked* and *nude*), clearly differentiating troublesome pairs (such as *disinterested* and *uninterested*), and generally setting the record straight in a delightful, easy, and familiar style. This guide to current American usage is accessible, authoritative, and eminently pragmatic.

499 Fowler's modern English usage. 3rd
ed. rev. R. W. Burchfield, ed. 896p.
Oxford, 2004. $

428.2   PE1628

The title of the modern version of this usage classic (first published in 1926) appears to morph from year to year; however, the purpose remains pretty much the same. Fowler's original work, revised by Gowers in 1965, has again been revised for a new generation of English speakers. Burchfield, a distinguished lexicographer, has in fact produced a recognizably new work, adding numerous entries that discuss recent foibles and perversities of usage. The latest *Fowler's* provides comprehensive and clear advice on the correct use of the complex communication tool we call the English language. Libraries owning the earlier editions will want to obtain this one as well.

500 Garner's modern American usage.
3rd ed. Bryan A. Garner. 942p. Oxford, 2009. $

423.1   PE2827

Originally titled *A Dictionary of Modern American Usage*, this guide offers advice on American English usage through individual word entries as well as essays on usage and style. Each of the more than 10,500 entries provides an example of the usage of the word, an illustrative quotation, and an appropriate citation. The essays address topics such as abbreviations, alliteration, etymology, and pronouns. A new feature of this edition is Garner's "Language-Change Index," which registers on a scale from one to five how widely accepted certain linguistic changes have become. More than 2,000 usages are ranked. The first edition of this work was designated an outstanding reference title by both ALA's Reference Sources Committee and *Choice*.

Rhyming Dictionaries

501 The complete rhyming dictionary.
Rev. ed. Clement Wood; rev. by Ronald J. Bogus. 627p. Doubleday, 1991. $

808.1   PE1519

This expanded and updated edition of the classic 1936 rhyming dictionary is both authoritative and comprehensive. It includes more than 60,000 entries, including one-, two-, and three-syllable rhymes. Within each section, words are arranged by vowel sound and then alphabetically.

502 New Oxford rhyming dictionary. 2nd ed. Clive Upton and Eben Upton. 448p. Oxford, 2012. $

423.1   PE1519

This edition contains rhymes for more than 45,000 words, including proper names, place names, and foreign terms used in English. Words are grouped by sound, and there is also a complete alphabetical index. In-text notes offer tips on using rhymes effectively, make suggestions for expanding the rhyming lists included in the book, and give examples of how poets past and present have used rhyme.

503 Words to rhyme with. 3rd ed. Willard R. Espy; updated by Orin Hargraves. 683p.

Facts on File, 2006. $

423.1   PE1519

Like its predecessors, the third edition has entries arranged by rhyming sound rather than by spelling. The approximately 100,000 words listed are divided into single, double, and triple rhymes. Included is a glossary where 9,000 of the more obscure words listed are defined. A 100-page "Primer of Prosody" introduces poetic techniques, making ample use of sample illustrations. This edition has added many new trademark words, common acronyms and abbreviations, and new technological terms. This is the most comprehensive and playful of the rhyming dictionaries and is for all word lovers.

Sign Language Dictionaries

504 The American sign language handshape dictionary. 2nd ed. Richard A. Tennant and Marianne Gluszak Brown. 461p. Gallaudet, 2010. $

419   HV2475

As the title implies, this dictionary organizes signs by hand shape rather than by alphabet. Some 1,900 signs are included, those most prevalent in sign conversation. The hand-shape approach allows the learner to progress from sign to word rather than vice versa. Each sign is clearly illustrated and explained in terms of five parameters: configuration, location, movement, orientation, and nonmanual markers. An index of English glosses at the end allows one to progress from English words to the appropriate hand shape, for those who wish to take that route. A DVD is included.

505 Gallaudet dictionary of American ✓ **sign language.** Clayton Valli, ed. 558p. Gallaudet, 2005. $

419   HV2475

Produced under the auspices of Gallaudet University, this dictionary presents some 3,000 alphabetically arranged illustrated entries. The illustrations are clear and easy to interpret. Listings of English synonyms throughout help to clarify usage. Of particular value, this dictionary comes with a DVD that offers a clear demonstration of each sign.

These video illustrations can be played at normal, reduced, or accelerated speed or set to play frame by frame.

506 Random House Webster's American sign language dictionary: Unabridged. Elaine Costello. 1200p. Random House, 2008. $

419 HV2475

This compendium of more than 5,600 words and signs was prepared by the founder of Gallaudet University Press. The dictionary includes a detailed introduction to the language that clearly explains its origins, its use, and its structure. It provides full-torso illustrations and includes separate sections on geographical signs and how numbers are signed. This most comprehensive of the signing dictionaries includes more than 3,000 cross-references.

Clichés and Metaphors

507 The Facts on File dictionary of clichés. 3rd ed. Christine Ammer. 556p. Facts on File, 2011. $

423 PE1689

This phrase dictionary traces the origins, explains the meanings, and illustrates the use of some 4,000 clichés commonly found in American English. Originally published in 1999 as *Have a Nice Day—No Problem!*, this delightful and engaging work is not as scholarly as Eric Partridge's *Dictionary of Clichés* (Routledge, 1978), but it is more intriguing and more fun. Entries are arranged alphabetically by the first major word in the phrase; a detailed index and numerous cross-references add to its usefulness.

508 Metaphors dictionary. Elyse Sommer and Dorrie Weiss, eds. 672p. Visible Ink, 2001. $

081 PE1689

This dictionary collects and elucidates some 6,500 metaphoric comparisons, from ancient times to the present, organized in 500 alphabetically arranged thematic sequences. An introduction discusses the various types of metaphor (mixed, extended, personification, etc.). There are separate listings for

the most common metaphors and metaphors from Shakespeare. The work includes author/speaker and subject indexes and a bibliography of sources.

Slang and Euphemisms

509 Dictionary of American slang. 3rd ed. Robert L. Chapman, Harold Wentworth, and Barbara Ann Kipfer, eds. 617p. HarperCollins, 2007. $

427 PE2846

This is a revised edition of a standard work, *Dictionary of American Slang* (Crowell, 1975). This version includes many slang expressions from the original work along with hundreds of new words from the intervening years. Notations include pronunciations, appropriate classification and dating labels, illustrative phrases, and numerous cross-references.

510 Encyclopedia of swearing: The social history of oaths, profanity, foul language, and ethnic slurs in the English-speaking world. Geoffrey I. Hughes, ed. 573p. M. E. Sharpe, 2006. $$

427 PE3724

This is a work that aims to provide a social history of foul language. Although focusing on American and British English, examples from all corners of the English-speaking world are included. The several hundred topical entries are arranged alphabetically; there are entries on historical periods, specific authors, and ethnic groups; sample topics include "Anatomical Insults," "Anglo-Saxon Terms," "Whore and Whoreson," and "Zounds!" A chronology, bibliography, and index are provided.

511 Green's dictionary of slang. Jonathon Green. 3v. Oxford, 2011. $$

429.09 PE3721

Seventeen years in the making, this dictionary, winner of the 2012 Dartmouth Medal, distinguishes itself by being based on historical principles. This means that each and every sense for every word or phrase is illustrated by a list of citations with example quotations, drawn from whatever medium yields them up, going back, as far as can be ascertained, to the first use for each slang sense. There are more than 53,000 entries, definitions of more than 100,000 words, and more than 400,000 citations.

512 The new Partridge dictionary of slang and unconventional English. 2nd rev. ed. Eric Partridge; rev. by Tom Dalzell and Terry Victor. 2v. Routledge, 2013. $$
427.09   PE3721

Marketed as "the successor to *The Dictionary of Slang and Unconventional English* by Eric Partridge," which first appeared in 1937, this new work contains 65,000 entries, from *A* to *Zymy*, in two volumes. Although this new dictionary focuses on post–World War II British and American slang, it is truly international in scope, incorporating entries from English-speaking nations around the world. Entries list the term, identify the part of speech, elucidate its meaning, indicate the country of origin, and provide quotations to illustrate usage. Published sources are given for most entries.

513 NTC's dictionary of American slang and colloquial expressions. 3rd ed. Richard A. Spears. 560p. NTC, 2000. $
427.973   PE2846

Spears has been monitoring American slang for more than thirty years. This offering is a straightforward dictionary with headwords listed alphabetically. Some 10,000 words and phrases are simply defined and simply illustrated. The value of this dictionary is that it focuses on our contemporary world and includes numerous terms from popular culture, pop technology, the Internet, and Generation X.

514 The Routledge dictionary of modern American slang and unconventional English. Tom Dalzell, ed. 1120p. Routledge, 2008. $
427   PE3721

Calling this volume an intended consequence of the larger *New Partridge Dictionary of Slang and Unconventional English* (2006), editor Dalzell (the coeditor of the previous volume) explains in his preface that the present work is a result of having extracted the American entries from *New Partridge* and ultimately reviewing each, excluding some,

enhancing others, and adding several thousand new entries—then trimming them down to meet the criteria of this volume, which consists of slang and unconventional terms used in the United States after 1945. The work contains 25,000 entries. Its price makes it a good alternative to the *New Partridge* for smaller collections.

Thesauri: Synonyms, Antonyms, and Homonyms

515 Historical thesaurus of the Oxford English dictionary. Christian Kay et al., eds. 2v. Oxford, 2009. $$
423.12   PE1591

Billed as the first historical thesaurus to be written for any of the world's languages, this work was forty years in the making. For scholars of the English language, it was worth the wait. The thesaurus looks at the range of meanings that a word has had over the ages and documents all the words in general English use over a period of many hundreds of years. Though based on the A–Z definitions in the *Oxford English Dictionary* (with additional material from *A Thesaurus of Old English*, 1995), it has a thematic arrangement. There are more than 236,000 categories and subcategories, and a numbering system is used to identify categories and hierarchical levels. In addition to being a history of words used to express a meaning over time, this is also meant to be used as a thesaurus for any period in the past.

516 Homophones and homographs: An American dictionary. 4th ed. James B. Hobbs, comp. McFarland, 2006. $
423   PE2833

New editions of this extraordinary work have been appearing regularly since 1986, and each new edition is more useful and more comprehensive than the last. Homophones are words that sound alike but have different spellings and meanings (*bear* and *bare*); homographs are spelled the same but have different meanings and are pronounced differently (*bass* and *bass*). This edition contains 9,040 homophones and 2,133 homographs. The work concludes with an extensive annotated bibliography. This American dictionary recognizes, celebrates, and expertly explicates that rather narrow range of vocabulary that initially confuses and ultimately delights.

517   Oxford American writer's thesaurus.
2nd ed. Christine A. Lindberg, comp.
1128p. Oxford, 2008. $
423   PE1591

This thesaurus from Oxford claims to be "the first to be developed by writers for writers." Included are the expected 30,000 synonyms and 10,000 antonyms, but what makes this thesaurus particularly interesting is the use of some 200 word banks, where collections of related nouns are grouped together under broad headings (e.g., under *bread* one might find, not synonyms, but *rye*, *pita*, *croissant*, *baguette*, or other specific examples), and the use of word spectrums, lists of 30 or more related words and phrases that run the gamut from, for example, *begin* to *end* or *lucky* to *unlucky*. Both these features are designed to help writers discover the perfect word for their particular context.

518   Random House Webster's word menu.
Rev. ed. Stephen Glazier. 800p. Random
House, 1998. $
423   PE1680

The *Word Menu* classifies some 65,000 words into relevant categories and subcategories. It can be used by anyone seeking to find related terms, equivalent terms, or just interesting words that are common to certain fields of endeavor. You won't find help with pronunciation, etymology, or usage; it is the richness of the relationships presented that is unique. Anyone who crafts with words or who loves words will find in this work a lasting companion.

519   Roget's international thesaurus. 7th
ed. Barbara Ann Kipfer and Robert L.
Chapman, eds. 1312p. HarperCollins,
2010. $
423   PE1591

Thoroughly revised and updated, the seventh edition reflects contemporary vocabulary, including slang, technical terms, and idiomatic expressions. This is a true thesaurus, based on the principles of Peter Mark Roget, arranged topically with an alphabetical index to the 330,000 entries. There are 1,075 categories in this edition; within each category, words are grouped by part of speech in the following order: nouns, verbs, adjectives, adverbs, prepositions, conjunctions, and interjections. Most important or most commonly used terms are indicated by boldface type. Roget's fundamental structure remains as useful as ever.

Style Manuals

**520   The Associated Press stylebook and
briefing on media law.** 45th ed. 416p.
Basic Books, 2011. $
808.06   PN4783

Called the "journalist's bible," *The Associated Press Stylebook* is a dictionary, handbook, and style guide, all in one. The more than 3,000 alphabetically arranged entries lay out the Associated Press rules on grammar, spelling, punctuation, and usage. The guide also provides practical advice on libel, right to privacy, and copyright as well as details about proofreader's marks and the Associated Press Agency.

**521   The Bluebook: A uniform system of
citation.** 19th ed. 511p. Harvard Law
Review Association, 2010. $
348.73   KF245
Prince's dictionary of legal citations.
8th ed. Mary Miles Prince. 559p. W. S.
Hein, 2011. $
349.73   KF246

The Bluebook is compiled by the editors of the *Harvard Law Review* in conjunction with the editors of the *Columbia Law Review*, *University of Pennsylvania Law Review*, and *Yale Law Journal* and serves as the standard source for style formats in U.S. law journals. *Prince's Dictionary* is a companion to the *Bluebook* and is meant to serve as a helpful interpretive tool when using that source.

522   The Chicago manual of style. 16th ed.
1026p. Chicago, 2010. $
808   Z253

The sixteenth edition of this standard style manual reflects the latest technological developments, discusses the new copyright laws, and provides more sample citations, including notes and bibliographic entries, and more guidance on the basics of style, including the use of numbers versus numerals, abbreviations, foreign words in an English-language context, and quotations. A reference staple since 1906, the current edition fully incorporates the electronic revolution while still providing expert advice on the fundamentals of manuscript preparation, punctuation, and spelling. This is the first edition to be published simultaneously in print and online.

523 The Columbia guide to online style.
2nd ed. Janice R. Walker and Todd Taylor. 312p. Columbia, 2006. $
808 PN171
Providing rules for electronic citation, guidelines for formatting documents for online publication, and tips on preparing texts electronically for print publication, this is the definitive guide to online style.

524 The elements of legal style. 2nd ed. Bryan A. Garner. 288p. Oxford, 2002. $
808 KF250
This is a practical guide for those who engage in legal writing and editing by one of the foremost authorities in the field. On the assumption that "legal writing shouldn't be lethal reading," Garner provides clear advice on such matters as punctuation, word choice, grammar and syntax, principles of legal writing, rhetorical figures, exposition and argument, and speaking. Although the focus is on legal writing, anyone interested in strong, healthy prose will benefit from consulting this work.

525 A manual for writers of research papers, theses, and dissertations. 8th ed. Kate L. Turabian; rev. by Joseph M. Williams et al. 464p. Chicago, 2013. $
808.06 LB2369
This is the standard guide for students preparing formal papers, including research papers, theses, and dissertations, in both scientific and nonscientific fields. The manual offers practical advice on the mechanics of writing (e.g., punctuation, spelling, and capitalization) as well as information on such matters as the parts of the paper, preparing and referring to tables and illustrations, and preparing a manuscript for submission. The citation practice of this edition conforms to sixteenth

edition of *The Chicago Manual of Style*. Libraries of all sizes should own at least one copy of this guide.

526 MLA handbook for writers of research papers. 7th ed. Joseph Gibaldi. 292p. Modern Language Association of America, 2009. $
808.027 LB2369
This handbook contains style rules covering such matters as abbreviations, footnotes, and bibliographies. In addition it discusses the mechanics of the research paper, including such issues as how to choose a term-paper topic, how to make effective use of the library, and the process of composing the research paper. The seventh edition contains information on new formats such as toons and strips, and appropriately devotes considerable attention to citing electronic publications.

527 New Oxford style manual. 2nd ed. 880p. Oxford, 2012. $
808.027 PN147
This addition to the community of style is actually a conjoining and reworking of two works, *New Hart's Rules* (2005) and *New Oxford Dictionary for Writers and Editors* (2005). Part 1 provides guidance on the mechanics of writing, such as grammar, punctuation, abbreviation, and quotation, as well as advice on larger matters—for example, copyright and the proper treatment of notes, references, and illustrations. Part 2 provides 25,000 alphabetical entries on words that frequently prove problematic to writers.
Publication manual of the American Psychological Association, **see 219.**

528 Scientific style and format: The CSE manual for authors, editors, and publishers. 7th ed. 658p. Council of Science Editors, 2006.
808 T11
Previously published as the *CBE Manual* (Council of Biology Editors), the new name and new edition reflect a broader scope. Described as the "authoritative reference for authors, editors, publishers, students, and translators in all areas of science," the manual covers both American and British styles. This edition is divided into four parts: publishing fundamentals, general style conventions, special scientific conventions, and technical elements of publication. There

are new chapters on the responsibility of authors, editors, and peer reviewers and on copyright.

Bilingual and Foreign-Language Resources

Bibliographies and Guides

529 A guide to world language dictionaries. Arnold Dalby, ed. 470p. Fitzroy Dearborn, 1998. $$
016.413   P361
Organized in alphabetical order by language, from Abkhaz to Zulu, this guide appraises the general and historical dictionaries of the world's 275 main written languages. Entries provide a description of the language, language family, geographic region where spoken, number of speakers, and alphabet. For major languages, dictionaries are listed under subheadings that differentiate historical dictionaries, modern standard dictionaries, regional dictionaries, slang dictionaries, and so forth. Also included are a history of dictionaries and an explanation of the International Phonetic Alphabet.

Databases and Indexes

530 Oxford language dictionaries online. Oxford. www.oxfordlanguagedictionaries .com. $$
This electronic language dictionary service offers searchable versions of Oxford's bilingual dictionaries covering English and Chinese, French, German, Italian, Russian, and Spanish. Users will find translations, audio pronunciations, explanations of phonetic symbols, and more. The Oxford Language Web feature adds translations in Arabic, Polish, Portuguese, Japanese, Korean, and Thai. The database also has study materials, including language learning and usage tools and resources as well as templates for various types of correspondence.

Arabic

531 Arabic–English lexicon. Edward William Lane and Stanley Lane-Poole,

eds. 264p. Gorgias Press, 2010. $$
492.7   PJ6640
This is the standard dictionary for classical Arabic, particularly useful for those studying and translating Islamic texts. The work of nineteenth-century scholars, it carefully references literary sources when known.

532 Elias modern dictionary: English–Arabic. Elias A. Elias and Edward E. Elias. 869p. Elias Modern Pub. House, 1993. $
492.73   PJ6640
This standard modern Arabic dictionary covers about 48,000 entries. First published in the 1920s, it includes both classical and modern Arabic vocabulary and usage. Entries are arranged alphabetically according to their root, with all derivatives subsumed under the root entry.

533 Oxford essential Arabic dictionary: English–Arabic, Arabic–English. 416p. Oxford, 2010. $
492.7321   PJ6640
Oxford has provided a compact dictionary that offers up-to-date coverage of all the essential day-to-day vocabulary of both languages, with more than 16,000 words, phrases, and translations. Arabic entries are listed according to alphabetical order, not by root, in order to make word searches easier. As with bilingual dictionaries for the more commonly taught languages, Oxford here includes supplemental material such as tables of verbs, pronunciation guides (using International Phonetic Association notation), notes on the Arabic numeric system, and so on.

Chinese

534 ABC Chinese–English comprehensive dictionary. John DeFrancis, ed. 1439p. University of Hawaii, 2003. $
495.1   PL1455
Unlike most Chinese–English dictionaries, which arrange entries by character, this dictionary took advantage of computer technology to list words in strict alphabetical sequence using Pinyin orthography. This updated edition includes more than 196,000 entries and is particularly useful when looking up a term whose pronunciation is known. There are charts to help locate characters whose pronunciation is not

known; conversion tables for Pinyin, Wade-Giles, and other orthographies; and much relevant information about the Chinese language.

535   The Oxford Chinese dictionary: English–Chinese, Chinese–English.
1011p. Oxford, 2010. $

423   PL1455

Translators and scholars from the United States, the United Kingdom, and China collaborated for six years to produce this bilingual dictionary offering more than 300,000 words and phrases and 370,000 translations. It has been produced using the latest lexicographic methods and is based on research in both the Oxford English Corpus and the LIVAC corpus from the City University of Hong Kong. The volume is arranged with Pinyin transcriptions in simplified Chinese characters and then traditional Chinese characters if they differ from the simplified form. Some 300 cultural notes give information about many aspects of life and culture in the Chinese- and English-speaking worlds. There are also more than fifty pages of lexical and usage notes. After the initial purchase, users have twelve-month access to an online dictionary service with regular updates of new words, audio pronunciations, and language learning help.

536   The Pinyin Chinese–English dictionary. 976p. Wiley, 1982. $

495.103   PL1455

Compiled by a staff of more than fifty Chinese and English linguistic specialists, the 125,000 entries are divided into single and compound characters. The dictionary reflects the straightforward presentation of Chinese characters adopted by the Pinyin system of English transliteration.

English as a Second Language

537   Merriam-Webster's advanced learner's English dictionary. 2032p. Merriam-Webster, 2008. $

423   PE1625

Intended for advanced students, this dictionary provides in-depth and up-to-date coverage of basic English vocabulary, grammar, and usage. It contains nearly 100,000 words and phrases, more than 160,000 usage examples, and more than 22,000

idioms. Supplemental information includes thirty pages of grammar.

French

538   Collins Robert French unabridged dictionary. 9th ed. 2142p. HarperCollins, 2012. $

443.21   PC2640

As the title implies, this dictionary is a collaboration between HarperCollins and the French publisher Robert. Updated frequently and with more than 820,000 entries and translations, it aims to provide the most complete coverage of contemporary French of any one-volume language dictionary. Included are the latest terms from business, technology, politics, and culture.

539   Harrap's new standard French and English dictionary. Rev. ed. Jean E. Mansion, ed.; rev. and ed. by Margaret Ledésert and R. P. L. Ledésert. 4v. Harrap, 1972–1980. $$

443.21   PC2640

This is a monumental work, exceptionally thorough, reliable, and accurate—indispensable to student and specialist alike. It is considered by many to be the most comprehensive and authoritative of the French–English bilingual dictionaries. Consists of four volumes divided into two parts: French–English (pt. 1, v. 1–2) and English–French (pt. 2, v. 2–3).

540   The Oxford-Hachette French dictionary: French–English, English–French. 4th ed. Jean-Benoit Ormal-Grenon and Nicholas Rollin, eds. 2112p. Oxford, 2007. $

443.21   PC2640

This is a superb dictionary of contemporary French. Usage examples are drawn from the everyday world of newspapers and advertising. Also included is a lengthy guide to effective communication in French, including correspondence, telephone, and e-mail.

German

541   Collins German unabridged dictionary. 7th ed. Maree Airlie and Joyce Littlejohn, eds. 2103p. HarperCollins, 2007. $$

433.21   PF3640

Now in its seventh edition, this popular dictionary aims to be up-to-date with the latest business, political, and technical terms. With its emphasis on colloquial usage, the Collins dictionary is particularly useful for language students.

542   Oxford German dictionary: German– English, English–German. 3rd ed. W. Scholze-Stubenrecht et al., eds. 1800p. Oxford, 2008. $

433.21   PF3640

The third edition, with more than 320,000 words and phrases and 520,000 translations, incorporates the use of color to enhance layout. The addition of usage boxes makes this a practical dictionary for learners; however, British English is favored. Other features include cultural notes and advice on e-mailing and text messaging.

Greek

543   A Greek–English lexicon: Ninth edition with a revised supplement. Henry George Liddell, Robert Scott, and Henry Stuart Jones, eds. 2446p. Oxford, 1995. $$

483   PA445

Frequently reprinted, this is the standard Greek and English lexicon, covering the language to about AD 600, omitting Patristic and Byzantine Greek.

Hebrew

544   The Complete Hebrew–English dictionary. Reuben Alcalay, ed. 2v. Miskal, 2000. $

492.43   PJ4833

Considered by many to be the most complete and authoritative Hebrew–English dictionary, it is particularly useful for textual study.

545   NTC's Hebrew and English dictionary. Arie Comay and Naomi Tsur. 1280p. NTC, 2000. $

492.4   PJ4833

This is a straightforward bilingual dictionary with about 100,000 entries. It focuses on contemporary

usage, excluding archaisms and poetic forms, using one-word translations. Included is a review of both English and Hebrew grammar.

546   The Oxford English–Hebrew dictionary. N. S. Doniach and Ahuvia Kahane, eds. 1120p. Oxford, 1998. $

492.432   PJ4833

This dictionary has been prepared for those studying the Hebrew of the twentieth century. It contains more than 50,000 entries and includes current idioms and phrases, slang, colloquialisms, and technical terminology.

Italian

547   Oxford-Paravia Italian dictionary. 3rd ed. 2800p. Oxford, 2010. $

453.21   PC1640

Oxford collaborated with one of the foremost publishers in Italy to produce this bilingual dictionary. Included are definitions of more than 700,000 words. Illustrative sentences demonstrate contemporary usage, and text boxes explain points of grammar.

Japanese

548   Kenkyusha's new English–Japanese dictionary. 6th ed. J. Koine, ed. 2886p. French and European Publications, 2002. $$

495.63   PL679

549   Kenkyusha's new Japanese–English dictionary. 5th ed. Masuda Koh, ed. 2827p. French and European Publications, 2003. $$

495.63   PL679

The fullest Japanese–English and English–Japanese dictionaries; romanized Japanese entries are alphabetized in transliterated form, followed by Japanese characters and their English equivalents.

Latin

550   Cassell's Latin dictionary: Latin– English, English–Latin. Donald P. Simpson, ed. 912p. Wiley, 1977. $

473   PA2365

This is an authoritative and durable favorite, first published in 1854. It has been frequently revised for new generations. The first part is designed to assist the reader; the second part, the writer of Latin.

551   Oxford Latin dictionary. 2nd ed. P. G. W. Glare, ed. 2v. Oxford, 2012. $$

473.21   PA2365

Based on fifty years of scholarship and an entirely fresh reading of original Latin sources, this comprehensive and authoritative dictionary follows the principles of the *OED*. It covers classical Latin from the earliest recorded words to the end of the second century AD and presents entries for approximately 40,000 words drawn from a collection of more than one million quotations. Included are proper names and major Latin suffixes. Quotes appear chronologically within each entry, showing whenever possible the earliest known instance of a particular usage.

Russian

552   English–Russian, Russian–English dictionary. 2nd ed. Kenneth Katzner. 1120p. Wiley, 1994. $

491.73   PG2640

This dictionary was compiled and published in the United States for American English speakers. There are 26,000 English entries and 40,000 Russian entries. It describes Russian parts of speech, grammar, usage, synonyms, and colloquial and idiomatic expressions and provides a glossary of geographical and personal names.

553   The Oxford Russian dictionary. 4th ed. Marcus Wheeler et al., eds. 1322p. Oxford, 2007. $

491.73   PG2640

This is an excellent, up-to-date, comprehensive one-volume bilingual dictionary compiled and published in the United Kingdom for English speakers. Now in its fourth edition, it contains 185,000 headwords and phrases, provides numerous illustrative examples, and claims to emphasize

"modern idioms and colloquial language." Abbreviations and acronyms are included.

Spanish

554   The American Heritage Spanish dictionary: Spanish/English, Inglés/Español. 2nd ed. 640p. Houghton Mifflin, 2001. $

463.21   PC4640

This bilingual dictionary emphasizes American English and Latin American Spanish. The second edition defines more than 120,000 words and phrases and includes contemporary popular and technical vocabulary. Useful features include grammar and usage notes, irregular verbs, abbreviations, pronunciation guides, and synonyms to distinguish meanings.

555   Collins Spanish dictionary: Complete and unabridged. 9th ed. Catherine Love and Gaëlle Amiot-Cadey, eds. 2087p. HarperCollins, 2009. $

463.21   PC4640

Now in its ninth edition, this respected unabridged dictionary explores some 240,000 headwords; definitions focus on contemporary usage; more than 1,000 sidebars provide readers with illustrations of life and culture in Spanish-speaking countries.

556   The Oxford Spanish dictionary: Spanish–English, English–Spanish. 4th ed. Beatriz Galimberti Jarman, Roy Russell, and Carol Styles Carvajal, eds. 2060p. Oxford, 2008. $

463.21   PC4640

Since the aim of this dictionary is to cover Spanish as it is spoken throughout the entire Spanish-speaking world, usage examples explicate meanings for specific geographic locations. There are more than 300,000 main entries, colorized for easy searching. This expanded edition includes terms from twenty-first-century life and technology; informative cultural notes are interspersed throughout the volume.

Science and Technology

9

JACK O'GORMAN

Science and technology sources have kept their prominence for scientists and engineers who rely on up-to-date and accurate technical information for their work. The issues for sci/tech librarianship include quality, costs, and coverage. Librarians need to be aware of the information needs of their clientele and strive to meet those needs within constrained budgets. In this chapter, I have endeavored to pull together the best reference sources in the scientific and technical disciplines. Hopefully, the sources listed will continue to be useful for reference collections of libraries of all sizes.

General Sources

Guides to the Literature

557 Science and technology resources.
James E. Bobick and G. Lynn Berard.
285p. Libraries Unlimited, 2011. $
025.5   Z711.6

This source will be beneficial to students of library science, practicing sci/tech librarians, and "researchers interested in acquiring an understanding and developing a working knowledge of science and technology collections." The first part of the book describes the scientific and technical communications process. In additional to traditional sources like encyclopedias and databases, it covers the gray literature, patents, standards and specifications, and handbooks. The second part of the book is a subject bibliography. Database descriptions contain annotations, but websites, dictionaries, and handbooks do not.

Databases and Indexes

558 Web of science. Thomson Reuters. http://thomsonreuters.com/web-of-science/. CP$
Scopus. Elsevier. www.elsevier.com/online-tools/scopus. CP$

Both of these databases offer excellent multidisciplinary scientific coverage. Medium-sized and larger academic libraries should have a subscription to one of these two products. Which one will depend on cost and consortial arrangements. Smaller academic libraries and public libraries may be able to get by with a free resource like Google Scholar (http://scholar.google.com).

Dictionaries and Encyclopedias

559 The American Heritage science dictionary. 695p. Houghton Mifflin Harcourt, 2011. $
503   Q123

The updated edition of this science dictionary belongs on the reference shelf of small and
medium-sized libraries. It defines more than
8,500 terms and includes a "Closer Look" for
certain terms as well as biographies and usage
definitions. Entries include photographs and
drawings, and definitions written to be under-
stood by nonspecialists. The 2011 edition incorporates recent developments and discoveries in
science.

560 Cool stuff 2.0 and how it works. Chris
Woodford. 256p. Dorling Kindersley,
2007. $
600   T48
This is an update of the 2005 title *Cool Stuff and
How It Works*. The author has also written *Cool
Stuff Exploded: Get Inside Modern Technology*.
Great for curious boys and girls and for adults who
want to know how something works. Just how
does a refrigerator work, or how do video games
work? This source presents a visual description of
the inner workings of modern technology. Includes
an appendix called "What's Next?" and a glossary
and index.

561 Dictionary of scientific principles.
Stephen Marvin. 631p. Wiley, 2011. $$
503   Q123
The author has compiled an extensive list of
principles derived from science and mathemat-
ics. Coverage includes psychology, management,
philosophy, art, and more. Two examples are the
Pollyanna principle from psychology, accord-
ing to which people give preference to pleasant
over unpleasant events, and the Bayes principle,
which is a technique to calculate the probability
of an unknown outcome. Contains about 2,000
entries and includes a principles-to-applications
listing. Unusual for a dictionary, it includes the
sources of the terms defined. This work pro-
vides a single source to define various scientific
principles.

**562 Encyclopedia of science, technology,
and ethics.** Carl Mitcham, ed. 4v.
Macmillan Reference USA, 2005. $$
503   Q175.35
Useful for those studying ethics in a modern context.
Introductory essays on topics such as technologies

of humility, ethics and technology, and research
ethics. Entries range from 200 to 5,000 words and
include books, journals, and websites. Access is via
the subject index, list of articles, a topical outline,
and cross-references. Appendixes include an annotated bibliography, Internet resources, glossary,
chronology, and codes of ethics from various engineering and scientific organizations.

**563 Encyclopedia of science and
technology communication.** Susanna
Hornig Priest, ed. 2v. SAGE, 2010. $$
501   Q225.2
Communication about science to nonscientists is
vitally important, especially considering some of
the public's skepticism about important scientific
concepts, such as evolution or climate change.
This encyclopedia focuses on issues around com-
munication in the sciences. Entries cover concepts
such as disasters, technology communication, and
evidence-based medicine and include biographies
of well-known science communicators such as
Thomas Kuhn and Bill Nye the Science Guy. The
audience includes science journalists and under-
graduate and graduate students studying science
communication. Includes indexes and bibliogra-
phies for further reading.

**564 General information concerning
patents: A brief introduction to
patent matters.** U.S. Patent and
Trademark Office. www.uspto.gov/web/
offices/pac/doc/general/. Free
A classic booklet, now available as a website. Your
library may want to include this site in the catalog
to refer patrons to authoritative patent information.
Contains general information on the application
for and the granting of patents, expressed in non-
technical language for the layperson. It is expressly
intended for inventors, prospective applicants, and
students. This site answers the most commonly
asked question about the operations of the U.S.
Patent and Trademark Office. Similar to this is
Basic Facts about Trademarks, at www.uspto.gov/
go/tac/doc/basic/.

565 The handy science answer book.
4th ed. Naomi E. Balaban and James E.
Bobick. 679p. Visible Ink, 2011. $
500   Q173

The new edition of this title asks and then answers more than 2,200 questions like, What is the difference between a rock and a mineral? What color is lightning? Are there any multiple Nobel Prize winners? This source is the perfect place to turn to answer questions like these. Arranged by broad categories like space, energy, the animal world, and health and medicine, it is also fun for browsing. Access is via the indexing for a specific topic. Other titles in the series include *The Handy Biology Answer Book*, *The Handy Physics Answer Book*, and *The Handy Math Answer Book*.

566 The McGraw-Hill dictionary of scientific and technical terms. 6th ed. 2380p. McGraw-Hill, 2003. $$
503   Q123

"The language of science and technology is expanding not only in its role in our culture; it is growing in its breadth and depth as scientific disciplines mature and whole new technologies, such as nanotechnology and genomics, arise." This seventh edition contains 115,000 terms, including more than 3,000 illustrations, and brief biographical listings for about 1,600 scientists. Synonyms, acronyms, and abbreviations are given within definitions as well as in alphabetical sequence as separate entries. Entries include pronunciation guide, U.S. and SI (metric) units, and an indication of the subject field. Contains appendixes on the SI system, table of the chemical elements, chemical nomenclature, mathematical notation, and other symbols.

567 Oxford dictionary of scientific quotations. W. F. Bynum and Roy Porter, eds. 712p. Oxford, 2005. $
503   Q173

Scientists, poets, novelists, and theologians talk about the craft of science. This source is like the *Oxford Dictionary of Quotations* (Oxford, 2005) with a scientific focus. Entries are alphabetical by author and include birth and death dates. Quotations are in chronological order, with original spelling and capitalization. The most important word of the quotation is indexed with an abbreviation of the author's name and page and quote number. A thoroughly researched and easily browsed volume.

568 Science online. Facts on File. http://online.infobaselearning.com. CP$

This is a compilation of more than 250 science books and encyclopedias. Its strength comes from the many Facts on File publications included in electronic form. It is well suited for undergraduate, high school, and even a middle school science audience. In addition to text, entries include videos, diagrams, definitions, biographies, and experiments. Publications included range in date from 1999 to 2011. Access includes a nice advanced search and browsing of science resources.

569 Sizes: The illustrated encyclopedia. John Lord. 374p. Harper Perennial, 1995. $
530.8   QC82

This source is a very readable guide to measurement. Just what is a pennyweight, and what does octane mean, and what is a bond rating? Charts, illustrations, and a clear layout help the reader decipher measuring units. Entries include the origin of a unit, how it is used, and cross-references. Includes graphical conversion charts and a subject index.

Biographical Sources

570 American men and women of science: A biographical directory of today's leaders in physical, biological, and related sciences. 25nd ed. 8v. R. R. Bowker, 1906–. $$$$
509.2   Q141

Brief biographical sketches of about 133,000 scientists and engineers active in the United States and Canada. About 3,000 of them are listed for the first time in this edition. Arranged alphabetically, with the discipline index using headings from the National Science Foundation's *Standard Taxonomy of Degree and Employment Specialties*. Useful in all libraries for biographical information on scientists. Also available online.

Astronomy
Dictionaries and Encyclopedias

571 Firefly encyclopedia of astronomy. Paul Murdin and Margaret Penston, eds.

472p. Firefly, 2004. $
520   QB14

According to the preface, "There are few sciences where professionals work so closely with amateurs, and this encyclopedia is evidence of that proximity." This work is drawn from professional astronomical literature, but the intended audience is the amateur astronomer, astronomy students, and interested readers. Entries are clearly written and include colorful photos and cross-references but no bibliography. This source uses dictionary-style entries, so it has no subject index.

572   National Geographic encyclopedia of space. Linda K. Glover et al. 400p. National Geographic, 2005. $
629.4   TL787.5

As one might expect from the National Geographic Society, this source is a colorful and visual representation of space and space travel. Deep space, the solar system, maneuvering in space, human spacecraft, the Earth and space commerce, and military uses of space are chapters in the book. As a special feature, experts on space have written short essays on such topics as a space elevator or a flight to Saturn. Browsable, informative, and fun.

573   NASA science. National Aeronautic and Space Administration. http://nasascience.nasa.gov. Free

This website is sponsored by the NASA Science Mission Directorate. It includes information about the Earth and the other planets and covers heliophysics, astrophysics, NASA missions and technology, and science news. Includes a NASA Astronomy Picture of the Day. Linking to the site from a library's catalog would help users get accurate, up-to-date, and interesting space information.

574   Night sky atlas. Robin Scagell. 96p. DK, 2007. $
523.8   QB63

The audience for this title may be younger children, but adults can also use it to find constellations in the sky. Plastic overlay sheets identify the stars and show the shape of the constellations. As can be expected from DK, contains colorful photos throughout. Includes interactive CD-ROM. This

title can be enjoyed either as a circulating book or as a reference book.

Chemistry

Bibliographies and Guides

575   The literature of chemistry: Recommended titles for undergraduate chemistry library collections. Judith A. Douville. 191p. Association of College and Research Libraries, American Library Association, 2004. $
016.54   Z675

This source is useful as a collection development tool for undergraduate chemistry collections. Basic chemistry and analytical, inorganic, organic, and biological chemistry are all covered in this guide. Most of the 1,000 entries have annotations.

576   Sudden selector's guide to chemistry resources. Elizabeth Brown. 93p. American Library Association, 2012. $
025.06   Z675

In this guide, Brown has assembled a brief guide to the chemical literature. It is part of the ALCTS (Association for Library Collections & Technical Services) Collection Management Section's Sudden Collector series. This is a guide to the literature of chemistry that will be useful for library science students and practicing librarians who have subject responsibilities in this field.

Dictionaries and Encyclopedias

577   Chemistry: Foundations and applications. J. J. Lagowski. 4v. 1246p. Macmillan Reference USA, 2004. $$
540   QD4

This strong chemistry reference source has more than 500 articles covering a broad range of chemical topics, including nanochemistry, biochemistry, energy, and medical applications. Terms used in the entries are defined in the margins. Entries are written in nontechnical language, usable by high school or college chemistry students. Charts, photos, bibliographies, and, of course, some equations are included in the entries. A valuable addition to the science collection of libraries of all sizes.

578 A dictionary of chemistry. 6th ed. John
Daintith, ed. 584p. Oxford, 2008. $
540.3   QD5

This chemical dictionary defines more than 4,700 terms and includes about 200 web links for further information on a topic. This title and its companion titles, *Dictionary of Physics* and *Dictionary of Biology*, are derived from Oxford's *Dictionary of Science*. The sixth edition includes physical chemistry and biochemistry terms. All units are expressed in SI (metric) units.

579 Encyclopedia of the elements:
Technical data, history, processing,
applications. Per Enghag. 1243p.
Wiley-VCH, 2004. $$
546   QD166

This title is more suitable for a university library reference collection than for a public library. Developed under the auspices of the Swedish National Committee for Chemistry and translated into English. Gives properties, uses, and the environmental impact of the elements, including the transuranic elements. For example, one chapter covers sodium and potassium. It includes facts about them; physical, thermodynamic, and nuclear properties; their discovery; the origin of the names; and uses.

580 McGraw-Hill concise encyclopedia of
chemistry. 663p. McGraw-Hill, 2004. $
540   QD4

This one-volume paperback makes a good guide for students of chemistry. Entries are taken from the *McGraw-Hill Encyclopedia of Science and Technology*. Of the 700 alphabetically arranged topics, many have graphics or charts accompanying the text. United States and SI (metric) units are used, and the work includes a subject index.

581 Van Nostrand's encyclopedia of
chemistry. 5th ed. Glenn D. Considine,
ed. 1831p. Wiley-Interscience, 2005. $$
540   QD4

While the fifth edition is still the latest available, a new edition is expected from Wiley-Blackwell. The fifth edition increased the number of entries and updated those entries. Cross-references, graphics, and the index have been redone from the fourth edition. It can be expected that the sixth edition will continue this fine editorial tradition. The work focuses on the following areas: process, raw materials, metals, energy, waste and pollution, instrumentation, chemicals in foods, materials, plans, and biotechnology. The result is a useful source for practicing chemists and chemistry students. *The Facts on File Encyclopedia of Chemistry* (Facts on File, 2005) might be a better choice for a high school audience.

Handbooks, Yearbooks, and Almanacs

582 CRC handbook of chemistry and
physics: A ready-reference book of
chemical and physical data. 92nd ed.
W. M. Haynes and David R. Lide, eds.
CRC Press, 1913–. $$
540   QD65

Format is one of the biggest changes in reference sources since the last edition of this work. The *CRC Handbook of Chemistry and Physics* is as useful as ever, but what format should your library get it in? It is available in print, as an e-book to rent or purchase, as a DVD, and online as an electronic product from CRC (www.hbcpnetbase.com). Which format is best for your library is a decision to be made locally. The scope of this work is "to provide broad coverage of all types of data commonly encountered by physical scientists and engineers, with as much depth as can be accommodated in a one-volume format." The index is particularly useful in getting to the data. This is the standard source for libraries to provide chemical information.

583 Lange's handbook of chemistry. 16th
ed. Norbert Adolph Lange and J. G.
Speight. 1000p. McGraw-Hill, 2005. $$
540   QD65

This title is a general reference source for chemists, chemical engineers, and college students. It is divided into four major sections: inorganic chemistry, organic chemistry, spectroscopy, and general information with conversion tables. Chemical properties like solubility, conductivity, enthalpies, and entropies are presented in the first two sections.

584   The Merck index: An encyclopedia of chemicals, drugs, and biologicals. 14th ed. Maryadele J. O'Neil et al., eds. 1756p. Merck, 2006. $$

615   RS51

This title is a good source for basic information on chemical substances. Entries give physical properties, chemical structure, and synonyms. To reflect the growing interdependence of chemistry, biology, and medicine, the work incorporates information on biochemistry, pharmacology, toxicology, and agriculture and the environment: "10,250 monographs describe significant chemical, drugs, and biological substances." CAS Registry Numbers have been added with this edition. This standard reference source is also available online. Visit http://scistore.cambridgesoft.com for more information.

585   NIOSH pocket guide to chemical hazards. Centers for Disease Control and Prevention, Department of Health and Human Services. www.cdc.gov/niosh/npg/. Free

The National Institute for Occupational Safety and Health (NIOSH) publishes this guide to chemical hazards and toxicity of 677 commonly encountered chemicals. Available online and as a PDF or self-extracting Windows file. Includes chemical names, synonyms, trade names, CAS, RTECS, and DOT numbers as well as chemical formula, exposure limits, and IDLHs (immediately dangerous to life and health values). Also included is first aid information. The sixth edition of *Reference Sources for Small and Medium-Sized Libraries* stated that this guide "belongs in the glove compartment of every construction and transportation vehicle, fire truck, and every library, depository or not, in this country." Now, mobile access to this work could be considered critical.

Perry's chemical engineers' handbook, **see 613.**

586   Sax's dangerous properties of industrial materials. 12th ed. Richard J. Lewis Sr. 5v. Wiley, 2012. $$$

604.7   T55.3

Information is the key to safe handling of chemicals. With that in mind, this title is useful in libraries where clientele are working with industrial chemicals. The twelfth edition contains information on about 28,000 commonly encountered

chemicals. According to the publisher, "Each entry includes a DPIM code, hazard rating, entry name, CAS number, DOT number, molecular formula, molecular weight, line structural formula, description of material and physical properties, and synonyms. The book also contains immediately dangerous to life or health (IDLH) levels for approximately 1,000 chemicals. It also covers exposure-level classifications for a number of regulatory agencies, from OSHA to the U.S. Department of Transportation."

Computer Science

Databases and Indexes

587   ACM digital library. Association for Computing Machinery. http://dl.acm.org. Free

As their website states, this source contains "full text of every article ever published by ACM and bibliographic citations from major publishers in computing." This translates into almost two million records about computer science. Includes access to the Special Interest Groups (SIGs) publications, e-books from the ACM, and the fourth edition of *The Encyclopedia of Computer Science*. Although they won't have access to the full text, nonmembers can still search and browse the ACM Digital Library. Consortial and individual library subscriptions are available.

Dictionaries and Encyclopedias

588   Berkshire encyclopedia of human computer interaction. William Sims Bainbridge, ed. 958p. Berkshire, 2004. $$

004   QA76.9

This source covers an important emerging area of computer science. It focuses on applications, approaches, breakthroughs, challenges, interfaces, and social implications of human-computer interaction (HCI). Entries show a multidisciplinary approach to HCI. Special features include sidebars, illustrations, glossary, bibliography of HCI books and journals, and a pop-culture appendix.

589   Encyclopedia of computers and computer history. Raúl Rojas, ed. 930p.

Fitzroy Dearborn, 2001. $$

004   QA76.15

When studying computer science, it is easy to lose sight of the tremendous growth in such a short time. This source chronicles that growth with entries like BIOS, data encryption, and biographies (John von Neumann, Bill Joy, etc.). Cross-references are in bold, and entries include selected writings for individuals and further readings. Topical bibliography and index included.

590   Encyclopedia of computer science and technology. Rev. ed. Harry Henderson. 580p. Facts on File, 2009. $

004   QA 76.15

The one- or two-page entries with bibliographies provide an overview of computer science topics. Reading level is appropriate for high school or college computer science students. Cross-references are indicated in the text, with subject index in the back. Entries give the background and usage on topics like Fortran, mathematics of computing, and data abstraction. Revised in 2009, the new edition contains about 180 new entries, including new programming languages, web design technologies, and open source software.

History of Science

Bibliographies and Guides

591   Reader's guide to the history of science. Arne Hessenbruch, ed. 934p. Fitzroy Dearborn, 2000. $$

509   Q125

This guide includes essays on 500 topics in the history of science. Entries deal with individuals, disciplines, and institutions on topics like ecology or materials sciences. Emphasis is on books, not articles, and coverage of the secondary literature of science. Contains thematic list, booklist, and general index.

Dictionaries and Encyclopedias

592   A dictionary of the history of science. Anton Sebastian. 373p. Parthenon, 2001. $

503   Q124.8

This is one of those titles that are important to have in a collection about the history of science. However, if it were housed in the circulating collection it would still be available to researchers. "The aim of this book is to give a brief historical understanding of the world around us on a scientific basis, so that we can relate to and appreciate it." Scientific terms from ancient to modern times are defined. Includes frequent cross-references from scientists who invented or discovered the item listed, and from other terms. For instance, the listing for *continental drift* refers the reader to *tectonic theory*.

593   Encyclopedia of the scientific revolution: From Copernicus to Newton. Wilbur Applebaum, ed. 758p. Routledge, 2000. $

509.4   Q125

The social and cultural context of the scientific revolution is considered in this source. The 441 articles track the progress of Copernicus, Galileo, Descartes, and their contemporaries. Developments over the sixteenth and seventeenth centuries in mathematics, astronomy, medicine, and even alchemy and astrology are chronicled. An important work for libraries of all sizes.

Handbooks, Yearbooks, and Almanacs

594   History of modern science and mathematics. Brian S Baigrie, ed. 4v. Scribner, 2002. $$$

509   Q125

Topical essays on the history of science and mathematics with twenty-three disciplines represented. Well indexed with books and websites in the bibliography. Useful for advanced high school, college students, and general adult readers.

595   The Oxford companion to the history of modern science. J. L. Heilbron, ed. 941p. Oxford, 2003. $$

509   Q125

This guide will help the reader browse through the history of science. Contains 609 signed entries with bibliographies, of which about 100 are biographical. Includes some black-and-white photos, ample cross-references, and indexing. For medium-sized and larger public and academic libraries. Also available via Oxford Reference Online.

Earth Sciences

Bibliographies and Guides

596 Earth science resources in the electronic age. Judith A. Bazler. 303p. Greenwood, 2003. $

025.06   QE48.87

This title presents earth sciences on the Internet. The first chapter covers the basics of finding information. The second one reviews quality websites. Other chapters include supplies, museums and summer programs, and career information in earth sciences. There is also a title in biology by the same author called *Biology Resources in the Electronic Age*.

Dictionaries and Encyclopedias

597 Encyclopedia of earth and physical sciences. 2nd ed. 13v. Marshall Cavendish, 2005. $$$

500.2   QE5

High school and public library readers will appreciate the coverage, layout, and design of this resource. Entries include colorful photos, definitions, "core facts," and short bibliographies. Sidebars include "A Closer Look," history of science, looking to the future, and science and society. Volume 13 includes conversion charts, a periodic table, a geologic timeline, Nobel Prize winners, a glossary, and an index.

Databases and Indexes

598 GeoRef. American Geosciences Institute. www.agiweb.org/georef. CP$

Produced by the American Geosciences Institute, this database contains more than 3.3 million citations. It provides access to the worldwide geoscience literature from 1933 to the present and North America from 1785 to the present. Available through a variety of vendors, including EBSCO, ProQuest, Dialog, Engineering Information,

GeoScienceWorld, and STN. Contact vendor for subscription information. Essential for geology researchers.

Handbooks

599 The encyclopedia of Earth. www .eoearth.org. Free

This resource was named a RUSA MARS best website in January 2013. The site "is a free, expert-reviewed collection of content contributed by scholars, professionals, educators, practitioners and other experts who collaborate and review each other's work." Coverage includes agriculture, climate change, geography, people, pollution, society, and many other topics. The content will support students and researchers with video and text about many facets of the natural world and life on Earth.

600 Encyclopedia of geology. Richard C. Selley, L. R. M. Cocks, and I. R. Plimer, eds. 5v. Elsevier/Academic, 2005. $$$$

551.03   QE5

This work is solid, both from the weight of the pages and the depth of scholarship, and forms the cornerstone of a geology reference collection. Other branches of earth sciences are covered by the *Encyclopedia of the Solar System*, *Encyclopedia of Ocean Sciences*, *Encyclopedia of Atmospheric Sciences*, and *Encyclopedia of Soils in the Environment*, also from the same publisher. Entries, written by experts from around the world, include graphs and maps, some in color; cross-references; and bibliographies. The reading level is that of the professional geologist or geology student. As such, it may be best suited for an academic library supporting a program in geology.

601 Gems of the world. Cally Oldershaw. 256p. Firefly, 2008. $

553.8   QE 392

The introduction of this work includes information about gems and their formation and mining. Much of the introduction is about the diamond industry. It also includes a history of gems, famous diamonds, and caring for gemstones and jewelry. The author is a gemologist who has written both popular books and textbooks on gems. The body of the book discusses more than 150 varieties of gems, arranged by color. Entries include shapes, distribution, background and history of the gem, characteristics, and color photos. Glossary and index are included.

602 Inside volcanoes. Melissa Stewart. 48p. Sterling Children's Books, 2011. $

551.21   QE521.3

This title presents useful volcanic information in an easy-to-read format that will appeal to children and adults. Stunning photos and clear illustrations show the dramatic power of these cracks in the Earth. The foldout format is visually pleasing, and short "I was there" accounts add to its impact. This title would also function well as a circulating book.

603 National Audubon Society field guide to North American rocks and minerals. Charles Wesley Chesterman. 850p. Alfred A. Knopf, 1979. $

552.097   QE443

Although older, this title has retained its usefulness and remained in print. In the introductory materials, "How to Use This Guide" states it is designed to be used "as a tool for identifying minerals, as a guide to identifying rocks, and as a convenient reference source for mineral collecting in the field." The small format, designed to be carried into the field, contains full-color plates identifying rocks and minerals and text describing color, hardness, occurrence, and other information. Indexes are by name and location. The 1979 edition was reprinted in 2010. However, if a library owns an older edition that is in good shape, it does not need to replace it.

604 Volcano Hazards Program. U.S. Geological Survey. http://volcanoes.usgs .gov. Free

This excellent website presents a wealth of information about volcanoes around the world. Includes current alerts for U.S. volcanoes, with update feeds, and features a *Volcano Hazards Program Fact Sheet* and reports such as *Airborne Volcanic Ash—A Global Threat to Aviation*. Another document provides a detailed account of the most voluminous

eruption of the twentieth century, the 1912 eruption of Novarupta-Katmai in Alaska. Contains a glossary of volcanic terms with photos. This site is useful for information about volcanoes for a variety of audiences, including the general public, and for geologists.

Oceanography

605 Oceans: A visual guide. Stephen Hutchinson and Lawrence E. Hawkins. 303p. Firefly, 2008. $

551.46   GC21

This reference book could double as a coffee-table book or also as a circulating title. Full of colorful aquatic photos, it covers all aspects of the oceans, including exploration, ocean life, human impact, and a fact line. Appropriate for libraries both big and small.

Climatology

606 Climate change. U.S. Environmental Protection Agency. www.epa.gov/climate change. Free

This site is the EPA's informational page about climate change. It has content about the impact of climate change on regions of the country, popular topics in climate change, climate news, why the climate is changing, and what we can do about it. This site will be useful for students and adult readers looking for unbiased information about the changing world in which we live.

607 Encyclopedia of climate and weather. 2nd ed. Stephen H. Schneider, Terry L. Root, and Michael D. Mastrandrea, eds. 3v. Oxford, 2011. $$

551.5   QC 854

Global climate change is even more important than when the first edition of this source was published fifteen years earlier. It contains 330 entries, all of which have been updated for the second edition. New articles include topics like the Intergovernmental Panel on Climate Change, tradable permits, and the Kyoto Protocol. Entries range from a page to several pages and include bibliographies. The audience is a "broad spectrum of readers, including the interested lay public, serious high school students, and college students," up to and including graduate students and professionals in the field. The editors are climate experts from Stanford University.

608 Encyclopedia of global warming and climate change. 2nd ed. S. George Philander, ed. 3v. SAGE, 2012. $$
363.738   QC 981
Climate research is very important to our future, which makes this title an important addition to a reference collection. This title is a traditional subject encyclopedia covering climate change. Contains about 750 articles with a broad interdisciplinary approach to climate change. Coverage includes state and country information as it relates to global warming and the climate policies of such leaders as George H. W. Bush, George W. Bush, and Barack Obama. Also included are entries on topics like charismatic megafauna and even RUSA's best free websites (in the entry on Internet media). The editor is a professor of geosciences at Princeton University and heads the African Centre for Climate and Earth System Science in Cape Town, South Africa.

Environment

609 Berkshire encyclopedia of sustainability. 10v. Berkshire, 2010–2012. $$$$
338.9   GE 140
This important new work covers the many aspects of sustainability from multiple disciplinary perspectives. It is published in ten volumes, which are sold separately and as a set, and is available electronically. The volumes cover the spirit, business, law, and politics of sustainability. They also covers natural resources, ecosystem management, and the measurement of sustainability. Three volumes cover regions: East and Southeast Asia, the Americas and Oceania, and Afro-Eurasia. The last volume, published in 2012, covers the future of sustainability. Entries present a page to several pages on the topic and include bibliographies for further reading. The graphic design includes background illustrations and sidebars in what would

otherwise be white space. Volume 10 has a master index, and there is also indexing volume by volume. The entries approach sustainability from an interdisciplinary perspective. For example, the entry for Confucianism in the *Spirit of Sustainability* (v. 1) and the entry on traditional knowledge (China) in *China, India, and East and Southeast Asia: Assessing Sustainability* (v. 7) both present information about Confucian ideas of sustainability. Continuing this example, one entry is written by a professor at Yale University, and the other by a professor at National Taiwan University. This illustrates the many voices found in this source. The reading level is appropriate for a wide range of audiences, including high school, college, and adult readers. This is an essential source for libraries.

610 Encyclopedia of American environmental history. Kathleen A. Brosnan. 4v. Facts on File, 2011. $$
This encyclopedia contains more than 770 entries by 350 expert contributors. It chronicles the interaction of Americans with their environment. Topics include environmental history and conservation but also the history of energy use in the United States, the Civil War, and waste management. It is written for high school, college, or adult readers. Entries include photos, maps, and bibliographies. Because energy and the environment will continue to be important topics, this encyclopedia is a valuable addition to reference collections of academic and public libraries.

Engineering

Bibliographies and Guides

611 The busy librarian's guide to information literacy in science and engineering. Katherine O'Clair and Jeanne R. Davidson, eds. 143p. American Library Association, 2012. $
507.1   Q181
This short guide to information literacy in the sciences and engineering will help librarians and researchers understand and enhance the information literacy of their students. According to the publisher, the book "highlights unique needs and

challenges for information literacy instruction within science/engineering curricula."

612 Guide to information sources in engineering. Charles R. Lord. 345p. Libraries Unlimited, 2000. $

025.06   T10.7

This is a thorough bibliography on engineering information. Organized by type of material (reference books, trade journals, etc.) and then by discipline. Lists more than 1,600 annotated entries. Also features a chapter on how engineers use information.

Handbooks

613 Perry's chemical engineers' handbook. 8th ed. Robert H. Perry and Don W. Green, eds. McGraw-Hill, 2008. $$

660   TP151

Here is another example of a very popular reference title that appears in multiple formats. Part of McGraw-Hill's Digital Engineering Library, it is also available from Ebrary, Knovel, and EBSCO, and, of course, in print. The organization of the eighth edition is similar to previous ones, but according to the preface the coverage has been extensively updated. Includes tables and unit conversions, fundamentals of engineering mathematics, chemical engineering fundamentals, waste management, safety, and hazardous materials. Very useful in both the lab and the library.

Standards

614 IHS. IHS. http://global.ihs.com. CP$

Occasionally, libraries will receive questions about standards. Only specialized libraries can afford to subscribe to standards from standards-issuing agencies like ASTM, IEEE, or the U.S. government. IHS/Global has 800,000 new and historical standards for sale, with more than half a million available as PDF files. Libraries can refer patrons to this site or, if they choose, purchase the standards the patron is looking for. According to its website, "IHS is the industry's most comprehensive source of hardcopy and PDF technical industry standards and government and military standards."

Electronics and Electrical Engineering

615 National electrical code, 2010–2011. 52nd ed. 870p. National Fire Protection Association, 2010–2011. $

621.31   KF5704

The National Fire Protection Association (NFPA) began publishing this well-known title in 1911. The newest edition has been approved as a national standard by the American National Standards Institute (ANSI) and supersedes all previous editions. The purpose of the code is the practical safeguarding of persons and property from hazards arising from the use of electricity. Coverage includes electrical equipment in homes, businesses, public buildings, and other structures, such as mobile homes, recreational vehicles, and industrial substations. Recommended for all libraries.

616 Wiley electrical and electronics engineering dictionary. Steven M. Kaplan. 885p. IEEE Press and Wiley-Interscience, 2004. $$

621.3   TK9

Defines 35,000 electronics and electrical engineering terms. Sponsored by the IEEE, this exhaustive dictionary will support computer scientists, networking professionals, and electrical engineers and students in those fields.

Manufacturing Engineering

617 Dictionary of engineering materials. Harald Keller and Uwe Erb. 1314p. Wiley, 2004. $$

620.1   TA402

What is it? What is it made of? How is it used? These are questions this dictionary can be used to answer. Almost 40,000 terms for both proprietary and common engineering materials are defined. *Rebar* and *laminate* are two terms defined here. Useful in materials science, engineering, and construction.

618 ThomasNet. Thomas Industrial Network. www.thomasnet.com. Free

Do you remember that big green set that used to

take up lots of reference shelf space? This old friend has morphed onto the web as ThomasNet, as the site says "powered by *Thomas Register* and *Thomas Regional*." Provides names and addresses of manufacturers, producers, importers, and other sources of supply in all lines and in all regions of the United States. It acts as a portal to company websites and is very handy for locating a manufacturing firm.

Vehicle Maintenance and Repair

619 ALLDATA.com. ALLDATA. www.alldata .com. CP$

This source's website describes itself by saying "ALLDATA is the industry's leading source of online factory Diagnostic and Repair Information used by 200,000-plus automotive technicians every day." Includes parts, locations, labor cost estimates, and difficulty estimates for repairs on almost all automobiles. OEM specs are given. ALLDATAdiy.com is the site for personal subscriptions to this service.

620 NADA used car guide. National Automobile Dealers Association. www .nada.com. Free

Consumers need information about cars. This site is an excellent place for value estimates, reviews, safety ratings, and other information. Includes cars, classic cars, boats, RVs, motorcycles, and more. In addition to VIN checks and other features, it can be used for car research and to find new and used cars for sale. Edmunds.com is another site that provides detailed reports about car values, so it can function as an alternative or second opinion to the NADA guide.

Life Sciences

Agriculture and Gardening

621 AGRICOLA. U.S. Department of Agriculture. http://agricola.nal.usda.gov. Free

AGRICOLA has two collections. One is the catalog of the National Agricultural Library. The other is a database of agricultural citations that includes journal articles, book chapters, and other reports. As the website states: "The records describe publications and resources encompassing all aspects of agriculture and allied disciplines, including animal and veterinary sciences, entomology, plant sciences, forestry, aquaculture and fisheries, farming and farming systems, agricultural economics, extension and education, food and human nutrition, and earth and environmental sciences." The catalog of the National Agricultural Library is freely available via the Internet. The journal component of AGRICOLA can be searched via the website, but patrons will have to use their local libraries to locate the resources. The database is also available from NTIS, Cambridge Scientific Abstracts, Dialog, EBSCO, Nerac, Ovid, ProQuest, and STN.

622 Agricultural statistics. U.S. Department of Agriculture. www.nass .usda.gov/Publications/Ag_Statistics/. Free

This source is a "reference book on agricultural production, supplies, consumption, facilities, costs, and returns." Tables on national and state data arranged by topic usually contain annual statistics for three to ten years and occasionally give foreign data for comparison. The USDA home page is also useful to visit (www.usda.gov/wps/portal/usdahome/).

623 .American Horticultural Society encyclopedia of plants and flowers. Rev. and updated ed. Christopher Brickell, ed. 744p. DK, 2011. $
635.90   SB403.2

A comprehensive dictionary describing more than 15,000 ornamental plants, with nearly 6,000 full-color illustrations, prepared by a team of 100 horticultural experts. Alphabetically arranged by botanical name, each description includes information on garden use, cultivation, propagation, pests, and diseases. The most authoritative single-volume reference source available.

624 50 high-impact, low-care garden plants. Tracy DiSabato-Aust. 168p. Timber Press, 2009. $
635.9   SB404.9

This guide to hardy, low-maintenance plants is perfect for people who love to garden but may not have much time to devote to it. Entries include scientific and common name as well as a description of the plant, its hardiness, height and spread, shade or sun preferences, and what it combines well with.

Color photos and a checklist of characteristics round out this guide, which may do well in either reference or the circulating collection.

625 Hortus third: A concise dictionary of plants cultivated in the United States and Canada. L. H. Bailey and Ethel Zoe Bailey. Macmillan, 1976. OP
582   SB45

The goal of this "Bible of nurserymen" is to provide an inventory of accurately described and named plants of ornamental and economic importance in continental America north of Mexico, including Puerto Rico and Hawaii. Brief directions for use, propagation, and culture of more than 20,000 species are included. Index lists more than 10,000 common plant names. It provides concise descriptions of all species and botanical varieties of cultivated plants. With reference collections being weeded, it is important that libraries retain this title. Although this title is out of print, it may be available on the secondary book market.

626 The National Arboretum book of outstanding garden plants: The authoritative guide to selecting and growing the most beautiful, durable, and care-free garden plants in North America. Jacqueline Hériteau. 292p. Simon & Schuster, 1990. OP
635.9   SB407

Gardeners will enjoy this older title, which could be moved into the circulating collection. It is a directory of more than 1,700 flowers, herbs, trees, and other proven plants selected by the National Arboretum as the most beautiful, durable, and carefree plants of their kind to grow in North America. Entries include plant description, growing information, gardening tips, and many color photographs. The National Arboretum also has a gardening information page available at www.usna.usda.gov/Gardens/gardeningr.html.

627 New encyclopedia of orchids: 1500 species in cultivation. Isobyl la Croix. 524p. Timber Press, 2008. $
635.9   SB409

This title was named an outstanding reference source in 2009 by RUSA. The author is a noted authority on orchids, has written several books,

and is a former editor of *Orchid Review*. Entries are by genus species names, using newer reclassified names for the orchids. Entries include synonyms, tribe, subtribe, etymology, and distribution. It is not surprising that this work contains beautiful color photography. Appendixes include glossary, bibliography, and indexes of scientific names and common names.

628 The New York Times 1000 gardening questions and answers: Based on the column "Gardeners Q. & A." Leslie Land. 852p. Workman, 2003. $
635   SB453

This gardener's guide is a one-stop reference for every gardening question. It can reside in either the circulating or the reference collection. A sample entry is about a tree stump in the yard. The guide informs the reader that neither salt, water, vinegar, nor kerosene will speed the trunk's decomposition. Manure will, but who wants that in their yard? It is recommended that you have the stump ground into mulch. However, a gardener could decorate and make use of the stump. Organized by type of garden—flower, landscape, kitchen, or potted—and includes a section on garden keeping plus an index. Libraries of all sizes should own a copy of this guide.

629 The organic gardener's handbook of natural pest and disease control: A complete guide to maintaining a healthy garden and yard the earth-friendly way. Rev. ed. Fern Marshall Bradley, Barbara W. Ellis, and Deborah L. Martin, eds. 408p. Rodale, 2010. $
632   SB453.5

This next entry is about common pesticides. What if you want to get bugs out of your garden naturally? This guide takes the gardener through the process of identifying symptoms and outlining solutions for pests and diseases. It includes a guide to garden pests and their natural enemies, ways to keep pests away from plants, and organic sprays and dusts. Useful either in reference or as a circulating title.

630 Pesticides: An international guide to 1,800 pest control chemicals. 2nd ed. G. W. A. Milne, ed. 609p.

Wiley-Interscience, 2006. $$

631.8   SB951

A total of 1,800 chemicals, including herbicides, bactericides, insecticides, and fungicides, that have been used in agriculture and public health are chronicled in this source. Entries include chemical name, formula, CAS Registry Number, European Inventory of Existing Commercial Chemical Substances (EINECS) number, and monograph number from the thirteenth edition of the Merck index. Synonyms, usage, toxicity, physical properties, and manufacturers are listed. Indexes for CAS Registry Number, EINECS number, and names and synonyms are included.

631 10,000 garden questions answered by 20 experts. 4th ed. Marjorie J. Dietz, ed. 1507p. Wings Books, 1996. $

635   SB453

A well-known garden guide, with botanical names revised in the fourth edition to conform to *Hortus Third*. Each chapter begins with introductory material in which questions with answers by specialists are grouped by subject (e.g., soils and fertilizers, perennials, houseplants). This is a good all-purpose garden book, particularly appropriate for public library collections.

Biology

BIBLIOGRAPHIES AND GUIDES

632 Biology resources in the electronic age. Judith A. Bazler. 286p. Greenwood, 2003. $

025.06   QH303.5

This resource is a useful guide to the Internet for biologists. Includes resources in biology, biology supplies online, museums, science centers, and summer programs and career information for biology students. Entries describe the site, indicate grade level, and review it at length. Includes glossary and index.

633 Sudden selector's guide to biology resources. Flora G. Shrode. 85p. American Library Association, 2012. $

025.2   Z675

This title is part of the ALCTS Collection Management Section's Sudden Collector series. It is a guide

to the literature of biology and will be useful for library science students and practicing librarians who have subject responsibilities in the life sciences. Although only eight-five pages, it presents websites, databases, and reference sources that will help guide librarians in developing their biology collections.

634 Using the biological literature: A practical guide. 3rd rev. ed. Diane Schmidt, Elisabeth B. Davis, and Pamela F. Jacobs. 474p. Marcel Dekker, 2002. $$

570   QH303.6

This source is a comprehensive bibliography of the biological literature. It includes biochemistry, molecular biology, genetics, microbiology, ecology, evolution, plant biology, anatomy, and zoology. The third revised and expanded edition incorporates more Internet resources. A fourth edition, from CRC Press, is forthcoming in 2014.

DATABASES AND INDEXES

635 BIOSIS. Thomson Reuters. http://thomsonreuters.com/biosis-citation-index/. CP$

BIOSIS is the major database in the biological sciences. Produced by Thomson Reuters, it is available from multiple vendors. Includes conferences, patents, books, review articles, and more than 5,500 journals. Searchable via detailed BIOSIS indexing, MESH subject headings, and CAS Registry Numbers. Related products include *Biological Abstracts/RRM (Reports, Reviews, Meetings)*, *BIOSIS Previews*, and *Zoological Record*. Back files available to 1926. This source is essential for all life sciences researchers.

DICTIONARIES AND ENCYCLOPEDIAS

636 Chronology of the evolution-creationism controversy. Randy Moore, Mark Decker, and Sehoya Cotner. 454p. Greenwood/ABC-CLIO, 2010. $

231.7   GN281.4

The 200th anniversary of Charles Darwin's birth in 2009 and the continuing controversy surrounding the teaching of evolution in the schools have kept this topic in the spotlight. This title is a chronology of creation and evolutionary highlights. It includes legislation, scientific discoveries, evolutionary evidence, and creation science. Entries are by year, and some have icons showing what kind of event they are. Includes glossary, a bibliography, and an index. Other recent works in this area include *Arguing for Evolution: An Encyclopedia for Understanding Science* (Greenwood, 2011), *More Than Darwin: An Encyclopedia of the People and Places of the Evolution-Creationism Controversy* (Greenwood, 2008), *Darwin's Universe: Evolution from A to Z* (University of California, 2009), and *All Things Darwin: An Encyclopedia of Darwin's World* (Greenwood, 2007).

637 Dictionary of bioinformatics and computational biology. John M. Hancock and Marketa J. Zvelebil, eds. 636p. Wiley-Liss, 2004. $$
570   QH324.2

Bioinformatics deals with the problems encountered with the information storage and retrieval of complex computational biological information. As this discipline has matured, the need for a dictionary for undergraduate and graduate students and professionals in the field became apparent. The editors, from the Mammalian Genetics Unit of the Medical Research Council and the Ludwig Institute for Cancer Research, both in the United Kingdom, complied this dictionary to present, as the preface notes, "fundamental concepts of bioinformatics and computational biology." It contains more than 600 entries and includes cross-references. Entries indicate definition and include related websites and further readings.

638 A dictionary of biology. 6th ed. E. A. Martin and Robert Hine. Oxford, 2008. $
570.3   QH302.5

More than 5,500 biological terms are defined in this one-volume paperback, with more than 400 new entries for this edition. Includes entries in biophysics, biochemistry, medicine, and paleontology. Its well-written definitions and occasional illustrations make this source a recommended title for libraries of all sizes. Its low cost makes it a great value. It is also part of Oxford Reference Online.

639 A dictionary of genetics. 8th ed. Robert C. King, Pamela K. Mulligan, and William D. Stansfield. 680p. Oxford, 2012. $
576.5   QH427

The eighth edition of this dictionary shows the rapidly growing nature of genetics and a commitment to keep up with this field. Entries are filed using a letter-by-letter alphabetization. Appendixes include classification, domesticated species, chronology, periodical names and addresses, Internet sites, genome sizes, and gene numbers. Also available in Oxford Reference Online.

640 Encyclopedia of biodiversity. Simon A. Levin, ed. 5v. Academic Press, 2001. $$$$
333.95   QH541.15

This important encyclopedia establishes a basis for research in this field. With 313 longer articles, it is well suited for researchers, students, and interested general readers. Entries include outline, glossary, body of the article, charts and graphs, cross-references, and bibliography. Volume 5 contains an extensive subject index, list of contributors, and glossary of key terms.

641 Encyclopedia of bioethics. 3rd ed. Stephen Garrard Post, ed. 5v. Macmillan Reference USA, 2004. $$$
174   QH332

The first edition of this encyclopedia was published about the time that genes were first being spliced. As biotechnology continues to progress, bioethics becomes more important. The third edition continues a tradition of excellence of coverage. Now in five volumes, it contains 450 entries, of which 110 are new. Emerging topics like cloning, stem cell research, and antiaging research are included. Most of the articles have updated bibliographies. Volume 5 has appendixes that include primary documents. This source was the inspiration for the *Encyclopedia of Science, Technology and Ethics*. Also available online.

642 Encyclopedia of biology. Don Rittner and Timothy Lee McCabe. 400p. Facts on File, 2004. $
570   QH309.2

This title is a practical one-volume encyclopedic guide to biology. Audience is high school, undergraduate, and general readers. Contains 800 entries on topics like cloning, the Krebs cycle, and the pH scale. Includes clear illustrations and photos.

643   Encyclopedia of life. http://eol.org. Free Libraries throughout the United States, Canada, Mexico, and the world can take advantage of free online sites that can enhance their local collection with outstanding research information. One such resource is the *Encyclopedia of Life.* This project is sponsored by the John D. and Catherine T. MacArthur Foundation and the Alfred P. Sloan Foundation and more than a dozen noted scientific institutions. Its mission is "to increase awareness and understanding of living nature through an Encyclopedia of Life that gathers, generates, and shares knowledge in an open, freely accessible and trusted digital resource." Every library should link to and support this excellent site.

644   Evolution: The story of life. Douglas Palmer and Peter Barrett. 367p. University of California, 2009. $
576.8   QH360.2
This colorful and appealing source covers the evolution of the world's fossil record from the Archean to the Holocene. It illustrates many recent advances in paleontology, such as early birds found in China and a small hominid from present-day Indonesia. It illustrates a habitat and features plants and animals found there. A "Tree of Life" section covers cladistics, and a gazetteer describes the fossil sites. The end papers offer a "Panoramic View" of the site illustrations. Book includes glossary, index, species listing, and foldout timeline. This source will appeal to readers interested in science.

645   The Facts on File dictionary of biology. 4th ed. Robert Hine. 406p. Facts on File, 2005. $
570   QH302.5
Libraries need a basic biology dictionary. This title contains 3,700 entries that define biological terms. Appropriate for high school, university, and public libraries. Includes pronunciation guide, cross-references, and illustrations for important entries.

Botany

646   Dirr's encyclopedia of trees and shrubs. Michael A. Dirr. 951p. Timber Press, 2011. $
635.9   SB435
According to the introduction, this work contains more than "3,500 photographs of species and cultivars in 380 genera, with an emphasis on the best new introductions of the past ten to 15 years." The lavish color photos of beautiful trees and shrubs are organized by genus species name, with the common name underneath. Includes a section on selecting plants for specific characteristics or purposes such as flower color, winter interest, shade tolerance, or grouping evergreens. Indexed by botanical names and common names.

647   Encyclopedia of North American trees. Sam Benvie. 304p. Firefly, 2002. $
582.16   QK110
Your library needs to have at least one book on trees, and this is a very good choice. Arranged by scientific name, entries include color photo, common name, and description of the tree's growth and habitat. Some trees have sidebars with key features. Appendixes include tree hardiness zones, a glossary, organizations, and an index.

648   Plant. Janet Marinelli. 512p. DK, 2005. $
580   QK45.2
The cover describes this text as "the ultimate visual reference to plants and flowers of the world." About 2,000 various plants are described, with photos. Habitat, origins, and the conditions for survival are covered. Sample topics include classifying plants, redefining the weed, and identifying invasive plants from around the world. Includes glossary, index, and photo credits.

Zoology

649   A dictionary of zoology. 3rd ed. Michael Allaby, ed. 689p. Oxford, 2009. $
590   QL9
Part of the Oxford Paperback Reference series, this title contains more than 5,000 zoological terms. A few of the areas covered include animal behavior,

ecology, cytology, and zoogeography. Audience is high school, college, and general interest readers. Also included in Oxford Reference Online.

650 Dinosaurs and other extinct creatures. Natural History Museum. www.nhm.ac.uk/nature-online/life/ dinosaurs-other-extinct-creatures/. Free
London's Natural History Museum has compiled this guide to dinosaurs. It includes a species directory of dinosaurs and other extinct animals, new discoveries, and galleries and models of popular dinosaurs. Be sure and take the quiz to see what kind of dinosaur you would be.

651 Grzimek's animal life encyclopedia. 2nd ed. Bernhard Grzimek, Neil Schlager, and Donna Olendorf, eds. 17v. Gale, 2003–2004. $$$$
590   QL7
The second edition of this comprehensive animal encyclopedia was very well received. Entries are arranged taxonomically and include photographs, range maps, and detailed information about many species of animals. Because of the emphasis on scientific names, it is critical to use the index. A web-based version is available from the publisher. This is an expensive source for libraries, but needed in a life sciences reference collection. It is also available as a database. Libraries on a tight budget could use the *Encyclopedia of Life* for similar information.

652 Insects: Their natural history and diversity. Stephen A. Marshall. Firefly, 2006. $
595.7   QL473
This title presents 718 pages of colorful photos and text about the diversity of insects. The focus is on insects found in the northeastern part of North America, but it can be more widely applied. Sections have introductory text, for example, twenty pages on true bugs and other hemipteroids. This example is then followed by fifty pages of photos about species in this family. Also contains an appendix with flow charts helping to identify different insects. Although useful as a reference book, libraries may prefer this source to be in circulating collections. A shorter *Firefly Encyclopedia of Insects and Spiders* (2002) is also available.

653 The Princeton field guide to dinosaurs. Gregory S. Paul. 320p. Princeton, 2010. $
567.9   QE861.4
Part of a series from Princeton University Press about the natural world, this guide presents dinosaurs in all their diversity. As the author notes in the preface, it is part of a paradigm shift "that observed that dinosaurs were not so much reptiles as they were near birds that often paralleled mammals in form and function." The first section of the book is about the biology of dinosaurs. The section presents information on almost all dinosaur species, including some unnamed ones. Entries are arranged by type of dinosaur and include an outline of the body with a representation of as much of the skeleton as has been found. Remains found, anatomical characteristics, age, and distribution information is also presented. This definitive guide will be useful as a circulating and reference book in public and academic libraries.

654 World Association of Zoos and Aquariums. WAZA. www.waza.org/en/ site/home. Free
This site serves as a conservation and wildlife sustainability resource center. It is sponsored by the World Association of Zoos and Aquariums and includes information about the WAZA conference, a virtual zoo, and a report on fighting extinction. It includes information on transporting and keeping various animals from bees to cheetahs. Includes links to distribution maps and ZooLex for zoo design.

Mathematics

Bibliographies and Guides

655 Guide to information sources in mathematics and statistics. Martha A. Tucker and Nancy D. Anderson. 348p. Libraries Unlimited, 2004. $
016.51   QA41.7
Bibliography for math and statistical information, with publication dates of items from the 1800s to the present. Electronic resources and paper resources included. Codes indicate whether items are for undergraduates, and it includes

bibliographic, electronic, statistical, and translated resources.

Databases and Indexes

656   MathSciNet. American Mathematical Society. www.ams.org/mathscinet/. CP$

MathSciNet is a subscription-based database sponsored by the American Mathematical Society. Offers "access to a carefully maintained and easily searchable database of reviews, abstracts and bibliographic information for much of the mathematical sciences literature." It grew out of the printed *Mathematical Reviews* and contains more than 2 million articles back to 1864. *MathSciNet* is the place to go for mathematical journal articles.

Dictionaries and Encyclopedias

657   The concise Oxford dictionary of mathematics. 4th ed. Christopher Clapham and James Nicholson. 510p. Oxford, 2009. $

510   QA5

This dictionary defines terms that high school and undergraduate mathematics students are likely to encounter in their studies. Alphabetical arrangement, boldface cross-references, formulas and graphs, and seven appendixes with trigonometric formulae and tables of series. Also available as a title in Oxford Reference Online.

658   Encyclopedic dictionary of mathematics. 2nd ed. Kiyoshi It , ed. 2v. MIT Press, 1993. OP

510   QA5

Under the auspices of the Mathematical Society of Japan, with assistance from the American Mathematical Society, MIT Press has published the most important mathematical encyclopedia in English—a concise, up-to-date collection of significant results in pure and applied mathematics. It has boldface cross-references and a lengthy subject index. Specialized libraries may also want to consider the *Encyclopedia of Mathematics*, a 1988 translation of a Soviet mathematical encyclopedia. The publication of the paperback edition should make the *Encyclopedic Dictionary*

of Mathematics more affordable to libraries. Libraries that own this title should retain it, even though it is older.

659   The words of mathematics: An etymological dictionary of mathematical terms used in English. Steven Schwartzman. 261p. Mathematical Association of America, 1994. $

510   QA5

This title is an etymological guide to 1,500 common mathematical terms, defined not in a technical sense but rather by their origins and literal meanings. As mathematics developed, words were borrowed and minted from Greek, Latin, Arabic, and English. Entries are arranged alphabetically, some with line drawings, and include forms and origins of terms with their modern meaning. This title is useful for both students and teachers of mathematics.

Websites

660   The math forum: Internet mathematics library. Drexel University. http://mathforum.org/library/. Free

This site is "an annotated catalog of mathematics and mathematics education websites." Sponsored by Drexel University.

Wolfram|Alpha, *see* **67.**

Biographical Sources

661   Biographies of women mathematicians. Agnes Scott College. www.agnesscott.edu/lriddle/women/. Free

Sponsored by Agnes Scott College, a women's college in Atlanta, this site presents biographies of notable women mathematicians. A useful site that can encourage young women to enter into the mathematics profession.

662   Notable mathematicians: From ancient times to the present. Robyn V. Young and Zoran Minderovic, eds. 612p. Gale, 1998. $$

510   QA28

The key number for this title is 303. That's how many noted mathematicians are featured. Other numbers include fifty women, fifteen minority mathematicians, and thirty scholars from outside the United States. Entries range from 450 to 1,000 words and include selected writings and further readings. A timeline, math awards, and a bibliography are also included, along with a subject index.

Physics

Dictionaries and Encyclopedias

663 **AIP physics desk reference.** 3rd ed. E. Richard Cohen, David R. Lide, and George L. Trigg, eds. 888p. Springer, 2003. $
530 QC61
This source functions as a handy physics handbook. The first edition was originally inspired by the Italian physicist Enrico Fermi. This third edition is "a concise volume of essential definitions, equations, and data from all the fields of physics." Useful in libraries of all sizes.

664 **A dictionary of physics.** 6th ed. John Daintith, ed. 616p. Oxford, 2009. $
530 QC5
With more than 3,800 physics terms, like group theory, particle beams, and harmonics, this title is an ideal low-cost, high-value physics dictionary. This is a practical purchase for libraries both big and small. The sixth edition contains more than 200 new entries. Also included with Oxford Reference Online.

665 **Macmillan encyclopedia of physics.** John S. Rigden, ed. 4v. Simon & Schuster Macmillan, 1996. $$$
530 QC5
Building blocks of matter: A supplement to the Macmillan encyclopedia of physics. John S. Rigden, ed. 530p. Macmillan, 2003. $$
539.7 QC793.2
The 900 articles, arranged alphabetically, offer clear explanations of the concepts, laws, and phenomena of physics as they relate to topics ranging from rainbows to earthquakes. These accessible essays do much to open the world and work of physics to

the general reader. Includes numerous biographical entries, tables, and an index. Supplemented by the 2003 publication *Building Blocks of Matter*.

Weapons and Warfare

666 **Americans at war: Society, culture, and the homefront.** John P. Resch, ed. 4v. Macmillan, 2005. $$
973 E181
This four-volume set covers the impact of war on American society, from the discovery of the New World to the present. The 395 articles were written for undergraduate students and general readers. Primary source documents are included in appendixes. A useful and informative encyclopedia.

667 **Armed conflict database.** International Institute for Strategic Studies. http://acd.iiss.org/armedconflict/. CP$
Sponsored by the London-based International Institute for Strategic Studies, this site tracks international and intranational armed conflicts. Entries include nonstate parties, state parties, and type of conflict and its status. Also included are number of internally displaced persons and refugees and timelines of events. Can be searched by map or by list of conflicts.

668 **The Department of National Defense and the Canadian Forces.** www.forces.gc.ca. Free
Canada's trillion-dollar economy and high standard of living make it a very successful country. Canadian Forces were allies with the United Kingdom and the United States in both World Wars, and Canada was a founding member of NATO and participated in the Afghanistan conflict as part of that force. This site presents information about the Canadian Army, Royal Canadian Air Force, and Royal Canadian Navy in both English and French. Information about Canadian defense topics, including *Canada First* (the forces' defense strategy document), its search and rescue operations, and protecting the country's sovereignty, can be found on this site.

669 **DOD dictionary of military terms.** www.dtic.mil/doctrine/dod_dictionary/. Free
As this site stated in August 2012: "The DOD Dictionary is managed by the Joint Education and

Doctrine Division, J-7, Joint Staff. All approved joint definitions, acronyms, and abbreviations are contained in Joint Publication 1-02, *DOD Dictionary of Military and Associated Terms* 08 November 2010, as amended through 15 July 2012." The search function includes both terms and definitions in its results, so a search for *sovereignty* includes a definition for *homeland defense*: "The protection of United States sovereignty, territory, domestic population, and critical defense infrastructure against external threats and aggression." Entries can be sorted by relevance or date. Includes links to the Joint Electronic Library, the Universal Joint Task List, and DOCNET (Doctrine Networked Education and Training).

670 How the Army runs: A senior leader reference handbook. U.S. Army War College. www.carlisle.army.mil/usawc/dclm/. Free

The U.S. Army War College updates this publication every two years. As the preface states: "This text is designed to explain and synthesize the functioning and relationships of numerous Defense, Joint, and Army organizations, systems, and processes involved in the development and sustainment of trained and ready forces for the Combatant Commanders." The intended audience is faculty and students at the U.S. Army War College, but its utility goes far beyond Carlisle, Pennsylvania. Chapters and sections include titles like the "Army Focus," "Army Organizational Life Cycle," "Army Organizational Structure," and "the Relationship of Joint and Army Planning."

671 The Oxford encyclopedia of maritime history. John B. Hattendorf, ed. 4v. Oxford, 2007. $$$

623.8   VK15

The introduction to this four-volume encyclopedia discusses the importance and sometimes overlooked subject of maritime history. Coverage includes art, economics, explorations, films, naval law and history, ships, boats, shipyards, and biographies of naval figures. Entries include bibliographies and some maps and illustrations. More than 900 extensive entries cover all aspects of maritime history.

672 United States Department of Defense. www.defense.gov. Free

This site presents a wealth of information about the United States military. Topics include news, upcoming events, the military budget, family support, the Pentagon channel, and DOD blogs. Headline categories include "Today in DOD," "About DOD," "Top Issues," "News," "Photos/Videos," and links to other military DOD websites. This site is a good place to go for top-level information about the U.S. Department of Defense and serves as an entry to more specific defense-related information.

10 Health and Medicine

BARBARA M. BIBEL

Because health-science information changes rapidly, it is important to maintain a current collection. Works listed here were the latest available editions at the time, but many are updated regularly. When ordering, always request the latest edition.

General Sources

Databases and Indexes

673 Centers for Disease Control and Prevention. www.cdc.gov. Free
This site offers a wealth of statistical information about diseases, births and deaths, and other health issues. It also provides health information for travelers, food safety, and environmental concerns.

674 ClinicalTrials.gov. U.S. National Institutes of Health. www.clinicaltrials .gov. Free
The National Library of Medicine maintains this site listing active clinical trials in the United States and 182 other countries. It is a good place for practitioners, patients, and researchers to find information about ongoing and completed trials. It also provides information about volunteering for clinical trials so that patients may make informed decisions.

675 Consumer health complete. EBSCO. www.ebscohost.com. CP$
This database contains full text for 250 health reference books and encyclopedias as well as articles, health reports, illustrations, and videos. EBSCO has related databases for alternative health, multilingual health information, and Salud en Español for Spanish-language information.

676 Health and wellness resource center. Gale. www.galecengage.com. CP$
The Health and Wellness Resource Center provides access to articles from thousands of medical journals and consumer publications as well as the full text of *The Gale Encyclopedia of Medicine* and related Gale medical encyclopedias. It also includes streaming videos, health news, and alternative health information.

677 Healthfinder.gov. U.S. Department of Health and Human Services. www.health finder.gov. Free
Healthfinder.gov offers basic information about wellness, diseases and conditions, and disease prevention. It includes directories for finding health services and practitioners, tools for tracking health, and health news. The site is available in Spanish.

678 National Institutes of Health. U.S. Department of Health and Human Services. www.nih.gov. Free

The nation's center for medical research offers information about diseases, news, ongoing research, and clinical trials. It is also a resource for those seeking grants to support health research.

679   NIH senior health. National Institute on Aging and U.S. National Library of Medicine. www.nihseniorhealth.gov. Free

This site is for seniors and it emphasizes the common health issues that they face. It includes videos and offers adjustable text size and contrast for the visually impaired.

680   MedlinePlus. U.S. National Library of Medicine. www.medlineplus.gov. Free

This outstanding resource for consumer health information offers health news, medical encyclopedias and dictionaries, information about diseases, conditions, and drugs and supplements, videos, tutorials, and health calculators. The site is available in Spanish, and there is a great deal of material in many other languages as well. There are directories of health practitioners and services and articles that are easy to read. *MedlinePlus* also has free directories of hospitals, physicians, dentists, specialty care centers, midwives, podiatrists, acupuncturists, dieticians, and other health care providers.

681   PubMed. U.S. National Library of Medicine. www.ncbi.nlm.nih.gov/pubmed. Free

This is the world's major database for access to articles from peer-reviewed academic medical journals. It contains more than 22 million citations in a variety of languages. Most are in English or have English-language abstracts. There is a subset, PubMed Central, with free, full-text articles.

682   Salem health. www.health.salempress.com. Salem Press. CP$

Salem Press offers the sixth edition of *Magill's Medical Guide* and related encyclopedias covering cancer, infectious diseases, complementary and alternative medicine, mental health, nutrition, genetic diseases, and addiction and substance abuse. Purchase of any print set includes unlimited remote access. The guides provide accurate, reliable consumer health information for general readers.

Dictionaries and Encyclopedias

683   Dorland's illustrated medical dictionary. 32nd ed. W. A. Newman Dorland. 2176p. Saunders, 2011. $
610.3   R121

This new edition of *Dorland's Illustrated*, for professionals and lay readers, includes thousands of new words, 500 new illustrations, and appendixes listing medical abbreviations, weight, measure, dosage, and temperature conversion; and reference laboratory values. Purchase includes free access to www.dorlands.com, which also has audio pronunciations. This is the standard professional source and authority for the National Library of Medicine's Medical Subject Headings (MESH).

684   Encyclopedia of medical devices and instrumentation. 2nd ed. John G. Webster, ed. 6v. Wiley, 2006. $$$$
610.28   R856

A unique encyclopedia that explains the structure and function of medical instruments and devices. It contains articles on everything from dialysis machines to CAT and MRI scanners. The language is somewhat technical but accessible to most readers.

685   The Gale encyclopedia of medicine. 4th ed. Laurie J. Fundukian, ed. 6v. Gale, 2011. $$$
610.3   RC41

Compiled by experienced medical writers, this encyclopedia has become a mainstay of the medical reference collection. It describes the most common medical disorders, conditions, tests, and treatments with both authority and thoroughness. The text and its language are aimed at the general reader, and the authors provide definitions and illustrations to enhance comprehension. This fills the gap that exists between single-volume medical encyclopedias and medical textbooks. The publisher offers related encyclopedias of surgery, cancer, genetic diseases, fitness, and mental disorders that are useful as well.

686   Goldman's Cecil medicine. 24th ed. Lee Goldman and Andrew I. Schafer, eds.

2v. Saunders, 2011. $$
610   RC46

**687 Harrison's principles of internal
medicine.** 18th ed. Dan Longo et al.,
eds. 2v. McGraw-Hill, 2011. $$
610   RC 46

These standard medical textbooks offer detailed information about the diagnosis and treatment of diseases affecting all of the systems of the human body. Although they are technical, lay readers use them, often with a medical dictionary, to learn more about various conditions and illnesses. Libraries should consider purchasing one of these.

**688 International dictionary of medicine
and biology.** E. Lovell Becker, Sidney I.
Landau, and Alexandre Manuila, eds. 3v.
Wiley, 1986. $$
610.3   R121

An unabridged dictionary of the biomedical sciences containing more than 150,000 terms and 159,000 definitions. It is written for professionals, but informed lay readers will be able to use it.

**689 Melloni's illustrated medical
dictionary.** 4th ed. Ida G. Dox et al.,
eds. 778p. Taylor and Francis, 2001. $
610.3   R121

The outstanding feature of this dictionary is the use of illustration as an integral part of the definitions. There are more than 3,000 high-quality line drawings sharing equal space with the text of the 30,0000 entries. The definitions are written for lay readers. This edition has increased coverage of medical abbreviations.

**690 Mosby's dictionary of medicine,
nursing, and health professions.** 9th
ed. Marie O'Toole, ed. 2240p. Elsevier,
2012. $
610.3   R121

This dictionary for paraprofessional and lay readers has been updated with more than 56,000 entries, 2,450 color illustrations, and forty-five appendixes. It contains a color anatomy atlas. There is a companion website with pronunciations and some of the appendixes.

**691 The Oxford dictionary of sports
science and medicine.** 3rd ed. Michael
Kent. 612p. Oxford, 2006. $
617.1   RC1206

Growing interest in sports and fitness makes this timely and useful. It contains 8,000 entries with brief definitions of terms used in sports science and medicine, reflecting the new technologies used in sports training and the importance of sports nutrition.

**692 Stedman's abbreviations, acronyms,
and symbols.** 5th ed. 1336p. Lippincott
Williams & Wilkins, 2012. $
610.14   R123

The new edition of this useful source highlights the terms and abbreviations mandated by the Joint Commission for standardized hospital abbreviations. It also includes slang terms and points out error-prone abbreviations that should not be used. There is an alphabetical section for abbreviations and a separate visual section for symbols organized by type: arrow, statistical symbols, genetic symbols, Greek alphabet, and so on.

693 Stedman's medical dictionary. 28th
ed. Thomas Lathrop Stedman. 2100p.
Lippincott Williams & Wilkins, 2005. $
610.3   R121

This source is a standard dictionary for health professionals. This edition has 107,000 entries and full-color illustrations. The definitions are concise and accurate. A total of forty-five consultants from various medical specialties reviewed the text.

Directories

694 National directory of chiropractic.
www.chirodirectory.com. Free

Lists more than 65,000 licensed chiropractors in the United States. Searchable by name and geographic location. MedlinePlus also has a directory of chiropractors from the American Chiropractic Association.

**695 The official ABMS directory of board
certified medical specialists.** Elsevier.
www.abmsdirectory.com. CP$

This website lists physicians who are board-certified in medical specialties. Search by name, specialty, or geographical location. The entries provide the name, contact information, education, and date certified. There is a free directory at www.abms.org, but it only provides the name of the physician and whether he or she is currently certified.

Handbooks, Statistics, and Diagnosis

696 Conn's current therapy 2013. Edward T. Bope and Rick D. Kellerman, eds. 1334p. Elsevier, 2013. Annual. $
615.5   RM101

Each year this book provides an overview of the latest developments in treating diseases and chronic conditions. It is written for physicians, but lay readers will find it useful. Also available as an e-book.

697 Current medical diagnosis and treatment. McGraw-Hill, 1961–. Annual. $
616.07   RC71

The Current Diagnosis and Treatment series keeps medical practitioners informed about the latest developments in their fields. Librarians and their patrons use them as ready-reference sources for current medical information. The medical volume is published annually. Related volumes for surgery, obstetrics and gynecology, and pediatrics are published on an irregular basis.

698 Injury facts. National Safety Council, 1921–. Annual. $
363.10   HA217

An annual compendium providing a wealth of information on different types of accidents in the United States. The majority are transportation related, but occupational and home accidents are also included. A bargain that belongs in all collections.

699 Lab tests online. American Association for Clinical Chemistry. www.labtestsonline.org. Free

This site provides peer-reviewed information about laboratory tests in lay language. It explains what the tests are, how they are performed, when they should be done, and what kind of preparation is required. It

also offers current relevant news and takes users on a tour of a clinical lab to see how it functions.

700 Mayo Clinic. Mayo Foundation for Medical Education and Research. www.mayoclinic.com. Free

This website offers reliable, current information on a wide variety of health topics, nutrition, and fitness as well as diseases and conditions. There is advertising.

701 The Merck manual home health handbook. 3rd ed. Robert S. Porter et al., eds. 2352p. Merck, 2011. $
615.5   RC81
The Merck manual of diagnosis and therapy. 19th ed. Robert S. Porter et al., eds. 3754p. Merck, 2011. $
615.5   RM127

These Merck manuals offer a wealth of information for both professional and lay readers. They now include color illustrations, new disease summaries, and clinical approaches. The home edition has comprehensive information on diseases, wellness, and alternative therapies in lay language. Both manuals, along with the *Merck Manual of Patient Symptoms*, *The Merck Veterinary Manual*, and the *Merck Manual for Pet Health* are available free at www.merckmanuals.com. The two medical manuals are available in twenty foreign languages as well, but the *Merck Manual of Diagnosis and Therapy* on the translation site is the seventeenth edition.

702 NORD. National Organization for Rare Disorders. www.rarediseases.org. $$

The National Organization for Rare Disorders provides information about more than 1,200 rare disorders as well as a directory of support groups and information about assistance with medication costs. The cost for an institutional subscription is about $500 per year. Individuals may access parts of the database for free.

703 Poisons and antidotes an A-to-Z guide. Rev. ed. Carol Turkington and Deborah Mitchell. 234p. Checkmark Books, 2009. $
615.9   RA1216

Covers poisonous snakes, plants, spiders, chemicals, drugs, and agricultural chemicals. It also deals with food poisoning. Symptoms, treatments, and descriptions are given for each of the substances. There are also directories of poison control centers, hotlines, organizations, and sources of educational materials. Indexes of toxicity ratings and poisons by symptoms complete the book.

704   Toxics A to Z: A guide to everyday pollution hazards. John Harte et al. 576p. University of California, 1991. $
615.9   RA1213

This book provides an overview of toxic substances and pollutants at home and in the workplace, the environmental implications of their use, methods of exposure, management, and regulation. There is an alphabetical listing of common toxins, including their characteristics and how to prevent exposure and protect oneself, as well as a bibliography. Free information is available from the National Library of Medicine's Household Products Database (http://householdproducts.nlm.nih.gov) and Tox Town (http://toxtown.nlm.nih.gov).

AIDS and STDs

705   AIDS sourcebook. 5th ed. Sandra J. Judd, ed. 682p. Omnigraphics, 2011. $
362.1   RC606.54

This book provides clear, direct information about AIDS and HIV infection for the lay reader. It includes historical and statistical data, current research, prevention measures, and special topics of interest to people living with AIDS. Sources for further assistance are listed for each topic.

706   Encyclopedia of sexually transmitted diseases. Jennifer Shoquist and Diane Stafford. 352p. Facts on File, 2003. $
616.95   RC200.1

More than 600 alphabetical entries cover specific diseases, their treatment, diagnosis, and prevention. A series of appendixes offers statistics, resource lists, and a bibliography.

707   Sexually transmitted diseases sourcebook. 5th ed. Amy L. Sutton, ed. 640p. Omnigraphics, 2012. $
616.95   RC200.2

This book offers the most current information

about the types of sexually transmitted diseases, their diagnosis, treatment, and prevention. It also covers current research on new therapies and vaccines.

Anatomy and Physiology

708   Atlas of human anatomy. 5th ed. Frank H. Netter. 640p. Saunders, 2010. $
611   QM25

Grant's atlas of anatomy. 13th ed. Anne M. R. Agur and Arthur F. Dalley. 888p. Lippincott Williams & Wilkins, 2012. $
611   QM25

Basic anatomy atlases are heavily used in both public and academic libraries. Netter's and *Grant's* atlases provide derailed coverage of the whole body by organ system in layers, starting from the outside and working inward. The illustrations are in color.

709   The complete human body: The definitive visual guide. Alice Roberts. 512p. DK, 2010. $
611   QM25

A basic introduction written in lay language and profusely illustrated with drawings, photographs, X-rays, and scans. It is organized by organ system and includes a companion DVD.

710   Gray's anatomy: The anatomical basis of clinical practice. 40th ed. Susan Standring, ed. 1576p. Churchill Livingstone, 2008. $$
611   QM23.2

This is the classic text and standard reference tool for human anatomy. The purchase includes access to a website with downloadable illustrations.

711   Textbook of medical physiology. 12th ed. Arthur C. Guyton and John E. Hall. 1120p. Saunders, 2011. $$
612   QP34.5

A classic textbook and reference source. It is written in technical language, but educated lay readers will be able to understand it. Functions of all human organs and systems are explained in great detail. The new edition has a full-color layout with many charts, tables, and clinical vignettes. It also has access to online text and supplemental material at www.studentconsult.com.

Cancer

712 The American Cancer Society.
American Cancer Society. www.cancer.org. Free

The American Cancer Society provides resources for cancer patients and their families. It includes information about types of cancer, treatment options, support groups, financial assistance, and survivorship plans.

713 Everyone's guide to cancer supportive care: A comprehensive handbook for patients and their families. Ernest H. Rosenbaum and Isadora Rosenbaum. 600p. Andrews McMeel, 2005. $

616.99   RC271

An oncologist and a medical assistant at the University of California San Francisco Comprehensive Cancer Center have written a book that goes beyond the basics of diagnosis and treatment, looking at the roles of spirituality, fitness, nutrition, and the will to live as factors in surviving and maintaining quality of life while fighting cancer.

714 Everyone's guide to cancer therapy: How cancer is diagnosed, treated, and managed day to day. 5th ed. Andrew Ko and Ernest Rosenbaum. 1024p. Andrews McMeel, 2008. $

616.99   RC263

This book explains various cancer treatments in common use, how they work, and their side effects, risks, and benefits. It is a useful, reassuring source accessible to all users.

715 The Gale encyclopedia of cancer. 3rd ed. Jacqueline L. Longe, ed. 2v. Gale, 2010. $$

616.99   RC54.5

This set provides the latest information on cancer diagnosis and treatment, including alternative therapies. It has information about rare cancers not found in other sources. It has a list of comprehensive cancer center locations, support groups,

government agencies, and research groups in the United States.

Children's Health

716 Caring for your baby and young child: Birth to age 5. 5th ed. Steven P. Shelov, ed. 928p. American Academy of Pediatrics, 2009. $

618.92   RJ61

This offers sound, common-sense advice for parents about all aspects of child rearing.

717 DrGreene.com. Greene Ink. www .drgreene.com. Free

This website by a pediatrician provides excellent advice on all aspects of child health and child rearing. The doctor takes a holistic approach and provides information about food purity and environmental toxins. There is advertising, but it is clearly labeled.

718 The Gale encyclopedia of children's health: Infancy through adolescence. 2nd ed. Jacqueline L. Longe, ed. 4v. Gale, 2011. $$$

618.92   RJ26

This encyclopedia has more than 600 articles about children from conception through eighteen years of age. It covers physical, psychosocial, and emotional development; diseases and disorders; and family life. Color illustrations enhance the text. A glossary, children's growth charts, and information about pediatric medications appear in appendixes.

Complementary and Alternative Medicine (CAM)

719 Alternative medicine: The definitive guide. 2nd ed. John W. Anderson et al., eds. 1233p. Celestial Arts, 2002. $

615.5   R733

A classic source on alternative therapies, this book contains an interesting essay on the future of medicine, a section on symptoms, and articles on forty-three alternative treatments with contributions by 380 doctors who use them. Some are physicians who incorporate complementary therapies; others are naturopaths, doctors of oriental medicine, and so forth.

720 The encyclopedia of natural medicine. 3rd ed. Michael T. Murray and Joseph E. Pizzorno. 1232p. Atria Books, 2012. $

615.5   RZ433

Written by two naturopaths, this encyclopedia provides detailed information about alternative therapy for common illnesses and chronic conditions. The authors are careful to indicate when the services of a traditional allopathic physician are needed (appendicitis, fractures, etc.).

721 The Gale encyclopedia of alternative medicine. 3rd ed. Laurie J. Fundukian, ed. 4v. Gale, 2009. $$$

615.5   R733

This encyclopedia has more than 800 articles covering 150 therapies, 275 diseases and conditions, and 300 herbs. It includes information on the efficacy of the treatments based on research done at the National Center for Complementary and Alternative Medicine and other institutions. These evidence-based data make it a valuable resource. It is also on Doody's Core Titles list for medical reference sources.

722 The National Center for Complementary and Alternative Medicine. U.S. Department of Health and Human Services. http://nccam.nih .gov. Free

The National Center for Complementary and Alternative Medicine is part of the National Institutes of Health. It conducts research on the safety and efficacy of complementary and alternative therapies. The website provides evidence-based information about therapies and herbs and their use in the treatment of diseases and conditions. It also offers information about the safety of CAM and tips for consumers to use when considering these treatments.

Drugs

723 The complete guide to prescription and nonprescription drugs. 2013 ed.

H. Winter Griffith; rev. and updated by Stephen W. Moore. 1120p. Perigee, 2012. Annual. $

615.1   RM671

A useful source containing the latest information about prescription and nonprescription drugs. It includes the latest information from the FDA, advice about storing and taking medications safely, drug interactions with foods and with other drugs, and adverse effects. "Lifestyle drugs" such as antiaging and sexual dysfunction medications are covered.

724 The complete guide to psychiatric drugs. Rev. ed. Edward H. Drummond. 352p. Wiley, 2006. $

615.78   RM315

This book provides the latest information on the diagnosis and treatment of mental illness and the drugs that may be prescribed. The author includes information on the use of drugs to treat women, minorities, children, and seniors and the increased risk of adverse effects in these groups. He also discusses alternative treatments.

725 Drugs.com. Drugs. com. www.drugs.com. Free

This site offers free, peer-reviewed information on more than 24,000 drugs, over-the-counter medications, and natural products. The information comes from Wolters Kluwer Health, the American Society of Health-System Pharmacists, Thomson Reuters Micromedex, and Cerner Multum. The site includes current health news, drug interaction information, and a pill identifier.

726 Encyclopedia of drugs, alcohol, and addictive behavior. 3rd ed. Pamela Korsmeyer and Henry R. Kranzler, eds. 4v. Macmillan, 2008. $$$

362.29   HV5804

Salem health: Addictions and substance abuse. Robin Kamienny Montvilo, ed. 2v. Salem Press, 2013. $$

362.29   RC563

These two encyclopedias cover the related topics of substance abuse and addictions with a multidisciplinary approach. They look at drugs and alcohol as well as gambling, eating disorders, and other behaviors such as kleptomania. They consider the social, political, economic, psychological, and medical issues and offer resources for further research. The Salem Health set includes online and remote access with purchase of the print version.

727 Encyclopedia of herbal medicine. Rev. ed. Andrew Chevallier. 366p. DK, 2000. $
615.32   RS164

A comprehensive reference guide to 550 herbs and their use as remedies for common ailments. It includes current scientific research as well as information about the major herbal traditions in various world cultures. Color illustrations and instructions for preparing herbal medicines complete the work.

728 Physicians' desk reference. Thomson Reuters. Annual. $
615.1   RS 75
Physicians' desk reference for herbal medicine. Thomson Reuters. $
615.32   RS164
Physicians' desk reference for non-prescription drugs. Thomson Reuters. Annual. $
615.1   RM671
Physicians' desk reference for nutritional supplements. Thomson Reuters. $
613.28   RM258

These sources provide detailed drug information from the pharmaceutical company package inserts. The *PDR* and *PDR for Nonprescription Drugs* are annual. The other volumes appear irregularly. All have color identification guides and are available online by subscription.

Nutrition and Diet

Bowes & Church's food values of portions commonly used, see **789**.

729 The encyclopedia of nutrition and good health. 2nd ed. Robert Ronzio. 736p. Facts on File, 2003. $
613.2   RA784

More than 2,500 alphabetical entries cover such topics as vitamins, processed foods, health disorders related to nutrition, allergies, and eating disorders.

730 Nutrition.gov. U.S. Department of Agriculture. www.nutrition.gov. Free

The USDA provides information on the contents of

food, nutrition, shopping, meal planning, weight management, food safety, and dietary guidelines.

731 Wellness foods A to Z: An indispensable guide for health-conscious food lovers. Sheldon Margen. 640p. University Health Publishing, 2003. $
613.2   RA784

This is a fine guide to maintaining health by eating properly. The author was a professor of nutrition at the University of California, Berkeley. He takes readers from market to kitchen and, finally, to the table, showing them how to select, store, and prepare fresh foods in a healthy, appetizing manner.

Physical Impairments

732 The encyclopedia of blindness and visual impairment. 2nd ed. Jill Sardegna et al. 356p. Facts on File, 2002. $
362.41   RE91

This book provides an overview of vision impairment. Entries cover medical, historical, and psychological subjects. There is a bibliography as well as a list of agencies for referral.

733 Encyclopedia of disability. Gary L. Albrecht, ed. 5v. SAGE, 2006. $$$
362.4   HV1568

An outstanding multidisciplinary resource that looks at all aspects of disability. Some 600 international scholars wrote more than 1,000 entries covering disability issues in law, medicine, economics, education, art, religion, and other fields. Volume 5 contains primary resource material. There are 200 biographies of disabled people and a large section devoted to the "experience of disability."

734 The illustrated guide to assistive technology and devices: Tools and gadgets for living independently. Suzanne Robitaille. 208p. Demos Health, 2010. $
681.7   HV1569.5
Home accessibility: 300 tips for making life easier. Shelley Peterman Schwarz. 144p. Demos Health, 2012. $
643.08   HV3020

These two books provide a wealth of information that will help those living with disability and their caregivers. They discuss devices that help with both physical and mental impairments as well as principles of universal design and modifying the home to make it both safer and more accessible.

735 National Institute on Deafness and Other Communication Disorders.
U.S. Department of Health and Human Services. www.nidcd.nih.gov. Free
The National Institute on Deafness and Other Communication Disorders at the National Institutes of Health provides information on all aspects of hearing impairment and speech and communication disorders. There are tips on preserving hearing and voice.

Women's and Men's Health

736 Conception, pregnancy and birth. 3rd ed. Miriam Stoppard. 376p. DK, 2008. $
618.2   RG525
Mayo Clinic guide to a healthy pregnancy. Roger W. Harms, ed. 509p. Mayo Clinic, 2011. $
618.2   RG525
Two excellent illustrated sources in lay language explaining conception, fetal development, labor, childbirth, and care of the newborn. The Mayo Clinic book includes information about decision making regarding circumcision and breastfeeding as well as returning to work after maternity leave.

737 Contraceptive technology. 20th rev. ed. Robert A. Hatcher et al. 906p. Bridging Gap Communications, 2011. $$
613.94   RG136
This book offers the latest information on contraception, sexuality, sexually transmitted diseases, and family planning. It is frequently revised.

738 The encyclopedia of men's health.
Glenn S. Rothfeld and Deborah S. Romaine. 400p. Facts on File, 2005. $
613   RG136
A physician trained in both traditional and alternative medicine and a medical writer have

produced an encyclopedia with more than 600 alphabetical entries covering all aspects of men's health. They examine the medical, scientific, social, and lifestyle issues that have an impact on men. Entries cover anatomy and physiology, diseases, nutrition, fitness, and stress reduction. The book has a glossary, a bibliography, and resource lists.

739 The encyclopedia of women's health.
6th ed. Christine Ammer. 496p. Facts on File, 2009. $
613.042   RA778
A concise encyclopedia of women's health, arranged alphabetically. It includes both traditional and alternative medical information. There are line drawings to illustrate anatomy and charts to summarize some information. Appendixes contain resource lists and a bibliography.

740 The Harvard Medical School guide to men's health: Lessons from the Harvard Men's Health Studies. Harvey B. Simon. 485p. Free Press, 2004. $
613.04   RA777.8
A physician looks at data from the Harvard Men's Health Studies and provides recommendations to help men improve their health. He examines diet, stress, and fitness and answers frequently asked questions about such issues as alcohol consumption and PSA tests to screen for prostate cancer.

741 The new Harvard guide to women's health. Karen J. Carlson, Stephanie A. Eisenstat, and Terra Ziporyn. 704p. Belknap Press, 2004. $
616   RA778
A comprehensive, thoughtful, clearly written encyclopedia covering more than 300 topics of special concern to women, from coffee and cancer to cosmetics and mental health. Well-depicted illustrations enhance the text. Suggestions for further information include websites, videos, and organizations.

742 Office on Women's Health. U.S. Department of Health and Human Services. www.womenshealth.gov. Free
This website provides a wide variety of health information for women. In addition to the usual

medical and health topics, there is information about insurance issues, lifestyle topics, current news, and health hotlines.

743   Our bodies, ourselves. Rev. ed. Boston Women's Health Book Collective, 944p. Touchstone, 2011. $

613   RA778

The fortieth-anniversary edition of this classic work offers in-depth coverage of women's health, addressing political and psychosocial issues as well as medical problems. It includes the latest information about the health care system, safer sex, and environmental health. There are notes at the end of each chapter, a resource list, and an extensive bibliography.

744   Our bodies, ourselves: Menopause. Boston Women's Health Book Collective. 368p. Touchstone, 2006. $

618.1   RG186

The producers of *Our Bodies, Ourselves* take an in-depth look at menopause. They treat it as a natural part of life and offer both scientific and psychosocial information as well as narrative testimony from diverse women to provide the tools that women need to make informed decisions about handling this transition.

11 *Households*

TERESE DESIMIO

New to this chapter in this edition are e-resources that can be offered as alternatives to print resources. While the e-resources may not be as comprehensive as the print resources, they can provide some good information in the event that access to print resources is not possible. All of the print resources listed are appropriate for a basic library reference collection or circulating collection and most are appropriate for home libraries. From cocktails to cockatiels, this chapter supports a wide variety of reader interests.

Beverages

745 The bartender's best friend: A complete guide to cocktails, martinis, and mixed drinks. Rev. ed. Mardee Haidin Regan. 400p. Wiley, 2010. $
641.8   TX951
Written by a bourbon expert, the first fifty-plus pages of this reference book are an introduction to bartending and include these sections: equipment, ingredients, glassware, basic garnishes, bartending techniques, drink-making techniques, stocking a home bar, and the cocktail party bar. Most of the book is 850-plus recipes arranged in alphabetical

order by drink name. The book ends with tips for the professional bartender, a bartender's glossary, bibliography, and index. Although not as comprehensive as *Mr. Boston*, it has more information for use in a home. The "companion website" isn't very useful at this time.

746 Beer. Michael Jackson. 288p. DK, 2007. $
641.2   TP577
Arranged similarly to *The Sotheby's Wine Encyclopedia*, the first sections are introductory and cover beer making, styles, and tasting. Most of the body of the book consists of sections on "Great Brewing Nations." Within each nation are smaller notable brewing regions, and within these are important breweries and their best beers. Information is succinct but attention grabbing. Includes a small glossary and index and very small print. Conveniently pocket-sized, it features a waterproof cover. A couple of small but informative high-quality photos are featured on each page along with occasional sidebars. Jackson, who died in 2007, is the world's best-selling author on beer.

747 BeerAdvocate. BeerAdvocate. beer advocate.com. Free
This website, described as a best beer website in major newspapers, was founded in 1996 by brothers Jason and Todd Alström. Now the website boasts of 2 million unique visitors per month. The brothers also publish *BeerAdvocate* magazine and

host several beer festivals a year. Highlights on this website include a busy discussion forum and a beer ratings and reviews section. Also interesting are the beer travel guides and the beer events and festivals sections. All sections are searchable, some have advanced search options. The "Beer 101" section is an exhaustive "beer-education." The website has minimal and unobtrusive advertisements.

748 Difford's encyclopedia of cocktails: 2,600 recipes. Simon Difford. 492p. Firefly, 2009. $

641.8   TX951

A big and beautiful book, this encyclopedia has color photos of every cocktail beside the recipe, of which there are six to seven per page. Bonus materials are the "Ingredients Index," which lists all of the cocktails that use the photographed ingredient, and the huge "Ingredients Appendix," which provides a photograph, a history, and a description of each ingredient. At the front of the book are chapters on bartending basics: techniques, equipment, glasses, garnishes, "14 Key Ingredients," and "Fridge & Pantry Essentials." Each succinct recipe provides this information: type of glass, garnish, and mixing method to use; list of ingredients; a comment about the drink and the origin of the drink. All recipes are rated on a scale of one (disgusting) to five (outstanding). The only missing content is nonalcoholic cocktail recipes. The author has been describes as "a London-based bartender with a cult following among cocktail enthusiasts." There's a companion website (www.diffordsguide. com). Highly recommended for all libraries.

749 Mr. Boston official bartender's guide: 75th anniversary edition. Jonathan Pogash, Rick Rodgers, and Ben Fink. 376p. Wiley, 2011. $

641.8   TX951

This classic reference for drink making, now in its seventy-fifth edition, was first published shortly after the repeal of prohibition. The first section of this current edition consists of an introduction called "Bar Basics": equipment, glassware, what to have in stock, techniques, serving (including theatrical moves), measures (tables and lists of equivalents), and recipes for syrups and other staples of drink making. Next are recipes for "Cocktail Classics." Then the 1,500 drink recipes are arranged alphabetically within these chapters: brandy, gin,

rum, tequila, vodka, whiskies, cordials and liqueurs, shooters, frozen drinks, hot drinks, eggnogs and punches, wine and beer in mixed drinks, and nonalcoholic drinks. The books ends with a list of resources, a glossary, an index, and a list of recipes. Designed as a handbook, it is a must-have for any bartender. It will also be a great library resource.

750 The Oxford companion to beer. Garrett Oliver, ed. 960p. Oxford, 2012. $

641.2   TP570

The editor of this award-winning resource is Garrett Oliver, brewmaster at the Brooklyn Brewery, "veteran judge of professional brewing competitions," and "one of the world's foremost authorities on the subject of beer." This is an encyclopedia with 1,000-plus A–Z entries in thirty-three subject categories including breweries and brewing companies, beers and beer styles, historically significant information about beer, biographies, and food and ingredients associated with beer. Entries are written by 166 of the "world's most prominent beer experts." A small section of color photos in the center of the book is pretty but not particularly informative. At the back of the book are these additions and appendixes: abbreviations; conversion tables; beer organizations and enthusiast clubs; beer festivals; websites, magazines, and newspapers; beer museums; directory of contributors; and an index. Highly recommended for all libraries.

751 Pocket wine book 2013. Oz Clark. 368p. Pavilion, 2012. $

641.22   TP548

Comprehensive and small enough to take to the wine shop with you, this guide has an encyclopedic A–Z listing of wines, producers, grapes, and wine regions. The author, an internationally known wine expert, is down-to-earth and injects his sense of humor into his writing. Highlights like "Best Producers" and "Best Years" make scanning easier. Some small black-and-white illustrations are included, but lack of color photos is not a problem. Lists and charts summarize information nicely. While symbols help keep text to a minimum, they are simple and easy to remember. The keys for symbols are on inside back and front covers for quick reference. There is cross-referencing throughout, a thorough index that takes up almost 10 percent of the book, and a glossary. Highly recommended for all libraries.

752 The Sotheby's wine encyclopedia. 5th
ed. Tom Stevenson. 736p. DK, 2011. $
641.2   TP548

Author Tom Stevenson has won Wine Writer of the
Year three times. Updated every two to four years,
this book is required reading for several wine expert
exams, but it is arranged in a way that makes the
information accessible to anyone interested in the
topic. Font size decreases as information becomes
more technical, so it is easy to get an overview by
reading the biggest font. The first 100 pages are an
introduction to winemaking techniques, history,
and factors affecting making of wine. The rest of
the book is broken down into the top eleven wine-
producing regions of the world. Smaller regions
and producers within the top regions are included.
For wine producers, the entries include ratings
and highlighted noteworthy wines. The graphics
are information-rich and so are the sidebars. Ends
with a "Guide to Good Vintages," a micropedia
(megaglossary!), and thorough index. This guide is
highly recommended for all libraries.

753 The webtender: An online bartender.
Webtender. www.webtender.com. Free

With more than 6,000 recipes, this website
has been published since 1995. It now features
several search engines: drink search, ingredient search, advanced search (so that you can
"search with extra parameters" and use Boolean
searching—be still my librarian heart!), and "In
My Bar," where you tell the search engine which
ingredients you have and it will produce a list of
all possible drinks you can make. You can also
browse drinks, see statistics ("a list of the most
popular drinks, voting chart and other useless
information"), and use an exhaustive bartender's
handbook. Recipes include alcoholic and nonalcoholic, hot and cold drinks, and punches.
The website is all text, with no photographs or
graphics of any kind, other than the few advertisements, but it is the most powerful searchable
database of drinks found to date.

Calendars

754 Chase's calendar of events. 56th ed.
752p. McGraw-Hill, 2013. $
394.26   R529

First published in 1957, the current edition has
12,500 entries and is the most comprehensive all-
purpose annual calendar reference in print. Entries
cover 4,000 "notable birthdays," 1,400 "historical anniversaries," 650 "national and international
holidays," 160 "religious holidays," and "thousands
of additional days of note from all over the globe."
The book starts with "Spotlight" sections covering
events of particular interest for the covered year.
The body of the book is arranged in January–
December order and features occasional sidebars
and black-and-white illustrations. Also included
are 20-plus appendixes on topics such as looking
forward, the Chinese calendar, wedding anniversary gifts, world map and time zones, astronomical phenomena, facts about the United States and
its elected officials, facts about Canada and Mexico, and major awards for the previous year. Also
included is a "fully searchable" CD-ROM (Windows only). McGraw-Hill hosts a free companion
website that has daily selections from the book
(www.mhprofessional.com/templates/chases/).

755 Earth calendar. Earth Calendar. www
.earthcalendar.net. Free

Although the author of this noncommercial website is not readily apparent, this resource is listed
on both the ipl2 and the Library of Congress virtual reference websites. It calls itself "a daybook
of holidays and celebrations around the world."
Sections include today, holidays by date, holidays
by country, and holidays by religion. The site has
some advanced searching capabilities and can list
holidays by day or month.

Construction

**756 Code check complete: An illustrated
guide to the building, plumbing,
mechanical, and electrical codes.** 2nd
ed. Redwood Kardon, Douglas Hansen,
Paddy Morrissey. 233p. Taunton Press,
2012. $
692.32   TH439

The publisher also offers *Code Check* books for
individual systems. This book and the individual systems books are each a "condensed guide to
the building portions of the 2009 International
Residential Code (IRC) for One- and Two-Family

Dwellings." This complete guide is intended for professionals as well as do-it-yourselfers, though it would likely take some practice for do-it-yourselfers to use this book efficiently. In order to fit all of the information into this neat, spiral-bound, compact format, lots of abbreviations have been used. The key to the abbreviations is on one of the first few pages rather than in an easy-to-view place like the inside covers, which are sadly blank. Comprehensive coverage includes references for each check-boxed code, black-and-white cutaway illustrations, glossaries at the end of each section, numerous tables, sidebars (e.g., "Common Complaints"), and a detailed table of contents rather than an index.

757 **Codes for homeowners: Your photo guide to electrical codes, plumbing codes, building codes, mechanical codes.** 2nd ed. Bruce A. Barker. 240p. Creative Publishing, 2012. $
690   TH4815.5
According to the publisher's description, "This new second edition of *Codes for Homeowners* is current with most national codes in force for the period of 2012–2014." Opening with the basics of codes and permits, the body consists of chapters that cover building safety and design, structural components, exterior components, heating and air conditioning, plumbing systems, and electrical systems. Entries feature plenty of informational photographs. The instructions for meeting code are succinct and numbered. Also included is an appendix of common mistakes, a section on conversions, and a small index. Published in cooperation with Black & Decker.

758 **The complete book of home inspection.** 4th ed. Norman Becker. 459p. McGraw-Hill, 2011. $
643   TH4817.5
Intended for homeowners, this is the fourth edition of a classic first published in 1980.The author is a founder of the American Society of Home Inspectors, one of several nationally recognized code organizations. Divided into "Interior Issues," "Exterior Issues," and "Other Issues," including energy considerations, environmental concerns, and green home technology. Each chapter is succinct, with clear headings, and has a checklist at the end. The checklists serve almost like bullet-point summaries

of the chapters. Some black-and-white illustrations and photos add detail. An appendix explains the requirements for certified home inspectors and includes a sample quiz. Includes the occasional cross-reference and a glossary and small index. Highly recommended for all libraries.

759 **Green from the ground up: Sustainable, healthy, and energy-efficient home construction; A builder's guide.** David Johnston and Scott Gibson. 336p. Taunton Press, 2008. $
690.83   TH880
Johnson is "a leader in the green building movement" whose approach to green building has "been embraced by professionals, municipalities, homeowners, and sustainability advocates nationwide." Chock full of practical advice using off-the-shelf building supplies, all aspects of construction are covered, with plenty of color photographs and clear illustrations. Written in plain language, this book could also be used by homeowners who want to consider greener alternatives when remodeling but may not satisfy green extremists. Also included are informational sidebars throughout and, at the end, a list of resources and good index.

760 **How to plan, contract, and build your own home.** 5th ed. Richard M. Scutella and Dave Heberle. 894p. McGraw-Hill, 2010. $
690   TH4815
This is the book that anyone considering building a house should read first. Even though the word *green* is not in the title it should be. The authors purposefully did not include the word because they think that in the near future green-ness will be assumed. The thirty-seven chapters in this book are divided into these parts: "Part 1: The Green Home," "Part 2: What to Build," Part 3: "How to Build It," "Part 4: Where to Build It," and "Part 5: Who Should Build It?" Making information easy to find are bullet-point considerations, lists of advantages and disadvantages to certain decisions, black-and-white illustrations, and a generous index. Highly recommended for all libraries.

761 **LEED materials: A resource guide to green building.** Ari Meisel. 223p.

Princeton Architectural Press, 2010. $
693.8   TH12.5
Based on the current *LEED Rating System* (version
3) published by the U.S. Green Building Council, this reference is much like a catalog. Chapters
cover site construction, wood and plastics, thermal
and moisture protection, doors and windows, finishes, furnishings, special construction, mechanical, and electrical. At the back of the book are
several indexes. Each entry gives the brand name of
a product, what it is, where it can be used, why it is
green, what LEED credits it gets, where to get more
information, and any special consideration needed
when using the product. Probably not many of
these products are available off the shelf at local
hardware stores, but this is still a useful guide to
the wide array of innovative green products homeowners and builders might consider using.
National electrical code, 2010–2011, see **615.**

**762   Residential construction performance
        guidelines: Consumer reference.** 4th
        ed. 139p. National Association of Home
        Builders, 2011. $
        690.83   TH4816
This spiral-bound publication by the National
Association of Home Builders could be a valuable
resource for consumers who want to understand
standard contracts and construction standards for
home building. Guidelines cover site work and
foundation; floors, walls, and roofs; plumbing and
electrical, including interior climate control; interior
and floor finishes; fireplaces and wood stoves; con-
crete stoops and steps; garages, driveways, and side-
walks; wood decks; and landscaping. Each entry for
these sections lists a theoretical observation about
the construction, a performance guideline, correc-
tive measure required by contractor (if contractor is
responsible), and variables that can affect the observation. Also included is a glossary at the end.

763   USGBC. U.S. Green Building Council.
        new.usgbc.org. Free
See the "Resources" section to download free ref-
erence guides, which include such titles as "LEED
Reference Guide for Green Building Design and
Construction: Healthcare Supplement with Global
ACPs," described as follows: "The comprehensive
reference guide provides tools to achieve certifica-
tion for new construction and major renovation

projects, including schools and core & shell development." These are large PDF documents.

**764   The visual handbook of building and
        remodeling: A comprehensive guide
        to choosing the right materials and
        systems for every part of your home.**
        3rd ed. Charles Wing. 632p. Taunton
        Press, 2009. $
        690   TH4813
The author has a PhD from MIT, has written numerous house-building books, had a show on PBS, and
has made hundreds of television appearances as a
house-building expert. This book is a perfect companion to home construction books, which usually
describe how to install materials correctly but don't
necessarily lay out all of the options available for
materials. Wonderfully plain language is used sparingly, and most of the book's content is presented
in high-quality tables, charts, illustrations, and lists.
Also included are sections on mortgages and financing, basic mathematics, conversions, and abbreviations, plus a glossary, sources, and a decent index.
Highly recommended for all libraries.

Consumer Affairs

ALLDATA.com, *see* **619.**

765   Cars.com. Cars.com. www.cars.com.
        Free
This website describes itself this way: "Visited by
more than 11 million car shoppers each month,
Cars.com is the leading destination for online car
shoppers, offering credible and easy-to-understand
information from consumers and experts to help
buyers formulate opinions on what to buy, where to
buy and how much to pay for a car." Major sections
include buy (sophisticated search engine), sell (place
a free add), research (reviews), finance calculators
("What can I afford?" and "What will my monthly
payment cost?"), and advice. A particularly valuable
resource is the free Kelley Blue Book Values.

766   Consumer protection (USA.gov). U.S.
        General Services Administration. www
        .usa.gov/topics/consumer.shtml. Free
This is an extensive consumer protection website
where "you can download or order a copy of the
2012 Consumer Action Handbook, access the

consumer directories, or file a complaint with government agencies." A link within this website called "Consumer Protection Publications" has these topics available: animals, cars, computers, consumer protection, education, employment, family, federal programs, food, going green, health, history, housing, money, small business, and travel.

767 Consumer Reports buying guide, 2013. 224p. Consumers Union, 2012. $
640.73   TX335

From the publisher: "Arm yourself with our exclusive ratings and recommendations for more than 1,800 brand-name products. This 224-page guide brings you expert reviews and advice on electronics, home appliances, garden supplies, even supermarket items. Plus, you'll have fingertip access to brand repair histories and shopping strategies to help make the most informed buying decisions wherever you go." No longer indexed, each product reviewed has a QR code and a website to go to for more information.

768 Consumer Reports car buying guide, 2012. 264p. Consumers Union, 2011. $
629.22   TL162

From the publisher: "This guide contains comprehensive advice to help you succeed, step by step: from determining your budget . . . to finding the right vehicle for your needs . . . to setting up the best financing . . . to avoiding dealer tricks . . . to getting the lowest price, even if you hate haggling." It includes ratings and reliability information on more than 270 vehicles.

769 Consumer Reports used car buying guide, 2012. 240p. Consumers Union, 2012. $
629.22   TL154

From the publisher: "Best & worst models and exclusive reliability ratings and unbiased reviews of 276 models, 2002–2011." This guide is a single issue of an annual subscription to *Consumer Reports* magazine, which may not be accessible to all but is important enough that libraries should provide access to it for their communities.

770 Consumer sourcebook. 27th ed. Matthew Miskelly, ed. 3v. Gale, 2012. $$$
381.33   HC110

From the publisher: "A subject guide to over 26,500 federal, state, and local government agencies and offices, national, regional, and grassroots associations and organizations, information centers, clearinghouses, publications, Internet resources, multimedia resources, media contacts, corporate contacts and related consumer resources in the fields of general consumerism, automotive matters, credit and personal finance, education, employment, environmental concerns, food and drugs, government performance, health care and promotion, insurance, legal affairs, manufactured goods and product safety, mass communications, real estate and construction, retail and commercial concerns, transportation and travel, utilities." From *Reference Book Reviews*: "This is an impressive and useful reference source for all libraries."

771 Household products database: Health and safety information on household products. U.S. Department of Health and Human Services. http://householdproducts.nlm.nih.gov. Free

From the site: "This database links over 12,000 consumer brands to health effects from Material Safety Data Sheets (MSDS) provided by manufacturers and allows scientists and consumers to research products based on chemical ingredients." Users can use a simple or advanced search or browser. This data base can be searched or browsed by category (which includes auto products, inside the home, pesticides, landscape/yard, personal care, home maintenance, arts and crafts, pet care, and home office) or by an A–Z index to product names, types of products, manufacturers, and ingredients.

772 United States Consumer Product Safety Commission. U.S. Consumer Product Safety Commission. www.cpsc.gov. Free

This is how this website describes itself: "CPSC is charged with protecting the public from unreasonable risks of injury or death associated with the use of the thousands of consumer products." Sections include "Recalls," "Safety Education," "Regulations, Laws & Standards," "Research & Statistics," and "Business & Manufacturing." Includes search function and forms for reporting an unsafe product.

Cooking

773 Betty Crocker cookbook: 1500 recipes for the way you cook today. 11th ed. Betty Crocker. 684p. Wiley, 2011. $

641.5   TX714

This cookbook is spiral-bound, has moisture-resistant covers and pages, and has twenty-three easy-to-grab tabs for each section. It is clearly intended to be used where the action is. First published in 1950, this is another teach-yourself-to-cook classic that includes much more than recipes: basic lists of equipment needed and ingredients to have on hand, definitions of cooking terms and techniques, food storage tips and charts, and quick guides at the beginning of each section. There are informational charts, sidebars, illustrations, and beautiful color photographs scattered throughout. It also features a large index and conversion/equivalent charts on the inside covers. Highly recommended for all libraries.

774 Cooks.com recipe search. FOURnet Information Network. www.cooks.com. Free

This Wikipedia-like recipe website has untold numbers of recipes, and it is hard to imagine that you couldn't find any recipe you want here. A search box allows keyword searching of the full text for all recipes, but no advanced searching or limiting. Probably best used by cooks with some experience, since you must judge for yourself what the best recipe is from the myriad results from a search. There is a user rating system, but it didn't seem extensively used at this time. Some distracting advertising is present.

775 The cook's illustrated cookbook: 2,000 recipes from 20 years of America's most trusted food magazine. 894p. America's Test Kitchen, 2011. $

641.59   TX715

A "compendium of greatest hits" from the twenty-year publication history of *Cook's Illustrated* magazine, this book could become as indispensable as the last huge recipe book from America's Test Kitchen, *The New Best Recipe* (2004). Critics say that it duplicates its predecessor too much but

acknowledge that it does include more recipes with much less information about the recipe-developing process. This means less reading to get to the actual recipe, which could be a good thing after all. The spare black-and-white illustrations are clear and informative. Numbered "Test Kitchen Tip" sidebars give good hints for ensuring the quality of your cooking results. The target reader is a somewhat experienced cook, and no beginner cook information is included.

776 Epicurious.com. Condé Nast. www.epicurious.com. Free

From the publisher of *Gourmet* and *Bon Appétit* magazines, this extensive recipe website offers browsing and basic or full-blown library-database-like advanced search options. It also hosts online classes from the Culinary Institute of America (for a fee). Also included is a section called "Articles & Guides," but extensive advertisements and an occasional pop-up in this section are just plain annoying. Most recipes are from the aforementioned magazines, but members can submit articles too.

777 The Good Housekeeping cookbook: 1,275 recipes from America's favorite test kitchen. 125th anniversary ed. Susan Westmoreland, ed. 752p. Hearst Books, 2010. $

641.59   TX715

Even lists of basic kitchen equipment needed for cooking are covered in this teach-yourself-to-cook classic. Also included are glossaries for wine, cooking terms, and ingredients. The body of the book contains the "triple tested" recipes. Guides at the beginning of the chapters for meats, fruits, and vegetables provide valuable information about choosing, buying, storing, and preparing these items. Other chapters include basic overview information that is likely to be very useful for new cooks. Many colorful photos and sidebars complement the nicely arranged textual information. Besides an extensive index, conversion/equivalent charts are printed on the inside covers. Highly recommended for all libraries.

778 How to cook everything: All you need to make great food. 2nd ed. Mark Bittman. 1044p. Wiley, 2008. $

641.5   TX714

Celebrating its tenth anniversary even though this is only the second edition, this book focuses on cooking what is "simple, straightforward, unpretentious, and easy" and strives not for what is brilliant but what is "good, wholesome, tasty, and varied." The first chapter is about kitchen basics and covers staple ingredients, equipment, and techniques. The remainder of the chapters consist of succinct but clear recipes. Back matter consists of sample menus for various meals, keyed to recipes in the book, and a huge index. Tables, lists, sidebars, black-and-white illustrations, and cross-references add detail throughout. This would be perfect for a person who is brand new to cooking.

779 Joy of cooking. 75th anniversary ed.
    Irma S. Rombauer, Marion Rombauer
    Becker, and Ethan Becker. 1132p.
    Scribner, 2006. $

    641.59   TX715
This is the seventy-fifth anniversary and the ninth and latest revision of a classic that the New York Public Library has selected as "one of the 150 most important and influential books of the twentieth century." It has 500 new recipes plus "4000 of the most beloved *Joy* classics retested and updated." Besides having all the information anyone needs to learn how to cook, it includes a huge reference section and an index. The reference section features an A–Z ingredients encyclopedia with descriptions and substitutions. Highly recommended for all libraries.

**780 Larousse gastronomique: The world's
    greatest culinary encyclopedia.** 1st
    American ed. Joël Robuchon and Prosper
    Montagné. 1206p. Clarkson Potter, 2009.
    $

    641.30   TX349
First published in 1938, this was Julia Child's favorite reference book, and for good reason. It contains an astounding number of A–Z entries, and 3,800 recipes are scattered throughout. New in this edition are more than a thousand educational color and black-and-white photographs and illustrations of foods that are likely to be accessible to home cooks. The entries include foods, terms, techniques, biographies, and advice on selecting, storing, and using as appropriate. At the back of the book are a general index and a recipe index.

**781 Modernist cuisine: The art and
    science of cooking.** Nathan Myhrvold,
    Chris Young, Maxime Bilet, and Ryan
    Smith. 6v. Cooking Lab, 2011. $$$

    641.01   TX651
Priced beyond most individuals' budgets, this six-volume resource is probably one of the most beautiful sets of cookbooks ever. The photographs of food and food preparation are without compare. Volumes include *History and Fundamentals* (v. 1), *Techniques and Equipment* (v. 2), *Animals and Plants* (v. 3), *Ingredients and Preparations* (v. 4), *Plated-Dish Recipes* (v. 5), and *Kitchen Manual* (v. 6). Cooking enthusiasts everywhere should see this, which is why all libraries should get it if they can. If this set is out of budget, all libraries should consider the *At Home* version in the next entry. Nathan Myhrvold has two PhDs from Princeton University, was the first chief technical officer at Microsoft, and has served as "Chief Gastronomic Officer" for Zagat Survey.

782 Modernist cuisine at home. Nathan
    Myhrvold, Maxime Bilet, and Melissa
    Lehuta. 456p. Cooking Lab, 2012. $$

    641.01   TX651
From the publisher: "*Modernist Cuisine at Home*. . . is destined to set a new standard for home cookbooks." User reviews seem to confirm that this is true. This luscious book, full of beautiful photographs and great information, includes two parts: part 1, "Stocking the Modernist Kitchen" (recommended countertop tools, cooking equipment, and ingredients to have on hand), and part 2, "The Recipes." Back matter includes further reading, a glossary of cooking terms, reference tables, step-by-step procedures, tables of "best bets," and an exhaustive index. A bundled set is available that includes a "Kitchen Manual," a spiral-bound reprint all of the recipes and reference tables on waterproof, tear-resistant paper.

Etiquette

783 Disability etiquette in the workplace.
    U.S. Department of Labor, Job
    Accommodation Network. purl.fdlp.gov/
    GPO/gpo13206. Free
The Job Accommodation Network is a service of the U.S. Department of Labor, Office of Disability

Employment Policy. This succinct guide, only nine pages long, covers important information often neglected in other etiquette guides. Covering numerous general types of disabilities, the information is mostly bullet-pointed and succinct. Also included is a list of other publications that might be useful to those who are looking for more information on the topic.

784   Emily Post's etiquette: Manners for a new world. 18th ed. Peggy Post et al. 736p. William Morrow, 2011. $

395   BJ1853

First published in 1922, this eighteenth edition was written by three of Emily Post's great- and great-great-grandchildren. It is completely updated for current times and stresses that respect, consideration, and honesty should always be absolute priorities. The book is elegant and pleasingly arranged, from font styles, colors, and spacing, to clear headings, sidebars, and accent illustrations. Much of the information is presented in charts, bullet points, and numbered lists. Major sections are as follows: "Etiquette Every Day" (includes social networking), "Life in the Workplace," and "Life Stages and Special Times." Besides a large index, the book includes a resources section with names and titles, official forms of address, how to dress for the occasion, sample invitations and announcements, a guide to food and drink, and a wedding budget planning chart. Highly recommended for all libraries.

How to be a perfect stranger: The essential religious etiquette handbook, see **117.**

785   Kiss, bow, or shake hands: The bestselling guide to doing business in more than 60 countries. 2nd ed. Terri Morrison, Wayne A. Conaway. 593p. Adams Media, 2006. $

395.5   HF5389

Content in this awesome reference book is arranged alphabetically by country. While it is intended for businesspeople, it would be a useful book to consult for anyone traveling internationally so that we might have fewer "ugly Americans" out and about. Sixty-two countries from Argentina to Vietnam are included. Each entry starts with a quiz with two or three questions called "What's Your Cultural IQ?" and then continues on with these headings: "Tips

on Doing Business," which lists a few things about the country in general that you should know about; "Country Background," which includes history, type of government, and language, plus a section that tries to describe the population's gestalt, their cognitive styles, how they organize and process information, what they accept for evidence, and their value systems; and, finally, "Business Practices," which tells about punctuality, appointments, negotiating, business entertaining, greetings, titles/forms of address, gestures, gifts, and dress. Scattered throughout are short "Cultural Note" boxes that add context. Just before the short index is a guide to international electrical adaptors. Recommended for all libraries.

786   United States protocol: The guide to official diplomatic etiquette. Mary Mel French. 472p. Rowman & Littlefield, 2010. $

395.5   JZ1436

Former president Bill Clinton says in his foreword to this book that it is "an authoritative user's manual for international relations [that] promises to become an indispensable reference—not only for those in Washington, but for all Americans in contact with people in other nations." This book is not simply a guide on how to address important people. Chapters titles include "Office of Protocol," "Order of Precedence Information," "U.S. Order of Precedence," "Titles and Forms of Address Information," "Titles and Forms of Address," "Official Visits with the President," "Official Entertaining," "Table Seating," "Flag Etiquette," "Ceremonies," "Conduct of Diplomacy," "Blair House," "Official Gift Giving," "Presidential Advance and Government Officials Information," "Internet Protocol," "Valuable Information" (facts about the United States), "Embassy Names and Other Office Information," and "Websites." Also included are a glossary and an index.

Festivals and Holidays

787   Holidays, festivals, and celebrations of the world dictionary: Detailing more than 3,000 observances from all 50 states and more than 100 nations. 4th ed. Cherie Abbey, ed. 1323p. Omnigraphics, 2010. $$

394.26   GT3925

Exhaustive coverage in this huge reference book includes extensive appendixes, indexes, and cross-referencing. Entries are for events for which people gather, and each entry has a paragraph or two describing the event and its history. Also provided for each entry are contacts (if available) and sources. Not included are birth or death anniversaries of individuals, unless an official event is associated with them.

788   **Holiday symbols and customs: A guide to the legend and lore behind the traditions, rituals, foods, games, animals, and other symbols and activities associated with holidays and holy days, feasts and fasts, and other celebrations, covering ancient, calendar, religious, historic, folkloric, national, promotional, and sporting events, as observed in the United States and around the world.** 4th ed. Helene Henderson and Sue Ellen Thompson. 1321p. Omnigraphics, 2009. $$

394.26   GT3930

The enormous title says what this book is all about. It covers 323 holidays, the entries for which are arranged in alphabetical order. Each entry provides succinct information on name of holiday, type of holiday, date of observation and where celebrated, symbols and customs, colors, and related holidays. After this basic information, several pages follow providing details about the origin and symbols of the holiday and resources for more information. A true reference book, it includes five appendixes: "Calendars throughout History," "Tourism Information Sources for North America," "Tourism Information Sources for Countries around the World," "Tourism Information Sources for Individual Festivals," and "Entries by Type." Lack of graphics is not a problem, and the massive index is a bonus. *Religious celebrations: An encyclopedia of holidays, festivals, solemn observances, and spiritual commemorations,* see **99.**

Foods

789   **Bowes & Church's food values of portions commonly used.** 19th ed. Jean

A. T. Pennington and Judith Spungen. 480p. Lippincott Williams & Wilkins, 2010. $

613.2   TX551

Authors of this edition, the nineteenth in over seventy years of publication, are a PhD RD and an RD. The value of this book is that it consolidates a number of data sources including the USDA's databases. The 6,300-plus entries are arranged alphabetically within thirty-two food group chapters, and each entry includes more than thirty columns of data in the following categories: weight (in grams and ounces), calories, macronutrients, minerals, and vitamins. An introduction has tables for DRI (Dietary Reference Intake), RDA (Recommended Dietary Allowance), and more; definitions; keys to abbreviations, symbols, and codes; and conversions and equivalencies. At the back, about 200 pages of supplementary data provide more information about the composition of foods, including things like amounts of amino acids, carotenoids, coenzyme Q, fatty acids, flavonoids, and more. While this book is intended for health professionals, the language is not overly scientific. Includes a searchable CD of all content.

790   **The complete food counter.** 4th ed., updated. Karen Nolan and Jo-Ann Heslin. 781p. Pocket Books, 2012. $

613.23   TX551

The authors' credentials (PhD and RD) and the arrangement of the data make this reference preferred over Netzer's *Complete Book of Food Counts.* Each of the more than 17,000 entries has these columns of data: portion, calories, protein, fat, cholesterol, carbohydrates, fiber, and sodium. The first section of the book is for brand-name products, non-brand-name products, and carry-out foods. The second section of the book consists of entries for restaurant chains. A quick guide to nutrition adds value.

791   **The culinarian: A kitchen desk reference.** Barbara Ann Kipfer. 616p. Wiley, 2011. $

641.3   TX349

This thick handbook-sized dictionary of food terms and culinary trivia is intended to be used as a "complement to your favorite cookbook." Some entries include a list (usually of varieties of the item); informational charts; sidebars like "Essentials,"

"Hint," or "Confusable," to alert you to things you must know about the entry for safety or quality; pen-and-ink illustrations; or cross-references. A small index comes after an A–Z section called "Perfect Flavor Parings."

792   A dictionary of food and nutrition.
3rd ed. David Bender. 255p. Oxford, 2009. $
641.03   TX349
The unique content in this food dictionary, which has 6,100-plus entries, is the comprehensive inclusion of food additives that have strange, unpronounceable scientific names and can include chemicals, naturally occurring substances like vitamins or molds, and toxins that can be present in food occasionally. It lists international as well as common American food items. Diseases that can be affected by food are also covered. Adding value are eight appendixes of charts and lists and the cross-referencing throughout. The author teaches biochemistry and molecular biology at University College London.

793   The food and culture around the world handbook. Helen C. Brittin. 384p. Prentice Hall, 2011. $
394.1   TX353
This reference book's content is arranged alphabetically by country and includes almost 200 of them. Each approximately two-page entry has very brief but thorough sections on geography; major languages; demographics; agriculture; natural resources; industries; history; influences on food; bread and cereals; meat, poultry, and fish; dairy products; fats and oils; legumes; vegetables; fruit; nuts and seeds; seasonings; dishes; national and other special dishes; sweets; beverages; and meals or street food or snacks. Includes a regional index for countries, grouping them by continent. Color world map on inside front and back cover has each county indicated.

794   The food substitutions bible: More than 6,500 substitutions for ingredients, equipment, and techniques. 2nd ed. David Joachim and Carol Sherman. 696p. R. Rose, 2010. $
641.5   TX652
David Joachim won the International Association of Culinary Professionals award for the first edition

of this book. All entries are alphabetically arranged and are also cross-referenced if appropriate. Each entry has introductory and reference information about the ingredient along with substitutions information. Many entries also have volume and weight measurement equivalents. Exhaustive coverage includes a guide to ingredients, which gives information about foods that have many varieties, like apples, beans, and chilies; and a guide to measurements, which includes equivalents for temperatures, can sizes, pan sizes, Imperial-to-metric conversions, common cooking volume and weights, and adjustments for high altitude.

795   The new complete book of food: A nutritional, medical, and culinary guide. 2nd ed. Carol Ann Rinzler. 474p. Facts on File, 2009. $
641.3   TX353
Although it covers only 300 common foods, this resource contains some unique information. Besides the usual nutritional values and how to buy, store, and prepare the food, it also lists the most nutritional way to serve the food, diets that might exclude it, how processing affects it, medical uses and/or benefits, adverse effects associated with it, and food/drug interactions. Each entry is two to five pages long. An appendix contains charts of "foods high in specific nutrients for specific diets," and a good index is included, too. The author, a prolific food writer, has included an impressive list of resources in the bibliography for this book.

796   The Oxford encyclopedia of food and drink in America. 2nd ed. Andrew Smith. 3v. Oxford, 2013. $$
641.59   TX349
The award-winning first edition of this title claimed to be "the most authoritative, current reference work on American cuisine." The three-volume new edition includes more than 1,400 entries covering American food consciousness in the twenty-first century. It adds more than 300 new entries on subjects such as food science and nutrition, molecular gastronomy, genetically modified foods, food controversies, regional foods, and food traditions of major American cities. The publisher states that all bibliographies and nonhistorical entries have been revisited.

797 StillTasty: Your ultimate shelf life guide. StillTasty. www.stilltasty.com. Free
This online resource gathers data from the USDA, FDA, and CDC as well as research from state government agencies and several "non-profit organizations that conduct studies on food storage and safety." It provides more information than just shelf life—for example, what to look for if the food may have gone bad. Users can use the search box to search for beverage or food names or browse by category. An FAQ section addresses common questions that aren't strictly about shelf life. Mercifully, the website also contains minimal and unobtrusive advertising.

Home Improvement

798 The complete guide to a clutter-free home: Organized storage solutions and projects. Philip Schmidt. 240p. Creative Publishing International, 2009. $
648   TX309
Library Journal says this book "presents strategies on letting go and organizing personal materials. Projects move from room to room throughout an entire house." The introductory chapter is short and sweet, describing first why clutter is a problem and then the basic techniques for dealing with it. While many of the techniques and storage ideas are not brand new, this book is unique in that it describes very succinctly the tried-and-true basics of home organization and also shows how to simply build storage solutions yourself. The projects mostly use off-the-shelf supplies, but some projects require more than basic carpentry skills. Each project includes lists of tools and materials needed and tables for the key components, with dimensions, quantities, and materials needed. Also included are plenty of informative color photographs, illustrations, and exploded diagrams. Published in cooperation with Black & Decker.

799 The complete guide to outdoor carpentry: More than 40 projects including furnishing, accessories, pergolas, fences, planters. 238p. Creative Publishing International, 2009. $
684.1   TH4961
Beautiful and clear photos and colorful exploded

illustrations are included for each of the forty projects. The projects are described by the publisher as fresh, stylish, sturdy, and inexpensive, yet require only simple tools and basic carpentry knowledge. Chapters include "Seating Projects," "Dining & Entertaining Projects," "Yard & Garden Projects," and "Yard Structures." Published in cooperation with Black & Decker.

800 The complete guide to room additions: Designing and building, garage conversions, attic add-ons, bath and kitchen expansions, bump-out additions. Chris Peterson. 250p. Creative Publishing International, 2011. $
643.7   TH4816.2
This large book features many quality color photographs and illustrations, typical for this publisher. Graphics include sequence photos, tip boxes, cutaways and schematics, exploded illustrations, and more. Specific projects include additions and bump-outs and attic, garage, and basement conversions. The front of the book features guides to planning, designing, and preparing. The back of the book includes conversion tables and an index. Also included are appropriate codes and practices. Published in cooperation with Black & Decker.

801 The complete photo guide to home improvement. 560p. Creative Publishing International, 2009. $
643   TH4817.3
This large book features many quality color photographs and illustrations, typical for this publisher. Graphics include sequence photos, tip boxes, cutaways and schematics, exploded illustrations, and more. A huge team of people worked to produce this reference, which includes "over 200 high-payback projects shown in complete detail." Covers home improvement skills and techniques, home improvement basics (like floors, walls, ceilings, windows, doors, and lighting), major remodeling (kitchen, bathroom, basements, and attics), and exterior improvements (roofing, siding, and trim). Also included are conversion charts and an index. Published in cooperation with Black & Decker.

802 Do-it-yourself home improvement: A step-by-step guide. Rev. ed. Julian

Cassell, Peter Parham, and Theresa Coleman. 544p. DK, 2009. $

643.72   TH4816

A typical graphically beautiful DK book, this reference includes quality photographs, colorful cutaway and exploded illustrations, and lots of ways to get information fast: checklists, charts, step-by-step photos and instructions, and sidebars highlighting special considerations. Comprehensive in coverage, this reference book could be used by beginning and advanced home improvers. The sides of the pages are color coded so that finding the major topics is easier. These include tools, equipment, and materials; alterations and repairs; kitchens and bathrooms; decorating and finishing; improving home performance; outdoor alterations and repairs; electrics; plumbing; and heating. Also includes a first aid and emergencies guide, a glossary, and an enormous index. Green alternatives are offered throughout. Highly recommended for all libraries.

803   The family handyman. Home Service Publications. www.familyhandyman.com. Free

The home improvement projects on this searchable website are divided into "parts of the house" (ceiling, doors, floor, roof, etc.) and "outdoors" (decks, garden, grill, patio, etc.). Projects include a time, complexity, and cost estimator; step-by-step instructions and photos; tools and materials lists; and user comments. The site is generously provided by the publishers of *Family Handyman* magazine, and so some advertising exists, but it is not obtrusive.

804   Ultimate guide: Home repair and improvement. 3rd ed. 607p. Creative Homeowner, 2011. $

643   TH4817.3

This large and heavy book features many quality color photographs and illustrations, typical for this publisher. Graphics include sequence photos, tip boxes, cutaways and schematics, exploded illustrations, and more. The sides of the pages are color coded so that you can quickly find the household system that the twenty-two chapters cover. The first sixty-plus pages are introductory, offering advice on safety and security, remodeling, and tools. The rest of the chapters cover everything from masonry

to shelving and storage to unfinished spaces. The projects listed are also color coded for money-saving and environmentally friendly qualities.

Housekeeping

805   The country almanac of housekeeping techniques that save you money: Folk wisdom for keeping your house clean, green, and homey. Richard Freudenberger. 254p. Fair Winds Press, 2012. $

648   TX324

From the publisher of *BackHome Magazine*, this resource collects information known to previous generations but usurped by the latest and greatest products and gadgets: "formulas for effective cleaning, gardening, and home maintenance" and ways to save on heating bills, repairs, and maintenance. Cleaning and maintenance is covered in part 1: kitchen and pantry, laundry room and linen closet, bathrooms, bedrooms and guest rooms, and basement and attic. Part 2 is about special interests: pets, crafts, and holidays. Part 3 covers the outdoors: exits and entries; garage and workshop; decks, patios, porches, and outdoor rooms; landscaping; and growing fruits, veggies, and herbs. Includes a good index.

806   Good Housekeeping stain rescue!: The A–Z guide to removing smudges, spots, and other spills. Anne Marie Soto. 287p. Hearst Books, 2012. $

648   TX324

This compact, spiral-bound book provides educational material as well as stain-removal methods. The first chapter, "Laundry Lowdown," talks about sorting, water temperatures, bleaches and enzymes, fabrics, leather, and laundry symbols. Chapter 2, called "First Aid for Stains," is mainly a list of supplies and tools to have on hand for stain battles. Chapter 3, "The A to Z Stain-Removal Guide," is the heart of the book at more than 200 pages. Chapter 4 discusses take-along stain treatments, aprons, bibs, door mats, headrest and armrest covers, storage, and mold/mildew. The last chapter covers caring for "heirloom textiles." Includes pretty photographs, numbered step-by-step instructions, sidebars, and a small index.

807 Home Ec 101: Skills for everyday living. Heather Solos. www.home-ec101 .com. Free

From the author: "Home-Ec 101 is an attempt to reach average people and teach them the domestic arts that make life a little less expensive, a little easier, and a little more enjoyable. . . . The founder of the site is Heather Solos, a professional blogger and author." Main sections on this website, which was launched in 2007, are called "Clean It," "Cook It," "Fix It," and "Wash It." Advertising is unobtrusive. Solos' book by the same name was published in 2011.

808 How to clean anything: The art of cleaning almost anything . . . How to Clean Anything. www.howtoclean anything.com. Free

The author of this blog, which was started in 1999, is apparently Jonas Stahr, CEO at Total Green Commercial Cleaning and Maintenance of Canada. Since it has been around this long, it should be a fairly stable website. Coverage is comprehensive and searching is good. Main areas covered include house cleaning, vehicles, animals, seasonal tips, recreational (e.g., barbecues), stain removal, and general cleaning. Some examples of interesting "How to Clean" entries: retainers, yoga mats, TOMS shoes, leaf stains on a driveway, and hamster cages.

809 Martha Stewart's homekeeping handbook: The essential guide to caring for everything in your home. Martha Stewart. 744p. Clarkson Potter, 2006. $

640   TX301

Even though this is an older book, it has no current equivalent in content or scope. Chapter 2, called "Room by Room," contains most of the content. It starts with checklists: "Six Things to Do Every Day" plus checklists for weekly, monthly, and seasonal housekeeping. Then exhaustive coverage of each room begins: suggested equipment and furnishings and how to choose, stock, organize, maintain, and clean everything you might find in the room. Chapter 3 describes routine cleaning and periodic maintenance. Chapter 4 covers all topics related to comfort and safety. Short chapters 5 and 6 are basically checklists and timelines for moving and

an alphabetical household materials guide. Full of not only checklists but numbered lists, tables, and black-and-white illustrations and photographs, this reference book also has a complete index. For more information, see www.marthastewart.com.

Interior Decoration

810 The color scheme bible: Inspirational palettes for designing home interiors. Anna Starmer. 255p. Firefly, 2012. $

747   NK2115.5

Booklist states about this title: "Design expert Starmer claims to have sifted through 16 million color possibilities to produce 200 combinations fit for a king and queen and their royal family. . . . The only issue? Too many selections—and too few ways to cross-index and cross-reference." Each entry features a main color, a few tonal varieties of the main color, accent colors (for an adjacent wall, woodwork, or upholstery fabric), and highlight colors (for a small injection of color). Included for each color scheme is an overview of the scheme, a description of it, what mood it evokes, and what inspired it. The first thirty-five pages introduce us to color: theory, light, emotions, inspirations, and design. Although this is apparently a reprint from the 2005 edition, it does not seem dated, and it fills a gap in its subject area.

811 Design ideas for your home. Alison Dalby. 176p. National Trust, 2013. $

728   NA7208

From the publisher: "This guide demonstrates how to use color in the home, running through the palette from greens, blues, reds, and yellows to pastels and neutrals. It then moves on to using patterns— such as stripes or florals—in fabrics, wallpapers, and floors, and describes how to use light in a home to best advantage, with insider tricks for creating task, background, or mood lighting using windows, lamps, and mirrors." It should be useful for home design ideas.

812 Step-by-step home design and decorating. Clare Steel. 400p. DK, 2012. $

747   NK2115

Chapters cover kitchen, bathroom, living room,

bedroom, hallway, home office, laundry room, and outside space. At the beginning is a "Where Do I Start" section. Also includes a couple of appendixes (resources and calculations), project templates, and an index. The best sequence of steps for working in each area is numbered, and then each step is detailed with color illustrations or photographs of furnishing options in beautiful DK style. The publisher's description doesn't exaggerate: "Comprehensive in its scope and utterly practical, *Step by Step Home Design and Decorating* is an indispensable single-volume reference for anyone restyling their home." Recommended for all libraries.

Maintenance and Repair

813 The complete guide to carpentry for homeowners: Basic carpentry skills and everyday home repairs. Rev. ed. Chris Marshall. 288p. Creative Publishing, 2008. $
694   TH5607

Graphic intensive, this reference features many quality photographs of cutaways and cross-sections and some exploded illustrations of carpentry projects. Charts, tables, and lists throughout make it easy to get information quickly. Chapters include an introduction (safety, workshop basics, building a workbench, building a sawhorse) and cover materials, tools and skills, basic carpentry (installing interior doors, door and window trim, base molding; framing basement foundation walls; and more), advanced carpentry (removing walls, doors, and windows; installing attic access ladder; framing and installing windows, doors, skylights, and bay windows; and more), and cabinets and countertops. Includes glossary and index. Published in cooperation with Black & Decker.

814 The complete guide to wiring. 5th ed. 351p. Creative Publishing, 2011. $
621.31   TK3284

This reference is "fully compliant with the most recent *National Electrical Code*." Chapters cover the basics of wiring (safety, how electricity works, and wiring components) and wiring projects (preliminary work, circuit maps, common wiring projects, and repair projects). There is also an appendix on home electronics and automation, common

mistakes, and conversions and a small index. More color photographs and illustrations than text, the high-quality visuals in this resource make concepts clear. Lists, tables, charts, and numbered instructions add further detail. Also included is a DVD with the PDF contents of the book (with warnings about copyright). Published in cooperation with Black & Decker.

815 The complete photo guide to home repair. 4th ed. 560p. Creative Publishing, 2008. $
643   TH4817.3

Now offered as a compact handbook, this dense little book covers major topics from the publisher's more specific guides, including plumbing, wiring, and carpentry. The specific guides, however, go into far more detail. This more general guide may work best for the less adventuresome home repairer. The bulk of this book is a section called "Systems Repairs." It covers repairs to plumbing, electrical, and heating, ventilation, and air-conditioning systems. Bonus sections are "Security, Safety & Health Upgrades" and "Workshop Reference" (workshop organizing, reference charts, maintenance schedule, glossary, and index). This resource is as graphic intensive as the more specific guides by this publisher listed in this section. Published in cooperation with Black & Decker.

816 Disaster recovery guides. American Red Cross. www.redcross.org/find-help/disaster-recovery. Free

Besides guides to human safety and recovery, this resource includes short guides for homes: "Checking Your Home: Structural Elements" and "Checking Your Home: Utilities, Systems, and Household Items." A "Tools and Resources" section includes an extensive guide to repairing your home after a flood. *The family handyman*, see **803**.

817 How your house works: A visual guide to understanding and maintaining your home. Updated and expanded ed. Charles Wing, 208p. RSMeans, 2012. $
643   TH4817

An amazing book by the author of *The Visual Handbook of Building and Remodeling*. As the publisher states, this title "uncovers the mysteries

behind just about every major appliance and building element in your house. Clear, full-color drawings show you exactly how these things should be put together and how they function, including what to check if they don't work." Topics covered include electrical systems, heating and air conditioning, plumbing, major household appliances, foundations, framing, doors and windows, sustainability inside and outside the house, clock thermostats, ventless gas heaters, moisture and mold, and passive solar heating. Witten in sparingly used plain language, the bulk of the book is presented in wonderful informational graphics, lists, and sidebars (with titles like "Before You Call the Plumber"). Has an index and detailed table of contents.
National electrical code, 2010–2011, **see 615.**

818 Popular Mechanics complete home how-to. The complete photo guide to home repair. Rev. ed. Albert Jackson and David Day. 514p. Hearst Books, 2009. $
643   TH4817.3

From the publisher: "Everything that concerns a house or apartment owner is included, with information on planning ahead; decorating; repairs and improvements; security; infestation, rot, and damp; electricity; plumbing; heating; outdoor care; and tools and skills." Color-coded chapters cover those topics, and there is a reference section and an index. Beautiful exploded and cutout color illustrations add detail, as do the photographs, charts, tables, and sidebars. Advice on prioritizing and codes is useful. This huge book seems to cover lots of unique issues—for example, repairing stained glass windows and plasterwork and installing a backup generator, a range hood, and a pond. Also included are aesthetics guides for things like painting and garden design.

819 Ultimate guide: Plumbing. 3rd ed. Merle Henkenius, Steve Wilson. 303p. Creative Homeowner, 2010. $
696   TH6124

This reference "complies with the latest plumbing codes" and includes quality photographs, cutout and exploded color illustrations, lists of tools and materials needed, and sidebars (tips, code details, ad green options). A safety guide is at the front of the book, and then guides to working with drain

and vent pipes follow. Part 1 has chapters on toilets, sinks, faucets, tubs, showers, water heaters, sump pumps and softeners, septic systems, wells, and sprinklers. Part 2 covers fundamentals like codes, how plumbing systems work, how to plan changes and additions, and how drains, vents, and traps work. The back matter includes a resource guide, glossary, index, and metric equivalents.

820 Ultimate guide: Trimwork. Neal Barrett et al. 287p. Creative Homeowner, 2010. $
694   TH5695

This reference is being included because no overall homeowner's carpentry guide includes the detail that this offers. Trimwork is almost always a highly visible aspect of a home, and so details on how to do quality trimwork may be important for home value. With plenty of color photographs and illustrations, charts, and lists, the book provides guides for putting trim on doors and windows, walls, floors, ceilings, columns, stairs, and mantels. Lots of sidebars accent important details. Additional useful sections include guides to safety, finishing, materials, tools, techniques, and resources; a glossary; and an index.

Parenting

821 Ain't misbehavin': Tactics for tantrums, meltdowns, bedtime blues, and other perfectly normal kid behaviors. Alyson Schafer. 288p. J. Wiley & Sons Canada, 2011. $
649   HQ769

The publisher describes Alyson Schafer as "bestselling author, psychotherapist, and leading parenting expert on tackling any child's worst behavior. . . . While acknowledging the daily reality that parents face, Schaefer's humor and experience make this book a must for parents who want to preserve the peace and also the joy of raising a child." The chapters are a laundry list of common behavioral concerns and advocate the "Democratic Approach" to solving problems. Lots of humor, examples, plain language, and insights into a child's thinking make this book compelling reading. The last chapter is a best practices family checklist.

822 Dr. Spock's baby and child care. 9th ed. Benjamin Spock; updated and rev. by Robert Needlman. 1152p. Gallery Books, 2012. $
649.1   RJ61

The first edition of this classic was published in 1946 and is now written by a Yale-educated pediatrician. The book is divided into sections on child development by age, from birth to eighteen years; food and nutrition; health and safety; "Raising Mentally Healthy Children"; "Common Developmental and Behavioral Challenges"; and "Learning and School." It also includes a medication glossary, a resource guide, and a comprehensive index. Unfortunately, it is text heavy with very little visually displayed information other than checklists and some bullet points. A companion website can be found at www.drspock.net.

823 Mayo Clinic guide to your baby's first year. Walter J. Cook, Robert V. Johnson and Esther H. Krych, eds. 573p. Good Books, 2012. $
649   TH61

This authoritative and comprehensive reference book is broken into six parts: part 1, "Caring for Your Baby" (feeding your baby, diapers, bathing and skin care, clothing, sleep and sleep issues, comforting a crying baby, and understanding your baby's temperament); part 2, "Baby's Health and Safety" (finding the right care provider, checkups, vaccinations, child care, traveling, home and outdoor safety, and emergency care); part 3, "Growth and Development Month by Month"; part 4, "Common Illnesses and Concerns"; part 5, "Managing and Enjoying Parenthood"; part 6, "Special Circumstances" (adoption, caring for multiples, premature baby, delayed development, Down syndrome, and other newborn conditions). Easy to read, with clear headings, quality color photographs, sidebars, and an index. It is amazing that all this information fits into this compact book.

The Merck manual home health handbook, see **701.**

824 1-2-3 magic: Effective discipline for children 2–12. 4th ed. Thomas W. Phelan. 224p. ParentMagic, 2010. $
649   HQ770.4

This is the twenty-fifth anniversary of this award-winning title written by a PhD clinical psychologist who is a nationally renowned expert on child discipline and attention deficit disorder. Demonstrating a welcomed sense of humor to distressed parents, his parts and chapters have titles like "Controlling Obnoxious Behavior (Job #1)." The intended audience is parents of more difficult children for whom the usual behavior modification guides don't seem to apply. He is upbeat and encourages a strong and positive relationship between parent and child. Examples of child behavior and conversations help to illustrate the problem and to show parents that they aren't the only ones with these problems. Also included are "Quick Tip" sidebars, further resources, and a generous index.

825 Parenting 24/7. University of Illinois at Urbana-Champaign. http://parenting247 .org. Free

This website describes itself this way: "Designed for parents and grandparents of children from birth through the teens, it provides feature articles with research-based information, video clips of parents and experts, breaking news and commentary, newsletters, and recommendations to the best parenting resources on the web." It is divided into sections for infants, preschoolers, school-age children, and teens. Each section features a list of common concerns that link to a list of resources that in turned link to articles, news items, Internet resources, and videos. Each section also includes lists of "Newsworthy" items and "Internet Sources" covering general information about the age group featured. Includes simple and advanced search options.

826 The parents' guide to psychological first aid: Helping children and adolescents cope with predictable life crises. Gerald Koocher and Annette La Greca, eds. 364p. Oxford, 2011. $
649   BF721

The 2010 President of the American Psychological Association said that this book offers psychologically sound and sensible approaches for children from toddlers to teens, including advice on health, family, school, social and peer issues, as well as anxieties and fears, sexual issues, and unique stressors. The focus on coping, resilience, and recovery from the emotional crises many children encounter in growing up is unique. Each chapter is clear and concise and includes a summary and a list of where to get more information. This book also covers many discipline problems and is written by a highly credentialed crowd of contributors.

Pets

827 **The complete care of baby animals: Expert advice on raising orphaned, adopted, or newly bought kittens, puppies, foals, lambs, chicks, and more.** 2nd ed., rev. and updated.
C. E. Spaulding and Jackie Clay. 295p. Skyhorse, 2011. $
636.08   QL83.2
Written by an experienced veterinarian with the help of an experienced veterinary field technician, this book seems to be the most current and comprehensive option for library collections. After a short introduction with a few stories about orphaned animals, sections 1–3 cover the animals. Section 1 is about farm animals and pets (foals, calves, piglets, lambs, kids, crias, pups, and kittens) and is clearly labeled that it is intended for wildlife rehabilitation centers or licensed breeders. Section 2 covers wild babies (fawns; fox, wolf, and coyote pups; bobcat and cougar kittens; raccoons and opossums; bear cubs; medium-sized and small rodents). Section 3 covers baby birds (raptors, song birds, shore birds, waterfowl, and domestic and wild poultry). Each of these sections explains how to approach, feed (even how to do feeding tubes!), house, and generally care for the orphan whether it is healthy or not (even how to give an enema!). Clear information stresses when to take the animal to a veterinarian. Includes feeding schedule charts and instructions on when to release wild orphans. Section 4 covers injuries to the animals caused by bites, cars, and guns and also discusses cuts and broken and amputated limbs. Section 5 covers exotic babies (monkeys, coatimundis, tamanduas, skunks, and armadillos). Multiple appendixes and an index add value and usability. Highly recommended for all libraries.

828 **The illustrated practical guide to small pets and pet care: Hamsters, gerbils, guinea pigs, rabbits, birds,** ✓

reptiles, fish. David Alderton. 256p. Southwater, 2008. $
636.08   SF511.5
Written by a prolific veterinarian author of pet care books, this book, with many beautiful color photographs, starts with the small mammals, providing for each an introduction (including a discussion of how the animal became a pet), health indicators, varieties, how to prepare appropriate housing (including simple construction directions), appropriate foods, handling, transporting, cleaning up, breeding, grooming, and, where appropriate, showing. A small section on small mammal health care precedes the next section, on birds. Information is arranged similarly for the rest of the animals. This book includes the full content from Alderton's *Exotic Pets* book. Additional reading materials are listed for each animal. A glossary and index are also provided. Highly recommended for all libraries.

829 **The Merck manual for pet health.** Merck. www.merckmanuals.com/pet health/. Free

830 **The Merck veterinary manual.** Merck. www.merckmanuals.com/vet/. Free
These free and comprehensive resources are based on the "Pet Owners" and "Veterinary Professionals" print editions, respectively. Merck provides these "as a service to the community"; and, in fact, "the online versions are updated periodically with new information and contain illustrations and audio and video material not present in the print versions." Both include a search box and cross-referencing. Totally Awesome!

The "Pet Owners" version includes sections on birds, cats, dogs, exotic pets, horses, and special subjects (emergencies, diagnostic tests and imaging, infections, zoonosis, drugs and vaccines, poisoning, pain management, travel, and more). A glossary is also included.

The "Veterinary Professionals" version covers behavior, circulatory system, clinical pathology and procedures, digestive system, emergency medicine and critical care, endocrine system, exotic and laboratory animals, eye and ear, generalized conditions, and the immune system.

831 **Petfinder.** Discovery Communications. www.petfinder.com. Free

From the site: "Petfinder is an online, searchable database of animals who need homes. It is also a directory of nearly 14,000 animal shelters and adoption organizations across the U.S., Canada and Mexico. Organizations maintain their own home pages and available-pet databases." Its mission: "1. Increase public awareness of the availability of high-quality adoptable pets; 2. Increase the overall effectiveness of pet adoption programs across North America to the extent that the euthanasia of adoptable pets is eliminated; 3.Elevate the status of pets to that of family member." The powerful default advanced search engine offers many ways to narrow the scope of your search. Updated daily.

Birds

832 The ultimate encyclopedia of caged and aviary birds: A practical family reference guide to keeping pet birds, with expert advice on buying, understanding, breeding and exhibiting birds. David Alderton. 256p. Southwater, 2011. $
636.68   SF461

This is a reprint of the unequaled classic by the prolific Dr. Alderton. From the publisher: this book "is an essential reference manual for bird-keepers of all levels—from the novice looking to keep a single pet bird indoors to the seasoned breeder wishing to extend an existing aviary collection. The first half of the book takes a practical look at the subject of bird care, including housing choices for different birds; constructing an aviary; buying birds and settling them in; feeding and handing; keeping birds healthy; exhibiting, breeding, and managing a stud. Every aspect of bird husbandry is discussed, and there are expert tips and step-by-step instructions to make learning new techniques clear and straightforward." Beautifully presented with high-quality color photographs, it also has further reading lists and an index. This book is highly recommended for all libraries.

Cats

833 The Cat Fanciers' Association. Cat Fanciers' Association. www.cfa.org. Free

This website describes itself as the "world's largest registry of pedigreed cats." Sections include breeds, cat care, cat shows, and for kids. The focus is almost entirely on information about breeds, so the best use of this website is to learn about cat breeds. The cat care section is inadequate.

834 The cat selector: How to choose the right cat for you. David Alderton. 176p. Barron's, 2011. $
636.8   SF442

Most of this book, which is filled with beautiful and charming photographs of cats, shows all the varieties of cats there are: colorful, lap, large, small, gorgeous, working, wild, talented, high-maintenance, and so forth. For each variety listed, encyclopedic entries of the breeds included give a history, characteristics, "At a Glance" sidebars, and notes and comments, in addition to an amazing photo of the breed. Following a brief section on caring for cats are two unique tools: "The Human Selector," where you answer questions about yourself and see what kind of cat is recommended, and "The Cat Selector," which is a table of all breeds with columns for rating cat features like active nature, grooming needs, suitable for older owners, and suitable for families. Also includes a glossary and further reading list. The small index helps you find a particular breed you are looking for. Covers 120 cat breeds.

835 Complete cat care: What every cat lover needs to know. Bruce Fogle. 192p. Mitchell Beazley, 2011. $
636.8   SF447

Dr. Fogle is another respected and prolific author of pet and pet care books. Starting off with a succinct "20 Essential Tips for a New Cat," these chapters follow: "Becoming a Cat Owner" (breeds), "A New Cat in the Family" (equipment and supplies needed), "Cats are Trainable," and "Cats Do What Cats Do" (a health care guide). Lots of beautiful photographs accent the informative text, tables, illustrations, and breed sidebars. It covers about 100 cat breeds. A thorough index is at the back.

Dogs

836 American Kennel Club. American Kennel Club. www.akc.org. Free

The website says this about its purpose: "AKC. org offers information on dog breeds, competition events, club search for training and services, dog ownership and registration to help you discover more things to enjoy with your dog." Includes information for puppies, dog owners, breeders, clubs and delegates, and dog shows and trials. The section for dog owners has good information on breeds, keeping your dog healthy, training and socialization, and finding a puppy. The focus is almost totally on purebred dogs.

837   Dog: The definitive guide for dog owners. Bruce Fogle. 384p. Firefly, 2010. $

636.7   SF427

This book got a starred review from *Booklist*, which said Fogle "may have produced the single best dog book of the decade." Dr. Fogle, an experienced veterinarian, describes in a conversational fashion his experiences with dogs. This title will be useful either in the reference or in circulating collections, and dog lovers may want to own a personal copy.

838   The dog selector: How to choose the right dog for you. David Alderton. 176p. Barron's, 2012. $

636.7   SF426

This beautiful book is identical in layout to Alderton's *Cat Selector*, listed in the preceding section, all the way down to the number of pages and price. It covers 130 breeds of dogs.

839   Encyclopedia of dogs. David Alderton. 383p. Parragon, 2010. $

636.7   SF426

This exhaustive resource covers about 420 breeds of dogs with quality photos and summary-type information for each breed: origin, height, weight, exercise level, coat care, organizations breed is registered with, and colors. A paragraph on the breed origins, a few comments, and several photographs wrap up each entry. The first 100 pages of the book are introductory and cover these topics: "The Nature of the Dog," "Dog Care," and "A Dog's Life" (characteristics of the major groups of dogs like working, herding, companion, etc.). At the back of the book are further reading lists, breed registries, a glossary, and an index.

840   Top dog. Kim Dennis-Bryan. 352p. DK, 2012. $

636.7   SF426

This reference, also written by a veterinarian, is very similar to Dr. Alderton's *Encyclopedia of Dogs*, but it includes some unique information that Alderton does not. For each of the 420 breeds listed here is this summary-like information: height, weight, life span, origin, and then a rating for amount of exercise required, amount of grooming required, ease of training, and level of sociability. Each dog gets about half a page, two or three small, high-quality pictures, a few comments, and notable information. At the back of the book are a thirty-five page care and training section, a glossary, and an index.

Fish

841   Encyclopedia of aquarium and pond fish. David Alderton. 400p. DK, 2008. $

639.34   SF456.5

This is a reprint of the 2005 edition, but it is still the definitive book on fish as pets. Detailed instructions on choosing, setting up, and maintaining the aquarium or pond is included. Beautiful photographs, charts, and summary boxes of species specifics (what they look like, food, species they cohabitate with, how big they grow) cover more than 800 freshwater, saltwater, coldwater, and tropical fish. Advice on compatibility of fish combinations, options for plants and invertebrates, a section on illness and treatment, and a thorough index round out the comprehensive coverage.

Horses

842   The encyclopedia of the horse. Rev. and updated ed. Elwyn Hartley Edwards, Bob Langrish, and Kit Houghton. 464p. DK, 2008. $

636.1   SF285

From the publisher: "Equestrian expert Elwyn Hartley Edwards traces the evolution of the horse, covering every major breed of horse and pony as well as the contribution the horse has made to civilization. The Visual Breed Guide portrays more than 150 of the world's major breeds of horse and pony photographed in specially commissioned full-figure portraits as well as hundreds of action shots. The origin, history, and uses of each breed are explained, and each breed is brought to life by historical anecdotes and fascinating, little-known facts." The first 100-plus pages give a fascinating history of horses and their influence on history. At the back of the book are short chapters on horse management and training and equipment plus a glossary and an index. Beautiful high-quality photographs, maps, and illustrations add tremendous value. Unique is the information on breeds. Highly recommended for all libraries.

843 The horse lover's bible: The complete practical guide to horse care and management. Tamsin Pickeral. 244p. Firefly, 2009. $

636.1   SF285.3

Written by an experienced horse trainer, this reference includes these chapters: "Horse Basics," "Choosing a Horse," "Identification and Security," "Housing," "Feeding," "Foot Care," "Tack," "Transporting," "Grooming," "Working Out," "Breeding and Foaling," and "Health and First Aid." Making it easy to read are color photos on each page, quick reference and tip boxes, margin definitions, sidebars, checklists, step-by-step photographs, and when-to-call-the-vet boxes. Unique are the overall instructions for keeping a horse.

844 Horse owner's veterinary handbook. 3rd ed. Tom Gore, Paula Gore, and James Giffin. 720p. Howell Book House/Wiley, 2008. $

616.1   SF951

Exhaustive coverage for horse owners and written in plain language, this reference includes chapters on emergencies, parasites, infectious diseases, the skin and coat, the eyes, the ears, the mouth, the feet, the musculoskeletal system, the respiratory system, the cardiovascular system, the urinary system, the nervous system, the digestive system,

nutrition and feeding, sex and reproduction, pregnancy and foaling, pediatrics, geriatrics, drugs and medications, and alternative therapies. At the back of the book are two appendixes—"Normal Physiological Data" and "Laboratory Tests"—and a glossary, list of tables, and a huge index. The few black-and-white photographs and illustrations are all that are needed to clarify the information. Highly recommended for all libraries.

Tools

845 The complete illustrated guide to everything sold in hardware stores. Steve Ettlinger. 486p. Bedford Street Media, 2011. $

683   TS405

This classic book, which may have never had an equal, has an interesting history. The first edition was printed in 1988, and the content in the 2011 e-book cited here is still the same. The 1988 edition was reprinted as a paperback in 2002. In 2003 Ettlinger published an even bigger book, the 1,097-page *Complete Illustrated Guide to Everything Sold in Hardware Stores and Garden Centers*. All are still good reference books for this topic. Contents in this 2011 version include seventy-seven chapters divided into eleven parts, on common hand tools; power tools; general hardware; general materials; paint, stains, finishes, wall coverings, and related products and tools; wood and wood products; wall, floor, and ceiling materials and tools; plumbing hardware, materials, and tools; electric products and tools; masonry materials, products, and tools; and safety equipment. Each entry starts with an "About" section and includes parts, other names, description, types, use, use tips, and buying tips. Includes two appendixes and a comprehensive index. The table of contents links to the sections, and there is linked cross-referencing throughout. Includes more than 1,000 items and has more than 600 pen-and-ink-type illustrations.

12 Visual Arts

EMMA ROBERTS AND SHEILA NASH

The visual arts are nonverbal in nature. They communicate through symbols, on two-dimensional surfaces, by three-dimensional objects, or through architecture, clothing, or furniture. This chapter presents information sources for such arts as architecture, photography, costumes, and comics. The changes to art information since the last edition obviously include Internet sources. Yet there is still a role for classic printed reference sources. This chapter covers everything from Oxford Art Online to *A World History of Photography*.

General Sources

Databases and Indexes

846 Art full text. EBSCO. www.ebscohost. com/academic/art-full-text. CP$

Some 475 international and domestic periodicals are indexed in this online database. It includes titles about architecture, graphic arts, pottery, textiles, antiques, landscape architecture, and many other disciplines. Full-text articles are available for 150 journals as far back as 1997, and additional journals are added over time. A Wilson subject thesaurus is used as well as name authority. In the citations of some articles, there are links to websites. Simultaneous searching is available for this file and the AMICO (Art Museum Image Consortium) Library, which provides access to more than 100,000 works of art that are cleared for educational use.

847 Art index retrospective. EBSCO. www .ebscohost.com/academic/art-index -retrospective/. CP$

This is an index to fifty-five years of nearly 600 periodicals in the fine, decorative, and commercial arts. The titles are in French, Italian, Spanish, German, Dutch, and English. A Wilson subject thesaurus is used along with uniform name authority. There are direct links to websites that are cited in articles. Covers the years 1929 to 1984.

848 Art museum image gallery. EBSCO. www.ebscohost.com/academic/art -museum-image-gallery/. CP$

There are high-resolution images in the fine and decorative arts of almost 100,000 images that include full descriptions, with provenance, multiple views, and details. It is worldwide in scope, with images from 3,000 BC to the present. The art images in rich digital resolution are cleared for educational use to illustrate items such as papers, assignments, lectures, and websites.

849 Avery index to architectural periodicals. CSA, 1934–. www.csa.com/

factsheets/avery-set-c.php. CP$

720   Z5945

This online index provides access to more than 2,500 American and international journals. Three-fourths of these journals are not indexed in any other source. Coverage is from 1934 to the present, with select coverage back to 1741. The periodicals include titles for landscape architecture, city planning, interior design and decoration, and historical preservation. There are more than 550,000 entries, including more than 13,000 obituaries going back to the 1800s. The ten-volume *Burnham Index*, from the Art Institute of Chicago and with a Midwestern emphasis, is also included.

850   Design and applied arts index. CSA, 1973–. www.csa.com/factsheets/daai -set-c.php. CP$

016.7   NK1160

This online index includes abstracts and bibliographic records for more than 500 design and applied-arts periodicals covering such diverse areas as advertising, vehicle design, product design, theater, web design, computer-aided design, animation, and fashion, from 1973 to the present. It includes more than 150,000 records, and approximately 1,200 more are added each month.

851   Oxford art online. Oxford. www.oxford artonline.com. CP$

Oxford Art Online includes the online version of Grove's *Dictionary of Art*, which provides easy access to 45,000 articles using keyword searching, with more than 23,000 subject entries and 21,000 biographies. More than 6,000 art images are available, and in addition there are 40,000 links to image databases and worldwide museum and gallery websites. This source also provides access to the digital versions of *The Concise Oxford Dictionary of Art Terms*, the *Encyclopedia of Aesthetics*, and *The Oxford Companion to Western Art*. Contact publisher for pricing information.

Websites

852   Artcyclopedia: The fine art search engine. John Malyon/Artcyclopedia. www.artcyclopedia.com. Free

This is a guide to museum-quality fine art that is found on the Internet. More than 2,900 art sites are indexed, and it has more than 9,000 artists. Access is provided to more than 160,000 works of art, and it can be searched by name, subject, nationality, and medium. Links open directly to images. Website started in 1996.

853   Artfact: Find, bid, win. Artfact. www .artfact.com. Free

The material in this great database is gathered from more than 500 fine auction houses throughout the world. The results include 10 million antiques, collectibles, and fine art. A variety of information may be included, such as abridged auction results and year, house, titles, description, estimated value, selling price, provenance, photos, and other information. It is used by everyone from librarians to gallery owners. It is free to register, but a subscription is required in order to see prices.

854   Art history resources. Christopher L. C. E. Witcombe. http://witcombe.sbc .edu/ARTHLinks.html. Free

Designed in 1995 by Christopher L. C. E. Witcombe, a professor at Sweet Briar College in Virginia, this metasite is a dictionary of art history resources on the web. It is arranged by movements and periods.

855   ArtLex art dictionary. Michael Delahunt. www.artlex.com. Free

This dictionary includes definitions of more than 3,600 terms dealing with styles, genres, techniques, and media. In addition there are more than 50,000 links and thousands of images. Artists are included only if they are a part of a definition.

856   ArtSource. Interactive Learning Paradigms. www.ilpi.com/artsource/. Free

Networked resources on art and architecture with original material submitted by librarians, artists, and art historians. Includes museum information, general resources, electronic exhibitions, organizations, online journals, libraries, and more. The site notes that the "*BEST* source of information is your local librarian."

857   AskART. AskART. www.askart.com/Ask ART/. Free

This site began in 1998 and has more than 42,000 American artists from the early sixteenth century to the present. Entries may include biographical information, references to books and periodical articles, auction records, images, and museum and gallery references. The auction results start in 1987. This very useful site also includes links to museum websites and a discussion board. It is used by gallery owners, researchers, artists, librarians, collectors, and insurers. Auction results and full biographies are available by subscription only.

858 The costume page. Julie Zetterberg
   Sardo. www.costumepage.org. Free
Started in 1995 and still maintained by Julie Zetterberg Sardo. This site includes her personal library of costumes as well as costuming-related links. The links are to more than 1,000 websites organized in sections such as historical, theatrical, ethnic, and making costumes.

859 The costumer's manifesto. Tara
   Maginnis. http://thecostumersmanifesto
   .com. Free
All the pages in this site may be used for nonprofit educational uses. Started in 1996 by Tara Maginnis, professor at the University of Alaska, Fairbanks, this site is now a wiki.

860 Getty research portal. Getty Research
   Institute. portal.getty.edu. Free
Still in its early stages, the Getty Research Portal is an online platform for accessing digitized art history texts in the public domain. The Getty Research Institute is collaborating with major libraries worldwide engaged in the digitization of art history books. A completely free resource, the portal provides a searchable union catalog that links to downloadable texts hosted in various online locations.

861 Great buildings collection.
   Architecture Week. www.greatbuildings
   .com. Free
More than 1,000 buildings and hundreds of architects worldwide can be searched or browsed in a variety of ways on this gateway site, which includes commentaries, images, architectural drawings, bibliographies, links, and more.

862 Heilbrunn timeline of art history.
   Metropolitan Museum of Art. www
   .metmuseum.org/toah/. Free
This site is a chronological, geographical, and thematic timeline of the history of world art that is illustrated mostly with images of the holdings in the Metropolitan Museum. Students, educators, and scholars seeking information from prehistoric art to the present day use it. There are charts of time periods, regional maps, an overview, and a list of key events. Users are able to compare art from around the world during any time period. There are links to other areas of the museum website as well as external sites. Copyrighted in 2000 and named "Best Research Site" by Museums and the Web, 2005.

**863 Maloney's antiques and collectibles
   resource directory.** David J. Maloney Jr.
   www.maloneysdirectory.com. CP$
Formerly available in print, this subscription-based directory of antiques and collectibles resources is unique in both scope and content. Fully searchable, indexed, and cross-referenced, object type categories include entries for specialist dealers, clubs, appraisers, restoration services, and more. There are more than 20,000 linked resources listed in more than 3,000 categories, as well as consumer awareness information.

**864 Mother of all art and art history links
   page.** University of Michigan, School of
   Art and Design. www.umich.edu/
   ~motherha/. Free
An online resource guide managed and produced by the School of Art and Design at the University of Michigan. It includes schools of fine arts, online exhibitions, art museums, databases, library catalogs, research resources in art history, and more.

865 NYPL digital gallery. New York
   Public Library, Astor, Lenox and Tilden
   Foundations. http://digitalgallery.nypl
   .org/nypldigital/. Free
There are more than 800,000 images here from the holdings of the New York Public library. Included are maps, posters, prints, photographs, illustrated books, illuminated manuscripts, ephemera, and more. Keyword and advanced search options are available. Many views may be available, and

images may be downloaded for personal research and study purposes only. Named "Best Research Site" by Museums and the Web, 2006.

866 SkyscraperPage.com. Skyscraper Source Media. http://skyscraperpage.com. Free

Begun in 1997, this site contains more than 31,000 diagrams of skyscraper structures, along with key information. Access points include a searchable database and interactive maps, and there is also a discussion forum for skyscraper enthusiasts. Also included are features on topics such as current construction, featuring side-by-side comparison of diagrams and statistics.

Architecture

867 African American architects: A biographical dictionary, 1845–1945. Dreck Spurlock Wilson, ed. 550p. Routledge, 2004. $$

720   NA736

A total of 168 alphabetical entries ranging from 250 to 4,000 words are cross-referenced and include photographs of the architects. Each entry includes a list of buildings with address at time of construction, date built, and, when possible, a selected bibliography. An appendix lists buildings by state. The format is modeled on *Concise Dictionary of American Biography* and includes the input of 100 contributors. This title is recommended for general readers, students, preservationists, historians, and architects.

868 Dictionary of architecture and construction. 4th ed. Cyril M. Harris. 1040p. McGraw-Hill Professional, 2005. $

720   NA31

Almost 25,000 definitions, more than 2,500 new, are included in this updated and expanded edition along with 200 new illustrations. This is a classic reference tool for students, librarians, researchers, historians, and practitioners, compiled by a well-known editor along with fifty expert contributors.

869 Dictionary of architecture and landscape architecture. 2nd ed. James

Stevens Curl. 992p. Oxford, 2007. $

720.3   NA31

Now up-to-date, this fully revised and expanded edition includes landscape terminology and biographies of modern architects. This source covers all of Western architectural history with more than 5,000 entries and more than 250 illustrations, more than fifty of them new. All entries include a bibliography providing suggestions for further reading. Good for students, professionals, and the general reader.

870 The elements of style: An encyclopedia of domestic architectural detail. 4th ed. Stephen Calloway and Elizabeth Cromley, eds.; rev. and updated by Alan Powers. 592p. Firefly, 2012. $

728   NK1165

More than 500 years of architectural style, both American and British, are covered in this well-illustrated "visual survey." It is organized by period then by style feature. The fourth edition includes an updated chapter covering the contemporary era and a new list of suppliers and resources. Glossaries are provided in American and British vernacular. Stephen Calloway, a curator at the Victoria and Albert Museum, edited this title with Cromley, Powers, and the input of many experts.

871 A history of architecture. 20th ed. Banister Fletcher; Dan Cruickshank, ed. 1794p. Architectural Press, 1996. $$

720.9   NA200

Sir Banister Fletcher's 100-year-old classic work has been updated, chapters expanded, and new chapters added. One-third of the book is new. This standard one-volume history of architecture includes new chapters on twentieth-century architecture in the Middle East, Asia, India, and the Soviet Union. Coverage of twentieth-century western Europe has changed dramatically, and there is now detailed coverage of pre-1900 Latin America and the Caribbean. Under Cruickshank's excellent editorship, these changes and others have been made. Half of this wonderful work is filled with more than 2,000 photographs and illustrations.

872 Illustrated dictionary of architecture. 3rd ed. Ernest E. Burden. 564p.

McGraw-Hill, 2012. $

720   NA31

A highly visual, full-color resource that focuses mostly on design and includes almost 8,000 definitions, 3,000 of which are new or updated, and more than 4,000 illustrations. This is a good ready-reference tool that covers styles, building elements and systems, and green building and also includes biographies and examples of the works of more than 300 architects.

873   The Penguin dictionary of architecture and landscape architecture. 5th ed. Nikolaus Pevsner, John Fleming, and Hugh Honour. 656p. Penguin, 2000. $

720   NA31

This basic reference with biographies, movements, styles, and terminology has been revised and expanded. There are also many new entries for landscape architecture, and it includes more American architects and architecture. Entries are as long as several pages and include cross-references and reading lists. Good for student assignments.

874   The Phaidon atlas of contemporary world architecture. Phaidon Press Editors. 824p. Phaidon Press, 2004. $$

724.7   NA680

The most outstanding world architecture in approximately seventy-five countries built between 1998 and 2002 is examined in this survey. It illustrates 1,052 buildings and is organized geographically. The atlas has more than 5,000 illustrations, 2,000 line drawings, 4,500 color images, and sixty maps. A committee of seven along with 150 international jurors helped to narrow down the list of 4,000 buildings.

875   The Phaidon atlas of 21st century world architecture. Phaidon Press Editors. 800p. Phaidon Press, 2008. $$

724.7   NA680

A comprehensive survey of 1,000 of the finest buildings completed since the year 2000, divided into six world regions and chosen by expert advisors and specialists from each. Each entry includes drawings and photographs as well as construction cost, client name, area of the

building, and geographical coordinates. There is extensive indexing and cross-referencing between entries.

876   A visual dictionary of architecture. 2nd ed. Francis D. K. Ching. 336p. Wiley, 2011. $

720.3   NA7205

This source is a series of illustrations along with definitions, and in this manner more than 5,000 architectural terms are defined. The terms are organized in sixty-eight groups and then defined with line drawings. Next to the drawings are brief definitions. Additional access is provided through an alphabetical index. This revised edition includes newer concepts and technology in architecture, design, and construction.

Art Dictionaries and Encyclopedias

877   The concise Oxford dictionary of art terms. 2nd ed. Michael Clarke. 288p. Oxford, 2010. $

703   N33

More than 1,800 terms used in the visual arts are described briefly in this dictionary. Periods and styles throughout time are well represented. This title explains materials, techniques, and foreign and philosophical terms. More than 100 new entries in this revised edition focus on modern and contemporary art materials and techniques. Updated entries are also available on the companion website, accessible via Oxford Art Online.

878   The design encyclopedia. 2nd ed. Mel Byars. 832p. Museum of Modern Art, 2004. $

745.2   NK1370

The last 130 years of design described in more than 3,600 entries. Covers the decorative arts, crafts, and industrial design. Biographies of major designers make up the greater part of the entries and include works, exhibitions, and bibliographies. Author Byars compiled information gathered by design experts from many sources, but the 700-plus color reproductions are mostly from the Museum of Modern Art's collection.

879 **Dictionary of art.** Jane Turner, ed. 34v. Oxford, 2003. $$$$
703 N31

Also known as "Grove's Dictionary of Art," this highly acclaimed thirty-four-volume encyclopedia is global in scope and includes all aspects of the visual arts throughout time. There are more than 41,000 signed articles by 6,000 contributors from 120 countries. The index has 670,000 entries and may be purchased separately. The longest biographies are up to thirty pages in length (Michelangelo). In deciding whether to purchase this title, need, cost, and space limitations must be considered. Many in-depth reviews are available online to help with this decision. This title is also available through a subscription to Oxford Art Online, and thousands of partial biographies are available for free at www.artnet.com.

880 **A dictionary of modern and contemporary art.** 2nd ed. Ian Chilvers and John Glaves-Smith. 784p. Oxford, 2010. $
709 N6490

More than 300 entries were added to the former *Dictionary of 20th Century Art* for this new edition, which now includes photography, installations, and performance art. There are now at least 2,000 entries, covering movements, styles, techniques, artists, critics, dealers, schools, and galleries. Work in public collections is indicated, and further reading and website recommendations are included.

881 **A dictionary of modern design.** Rev. ed. Jonathan M. Woodham. 544p. Oxford, 2006. $
745.403 NK1165

A well-designed concise history as well as a dictionary that spans the mid-nineteenth to the end of the twentieth century. There are more than 2,000 entries on movements and individuals. Ceramics, furniture, graphics and designers, manufacturers, movements, and museums are included. Each alphabetical section begins with an example of design. No other illustrations are included. The dictionary section is followed by a topical bibliography, timelines, and a name index.

882 **Dictionary of subjects and symbols in art.** 2nd ed. James Hall. 400p. Westview

Press, 2007. $
703 N7560

One volume covers religious, classical, and historical themes, the figures of moral allegory, and characters from romantic poetry represented in Western art. Subjects are placed in context and cross-referenced to provide greater meaning. Recommended for students and the general public, the second edition includes images chosen by the author.

883 **Encyclopedia of American folk art.** Gerard C. Wertkin, ed. 704p. Routledge, 2003. $$
745 NK805

More than three centuries of folk art are surveyed in this source. Folk art is only one name used; others are outsider art, vernacular art, visionary art, and self-taught art. A total of ninety-two specialists along with individuals at the American Folk Art Museum have contributed approximately 600 cross-referenced and indexed articles and bibliographies. Categories covered are artists, materials, and movements, with articles ranging in length from one paragraph to one page. There are 100 black-and-white photos throughout as well as eight sixteen-page full-color inserts.

884 **The Oxford dictionary of art and artists.** 4th ed. Ian Chilvers. 720p. Oxford, 2009. $
703 N33

This concise title contains more than 2,500 entries on styles and movements, materials and techniques, and museums and galleries, as well as biographies of artists, dealers, collectors, critics, and patrons. Entries cover the history of Western art from ancient Greece to the present day. This title is suitable for reference as well as browsing.

885 **Self-taught, outsider, and folk art: A guide to American artists, locations, and resources.** Betty-Carol Sellen and Cynthia J. Johanson. 334p. McFarland, 1999. $
745 NK805

This title is in two parts. The first is a state-by-state guide to galleries, auctions, festivals, museums, organizations, and other resources for outsider art. The second part is alphabetical and has information on hundreds of artists. Each entry has style, techniques, and personal information. Contact information and the information in the first section may be out of date because of the 1999 publication date, but it is still a useful tool.

886 Symbols and allegories in art. Matilde Battistini. 384p. J. Paul Getty Museum, 2005. $

703   N7740

Part of the Getty's Guide to Imagery series, this title is divided into four sections, on time, man, space, and allegories or moral lessons. An example image is included with each entry, in which relevant details are highlighted, and margin notes include name derivation, characteristics, religious and philosophical traditions, and related gods and symbols. There is also an index and bibliography.

887 The Thames & Hudson dictionary of art terms. 2nd ed. Edward Lucie-Smith. 240p. Thames & Hudson, 2004. $

703   N33

Redesigned and revised, this dictionary has more than 2,000 terms used in the arts. There are 400 illustrations and diagrams of architectural terms. It defines words and phrases throughout the world and throughout history. It now includes terms connected with computer technology.

Art Directories

888 Artists communities: A directory of residencies that offer time and space for creativity. 3rd ed. Alliance of Artists Communities Staff. 336p. Allworth Press, 2005. $

700   NX110

This book is organized in such a way that the interested artist can navigate through the detailed profiles for ninety-five leading communities in the United States and more than 350 programs throughout the world and make an informed choice.

889 2013 artist's and graphic designer's market. 38th annual ed. Mary Burzlaff Bostic, ed. 672p. North Light Books, 2013. $

706   N8600

More than 1,700 listings are in this serial publication geared toward amateur and professional artists and graphic designers and filled with marketing information. There are eleven sections, from greeting card companies to book publishers. This year's edition includes new articles on topics such as strategic planning, as well as new special features and interviews.

Art Histories

890 Atlas of world art. John Onians, ed. 352p. Oxford, 2004. $$

709   GE1046

Onians has compiled and edited the work of more than sixty art historians, archaeologists, and others to track world art throughout time, from prehistory to the present. The atlas is arranged chronologically and then regionally and includes roughly 150 double-page spreads. More than 300 color maps are included. Color reproductions are spread throughout as well as lengthy captions when necessary.

891 The Collins big book of art: From cave art to pop art. David G. Wilkins, ed. 528p. Collins Design, 2005. $

709   N7425

This history of European art is supplemented by the art of women, people of color, and non-Western civilizations. The first section of this book is a chronology that covers art from cave paintings through the sixties and is well illustrated with more than 1,200 works of art. A timeline is located across the top of this section. The second section expounds on themes in art and shows how art has illustrated those themes. The lengthy reference section includes many indexes. The way in which the book is arranged allows people to access information according to interest. The book is informative and can be enjoyed on many levels.

892 Janson's history of art. 8th ed. Anthony Janson; Penelope J. E. Davies et al., eds. 1184p. Pearson, 2010. $$

709   N5300

The eighth edition has been revised to include current scholarship and new discoveries. It is limited to the Western tradition, with a chapter on Islamic art and its relationship to Western art. The following is from the press release: "This edition maintains an organization along the lines established by Janson, with separate chapters on the Northern European Renaissance, the Italian Renaissance, the High Renaissance, and Baroque art, with stylistic divisions for key periods of the modern era. Also embedded in this edition is the narrative of how art has changed over time in the cultures that Europe has claimed as its patrimony."

893 Styles, schools, and movements. 2nd ed. Amy Dempsey. 312p. Thames & Hudson, 2011. $

Some 300 schools and movements are organized chronologically, beginning with impressionism and ending with a few movements in the twenty-first century. Two hundred secondary entries are cross-referenced to the 100 main entries. The main entries are one to three pages in length and include key collections and book lists for further study. Many illustrations support the text. There is also helpful supplemental material, including a foldout timeline and an in-depth index.

Art Biographical Sources

894 African American art and artists. 3rd ed. Samella S. Lewis. 360p. University of California, 2003. $

704.03   N6538

This classic work now surveys the works and lives of artists from the eighteenth century to 2003. A new introduction by Mary Jane Hewitt includes a lot of information about the author, Samella S. Lewis. A new section describes 1990–2002; the other five sections are much the same. There is also an expanded conclusion and bibliography.

895 Artists from Latin American cultures: A biographical dictionary. Kristin G. Congdon and Kara Kelley Hallmark. 344p. Greenwood, 2002. $

709   N6502.5

Approximately seventy-five Latin American artists from the United States, Central America, South America, and the Caribbean are listed in this dictionary. There are artists working in many areas, including installation artists and performance artists. Includes biographical material, information

on artists' works, and places to view their works. There are many photographs in color and black and white.

896 Dictionary of women artists. Delia Gaze, ed. 2v. Routledge, 1997. $$

709.2   N8354

More than 550 women artists, including painters, sculptors, photographers, and applied artists from medieval times to the present and born before 1945, are included in this dictionary. All entries are illustrated and include biographical information, an exhibition list, primary and secondary bibliographies, and a signed essay by one of several hundred art historians. This is the most comprehensive work on women artists working in the Western tradition.

897 North American women artists of the twentieth century: A biographical dictionary. Jules Heller and Nancy G. Heller, eds. 736p. Garland, 1997. $

709.2   N40

Approximately 1,500 women artists from Canada, the United States, and Mexico are in this dictionary. Twentieth-century artists born before 1960 and working in a broad range of fields are included. Entries average 330 words and include background, media, exhibitions, awards, and brief bibliographies. There are 100 black-and-white photos.

Cartoons and Comics

898 Comic book encyclopedia: The ultimate guide to characters, graphic novels, writers, and artists in the comic book universe. Ron Goulart. 384p. Harper Entertainment, 2004. $

741.5   PN6707

Covering the 1930s to the publication date, this book includes characters, artists, writers, and the history of comic books, strips, and graphic novels. The reproductions are in color where appropriate and are excellent in quality. The superhero is emphasized and gets more in-depth coverage, but also included are some independent comic characters as well as some children's characters. If your library can only get one title, this might be a good choice, as Marvel, DC, and others are all included.

899 Critical survey of graphic novels: Independents and underground classics. Bart H. Beaty, ed. 3v. Salem Press, 2012. $$

741.50   PN6725

A three-volume set arranged alphabetically by title, this is a useful source for enthusiasts and reference. Each title entry includes bibliographic information, publication history, and sections on plot, characters, artistic style, themes, and impact, to provide an in-depth profile of the works. A bibliography and further reading suggestions are included at the end of each entry, and there are biographical inserts for writers as they are introduced. Volume 3 includes a general bibliography, a guide to online resources, a timeline, major awards, works by artist, author and publisher, and an index.

900 The DC Comics encyclopedia: The definitive guide to the characters of DC Universe. Updated and expanded ed. Scott Beatty et al. 400p. DK, 2008. $

741.5   PN6725

With coverage from the inception of DC Comics in the 1930s through the early 2000s, this encyclopedia features more than 1,000 characters. It is well illustrated and includes the date of first appearance, category (hero, villain, techno-sorcerer, etc.), and personal information about each character. Also includes many cross-references.

901 Encyclopedia of comic books and graphic novels. M. Keith Booker, ed. 2v. Greenwood, 2010. $$

741.50   PN6707

A two-volume encyclopedia including more than 300 signed entries on the history and creators associated with this genre. Arranged alphabetically, entries range from one or two paragraphs to several pages in length with a selected bibliography. There is a general index, an alphabetical list of entries, and a topical entry guide; the second volume includes an extensive bibliography. There are a limited number of black-and-white illustrations throughout the text. The tone is academic but accessible, and the title is useful for reference as well as browsing.

902 Manga: The complete guide. Jason Thompson. 592p. Del Rey, 2007. $

741.5   PN6790

More than 900 manga series are profiled in this title, which also rates them from zero to four stars. Each entry is one to two paragraphs long, includes background information on creators and series, and has guidelines for age-appropriateness. There is a discussion of the history of manga at the start of the book, and a glossary and artist index at the back, along with information on the Japanese language as used in manga.

903 The Marvel encyclopedia. Updated and expanded ed. Alastair Dougall, ed. 400p. DK, 2009. $

741.5   PN6725

Marvel published the *Fantastic Four* in 1961 and has continued to create one classic after another. This illustrated volume includes more than 1,000 characters with essential facts and full details, including allies, enemies, and powers. This is an updated edition, featuring new images and text, to celebrate seventy years of Marvel. Five additional volumes featuring the X-Men, the Hulk, Spider-Man, Marvel Knights, and the Fantastic Four have been published. These volumes go into more detail than the encyclopedia and feature all friends and foes.

904 U-X-L graphic novelists: Profiles of cutting-edge authors and illustrators. Tom Pendergast and Sara Pendergast; Sarah Hermsen, ed. 3v. U-X-L, 2006. $$

741.50   NC1305

Seventy-five alphabetically arranged articles make up this three-volume reference title, including profiles of authors, illustrators, and author-illustrators. Entries are several pages long and include black-and-white and color illustrations as well as further reading suggestions. The introduction provides historical perspectives, and there is also a separate essay on manga, an annotated directory of publishers, a glossary of terms, and a detailed index. The set is aimed at middle and high school students and is highly accessible.

Costume and Fashion

905 Accessories of dress: An illustrated encyclopedia. Katherine Lester and Bess Viola Oerke. 608p. Dover, 2004. $

391.4   GT2050

This is an unabridged republication of the 1940 title *An Illustrated History of Those Frills and Furbelows of Fashion Which Have Come to Be Known As: Accessories of Dress*. It describes the personal accessories that men and women have used throughout time. More than 600 figures and fifty plates from magazines, books, and paintings illustrate such items as shoes, hats, and wigs. If your library happens to own the older edition, you may retain it with confidence.

906 The Berg companion to fashion.
Valerie Steele, ed. 800p. Berg Publishers, 2010. $
746.5   GT511

More than 300 in-depth entries cover a large range of topics, including designers, articles of clothing, key concepts, and styles, in this one-volume title. A key source for ready reference and useful for students, general readers, and anyone interested in the meaning, history, and theory of fashion. Valerie Steele, the author of many fashion titles, is the director and chief curator of the Museum at the Fashion Institute of Technology.

907 The complete costume dictionary.
Elizabeth J. Lewandowski. 622p. Scarecrow, 2011. $$
391   GT507

More than 20,000 fashion and costume terms, with more than 300 illustrations, are included in this extensive volume. The alphabetical listing features definitions, period, and country of origin. This is followed by three appendixes, which list garments by type, country, and type by era. There is also a selected bibliography that cites costume history texts, journal articles, historical publications, and more. This would be useful for the student, scholar, or general reader.

908 The complete fashion sourcebook.
John Peacock. 424p. Thames & Hudson, 2006. $
391   GT596

The well-known drawings of Peacock illustrating fashion from the 1920s through the 1980s are now in one rather than seven volumes. The year-by-year format includes day and evening wear, sports and leisure wear, accessories, underwear, and wedding attire, and each garment is described. There

is a chart showing how shapes and styles evolved, biographies of well-known designers, and a bibliography. This is a very useful tool for reference and circulation.

909 Contemporary fashion. 2nd ed.
Richard Martin, ed. 768p. St. James Press, 2002. $$
746.9   TT505

This revised edition of the 1995 title covers more than 400 designers and companies from the forties through 2002. There are approximately fifty new entries in this edition and double the photographs; all are black and white. Each entry is alphabetically arranged, and after a short biography or history, there is a bibliography and a signed article or essay. The more than seventy contributors are critics or scholars in fashion and costume. Not recommended for small libraries unless there is an institution nearby with a fashion curriculum.

910 Costume and fashion: A concise history. 5th ed. James Laver. 312p. Thames & Hudson, 2012. $
391   GT511

Laver's 1965 guide to the most important markers in the history of costume, beginning in ancient times, is much the same except for the revision of the final chapter. This chapter has been revised by Amy de la Haye of the Victoria and Albert Museum and covers the fashion industry in the twenty-first century, including issues such as stylists and celebrity endorsements. It is a good introductory tool that is highly pictorial. This source has a slight British bias and sometimes uses different terminology from other fashion reference tools. Good for an overview or as a circulating item.

911 A dictionary of costume and fashion: Historic and modern. Mary Brooks Picken. 446p. Dover, 1998. $
746.9   TT503

Defining more than 10,000 words and including more than 700 detailed illustrations, this lexicon provides current and historic usage. The terms are arranged alphabetically or in categories such as elements of dress, parts of dress, design, or style. Great ready-reference tool for finding definitions of fashion and dress.

912 Encyclopedia of clothing and fashion. Rev. ed. Valerie Steele. 3v. Scribner, 2004. $$$

391   GT507

Culture and fashion throughout history are covered in this set. There are more than 600 alphabetically arranged articles, almost 600 black-and-white illustrations, and some color plates. Each article has a brief bibliography and may cover the history of clothing and textiles, periods, styles, trends, designers, and fashion houses. Articles range from one-half page to several pages. Steele, of the Fashion Institute of Technology Museum, and more than 300 contributors have composed this resource. At the back of volume 3 there is a timeline, outline of topics, and a detailed index. These volumes will be useful to students from high school through college and the general public.

913 Encyclopedia of world dress and fashion. Joanne B. Eicher. 10v. Oxford, 2010. $$$$

391   GT507

This ten-volume encyclopedia contains 854 articles, written by 585 authors from sixty different countries, and 2,000 black-and-white illustrations. The first nine volumes focus on specific geographical regions, and the tenth concentrates on global perspectives and also has a timeline and a cumulative index. Each volume has its own index. The writing is scholarly but also aimed at the general reader, with attention given to differences in terminology for articles of dress across different countries. Article length ranges from one to ten pages. An online version, the *Berg Fashion Library*, is also available.

914 Fashion A to Z: An illustrated dictionary. Alex Newman and Zakee Shariff. 240p. Lawrence King Publishers, 2009. $

391   TT503

An accessible and up-to-date dictionary of fashion terminology, suitable for students and the general reader. Terms included cover the craft and technology involved in garment construction, shapes, and processes. The more than 2,000 concise entries are arranged alphabetically and interspersed with illustrations.

915 Fashion in costume, 1200–2000. 2nd ed. Joan Nunn. 288p. New Amsterdam Books, 2000. $

391   GT580

Costumes of the Western world are covered in this title. Each chapter covers a particular period and includes an introduction and descriptions of accessories and dress worn by men, women, and children. This is an illustrated reference book that includes more than 800 line drawings by the author. The last two decades are covered in this edition. It is a good tool for the general reader, those interested in designing costumes, and students of fashion, the arts, and culture.

916 Fashions of a decade. Facts on File Staff. 8v. Facts on File, 2006. $$

391   GT596

This set of eight books covering the 1920s through the 1990s is geared to young adults. Each decade is well illustrated with ads, other graphics, and photographs from the times. Each book begins with an introduction that includes trends in the arts and sciences, lifestyles, politics of the decade, and changes in fashion. This is followed by eight topics on specific themes, followed by a glossary, bibliography, chronology, and index.

917 In an influential fashion: An encyclopedia of 19th and 20th century fashion designers and retailers who transformed dress. Ann T. Kellog et al. 392p. Greenwood, 2002. $

391   TT505

More than 160 designers and companies are featured in this book. An emphasis was placed on those who influenced current society or the fashion industry and with a focus on the United States. Where appropriate this source includes the economic side of fashion, with items such as licensing agreements and innovations in marketing. All entries range in length from one to two pages and are followed by a short reading list. Black-and-white illustrations were created specifically for this title. Appendixes include a chart of designers and the period they were active, designers by country and specialty, college and design programs, and costume collections.

918 Shoes: The complete sourcebook. John Peacock. 168p. Thames & Hudson,

2005. $

391.41   GT2130

This is a very useful pictorial source featuring more than 2,000 color illustrations. There are examples of shoes for men and women from all eras arranged chronologically and including descriptions of materials, details, and styles. There is a time chart showing development throughout history, biographies of leading designers and manufacturers, and a bibliography. Peacock is an experienced costume and fashion designer.

Decorative Arts and Antiques

919   The elements of design: A practical encyclopedia of the decorative arts from the Renaissance to the present. Noel Riley and Patricia Bayer, eds. 544p. Free Press, 2003. $

745.4   NK750

The chapters of this very visual survey are organized by time period. Each period covers a variety of objects, such as furniture, textiles, silver, glass, and ceramics. More than 3,000 images help to illuminate the periods. Also included are biographies and information regarding conservation. Different individuals authored the various sections. This source provides a good overview of the time periods covered.

920   Furniture in history: 3000 B.C.–2000 A.D. 2nd ed. Leslie Piña. 480p. Prentice Hall, 2009. $$

749.9   NK2270

Redesigned for this edition, this title focuses on a theme of innovation and change in its discussion of the history of furniture in the West. Hundreds of illustrations are included, many from the Cleveland Museum of Art. Chapters include chronologies and historical highlights as well as designer contributions. Visually appealing to both the researcher and browser, this also makes a good reference tool.

921   An illustrated dictionary of ceramics. Harold Newman and George Savage. 320p. Thames & Hudson, 2000. $

738   NK3770

More than 3,000 words or phrases describing styles, materials, patterns, and ceramic processes are explained. There is also a list of English and European factories, including dates, marks, and people. It includes many illustrations that are well labeled. This is the same edition as the 1985 paperback edition.

922   Materials and techniques in the decorative arts: An illustrated dictionary. Lucy Trench, ed. 576p. Chicago, 2000. $

745   NK30

As the title states, this dictionary describes the materials and techniques used in the decorative arts. The main materials are ceramics, glass, paints, stone, wood, metals, textiles, and paper, but many additional materials are included. There are *see* references and cross-references that help users to navigate easily. It is a good source for collectors, decorators, curators, and others. The contributors come from many areas of specialty, including art history and science. The bibliography includes items arranged by materials in addition to general titles.

Graphic Design and Illustration

923   Graphic design time line: A century of design milestones. Steven Heller and Elinor Pettit. 256p. Allworth Press, 2000. $

741.409   NC988

This useful reference work chronicles the key moments in graphic design history, in terms of style, technology, movements, schools, and individual designers' work. Seventy-five black-and-white illustrations complement the text, and there are two-page spreads for each year of the century, from 1900 to 2000. Useful for students, designers, and general readers.

924   The Thames & Hudson dictionary of graphic design and designers. 3rd ed. Alan Livingston and Isabella Livingston. 260p. Thames & Hudson, 2012. $

741.603   NK997

This book includes all areas of graphic design from 1840 to the present as well as developments in the field as far back as the first use of typography and printing presses. Movements, styles, techniques, artists, designers, and printers are defined or described. This edition includes more than 200 new entries, with more than 550 illustrations and a chronological chart.

Photography

925 The Abrams encyclopedia of photography. Quentin Bajac and Christian Caujolle. 288p. Harry N. Abrams, 2004. $
770   TR9

In four sections, this volume surveys the nearly 200 years of the history of photography. Prior to the sections is a list of important dates in photographic history. The first three sections are chronologically divided, and the last section includes biographies. The most coverage that a photographer receives is nearly two pages. The various themes that recur in photographs, such as landscapes, photojournalism, fashion, and nudes, are examined. There are more than 200 photographs included. This title is recommended for communities that have larger art collections or that serve students involved in the visual arts.

926 Encyclopedia of twentieth-century photography. Lynne Warren, ed. 3v. Routledge, 2005. $$$
770   TR642

This three-volume set examines the last 100 years of photography. Six sections cover areas such as history, equipment, terminology, processes, and people. Each volume contains more than 100 black-and-white photos, a color insert, and a glossary of terms. There are some articles written by experts that average five pages.

927 The Focal encyclopedia of photography. 4th ed. Michael R. Peres, ed. 880p. Focal Press, 2007. $$
770.3   TR9

A comprehensive single-volume title focusing on the history, applications, and processes of photography. This edition includes a searchable CD-ROM and more than 450 color images. More complex technical terms are illustrated with diagrams, and there are several technical appendixes, making this a good source for hard-to-find explanations of photographic terminology.

928 A history of women photographers. 3rd ed. Naomi Rosenblum. 416p. Abbeville Press, 2010. $
770   TR139

This history is a necessary edition for chronicling the accomplishments of women throughout the entire history of photography. Arranged chronologically, more than 250 photographers are examined, and examples of their works are included. The biographies are very detailed and include annotated bibliographies. This work has become a standard and a vital acquisition for any library that has an interest in art history or photography. The new edition has been expanded to include women working in the twenty-first century, and there are revisions throughout the text.

929 Photographers A–Z. Hans-Michael Koetzle. 444p. Taschen, 2011. $$
770.9   TR139

An accessible and comprehensive biographical encyclopedia with more than 400 entries, this volume presents an overview of twentieth-century photographers. The focus is on North American and European photographers, but the scope is worldwide. Illustrated with facsimiles from books and magazines, this makes a good reference and browsing item.

930 2013 photographer's market. Mary Burzlaff Bostic, ed. 688p. North Light Books, 2012. $
770.68   TR9

This is a serial publication that provides marketing information for amateur and professional photographers. More than 2,000 opportunities are listed, with contacts, needed items, and guidelines for submission.

931 A world history of photography. 4th ed. Naomi Rosenblum. 712p. Abbeville Press, 2008. $
770.9   TR15

More than 800 selected photographs chronicle the development of photography, both chronologically and thematically. Topics such as portraiture, documentation, advertising, and photojournalism are included, and this revised edition includes a new chapter on contemporary photographers.

13 *Performing Arts*

CAROLYN M. MULAC

Unlike the visual arts, which need only to be seen, performing arts need to be heard as well, and preferably in real time. The performing arts included here are dance; film and video; television, radio, and telecommunications; and theater. Because of the large number of reference books in the field, music is treated separately in another chapter. Although the majority of reference sources listed here are still available in print, an effort has been made to include more web-based sources in this edition.

General Sources

Bibliographies and Guides

932 The performing arts: A guide to the reference literature. Linda K. Simons. 244p. Libraries Unlimited, 1994. $
016.791   Z6935

An annotated bibliography of more than 700 reference sources on theater, dance, and musicals, but not film or television. Most sources listed are in English and have been published since the mid-1960s. Includes bibliographies, indexes, encyclopedias, core periodicals, libraries and archives, and professional organizations. Author-title and subject indexes.

Databases and Indexes

933 GloPAD. GloPAC. www.glopac.org. Free

The Global Performing Arts Database—GloPAD—is maintained by GloPAC, the Global Performing Arts Consortium. It is "a multimedia, multilingual, Web-accessible database containing digital images, texts, video clips, sound recordings, and complex media objects (such as 3-D images) related to the performing arts from around the world." GloPAD was developed with a grant from the Institute of Museum and Library Services administered through the Cornell University Library.

934 A guide to critical reviews. James M. Salem.
Part 1: American drama, 1909–1982. 3rd ed. 669p. Scarecrow, 1984. $
016.8092   Z5781; PN2266
Part 2: The musical, 1909–1989. 3rd ed. 828p. Scarecrow, 1991. $
016.8092   ML128
Part 3: Foreign drama, 1909–1977. 2nd ed. 420p. Scarecrow, 1979. OP
016.7920   Z5782
Part 4: The screenplay from *The Jazz Singer* to *Dr. Strangelove*. 2034p. Scarecrow, 1971. $
809.2   PN1995

Part 4, supplement 1: The screenplay, 1963–1980. 708p. Scarecrow, 1982. $
016.80   PN2266
These volumes supply citations to reviews in general periodicals and the *New York Times*, with some coverage of regional and specialty periodicals. The reviews are of particular productions rather than general literary criticism. Each volume includes a number of special lists of awards, long runs, and so forth, as well as several indexes.

935   **Performing arts encyclopedia: Explore music, theater, and dance at the Library of Congress.** Library of Congress. www.loc.gov/performingarts/. Free
The PAE, or Performing Arts Encyclopedia, "is a guide to performing arts resources at the Library of Congress." Here you will find information about the LC's collections of films, recordings, photographs, audio recordings, sheet music, scores and more. There are digitized items, web pages, finding aids, databases for performing arts resources and more. Also included is the Performing Arts Resource Guide, which supplies entries for numerous online sources and websites and links when available.

Directories

936   **SIBMAS: International directory of performing arts collections and institutions.** International Association of Libraries and Museums of the Performing Arts. www.sibmas.org. Free
From the Société Internationale des Bibliothèques et des Musées des Arts du Spectacle (SIBMAS), a listing of several thousand institutions around the world describing their collections in the areas of radio, television, cabaret, ballet, opera, music, circus, film, pantomime, and theater. May be browsed by name, collection, or location.

Biographical Sources

937   **African Americans in the performing arts.** Rev. ed. Steven Otfinoski. 288p. Facts on File, 2010. $
791.08   PN2286

Offers brief biographies of prominent African Americans in the performing arts from the early twentieth century to the present. Each entry includes suggestions for further reading, and there is also a general bibliography.

938   **Contemporary theatre, film, and television.** Gale Cengage, 1984–. $$
791   PN2285
A comprehensive biographical guide continuing the coverage of the seventeen editions of *Who's Who in the Theatre* (1921–1981) and expanding it to include choreographers, composers, critics, dancers, designers, executives, producers, and technicians along with theater, film, and television performers. Starting with volume 3, there are cumulative indexes in each volume that also index *Who's Who in Theatre* and *Who Was Who in the Theatre* (Gale, 1978). Volumes 1–52 are now available from the publisher in an e-book version, as are individual volumes thereafter.

Awards

939   **Academy of Motion Picture Arts and Sciences.** Academy of Motion Picture Arts and Sciences. www.oscars.org. Free
Oscar's searchable home in cyberspace; this is the official website of the Academy of Motion Picture Arts and Sciences. On it you will find databases of award winners and nominees, acceptance speeches, motion picture credits, and motion picture scripts. You can also search the Margaret Herrick Library catalog and its inventories of special collections and photographs. Also searchable is a database of the library's production art holdings, including animation art, storyboards, paintings, and costume design.

940   **Emmys: Academy of Television Arts and Sciences.** Academy of Television Arts and Sciences. www.emmys.com. Free
The official cyber home of the Emmy and the Academy of Television Arts and Science. According to the website, "The mission of the Academy of Television Arts and Sciences is to promote creativity, diversity, innovation and excellence through recognition, education and leadership in the advancement of the

telecommunication arts and sciences." Includes a searchable Primetime Emmy Awards database.

941 Entertainment awards: A music, cinema, theatre, and broadcasting guide, 1928 through 2003. 3rd ed. Don Franks. 623p. McFarland, 2005. $

792   PN2270

The third edition of a complete listing of major performance awards through 2003, including Oscars, Tonys, Obies, Emmys, Peabodys, and more.

942 Tony awards. League of American Theatres and Producers and the American Theatre Wing. www.tonyawards.com. Free

The American Theatre Wing's repository of theater excellence on the web. Includes a video library, press releases, events calendar, and other information about the awards. You'll find summaries of the awards ceremonies back to 1947, facts and trivia, photo galleries, and more.

Dance

Bibliographies and Guides

943 CyberDance: Ballet on the net. Rose Ann Willenbrink. www.cyberdance.org. Free

From the site: "An extensive internet dance database containing thousands of links to classical ballet and modern dance resources on the Internet."

944 Voice of dance. www.voiceofdance.com. Free

Founded by Lori Smith Sparrow and Warren Hellman in 1997, and often referred to as "the Google of the dance world," this comprehensive site covers ballet, ballroom, hip-hop, Irish, modern, salsa, tap, world dance, and jazz. There are numerous links to resources for dance fans and professionals alike.

Dictionaries and Encyclopedias

945 American Ballet Theatre's online ballet dictionary. Ballet Theatre

Foundation. www.abt.org/education/dictionary/index.html. Free

American Ballet Theatre Company dancers demonstrate terms from the *Technical Manual and Dictionary of Classical Ballet* (Dover, 1982). A total of 170 ballet terms are demonstrated on this site.

946 Concise Oxford dictionary of ballet. 2nd ed. Horst Koegler, ed. 503p. Oxford, 1984. OP

792.803   GV1585

Provides short entries on all aspects of ballet, including people, companies, and technical terms as well as modern, ethnic, and ballroom dance. Originally translated and adapted from Friedrich's *Ballet lexicon von A–Z* (1972), this is an update of the second edition, published in 1982. Libraries that may be weeding their reference collections will want to retain this classic title.

947 International dictionary of ballet. 2nd ed. Martha Bremser, ed. 2v. St. James Press, 2005. $$

792.8   GV1585

More than 700 entries on dancers, choreographers, designers, teachers, ballet companies, and ballets accompanied by lists of related publications and signed, critical essays. Includes black-and-white photographs and other illustrations and indexes by professions, institutions, and nationalities.

948 International dictionary of modern dance. Taryn Benbow-Pfalzgraf, ed. 900p. St. James Press, 1998. $

More than 400 signed entries about choreographers, companies, dancers, teachers, schools, works, trends, and more, accompanied by black-and-white photographs. Includes a chronology of developments in modern dance and a bibliography. This is another older title that should be retained in libraries.

949 International encyclopedia of dance. Selma Jeanne Cohen, ed. 6v. Oxford, 2004. $$

792.6   GV1585

A slipcased paperback edition of a classic work of dance scholarship first published in 1998. More than 2,000 articles by 600 scholars cover virtually every kind of dance, dance production, and dance company from every country, culture, and period of world history. Enhanced by more than 2,300 photographs, drawings, and other illustrations.

950 Oxford dictionary of dance. 2nd ed. Debra Craine and Judith Mackrell. 512p. Oxford, 2010. $

792.803   GV1580

Offers a comprehensive treatment of many aspects of dance in more than 2,600 articles. Traditional and modern forms of dance, dance company histories, and technical terms are among the topics covered in this compact and affordable volume.

Directories

951 Balletcompanies.com. Dick Heuff. www.balletcompanies.com. Free

In addition to more than 3,000 links to ballet and dance companies around the world, you'll find the latest in ballet and dance news on this ballet search engine.

Handbooks

952 The dance handbook. Allen Robertson and Donald Hutera. 278p. Macmillan, 1990. $

793.3   GV1601

Comprised of entries on 200 major dancers, dance companies, choreographers, and dances that include critical commentary as well as factual information. A brief glossary of terms and a bibliography are included along with a directory of dance magazines, companies, and festivals.

953 101 stories of the great ballets: The scene-by-scene stories of some of the most popular ballets, old and new. George Balanchine and Francis Mason. 560p. Doubleday, 1975. $

792.8   MT95

Based on Balanchine's *Complete Stories of the Great Ballets* (Knopf Doubleday, 1975), this handbook includes old favorites and newer works up to 1975. Concise, detailed stories are accompanied by production information—for example, the date and place of premiere, choreographer, principal dancers, designers, and music.

Film and Video

Bibliographies and Guides

954 Film and television: A guide to the reference literature. Mark Emmons. 384p. Libraries Unlimited, 2006. $

016.791   Z5784

A comprehensive annotated bibliography supplying for television and film research what Simons does in *The Performing Arts: A Guide to the Reference Literature.*

Databases and Indexes

955 IMDb. Internet Movie Database. www .imdb.com. Free

This well-known site offers fans the complete details on thousands of films, including made-for-television movies and series. There are reviews by readers as well as professional film critics, box office grosses, trivia, film openings, the current television schedule, and more.

Dictionaries and Encyclopedias

956 A dictionary of film studies. Annette Kuhn and Guy Westwell. 516p. Oxford, 2012. $

791.43   PN1993.45

Many of the more than 500 detailed entries on film terms, concepts, history, movements, and so forth, include suggestions for further reading as well as web links updated on a companion website. A good choice for film students and film buffs alike.

957 Dictionary of film terms: The aesthetic companion to film art. Frank E. Beaver. 363p. Peter Lang, 2005. $

791.43   PN1993.45

An updated version of a 1984 publication concentrating on aesthetics rather than technology. Current films are used as examples in many of the entries.

958 Film cartoons: A guide to 20th century American animated features

and shorts. Douglas L. McCall. 267p. McFarland, 2005. $

016.791 NC1766

An alphabetically arranged listing of some 1,614 animated films, including synopses, credits, and voices. Offers extended discussions of 180 full-length features. A reprint of the 1998 hardcover edition.

959 The film encyclopedia. 7th ed. Ephraim Katz and Ronald Dean Nolen. 1584p. HarperCollins, 2012. $

791.43 PN1993.45

The seventh edition of a well-respected reference work offering thousands of entries on film stars, directors, producers, screenwriters, cinematographers, studios, styles, genres, and schools of filmmaking. Definitions of film terms and jargon are included. Now also available as an e-book.

960 International dictionary of films and filmmakers. 4th ed. 4v. Gale Cengage, 2004. $$$$

791.43 PN1997.8

Originally a four-volume print set now available only in eBook format through the Gale Virtual Reference Library. This version supplies all the content of the original set as well as more than 260 new entries and more than 200 updated entries. Articles discuss films, directors, actors and actresses, writers, and production artists.

961 The literary filmography: 6,200 adaptations of books, short stories, and other nondramatic works. Leonard Mustazza. 739p. McFarland, 2006. $

016.791 Z5784

Extensive list of English-language literary works adapted as theatrical and television films. Entries indicate directors, screenwriters, casts, and availability in DVD or VHS. Includes a selected bibliography and an index of persons.

962 Magill's cinema annual. Gale Cengage, 1983–. Annual. $$

791.43 PN1993.3

A yearly retrospective offering synopses on contemporary English- and foreign-language films released in the United States. Includes critical reviews, credits, awards, and Motion Picture Association of America ratings.

963 New historical dictionary of the American film industry. Anthony Slide. 288p. Scarecrow, 2001. $

384.80 PN1993.5

This revised and updated edition of Slide's *The American Film Industry* offers descriptions of film techniques and genres, definitions of industry terms, information on film companies and organizations, and more.

964 RogerEbert.com. Roger Ebert et al. www.rogerebert.com. Free

Thousands of movie reviews; hundreds of essays, interviews, and articles; and a number of special features—most of them by the late Roger Ebert, "the best known and most widely read film critic in the world."

Directories

965 Bowker's complete video directory. 4v. Grey House, 2012. $$$

016.29 PN1992.95

Now published by Grey House, this comprehensive directory continues to provide descriptive information for thousands of feature films and educational and special interest videos and documentaries. Offers indexes by manufacturer and distributor names and one by subject covering more than 500 categories.

Handbooks and Almanacs

966 International motion picture almanac. Quigley, 1956–. Annual.

791.43 PN1993.3

Provides biographical sketches of movie personalities, lists of services, distributors, film corporations, companies, theaters, suppliers, organizations, markets, and government agencies, primarily in the United States. Lists films of the previous decade and reviews the previous year in film awards, polls, and festivals. Free access to an electronic edition is offered with the purchase of the print volume.

967 Leonard Maltin's movie guide 2013: The modern era. Leonard Maltin. 1664p. Plume, 2012. $
791.43   PN1992.8

The television film critic's take on thousands of movies in detailed entries that indicate availability on video, exact running times, and MPAA code ratings. Special features include a useful list of online and mail-order vendors that buy and rent videos. Now also available in an e-book edition.

968 Screen world 63: The films of 2011. Barry Monush. 450p. Hal Leonard Corporation, 2012. $
791.43   PN1993.3

Since 1949, *Screen World* has chronicled the year in cinema, listing "every significant American and foreign film released in the United States" with full details, cast and production credits, brief plot synopses and black-and-white photographs.

969 Videohound's golden movie retriever: 2013. Jim Craddock. Gale Cengage, 2012. $
791.43   PN1993.3

This perennial favorite lists more than 23,000 films available on video and rates the best and worst among them. Contains no less than ten indexes, by writer, cast, director, and so on. Now also available in an e-book format through the Gale Virtual Reference Library.

Biographical Sources

970 Halliwell's who's who in the movies: The only film guide that matters. 4th ed. John Walker. 656p. HarperCollins, 2006. $
701.43   PN1994.45

The latest edition of this popular work is out of stock indefinitely according to *Books in Print*, but it is available for order through Alibris. Its thorough coverage includes entries on actors, actresses, directors, producers, and other film personnel.

971 The new biographical dictionary of film. 5th ed. David Thomson. 1033p. Knopf Doubleday, 2010. $
920   PN1998.2

Nearly 1,500 entries on the lives and careers of actors and actresses, directors, writers, and producers important in the history of cinema in this updated edition of a reliable film reference work.

972 Who was who on the screen. Evelyn Mack Truitt. 438p. R. R. Bowker, 1984. OP
791.43   PN1998

An authoritative and unfortunately out-of-print biographical directory of 13,000 screen personalities who died between 1905 and 1981. Entries include original and screen names, birth and death dates and places, cause of death, screen credits, and more. If it's already in the collection, keep it, and if not, consider acquiring a used copy from an online vendor.

Television, Radio, and Telecommunications

Dictionaries and Encyclopedias

973 Broadcast communications dictionary. 3rd ed. Lincoln Diamant, ed. 266p. Greenwood, 1989. $
384.54   PN1990

Several thousand common technical and slang terms from radio and television programming and production, network and cable operations, and audio- and videotape productions.

974 Children's television, 1947–1990: Over 200 series, game and variety shows, cartoons, educational programs, and specials. Jeffery Davis. 295p. McFarland, 1995. $
791.45   PN1992.8

A select encyclopedia covering children's programming. Entries are arranged under broad categories, such as "Cartoon Shows," "Kindly Hosts and Hostesses," "Puppets, Marionettes, and Dummies," and more. Appendixes include a chronology and a list of awards. Also available as an e-book.

975 Complete directory to prime-time network and cable TV shows, 1946–present. 9th ed. Tim Brooks and

Earle F. Marsh. 1856p. Random House, 2007. $

791.45   PN1992.18

The latest edition of one of the most useful and affordable reference works on television programs covers thousands of series on commercial networks. Entries include type of show, broadcast history, cast, plot or format, and spin-offs. Appendixes list each season's prime-time schedules, award winners, and more.

976 Encyclopedia of radio. Christopher H. Sterling. 3v. Routledge, 2003. $$$

791.44   TK6544

Produced in association with the Museum of Broadcast Communications in Chicago, this comprehensive set offers in-depth articles about all aspects of radio, including its history and development and its roles in advertising, entertainment, popular media and propaganda, and more. Also available as an e-book.

977 Encyclopedia of television. 2nd ed. Horace Newcomb. 4v. Fitzroy Dearborn, 2005. $$$

384.55   PN1992.18

Commissioned by the Museum of Broadcast Communications in Chicago, and drawing heavily on its archives, the second edition of this comprehensive work provides an excellent starting point for investigating almost any aspect of television or the television industry. The entire first edition of this landmark work is also available online at no charge at www.museum.tv/eotv/eotv.htm.

978 Movies made for television, 1964– 2004. Alvin H. Marill. 5v. Scarecrow, 2005. $$

Movies made for television, 2005– 2009. Alvin H. Marill. 192p. Scarecrow, 2010. $

791.45   PN1992.8

The five-volume set consists of four volumes of detailed listings for several thousand made-for-TV movies arranged alphabetically within each of four time periods (1964–1979, 1980–1989, 1990–1999, 2000–2004). The fifth volume is a comprehensive index. The latest one-volume edition provides the same kind of information for another 400 TV movies from 2005 to 2009 and is also available as an e-book.

979 The Museum of Broadcast Communications. Museum of Broadcast Communications. www.museum.tv. Free

The online home of one of the three broadcast-history museums in the United States. The Museum of Broadcast Communications in Chicago is also home to the Radio Hall of Fame. Search the archives catalog and view or listen to television and radio programs online.

980 On the air: The encyclopedia of old-time radio. John Dunning. 840p. Oxford, 1998. $

791.44   PN1991.3

This one-volume encyclopedia is an amplified and reorganized version of the author's *Tune in Yesterday* (Prentice Hall,1976) covering some 1,500 programs from radio's golden age. Features include broadcast details and behind-the-scenes information. Libraries should retain this title for queries about this topic.

981 Television cartoon shows: An illustrated encyclopedia, 1949 through 2003. 2nd ed. Hal Erickson. 1054p. McFarland, 2005. $

791.45   PN1992.8

In the second edition of this comprehensive source, coverage has increased by ten years. Entries include show titles, network, studio, producer, voice credits, and a critical essay with plot description, commentary, and other information.

982 Television production handbook. Roger Inman and Greg Smith, 1980– 2009. www.tv-handbook.com. Free

Originally intended as a guide for people using public and government access cable television channels, this site introduces the basics of television production (e.g., composition, light, and basic audio and video). Although it may not be duplicated or distributed, a hard-copy version is available for purchase.

Directories

983 The complete television, radio, and cable industry directory. 2013 ed. 2000p. Grey House, 2012. $$

384.54   HE8689

Known for more than seventy years as Bowker's *Broadcasting Yearbook* and then its *Broadcasting and Cable Yearbook*, this directory was renamed when acquired by Grey House Publishing. The content is the same, consisting of comprehensive listings of U.S. and Canadian radio and television stations, satellite services, programming and production services, advertising and market services, and much more. An online subscription is also available.

984 Television and cable factbook: The authoritative reference for the television, cable, and electronics industries. 2013 ed. 4v. Warren Communication News, 2012. $$$$
384.55   TK6540

Covering cable systems, television stations, media ownership, and media services, this extensive and expensive directory provides the latest in industry information. A one-year, one-user online version is also available.

Handbooks and Almanacs

985 International television and video almanac. Quigley, 1987–. Annual. $$
384.55   HE8700

Provides listings of TV and cable industry personnel and personalities, services, distributors, press contacts, shows, series, movies, stations, publications, equipment, expenses and advertising, TV households and more. Free access to an electronic edition is offered with the purchase of the print volume.

986 World radio TV handbook. WRTH Publications. Annual. $
621.38   TK6540

Listings of long-, medium-, and shortwave television and radio broadcast frequencies, operating times, and addresses for every country in the world. Lists English-language and world satellite broadcasts and includes maps of principal transmitter sites.

Theater

Bibliographies and Guides

987 DPS. Dramatists Play Service, Inc. www.dramatists.com/text/catalogues.html. Free

This website offers freely available and downloadable catalogues of plays and the Play Finder, where you can "purchase books, apply for rights, search our catalogue of over 3,000 titles." The "Page to Stage" feature lets you search upcoming productions by author, title, city or state. There are also author bios that may be copied for use in programs.

988 Playbill. Playbill. www.playbill.com. Free

The place to go on the web for the latest news from Broadway and beyond. Special features include the Playbill Vault ("the largest Broadway database on the Internet"), the week in review, "On This Date," Broadway grosses, and much more.

989 Samuel French: Make theatre happen. Samuel French. www.samuelfrench.com. Free

New features on this revamped website include "Now Playing," where you can search an interactive map to find specific productions nationwide. There is an extensive catalog of plays for sale and searchable by specific criteria (e.g., type of play, set requirements, setting/period, duration, sets, etc.) and a place to apply for performance rights. A live chat feature is also included.

Databases and Indexes

990 Index to children's plays in collections. 2nd ed. 227p. Scarecrow, 1977. OP
Index to children's plays in collections, 1975–1984. 3rd ed. 124p. Scarecrow, 1989. $
016.8   PN1627

Some 950 plays from sixty-two collections have been added to the first edition (1972). The 1986 edition extends access by indexing 540 plays from forty-eight collections published between 1975 and 1984, to bring the series total to 1,990 plays.

991 Index to plays in periodicals. 2nd ed. Dean H. Keller. 836p. Scarecrow, 1979. $$
Index to plays in periodicals, 1977–1987. Dean H. Keller. 399p. Scarecrow, 1990. $
016.80   PN1721

The 1979 volume contains references to more than 9,500 entries found in 267 periodicals through 1976. The 1990 volume has 4,605 plays from 104 periodicals. Both volumes are arranged by author and contain citations to plays and title indexes.

992 Internet Broadway database.
Broadway League. www.ibdb.com. Free
"The official database for Broadway theatre information," created by the research department of the Broadway League in association with Theatre Development Fund and New York State, documents past and current shows.

**993 Ottemiller's index to plays in
collections: An author and title index
to plays appearing in collections
published since 1900.** 8th ed. Denise L. Montgomery. 816p. Scarecrow, 2011. $$
016.80   PN1655
The previous edition of this standard work for locating plays covered 1900–1985; this edition extends coverage to 2000 and beyond. More than 3,500 new plays and 2,000 new authors have been added. Also available as an e-book.

994 Play index. EBSCO. CP$
016.81   PN1627
Once a print index produced by H. W. Wilson, this title is now a searchable database covering approximately 31,000 classic, historical, and contemporary plays from 1949 to the present. Citations include descriptive annotations.

Dictionaries and Encyclopedias

**995 American musical theatre: A
chronicle.** 4th ed. Gerald Bordman and Richard Norton. 1032p. Oxford, 2010. $$
782.1   ML1711
A comprehensive history covering the American musical theatre from its origins in 1735 to the 2010 Broadway season. Chronologically arranged entries provide opening dates, theaters, plot synopses, and notable performers, directors, producers, and musicians.

**996 American plays and musicals on
screen: 650 stage productions and
their film and television adaptations.**
Thomas S. Hischak. 351p. McFarland, 2005. $
791.43   PS338
A guide to film and television version of hundreds of stage productions. Entries supply full credits for both stage and film versions. Critical commentaries assess the success of transitions from stage to screen.

**997 Broadway plays and musicals:
Descriptions and essential facts of
more than 14,000 shows through
2007.** Thomas S. Hischak. 644p. McFarland, 2009. $$
792.09   PN2277
Detailed descriptions of thousands of Broadway shows include critical reception and indicate the significance of each production in the history of New York theater. Also available as an e-book.

**998 The Cambridge guide to American
theatre.** 2nd ed. Don B. Wilmeth, ed. 774p. Cambridge, 2007. $$
792.09   PN2221
More than 2,700 cross-referenced entries cover American theater from its origins to the present. Special features include a bibliography of major theater sources and a biographical index listing more than 3,200 people.

999 The Cambridge guide to theatre. 2nd ed. Martin Banham. 1247p. Cambridge, 1995. OP
792.09   PN2035
This guide covers the history and current practice of theater throughout the world, broadly interpreted to include other popular stage entertainment, such as puppetry and the circus. If your library owns this title, you should retain it.

**1000 The encyclopedia of the musical
theatre.** 2nd ed. Kurt Ganzl. 3v. Gale Cengage, 2001. $$$
782.14   ML102
First published in 1994, this substantial source has grown to three volumes packed with interesting, accessible articles spanning two centuries of musical theater history. Color photographs and black-and-white illustrations accent the detailed entries.

1001 The Oxford companion to the American theatre. 3rd ed. Gerald Bordman and Thomas S. Hischak. 696p. Oxford, 2004. $

Alphabetical listing of major American plays, long-running foreign plays, and theatrical notables, such as actors, authors, producers, and others. Thoroughly cross-referenced.

1002 Stage it with music: An encyclopedic guide to the American musical theatre. Thomas S. Hischak. 328p. Greenwood, 1993. $

792.60   ML102

A comprehensive one-volume source providing nearly 900 entries spanning 1866 to 1992. Articles cover individual shows, actors, directors, producers, composers, choreographers and other theater people. There are indexes by subject, name, show, and song title. Also available as an e-book.

Handbooks and Almanacs

1003 The best plays theater yearbook, 2007–2008. 650p. Limelight Editions, 2009. $

792   PN6112

Since 1920 this annual chronicle of the theater season on, off-, and off-off Broadway and around the country has also featured the ten best plays of the season. This volume covers new productions that opened between June 1, 2007, and May 31, 2008.

1004 Theatre world: Volume 67, 2010–2011. 496p. Theatre World, 2012. $

792   PN2277

Long-running publication that provides a record of performances, casts, and other production information for New York and American regional theater. It also includes photographs and a listing of actors with brief biographical information.

14 *Music*

EMILY A. HICKS

Music reference sources continue to evolve, in part because of technological developments and a broadening interest in non-classical genres, including world music. A small number of classic works in print remain on the list because of their unique contributions to the field, even though they may not be widely available. A growing number of seminal works have found new life as electronic texts or in databases. General sources are listed first, followed by sources specific to one or two genres of music. Major categories include blues and jazz, classical, country and gospel, popular and rock, and world music. Works encompassing more than two genres of music are included in the "General Sources" section. Entries include information about print and electronic versions with URLs to databases, as appropriate.

General Sources

Bibliographies and Discographies

1005 A basic music library: Essential scores and sound recordings. 4th ed. Music Library Association, comp. 752p. American Library Association, 2013. $$
016.78026   ML113

Now in its fourth edition, this essential selection and buying guide has been completely revised and reorganized. Coverage has been updated with new music published since the 1997 edition and expanded to include CDs, DVDs, and songbooks in addition to printed music. The volume is organized into three general categories—classical music, popular music, and world music. All genres of music, instruments, and types of scores are included. This reference work continues to be an important tool for building and evaluating music collections of all sizes.

1006 Song sheets to software: A guide to print music, software, instructional media, and web sites for musicians.
3rd ed. Elizabeth C. Axford. 274p. Scarecrow, 2009.
780.26   ML74.7

Now in its third edition, this unique guide lists song sheets in print, music software, instructional media, and music-related websites for use by music educators or anyone wanting to learn more about music. Topics include digital sheet music, online collections of historical sheet music, and video game music. Also provides information on instructional DVDs and CD sets covering a range of topics such as scoring and notation programs, composition and songwriting software, digital recording and editing, computer-aided instruction, and music theory. The volume also includes a brief history of printed music, essays on music royalties and copyright laws, a list of technical terms, and an updated bibliography. Electronic version also available.

Biographical Sources

1007 Women composers and songwriters: A concise biographical dictionary.
2nd ed. Gene Claghorn. 247p. Scarecrow, 1996. $
780   ML105
This work updates and expands the content of the author's 1984 publication, *Women Composers and Hymnists*. Alphabetical entries provide brief biographical sketches of approximately 950 female composers and lyricists of a wide range of music, including jazz, blues, classical, rock, and sacred. Birth and death dates, career highlights, and major works are included. Also available as an e-book.

Databases and Indexes

1008 African American music reference.
Alexander Street Press. http://aamr.alexanderstreet.com. $$$$
This database from Alexander Street Press provides access to reference texts, sheet music, lyrics, liner notes, images, biographies, chronologies, and discographies chronicling the history and culture of the African American experience through music. Periodic updates will expand the coverage of jazz, blues, spirituals, rhythm and blues, gospel, civil rights songs, slave songs, hip-hop, and ragtime as well as associated songwriters, artists, and groups. This resource is available as part of Music Online from Alexander Street Press and is cross searchable with all of the Alexander Street Press music databases to which the library subscribes. This database is available either by annual subscription or through one-time purchase of perpetual rights, with prices scaled to budget and full-time enrollment.

1009 Music index. EBSCO. www.ebscohost.com/public/music-index. $$$$
Formerly the *Music Index Online* from Harmonie Park Press, this resource provides comprehensive indexing and abstracting for almost 500 music periodical titles as well as selective coverage of music-related material from an additional 200 titles. All musical styles and genres are covered, from 1970 to the present. A subject list organizes topical and geographic headings about classical and popular music. News and articles about music, performers, and the industry are included. Reviews of books, recordings, and performances are indexed. First performances and obituaries are also noted.

1010 RILM abstracts of music literature.
EBSCO. www.ebscohost.com/academic/rilm-abstracts-of-music-literature. $$$$
This bibliography provides citations, abstracts, and indexing for a broad range of resources, including journal articles, books, conference proceedings, dissertations, critical editions, essay collections, technical drawings, reviews, sound recordings, motion pictures, and Internet resources. Included materials date from 1967 to the present, with selected retrospective coverage dating back to the early nineteenth century. Subject coverage is comprehensive for music and includes a wide variety of interdisciplinary topics as well. Publications in more than 200 different languages (Roman and non-Roman) are included with English titles and English abstracts. Many entries also include the abstract in the original language of publication as well.

Dictionaries and Encyclopedias

1011 Baker's student encyclopedia of music. Laura Diane Kuhn, comp. 3v. Schirmer Books, 1999. $$$
780   ML100
This three-volume comprehensive encyclopedia provides more than 5,500 concise entries on a broad range of music, musicians, composers, conductors, musical terms, and musical styles aimed at the junior high school level and up. These easy-to-read volumes include timelines for major historical figures, icons denoting entries for people or instruments, sidebars, and illustrations. Each volume contains an index and a full-color insert featuring a musical topic, such as popular performers and music around the world. Coverage includes classical, rock, rap, jazz, reggae, hip-hop, country, folk, popular, world, and New Age music. This

resource, along with *Baker's Dictionary of Music*, *Baker's Biographical Dictionary of Musicians*, and numerous other music reference titles, is available as part of the Alexander Street Press Classical Music Reference Library. This database covers the history of Western classical music with more than 40,000 pages of material and is available either by annual subscription or through one-time purchase of perpetual rights, with prices scaled to budget and full-time enrollment.

1012 The book of world-famous music: Classical, popular, and folk. 5th ed. James J. Fuld. 752p. Dover, 2000. $
016.78   ML113
First published in 1966, this useful resource compiles historical information for nearly 1,000 of the world's most famous songs, including origins, composers, first lines of music, and copyright dates. Now in its fifth edition, the text has been updated and expanded to include new biographical and bibliographical data. Supplementary information includes first performers, performance dates, and recordings. A broad range of musical compositions spanning 500 years are covered, including "Happy Birthday to You," "Greensleeves," "My Old Kentucky Home," and Beethoven's Symphony no. 5. The volume includes an extensive introduction to the work, an index, and selected illustrations.

1013 Encyclopedia of national anthems. 2nd ed. Xing Hang, comp. 2v. Scarecrow, 2011. $$
782.4   M1627
This welcome revised edition reflects the changes to country names, boundaries, and anthems since the 2003 edition. Entries are arranged alphabetically and include general country information as well as maps, flag images, and music scores. Lyrics are presented in the original language and English, with a transliterated phonetic version if necessary. Information about the composers, lyricists, and anthem adoption are also included. Endnotes and a bibliography complete the set, making this resource a good starting point for more in-depth study.

1014 The Facts on File dictionary of music. 4th ed. Christine Ammer. 495p. Facts on File Infobase, 2004. $
780   ML100

This resource, formerly *The HarperCollins Dictionary of Music*, provides basic explanations of musical terms, instruments, and genres as well as brief biographical sketches of selected composers and performers. Lists of major composers and works are included. Pronunciation help is provided for foreign names and words. Not as scholarly as some other, similar works, but a good option for smaller libraries serving high school students. Electronic version available.

1015 The Grove dictionary of musical instruments. 2nd ed. Laurence Libin, ed. 5v. Oxford, 2014. $$$
781.91   ML102
The second print edition of this work expands from three to a projected five volumes and covers a broad range of cultures, music styles, and time periods. Instruments are described individually and within the context of the family of instruments to which they belong. History, construction, musical function, restoration, maintenance, and performance technique are noted. Information about instruments from non-Western and developing countries is also included. New and revised content is available electronically in Grove Music Online, available via the Oxford Music Online gateway. Grove Music Online has full-text searching and links to related resources, including images and examples of musical styles and concepts. The convenient online platform makes regular updates and additions to the content possible.

1016 The Harvard dictionary of music. 4th ed. Don Michael Randel, ed. 978p. Belknap Press, 2003. $
780   ML100
The fourth edition of this classic music reference work has reverted back to its original title, dropping the word *new*, added to the previous edition. Although the focus is still Western classical music, many existing entries have been updated and new entries added, giving greater attention to world and popular music and reflecting new developments in musical scholarship. Entries range from one or two words to encyclopedia length. The volume includes a list of contributors, bibliographical abbreviations, drawings, and musical examples. Electronic version available.

1017 Music since 1900. 6th ed. Laura Diane
  Kuhn and Nicolas Slonimsky, eds. 1174p.
  Schirmer Reference/Gale, 2001. $$

780.9   ML197

This sixth edition, the first published since famed
musicologist Nicolas Slonimsky died in 1995,
retains his unique mark while updating entries
to reflect the end of the twentieth century. This
detailed reference chronologically records signifi-
cant events in the history of music during the entire
twentieth century, including deaths, performances,
festivals, publishing milestones, and music-related
documents from around the world. Entries provide
pertinent details in a single sentence. Some entries
contain further information from letters and other
documents as well as Slonimsky's own insights.
The volume includes a list of letters and docu-
ments, a dictionary of terms, and an index. This
entertaining work provides a wealth of information
about classical music, composers, and musicians.
This edition has more than 1,500 new entries.

1018 The new Grove dictionary of music
  and musicians. 2nd ed. Stanley Sadie
  and John Tyrrell, eds. 29v. Oxford, 2001.
  $$$$

780.3   ML100

The second edition of this indispensable reference
work arrived simultaneously in print and online
in 2001. Even grander in size and scope than the
laudable twenty-volume 1980 edition, this print
edition expands to twenty-nine volumes, with
entire volumes devoted to the appendixes and
the index. This edition expands its coverage of
non-Western music, such as Latin American and
African music, and covers recent developments in
musicology. Although Grove Music Online began
as the online version of the second edition of *The
New Grove Dictionary of Music and Musicians*, reg-
ular updates and additions continue to expand the
content. Grove Music Online, now available via the
Oxford Music Online gateway, also includes *The
New Grove Dictionary of Opera* and the second
edition of *The New Grove Dictionary of Jazz* as well
as access to the newly revised, online-only edition
of *The Oxford Companion to Music* and the second
edition of *The Oxford Dictionary of Music*. Many
recent additions to Grove Music Online come from
two print works: *The Grove Dictionary of American
Music*, 2nd ed. (published in late 2013), and *The*

Grove Dictionary of Musical Instruments, 2nd ed.
(5v., due out in early 2014). A variety of search
options, including full-text, are available. Musical
examples and links to related resources are also
provided. As with its print predecessor, Grove
Music Online continues to be the definitive source
for music scholars. The frequent updates and addi-
tions to the online content as well as the search-
ing capability across multiple reference works and
links to related resources make the investment in
Grove Music Online worthwhile.

1019 The Oxford companion to music.
  Rev. online-only ed. Alison Latham, ed.
  Oxford, 2011. $

780   ML100

This classic reference work, published since 1938,
moved online with the 2002 revised print edi-
tion and its content is now offered electronically
with a subscription to Grove Music Online, avail-
able via the Oxford Music Online gateway. Grove
Music Online has full-text searching and links to
related resources, including images and examples
of musical styles and concepts. The convenient
online platform makes regular updates and addi-
tions to the content possible. Entries on a broad
range of topics, including biographies of compos-
ers and musicians, instruments, works, musical
genres, and areas of current research are included.
Western classical music is treated expansively, with
jazz, dance, and popular music included as well.
Alphabetical entries range from short definitions
of musical terms to extensive articles on musical
forms and styles.

1020 The Oxford dictionary of music. 6th
  ed. Tim Rutherford-Johnson, Michael
  Kennedy, and Joyce Bourne Kennedy,
  eds. 976p. Oxford, 2012. $

780.3   ML100

Formerly *The Concise Oxford Dictionary of Music*,
this classic work has been comprehensively revised,
updated, and expanded to include additional cov-
erage of popular music, ethnomusicology, record-
ing technology, and recent composers. Musical
terms, works, composers, musical instruments,
and performers are included. Entries are alphabeti-
cal with cross-references, and a list of abbreviations
used is included. Written for general readers as
well as professionals, this volume is now offered

electronically with a subscription to Grove Music Online, available via the Oxford Music Online gateway. Grove Music Online has full-text searching and links to related resources, including images and examples of musical styles and concepts. The convenient online platform makes regular updates and additions to the content possible.

1021 The Oxford dictionary of musical terms. Alison Latham, ed. 224p. Oxford, 2004. $

780   ML108

This affordable A–Z listing provides succinct definitions of more than 2,500 musical terms commonly used in Western music, including jazz and popular music genres. Based on *The Oxford Companion to Music*, this dictionary encompasses a broad range of subjects, including genres, musical periods, scales, pitch, rhythm, and tempo. Entries provide etymologies and cross-references. Some entries include music examples and tables. This book is ideal for students, teachers, musicians, concertgoers, and anyone wanting a quick reference guide to musical terms.

Directories

1022 Songwriter's market. Writer's Digest Books, 1979–. Annual. $

338.47   MT67

This guide to where and how to market songs published its thirty-sixth edition for 2013. The annual directory contains hundreds of listings for record companies, music publishers, music producers, booking agents, and others connected to the industry. The resource also includes interviews with music professionals and articles about songwriting and the music business. Guidance for getting started in the music business, including how to submit your songs and register your copyright online, is also included. Music company entries contain contacts, addresses, submission instructions, and musical genres of interest. The guide indicates new listings, companies accepting submissions from beginners, awards, changes to contact information, and firms that put music in films or television shows. Multiple indexes, lists of related websites and publications, and information about contests, awards, grants, workshops, and conferences are also included.

Handbooks

1023 All you need to know about the music business. 8th ed. Donald S. Passman. 512p. Free Press, 2012. $

780.23   ML3790

The music industry has experienced seismic shifts in the twenty years since this book was first published. Now in its eighth edition, this resource continues to be an invaluable tool for anyone in, or looking to break into, the music business. The writing style is clear and easy to read, even when describing complex legal matters. The author's experience as a music lawyer provides good insight into the legal aspects of publishing, contract negotiations, and touring. Frequent updates help keep the text relevant to current trends such as digital downloads.

1024 This business of music: The definitive guide to the business and legal issues of the music industry. 10th ed. M. William Krasilovsky and Sidney Schemel. 528p. Watson-Guptill, 2007. $

338.4   ML3790

Now in its tenth edition, this resource continues to be an authoritative reference to the legal, economic, and financial issues of the music industry, addressing such topics as the implications of MP3, P2P sharing, digital downloads, copyright revisions, antibootlegging initiatives, public domain, and marketing and selling music. Contains an updated directory of websites for music business information and research sources. An index and appendixes with excerpts from the Copyright Act, a list of music industry organizations, and contract checklists are also included. Electronic version available.

Blues and Jazz

Bibliographies and Discographies

1025 The Penguin guide to jazz recordings. 9th ed. Richard Cook and Brian Morton. 1646p. Penguin, 2008. $

781.65   ML156.4

This substantial work continues to be a comprehensive compilation of jazz recordings. The authors have reassessed and updated each artist's entry and expanded the lists of CDs. Entries are alphabetical by artist with brief biographical information and chronological disc reviews. A four-star rating system is used, and a crown symbol indicates the authors' personal favorites. Approximately 200 recordings that the authors consider essential to any jazz library are identified as a core collection.

Dictionaries and Encyclopedias

1026 Encyclopedia of the blues. Edward Komara, ed. 2v. Routledge, 2006. $$
    781.643   ML102
This two-volume set covers the blues from its roots in African and American music to the twenty-first century, making this resource essential for students of the blues. Entries are alphabetical and vary in length, with many including bibliographies and discographies. Topics include songs, artists, songwriters, record labels, instruments, and musical forms and characteristics. Related social, cultural, and political issues dealing with race, gender, and discrimination are also included. Electronic version available.

1027 The new Grove dictionary of jazz. 2nd ed. Barry Dean Kernfeld, ed. 3v. Oxford, 2002. $$
    781.65   ML102
This second edition builds on the impressive first edition (1988), expanding to three volumes and adding 2,750 new entries, including 1,500 on musicians who emerged in the 1980s and 1990s. This one-stop resource to all things jazz provides alphabetical entries for composers, performers, instruments, terms, record labels, venues, and more. Many entries include bibliographies and selected recordings when applicable. The work includes illustrations, listings of abbreviations, comprehensive bibliography of resources on jazz, calendar of births and deaths, and list of contributors. This work is available online along with *The New Grove Dictionary of Music and Musicians* and *The New Grove Dictionary of Opera*, making regular updates and additions to the content possible. Grove Music Online, now available via the Oxford Music Online gateway, has full-text searching and links to related resources, including examples of musical styles and concepts.

Classical Music
Bibliographies and Discographies

1028 The Penguin guide to the 1000 finest classical recordings: The must-have CDs and DVDs. Ivan March, Edward Greenfield, Robert Layton, and Paul Czajkowski. 418p. Penguin Group, 2011. $
    781.68   ML156.9
In 2010 the authors of *The Penguin Guide to Recorded Classical Music* determined that the guide in its present comprehensive form was no longer manageable. Their solution was to cull the list down to the 1,000 best recordings, resulting in this new work. Entries are alphabetical by composer, with brief biographical data and notes about the chosen recordings. The foreword provides a brief history of recorded sound from Edison's cylinder phonograph to the DVD. A timeline of included composers and overviews of ballet and opera are also included. This scaled-back, more-focused guide continues to be an important resource for collectors of significant classical recordings.

Biographical Sources

1029 Baker's biographical dictionary of musicians. 9th ed. Nicolas Slonimsky and Laura Diane Kuhn, eds. 6v. Schirmer Reference, 2001. $$$
    780   ML105
This classic reference work celebrates its 100-year mark with an expanded centennial edition. Also called the ninth edition, this publication is the first since the death of editor Nicolas Slonimsky, in 1995. The six-volume set contains almost 2,000 new entries on rock, popular, jazz, and country music, which had not been extensively covered in previous editions. Coverage of the nonclassical genres continues to be selective. Existing classical entries have been revised and more than 1,000 new classical entries added, for a total number of entries in excess of 15,000. Signed entries are alphabetical and range in length from one paragraph to multiple pages. Works or discographies are included as appropriate. Indexes for genre, nationality, and

women composers and musicians are included. This resource, along with *Baker's Dictionary of Music*, *Baker's Student Encyclopedia of Music*, and numerous other music reference titles, is available as part of the Alexander Street Press Classical Music Reference Library. This online database covers the history of Western classical music with more than 40,000 pages of material and is available either by annual subscription or through one-time purchase of perpetual rights, with prices scaled to budget and full-time enrollment.

1030 Dictionary of American classical composers. 2nd ed. Neil Butterworth. 548p. Routledge, 2005. $$

780   ML106

This volume provides synopses of more than 650 composers active in the United States from the eighteenth to the twenty-first century. Alphabetical entries include biographical data, work lists, and critical examination of key works and influence. Many entries have been checked for accuracy by the composers. A selective list of American composers and their students is provided. Illustrations (including 200 black-and-white photographs), a bibliography, and an author index are also included. Unfortunately, the index is not searchable by topic or musical composition. The work's focus on American composers makes it a unique and worthwhile addition to any music collection.

1031 The lives and times of the great composers. Michael Steen. 992p. Oxford, 2004. $

780   ML390

This volume presents fifty notable composers of classical music within the social, cultural, musical, and political contexts of their times. Beginning with Handel and Bach, this work encompasses 350 years of European history. Each narrative chapter presents a series of sketches from the lives of one or more composers. Readers desiring full biographical accounts or in-depth analysis of individual musical works should look elsewhere. The usefulness of this text is the insights into when, where, and how the composer lived. The volume includes color plates, a map of composers' birthplaces, bibliographical references, and an index.

Databases and Indexes

1032 Naxos music library. Naxos Digital Services. www.naxosmusiclibrary.com. CP$

The Naxos label is known for its high-quality, budget-priced classical CDs. This affordable database contains more than 1.1 million tracks of streaming audio from more than 200 labels. In addition to covering the full range of the classical repertoire, the collection includes jazz, New Age, world, folk, and Chinese music. Access is through annual subscription. Subscribers have access to new material as it is released, typically more than 1,000 CDs per year. Users can read notes on the works being played as well as biographical information on composers or artists. Features include custom playlists, static URLs, near-CD quality sound, and extensive searching capability by composer, artist, period, year of composition, instrument, or genre. Subscribers can add the Naxos Music Library Jazz, featuring the Fantasy label; the Naxos Spoken Word Library, containing recordings of classic literary works; and Naxos Web Radio, a streaming service of preprogrammed playlists, for relatively modest additional fees.

Dictionaries and Encyclopedias

1033 Encyclopedia of American opera. Ken Wlaschin. 486p. McFarland, 2009. $

782.10   ML102

The distinctly American focus of this resource makes it stand out from other opera reference works. Features include a brief history of American opera and entries on composers, performers, operas, opera companies, and individual arias. Audio and video recordings, plot summary, cast lists, and premiere dates are included as appropriate. Entries detailing the history of opera in each state, such as important works and premieres associated with the state, are also included. The author's interpretation of what constitutes an opera is very broad, so several musicals are included as well.

1034 The new Grove dictionary of opera. Stanley Sadie, ed. 4v. Oxford, 1992. $$

782.1   ML102

Covering virtually every aspect of Western opera, from composers, conductors, performers, and directors to genres, costumes, terminology, and venues, this work is available electronically along with *The New Grove Dictionary of Music and Musicians* and *The New Grove Dictionary of Jazz*. Grove Music Online, available via the Oxford Music Online gateway, has full-text searching and links to related resources, including examples of musical styles and concepts. Biographical entries include vital statistics and lists of operatic works. The convenient online platform makes regular updates and additions to the content possible.

1035 The new Penguin opera guide. Rev. ed. Amanda Holden. 1142p. Penguin, 2001. $

782.1   ML102

The Penguin concise guide to opera.
Amanda Holden. 593p. Penguin, 2005. $
782.1   ML102

The New Penguin Opera Guide, first published in 1993 as *The Viking Opera Guide*, is a comprehensive, one-volume encyclopedia of composers and works from the sixteenth century through the twentieth century. In total, the volume includes almost 2,000 works by 850 composers, covering all forms of opera and a wide range of composers, from Mozart and Wagner to contemporary composers Holliger and Tan Dun. Alphabetical by composer's surname, articles summarize the composer's operatic career and contribution to the field with entries for major works listing title, background, plot synopsis, libretto, duration, premiere information, cast, orchestra, and musical analysis. Brief bibliographies and selected recordings are included. A glossary, list of contributors, index of librettists, and index of opera titles conclude the volume. *The Penguin Concise Guide to Opera* includes the most popular composers and frequently performed works from the full version.

1036 The Oxford dictionary of musical works. Alison Latham, ed. 224p. Oxford, 2004. $

780   ML100

This inexpensive, accessible dictionary, based on *The Oxford Companion to Music*, provides brief entries of more than 2,000 musical works, encompassing a wide range of genres, including opera, ballet, choral music, orchestral pieces, chamber ensembles, hymns, national anthems, and traditional melodies. Entries provide the genre, composer, librettist, number of movements or acts, scoring, historical context, and important dates, such as composition date or first performance. An appendix lists the composers included in the volume. This handy quick-reference work provides essential details about frequently performed and recorded works and is ideal for anyone wanting more information about the music he or she listens to or performs.

Country and Gospel Music

Bibliographies and Discographies

1037 Joel Whitburn presents hot country songs, 1944–2008. Joel Whitburn, ed. 674p. Record Research, 2009. $

016.78   ML156.4

Previously published as *Joel Whitburn's Top Country Songs, 1944–2005*, this edition lists more than 2,400 artists and 19,000 songs that debuted on *Billboard*'s country singles charts from 1944–2008. Entries are alphabetical by artist and include brief biographical information, song title, date song debuted on the chart, peak chart position, number of weeks on the chart, and record label. A special record breakers section lists top artist and record achievements, including peak chart position of songs and a chronological list of number-one hits. The illustrated, easy-to-use volume provides quick access to country music trivia at an affordable price.

Dictionaries and Encyclopedias

1038 Encyclopedia of American gospel music. W. K. McNeil, ed. 512p. Routledge, 2005. $

782.25   ML102

This encyclopedia defines American gospel music as "songs reflecting the personal religious experience of people" and covers both the African American and white gospel traditions. Significant events, musical instruments, musical styles, radio stations, record labels, publications, societies, and biographical profiles of performers, composers, and writers are included. The influence of gospel music on other genres of music and culture is examined. Entries are alphabetical and include selected bibliographies, Internet sites, and discographies. The volume also includes illustrations, end-of-article cross-references, and an index.

1039 Encyclopedia of country music: The ultimate guide to the music. 2nd ed. Country Music Hall of Fame and Museum, comp.; Paul Kingsbury, Michael McCall, and John W. Rumble, eds. 696p. Oxford, 2012. $
781.64   ML102

This work, first published in 1998, includes approximately 1,200 concise alphabetical entries on the singers, songwriters, record companies, and industry insiders that have made country music one of the most popular musical genres in North America today. Compiled by the Country Music Hall of Fame and Museum, this guide presents ninety years of country music history, from the earliest "hillbilly" recordings in the 1920s to the current mainstream success of Taylor Swift and Carrie Underwood. Entries include biographical data, professional milestones, representative recordings, and cross-references. Black-and-white photographs are included along with sixteen pages of color album art. The volume includes lists of best-selling albums, award winners, Country Music Hall of Fame members, and Grand Ole Opry members. An index is not included.

Popular and Rock Music

Bibliographies and Discographies

1040 The Billboard book of top 40 hits: Complete chart information about America's most popular songs and artists, 1955–2009. 9th ed. Joel Whitburn. 912p. Billboard Books, 2010. $
016.78   ML156.4

Now in its ninth edition, *The Billboard Book of Top 40 Hits* features America's most popular songs and artists from the beginning of the rock era through 2009. This work lists every song that charted in the top forty on Billboard's pop-singles charts since January 1, 1955, alphabetically listed by both artist

and song title. Artist entries include biographical information, chart information, and original label name and catalog number. A special record-holders section lists top artist and record achievements, including the top 100 hits of the rock era, the top 25 number-one hits by decade, the top 100 artists from 1955 to 2009, the top 25 artists by decade, and the number-one singles listed chronologically from 1955 to 2009. From "Rock Around the Clock" by Bill Haley and His Comets to "Poker Face" by Lady Gaga, this illustrated volume provides quick access to six decades of top-forty trivia at an affordable price.

1041 The Green book of songs by subject: The thematic guide to popular music. 5th ed. Jeff Green. 1569p. Professional Desk References, 2002. $
016.78   ML156.4

Now in its fifth edition, *The Green Book of Songs by Subject* organizes more than 35,000 songs into nearly 1,800 themes, such as desire, sadness, marriage, politics, animals, cars, and love. Entries span 100 years and cover all genres of popular music, including rock, country, R&B, rap, hip-hop, jazz, oldies, contemporary hits, popular standards, television themes, and advertising jingles. Compiled over twenty-five years by a music-industry professional, this thematic guide lists songs, artists, selected discographies, and record labels. This fifth edition includes 4,000 search terms and keywords in an expanded index with cross-references.

1042 Hot R&B songs, 1942–2010. Joel Whitburn. 914p. Record Research, 2011. $
016.78   ML156.4

Previously published as *The Billboard Book of Top 40 R and B and Hip-Hop Hits*, this edition lists top-forty music-chart information for the most popular rhythm and blues (R&B) and hip-hop songs and artists from October 24, 1942, through 2010. In 1942, *Billboard* magazine created the "Harlem Hit Parade," which charted the musical genre that would become R&B. By 1963, in the wake of rock and roll, the R&B and pop charts were so similar that the R&B chart was discontinued. Billboard's R&B chart was revived in 1965 and featured hits by James Brown, Aretha Franklin, and the Supremes. Rap music entered the charts in 1979 with "Rapper's Delight" by the Sugarhill Gang and was popularized in the following decades by Run-D.M.C., LL Cool J, and others. Entries are alphabetical by artist or group name and include brief biographical data, date of song debut in the top forty, highest chart position achieved, total weeks in the top forty, and original record label information. The volume also includes an alphabetical song list and lists of top artist and record achievements.

Biographical Sources

1043 Baker's biographical dictionary of popular musicians since 1990. 2v. Schirmer Reference, 2004. $$

781.64   ML102

This excellent companion to *Baker's Biographical Dictionary of Musicians* focuses on artists who have had an impact on the popular music scene since 1990. In contrast to *Baker's Biographical Dictionary of Musicians*, which emphasizes classical composers and their works, this dictionary focuses on the musical recordings of the included artists. Written for the general audience, the entries provide an overview of each artist's career with birth and death data, genre, best-selling recordings since 1990, and selected discography. The majority of the almost 600 artists included are from the rock/pop, rap, hip-hop, and rhythm and blues genres, although country, classical, jazz, world, and Latin artists are also included. Some artists, such as Britney Spears and the Backstreet Boys, are included for their commercial success, while others, like the Beatles and Nirvana, are included for their innovation and influence. The London Symphony Orchestra is included because of its prolific recordings—it released almost 100 albums in the 1990s alone. It has a long history of recording movie soundtracks, including *Superman*, *Raiders of the Lost Ark*, and *Star Wars*, and has accompanied a long list of popular artists. The appendix provides historical context with essays on grunge, rap, the transformation of commercial radio, and the music industry. A glossary, genre index, and general index are also included. Electronic version available.

Databases and Indexes

1044 The Children's song index, 1978–1993. Kay Laughlin et al., comps. 153p.

Libraries Unlimited, 1996. $

016.78   ML128

This reference tool compiles 2,654 children's songs found in seventy-seven American songbooks listed in the *Cumulative Book Index, 1977–1994*, under the subject heading "Children's Songs." The work contains a list of songbooks included, a song-title index, an index of first lines, and a subject index with subject thesaurus. Electronic version available.

1045 Popular song index. Patricia Pate Havlice. 933p. Scarecrow, 1975. $
First supplement. 386p. 1978. $
Second supplement. 530p. 1984. $
Third supplement. 875p. 1989. $
Fourth supplement, 1988–2002. 2v. 2005. $$

016.78   ML128

The fourth supplement to this indispensable resource indexes 333 collections of popular songs published from 1988 to 2002 in different genres, including rock, folk, country, blues, show tunes, children's songs, and movie soundtracks. Songs are listed by title, first line, and first line of the chorus, with an index of composers and lyricists. The original volume indexes 301 song collections published between 1940 and 1972. The first three supplements reference collections published primarily between 1970 and 1987.

1046 SongCite: An index to popular songs. William D. Goodfellow. 433p. Garland, 1995. $
Supplement 1. William D. Goodfellow. 400p. Garland, 1999. $

016.78   ML128

Building on the venerable *Song Index*, by Minnie Sears (1926; reprint, Shoe String Press, 1966), and the *Popular Song Index*, by Patricia Pate Havlice, the original edition indexes more than 7,000 compositions from 248 collections of popular songs published between 1988 and 1994. Criteria for inclusion include publication date, a song's popular appeal, and the lack of indexing in a similar work. A variety of popular music genres are represented, including rock, country, show tunes, jazz, folk, gospel, and holiday music. The resource contains a bibliography of indexed collections with corresponding codes, an index of titles and first lines, an index of composers, and an index of works from musicals, films, and television. The supplement indexes 6,500 popular songs published in 201 collections between 1990 and 1996. The inclusion of first lines as well as titles makes this resource particularly useful.

Dictionaries and Encyclopedias

1047 American popular music. 8v. Richard Carlin, ed. Facts on File, 2006. $$

781.64   ML102

This eight-volume set devotes one volume to each of seven music genres—blues; classical; country; folk; jazz; rhythm and blues, rap, and hip-hop; and rock and roll—and rounds out the collection with a comprehensive index. Subjects include songs, musicians, instruments, organizations, seminal recordings, record companies, venues, and related sociopolitical issues. Each volume includes photographs, chronology, discography or bibliography, glossary, and index. This work provides an ideal starting point for junior high and high school students researching musical topics. Electronic version available.

1048 The American songbook: The singers, songwriters, and the songs. Ken Bloom. 320p. Black Dog and Leventhal, 2005. $

782.42   ML3477

This visually striking volume presents an illustrated history of twentieth-century American popular song and the 200 most prominent performers and songwriters of the era, including Louis Armstrong, Bing Crosby, Rosemary Clooney, Ella Fitzgerald, Stephen Foster, Richard Rodgers, Duke Ellington, and Cole Porter. Each entry contains information about the artist's life and career, famous songs, important contributions, record covers, anecdotes, quotes, and photographs. Hundreds of songs and related topics are featured throughout the book. Coverage is not comprehensive but provides a good overview, particularly of Tin Pan Alley artists. The volume includes song lists, capsule biographies, and an index.

1049 The encyclopedia of popular music. 4th ed. Colin Larkin, ed. 10v. Oxford, 2006. $$$$

781.64   ML102

The fourth edition of this monumental work expands on previous editions by adding more than 6,000 new entries for a total of 27,000 entries.

Coverage includes the popular music of the United States and United Kingdom in the twentieth and twenty-first centuries, including rock, pop, country, jazz, soul, blues, reggae, show tunes, techno, rap, and world music. Entries vary in length from a paragraph to several pages and cover individuals, bands, recordings, musical theater, films, record labels, and related topics. A useful album rating system ranks albums from outstanding (five stars) to poor (one star). This work's comprehensive nature makes it a worthy addition to library collections. Its inclusion via the Oxford Music Online gateway only enhances its usefulness.

1050 Encyclopedia of rap and hip hop culture. Yvonne Bynoe. 449p. Greenwood, 2006. $

782.421649   ML102

This comprehensive work covers the four components of hip-hop—MCing (or rapping), B-boying (or break dancing), DJing, and aerosol art (or graffiti)—providing a much-needed reference source about the thirty-year-old genre. The A–Z listing includes artists such as Dr. Dre, the Beastie Boys, Eminem, and the Sugar Hill Gang, who released the first commercially successful rap record, "Rapper's Delight," in 1979. Also included are entries for subjects (gangsta rap, censorship); record labels (Def Jam Recordings, Death Row Records); films (*Boyz n the Hood*, blaxploitation); and musical techniques (scratching, beatboxing). Entries range from a paragraph to several pages, with cross-references and select illustrations. The volume includes a well-written introduction on the history of hip-hop, a selected discography of rap, a selected bibliography, an index, and the Hip Hop Declaration of Peace, presented to the United Nations in 2002.

1051 Encyclopedia of television theme songs. Mark A. Robinson. 207p. McFarland, 2011. $

781.5   ML102

This entertaining resource contains approximately 1,000 entries organized alphabetically by TV series. Individual entries list the theme song with composer, lyricist, performer, cast credits, television network, years of original run, and program description. Anecdotes and other information about each theme song such as the theme's popularity and any awards are included. Electronic version available.

1052 The Grove dictionary of American music. 2nd ed. Charles Hiroshi Garrett, ed. 8v. Oxford, 2013. $$$$

780.973   ML101

The second print edition of this influential work is twice the size of the first edition, reflecting, in part, the growth of scholarship about American music since its initial publication in 1986. Topics covered include music education, musical terms, dance styles, musical instruments, the history of American orchestra, and biographies of performers, composers, and music patrons. New and revised content is also available electronically in Grove Music Online, available via the Oxford Music Online gateway. Grove Music Online has full-text searching and links to related resources, including images and examples of musical styles and concepts. The convenient online platform makes regular updates and additions to the content possible.

1053 The Rolling Stone encyclopedia of rock & roll: Revised and updated for the 21st century. 3rd ed. Holly George-Warren, Patricia Romanowksi, and John Pareles, eds. 1114p. Fireside/Simon & Schuster, 2001. $

781.66   ML102

Now in its third edition, this authoritative encyclopedia covers rock and roll artists from the 1950s to the twenty-first century. The scope of this work is broad and includes artists as diverse as Elvis, Britney Spears, Eminem, and 'N Sync. The new edition includes revisions to the 1,800 existing entries and more than 100 new entries. Alphabetical entries contain vital statistics, discography, and critical essays detailing the performer's career and contribution to the field. Considered the premier guide to the history of rock and roll, this work is the official source of information for the Rock and Roll Hall of Fame and Museum.

World Music

Databases and Indexes

1054 Smithsonian Global Sound for libraries. Alexander Street Press. glmu.alexanderstreet.com. $$$$

This database is available on the web through annual subscription and contains more than 35,000 tracks of music, spoken word, and other sounds, including the Smithsonian Folkways collection, founded by Moses Asch. The variety of recordings is immense, from a frog being eaten by a snake to classical violin instruction. The virtual encyclopedia also includes readings of plays, poetry, and other literary works, some spoken by the authors themselves. The children's collection includes songs, games, stories, and sing-alongs from around the world. The majority of the recordings are North American in origin. Controlled vocabularies enable users to browse by a variety of fields, including country, cultural group, genre, or instrument. The service allows the creation of password-protected, custom playlists and course folders with static URLs. The publisher also offers two subsets: Smithsonian Global Sound for Libraries—North America, with 19,000 tracks, and Smithsonian Folkways Recordings Online, covering approximately 325 CDs from the Folkways collection. This resource is available through annual subscription from Alexander Street Press and is cross-searchable with all of the Alexander Street Press Music Online databases to which the library subscribes.

Dictionaries and Encyclopedias

1055 Continuum encyclopedia of popular music of the world. 8v. John Shepherd, David Horn, and Dave Laing, eds. Continuum, 2003–. $$$$

781.63   ML102

This ambitious set, projected to be twelve volumes, presents the world's popular music from a geographical and cultural perspective. Each volume is organized around a topic or geographic area. Scholarly articles are written by contributors from all over the world and contain extensive bibliographies and discographies. Geographic volumes include high-level historical surveys of regional and national popular music as well as narrowly focused entries about the music of a particular city. Electronic version available.

1056 The Garland encyclopedia of world music. 10v. Bruno Nettl and Ruth M. Stone, eds. Routledge, 1997–2002. $$$$

780.9   ML100

1057 The concise Garland encyclopedia of world music. 2v. Ellen Koskoff et al., eds. Routledge, 2008. $$

780.3   ML100

This impressive ten-volume set is the leading resource for ethnomusicology research. Each volume focuses on a specific region of the world and examines the influence of music on the society, art, and culture of that region's people. Entries are written by international, multidisciplinary scholars and include photographs, drawings, maps, and musical notations. Each volume includes an accompanying CD with relevant music examples. Indexes and glossaries are also included. This groundbreaking resource was awarded the Dartmouth Medal and was named one of *Library Journal*'s 50 Reference Sources for the Millennium.

This resource is also available from Alexander Street Press as part of Music Online and is cross-searchable with all of the Alexander Street Press music databases to which the library subscribes. This online database is available either by annual subscription or through one-time purchase of perpetual rights, with prices scaled to budget and full-time enrollment. Libraries that cannot afford the ten-volume survey will definitely want to acquire the *Concise Garland Encyclopedia of World Music*. This two-volume set retains the global perspective and scholarly integrity of the original content, but presents topics in language that is more accessible to a general audience. The volumes continue to be organized geographically and include photos, maps, diagrams, musical notations, selected audio examples, and brief bibliographies.

15 *Crafts and Hobbies*

CAROLE DYAL

Works published for crafters and hobbyists can be wonderfully entertaining. While they may not be as scholarly or academic as other reference materials, they must be well organized and easy to use. Instructions must be clear but also inspirational for the enthusiast. Many of the works in this chapter are appropriate not only for the reference collection but also for the circulating collection. A rich source for any crafter or hobbyist is the Internet. A keyword search will produce unlimited websites with extraordinary amounts of information, ideas, and guidance for any hobby or craft; indeed, many of the publishers of the guides noted here produce elaborate websites with much additional information. However, the Internet does not often supply the kind of overview and general context that crafters and hobbyists need to grasp the essence of their field of interest, nor does it provide the portability and durability that hard copy allows.

General Sources

Handbooks

1058 Favorite hobbies and pastimes: A sourcebook of leisure pursuits. Robert S. Munson. 366p. American Library Association, 1994. $
790.1   GV1201.5

A book of descriptions and information sources for eighty-four hobbies and pastimes. Entries are arranged alphabetically and range from three to six pages; they provide an overview of the pastime or hobby and often include a brief history as well as specifics detailing rules and equipment or tools needed. Entries close with a brief bibliography listing reference books, periodicals, and associations for the hobbyist. For those who like to browse library shelves, a listing of library classification call numbers is given, and a subject index provides a further subdivision of the various entries.

1059 Health hazards manual for artists. 6th ed. Michael McCann and Angela Babin. 181p. Lyons Press, 2008. $
615.9   RC963.6

Supplies commonly used by artists and crafters are often highly toxic. This guide describes the relationship of such toxic materials to specific diseases and gives the threshold limit values for many common chemicals used in art and hobby materials, including raw materials, pigments and dyes, solvents, and plastics. New chapters include limits for metals and minerals as well as basic first aid suggestions. Safe substitutes for toxic materials are listed. Precautions are clearly articulated, including protective equipment and proper disposal of materials. Organizations and published works of relevance are described.

1060 Martha Stewart's encyclopedia of crafts: An A-to-Z guide with detailed instructions and endless inspiration. Martha Stewart. 416p. Crown/Potter Craft, 2009. $

745.5   TT157

More than 400 pages with thirty-two chapters of various craft techniques from albums and scrapbooks to wreaths will inspire the beginner as well as the seasoned crafter. Each chapter begins with an overview and description of a specific theme followed by materials needed, safety tips, and care and handling tips, with a detailed listing of supplies. Several specific projects per technique are included with step-by-step instructions and gorgeous photographs to illustrate the various steps. The general section describing tools and materials will be very helpful for the novice crafter. Templates for many of the designs, an extensive list of tools and sources, and a buyer's guide for specific projects are included as appendixes. The index is comprehensive.

Crafts

Beading

1061 The bead directory: The complete guide to choosing and using more than 600 beautiful beads. Elise Mann. 256p. Interweave Press, 2006. $

745.58   TT860

Chapters are arranged by bead composition, including glass, stones, wood, and ceramics, for more than 600 individual beads. Beads are pictured from all angles to allow foolproof identifications. Descriptions include dimensions, possible colors, weight, possible uses, and special care. Suppliers are listed in both store locations and websites. Well indexed.

1062 Beadwork: A world guide. Caroline Crabtree and Pam Stallebrass. 208p. Rizzoli, 2002. $

745.58   NK3650

This volume is beautifully illustrated with beading techniques and beading examples from cultures around the world. A history of beading is followed by various manufacturing centers and historical trading patterns. Examples of beadwork from four main geographical areas (Africa, America, Asia, and Europe) make up the majority of the book. There is a bibliography by country as well listings of beading collections. Tips for collecting and for the proper storage of beads are included. The section on construction and techniques is appropriate for the more experienced beader, but beaders of all levels will be inspired by the extensive and diverse examples of beadwork from around the world. The extensive index is by country and also by technique.

1063 The encyclopedia of beading techniques: A step-by-step visual guide, with an inspirational gallery of finished works. Sara Withers and Stephanie Burnham. 160p. Running Press, 2005. $

745.5   TT860

This is a true step-by-step visual guide to beading. The first section focuses on tools and materials, including how to identify and select beads, threads, and tools. Small color photographs are shown with detail explaining each item. In section 2, various techniques, including traditional and contemporary methods, are well illustrated with step-by-step instructions. Section 3 will serve as an inspiration to beaders, featuring more than thirty pages of finished examples of each type of beading covered in the second section. A short list of resources, including societies, suppliers, and websites, is included. Well indexed.

1064 The illustrated bead bible: Terms, tips, and techniques. Theresa Flores Geary. 406p. Sterling, 2008. $

745.58   TT860

This comprehensive guide to the world of beads is very well organized and easy to use. The introduction gives a quick overview of the culture and history of beads. Part 2 is more than 300 pages and provides an A–Z listing of beads and beading terms with very clear photographs for bead types. Part 3 is a section of beading techniques and tips presented as questions and answers in an easy style that is fun to read straight through. This is followed by a section of beading tables and charts that go into some detail on bead types, finishes, and appearance. The final section is a how-to with simple and clear illustrations for beading, embellishments, knotting, and finishing. An extensive bibliography, including Internet resources, is included. The index is good and includes many cross-references.

1065 Teach yourself visually: Beadwork; Learning off-loom beading techniques one stitch at a time. Chris Franchetti Michaels. 245p. Visual/Wiley, 2009. $

745.58   TT860

An excellent guide for the beginning or intermediate beader, this volume is a step-by-step course for dozens of beading patterns. Each step is illustrated with a detailed photograph or drawing. Tips and frequently asked questions are included throughout the directions. The first two chapters are an introduction to beadwork and basic skills and techniques, from simple stitches to finishing techniques. The last chapters demonstrate specific projects. There is an online appendix available through the publisher's website that includes Internet resources, detailed bead sizes, common units of sales for seed beads, protective coatings, and troubleshooting. These additional nine pages should have been included as part of the printed volume with online updates.

Ceramics

1066 The ceramics bible: The complete guide to materials and techniques. Louisa Taylor. 287p. Chronicle, 2011. $

738.14   NK4235

This is a beautiful as well as practical resource and guide for anyone interested in working with clay. The photographs are so lovely; it could pass for a coffee-table book. The first section covers materials and tools, including safety procedures. The next section gives an overview of forming and building techniques. Glazing and firing techniques are followed by decorative and finishing techniques. Profiles of

ceramic artists with photographs of their pieces are included throughout the book. The artists' works serve as examples of procedures discussed but also provide inspiration. The book concludes with a section of useful resources, including places for formal study, suppliers, and a select bibliography. A true how-to reference beautifully presented.

Knitting and Crocheting

1067 Big book of knitting stitch patterns. Sterling Publishing Company Staff. 288p. Sterling, 2004. $

746.43   TT820

This book contains more than 550 knitting patterns made from nearly 150 different stitches. Basic stitches and patterns are covered extensively; other patterns are presented two per page. A black-and-white knitting chart as a well as a color photograph of each pattern is included. Patterns are presented alphabetically within traditional categories. In addition to basic, classic, crossover, creative, lace, textured, and slipstitches are multicolored and jacquard patterns.

1068 Crochet stitches visual encyclopedia: 300 stitch patterns, edgings, and more. Robyn Chachula. 272p. Wiley, 2011. $

746.43   TT820

This is not a how-to crochet book. This is an encyclopedia of more than 300 stitch patterns ranging from basic stitches, textured stitches, lace patterns, multicolor patterns, squares, and snowflakes to simple and special edgings. The color photos are straightforward and clear. The instructions are presented with traditional crochet symbols and diagrams, so a knowledge of basic techniques will be necessary to use the patterns. However, the comprehensiveness and coherent organization of the stitches makes this a valuable reference tool for any crocheter.

1069 Reader's Digest knitter's handbook: A comprehensive guide to the principles and techniques of handknitting. Montse Stanley. 318p. Reader's Digest, 2001. $

746.43   TT820

A truly comprehensive compendium of knitting techniques. At once clearly written and remarkably detailed, this work will appeal to both beginners and advanced students. Includes gauge charts and pattern instructions. Extra detail for finishing touches, including button holing and edging, is provided. Also included is a "Help" section to diagnose and remedy common knitting problems. All techniques discussed are well illustrated.

1070 A treasury of knitting patterns.
Reprint ed. Barbara G. Walker. 320p. Schoolhouse Press, 1998. $
746.4   TT820
A second treasury of knitting patterns. Reprint ed. Barbara G. Walker. 398p. Schoolhouse Press, 1998. $
746.4   TT820
Charted knitting designs: A third treasury of knitting patterns. Reprint ed. Barbara G. Walker. 269p. Schoolhouse Press, 2010. $
746.432   TT820
A fourth treasury of knitting patterns. Barbara G. Walker. 241p. Schoolhouse Press, 2001. $
746.4   TT820
These are reprints of classic knitting stitch pattern compendia illustrated with closeup photographs of stitches along with explicit directions on how to knit more than 500 patterns. Includes simple knit-purl combinations, ribbings, color-change patterns, slip-stitch patterns, twist-stitch patterns, fancy texture patterns, patterns made with yarn-over stitches, eyelet patterns, lace, cables, and cable-stitch patterns. Includes information on the origin and use of patterns. Indexed.

1071 Ultimate crochet bible: A complete reference with step-by-step techniques. Jane Crowfoot. 304p. Sterling/ Collins & Brown, 2010. $
746.43   TT820
This is a wonderful and comprehensive guide to the art and craft of crochet. Beginners as well as advanced practitioners will enjoy this detailed presentation. The book opens with a history of crochet and goes through a detailed discussion of hook selection and other equipment, including yarns. The next 250 pages are a detailed manual of

various stitches and patterns. The section after that demonstrates professional finishing techniques, including joining pieces. Tips for care and storage of finished items are given. A glossary of terms and an index complete the guide.

1072 Vogue knitting: The ultimate knitting book. 280p. Sixth & Spring Books, 2002. $
746.43   TT820
A basic encyclopedia of knitting that is clearly written and easy to comprehend. Includes a history of knitting and a stitch dictionary that illustrates more than 120 popular stitches. Describes knitting supplies and basic techniques, including how to design garments. Includes 1,600 full-color illustrations.

Needlework

1073 The complete encyclopedia of needlework. 4th ed. Thérèse de Dillmont. 702p. Running Press, 2002. $
746.4   TT705
Originally published in France in the nineteenth century, this work offers a very traditional approach to stitchery, describing needlework ranging from linen and silk embroidery to tapestry. Provides directions for both simple and advanced techniques of every kind of needlework, including sewing and knitting.

1074 The complete encyclopedia of stitchery. Mildred Graves Ryan. 689p. Sterling, 2005. $
746.4   TT760
Firefly's step-by-step encyclopedia of needlecraft: Patchwork, embroidery, quilting, sewing, knitting, crochet, appliqué. Louise Dixon, ed. 320p. Firefly, 2011. $
746.4   TT705
The needlecraft book. Maggi Gordon, Sally Harding, and Ellie Vance. 400p. Dorling Kindersley, 2010. $
746.4   TT705
These three volumes are all very good comprehensive guides for beginners as well as experienced crafters. Each one has overviews of various modern

techniques arranged by general categories (e.g., knitting, embroidery, and needlepoint). The *Complete Encyclopedia* includes rug making and tatting. *Firefly's Step-by-Step Encyclopedia* includes many extra tips for machine work.

1075 The complete illustrated stitch encyclopedia. Crafter's Choice Staff. 320p. Sterling, 2004. $
746.44   TT771
This encyclopedia is very well illustrated with easy-to-follow directions for more than 250 hand stitches. Each technique is demonstrated and explained in full. The introduction includes a fabric guide and describes the particular language of the various stitches. The stitches are then presented by type, from embroidery to needlepoint to special techniques to finishing, which includes tassels and fringes. Examples and finished projects are pictured after each section. The index is easy to use.

1076 The needlepoint book: A complete update of the classic guide. Rev. ed. Jo Ippolito Christensen. 448p. Touchstone, 1999. $
746.4   TT771
Originally published in 1976, this resource is a complete guide to the craft of needlepoint. A sixteen-page section of projects photographed in color are inspirational. Updates include new fabrics and fibers and how to work with them. More than 1,300 illustrations are shown with more than 370 stitches. Common errors with suggestions of how to avoid them are given. A true classic.

1077 Stitch sampler. Lucinda Ganderton. 160p. Dorling Kindersley, 2006. $
746.46   TT770
Some 234 stitches are illustrated in a "gallery of stitches." The small color photographs in the gallery magnify each stitch, list the name, and refer the sewer to the exact page for instructions. The instructions are two to a page and give alternative names for the stitches, level of expertise required, various uses for the stitch, and what the method of stitch is as well as step-by-step instructions with simple and clear color photographs. Technique variations are often provided as well as appropriate

materials. The introduction gives an overview of materials, tools, and equipment needed.

1078 The ultimate A to Z companion to 1,001 needlecraft terms: Appliqué, crochet, embroidery, knitting, quilting, sewing. Marie Clayton. 192p. St. Martin's Griffin, 2008. $
746.4   TT715
This book serves as a handy reference for more than 1,000 needlecraft terms. New terms for old techniques as well as old terms for "forgotten" techniques are included. Simple yet effective drawings accompany many terms. Cross-references are given as well as explanations of multiple meanings for some entries. Sewing pattern symbols are defined as well as international care instruction symbols. Includes measurement conversion charts and common abbreviations. A compact but comprehensive compendium for any needlecraft collection.

Quilting

1079 Complete guide to quilting. Better Homes and Gardens, 320p. Meredith Books, 2012. $
746.46   TT835
Complete guide to quilting techniques: Essential techniques and step-by-step projects for making beautiful quilts. Pauline Brown. 256p. Reader's Digest, 2006. $
746.46   TT835
Quilting: The complete guide. Darlene Zimmerman. 255p. Krause, 2007. $
746.46   TT835
Quilter's complete guide. Rev. ed. Marianne Fons and Liz Porter. 272p. Leisure Arts, 2000. $
746.97   TT835
All of these titles are excellent comprehensive guides to quilting, describing requisite equipment and supplies and introducing quilting skills in an accessible how-to approach. Layouts and quilt planning with yardage charts are given. In each case, several examples are included along with practical projects.

1080 Encyclopedia of pieced quilt patterns.
Barbara Brackman, comp. 551p.
American Quilter's Society, 1993. $
746.46   TT835

Spanning the years 1830–1980, this encyclopedia presents the most complete index to published American quilt designs in existence. A simple black-and-white graphic illustration is provided for each pattern indexed. Designs are presented in twenty-five clearly differentiated categories (one patch, strip, four patch, wheels, fans, etc.), each with several subdivisions. Provides the original publication source of reference for each pattern. This is both a practical tool and a historical catalog. A masterpiece. Extensive bibliography.

1081 5,500 quilt block designs. Maggie
Malone. 448p. Sterling, 2005. $
746.46   TT835

This is a visual feast for quilters of all levels. The color line drawings are clearly organized by pattern type, from traditional nine-patch patterns to more elaborate twenty-four-patch patterns. Circle and curve patches are included as well as octagons and stars and alphabets. International signal flags are also shown. Each section begins with a grid that can be used to create the pattern. The color illustrations very clearly display each pattern. Alternative names for patterns are given, and a key at the beginning of the book reveals when the pattern first appeared and in what publication. Not as comprehensive for research as the *Encyclopedia of Pieced Quilt Patterns* but a wonderful addition to any quilting collection. The index is by pattern name.

**1082 The quilter's album of patchwork
patterns: More than 4050 pieced
blocks for quilters.** Jinny Beyer. 488p.
Breckling, 2009. $
746.46   TT835

Quilt patterns from the 1800s to 1970 have been carefully sorted and organized for this inspirational volume. Blocks are first sorted by straight lines and then curved lines. The straight line blocks are then organized by grid type (2x2, 3x3, etc.). Curved blocks follow, then hexagons, continuous patterns, one-patch blocks, and miscellaneous blocks. There is a good introduction to drafting designs using base grids that is made even more useful by

transparent stencils in a back pocket with grid lines drawn on them. A thorough bibliography of the historical sources for the original blocks is included. Block names are indexed.

Scrapbooking and Cardmaking

**1083 Creating keepsakes: The encyclopedia
of scrapbooking.** 318p. Leisure Arts,
2005. $
745.59   TR645

From the editors of Creating Keepsakes *Scrapbook Magazine*, this is a principal guide for scrapbooking. A brief history of scrapbooks in America going back to the mid-1800s begins this volume. Basics from a tool guide to advanced embellishments are discussed and illustrated. The table of contents is quite thorough and can be used as an alternative to an index. Appendixes cover archiving tips as well as computer applications. A listing of resources, a glossary, and an index complete this useful book.

**1084 The encyclopedia of scrapbooking
tools and techniques.** Susan Pickering
Rothamel. 320p. Sterling, 2009. $
745.59   TR645

This encyclopedia begins with a history timeline of scrapbooks that goes back further than the *Creating Keepsakes* volume. From John Locke's 1705 *New Method of Making Commonplace Books* to the late 1980s, scrapbooking has a fun history. Topics are arranged alphabetically with generous color illustrations. Every essential scrapbooking tool or technique is described in this thorough reference work. Sections on storage tips and photograph preservation are included. The acknowledgments include many websites for additional information as well as companies, including telephone numbers, for supplies. Scrapbooking publications and magazines are listed. In addition to a regular index is a twelve-page project index for quick reference to the multitude of projects and ideas presented.

**1085 Ultimate cardmaking: A collection
of over 100 techniques and 50
inspirational projects.** Sarah Beaman.
192p. Collins & Brown, 2008. $
745.59   TT872

This is a straightforward and basic guide to card-making. Tools and materials are photographed and clearly described. The descriptions of more than 100 specific techniques include multiple photographs to cover each step. The written instructions are easy to follow. Two-thirds of the book is dedicated to inspiring projects incorporating the techniques described earlier on. Quick and simple as well as elaborate and time-consuming cards are described. This is a solid, well-designed guide for the cardmaking crafter.

Sewing

1086 Claire Shaeffer's fabric sewing guide.
2nd ed. rev. Claire B. Shaeffer. 525p.
Krause, 2008. $
646.4   TT557

This is the most comprehensive guide to the selection, wear, care, and sewing of all fabrics. Part 1 describes fiber content, including natural fibers, man-made fibers, leathers, synthetic suedes, vinyls, furs, and feathers. Part 2 discusses fabric structure: woven fabrics, knits, and stretch-woven fabrics. Part 3 discusses all manner of fabric surface characteristics, including special-occasion fabrics such as satin and taffeta, sequined and beaded fabrics, and lace and net; napped and pile fabrics; felt and felted fabrics; reversible fabrics; quilted fabrics; and fabrics with designs, such as plaids, stripes, and prints. Part 4 discusses linings and interfacings. Part 5 describes sewing techniques, such as seams, hems, edge finishes, closures, and hand stitches. Part 6 is a fabric and fiber dictionary. There are several useful appendixes, including one on burn tests for fiber identification, as well as many other useful tips. A resource section, glossary, bibliography, and lengthy index complete this fine resource.

1087 Complete book of sewing: A practical step-by-step guide to every technique.
Rev. ed. Chris Jefferys et al. 320p.
Dorling Kindersley, 2006. $
646.2   TT705
Complete photo guide to sewing: 1200 full-color how-to photos. Rev. ed. Singer Sewing Machine Company, eds. 352p. Creative Publishing International, 2009. $
646.2   TT713

New complete guide to sewing: Step-by-step techniques for making clothes and home accessories. Reader's Digest Editors. Updated ed. 384p. Reader's Digest, 2011. $
646.2   TT705

These basic sewing guides complement each other well. The Dorling Kindersley volume is fully illustrated with color photographs, color drawings, and charts. Chapters begin with an easy-to-follow guide to the ensuing sections and techniques. Tools, patterns, notions, fabrics, general techniques, and professional techniques, including finishing and tailoring, are included. A small section on mending is useful. The glossary and index are extensive. The Reader's Digest volume contains more color line drawings but is very easy to follow. Projects are included for each section that well illustrate the particular techniques described. There is also a section on pattern altering for men, lacking in the others. The sections on sewing supplies and fabric selection are in color, and the fabric guide is quite useful. The *Complete Photo Guide* is a step-by-step guide to sewing. Each step is clearly illustrated with a color photograph. Chapters begin with a text overview followed by specific directions. Because each book is slightly different in approach, sewers may want to compare illustrations and directions from each volume for an exceptionally thorough understanding of each technique.

1088 Encyclopedia of sewing machine techniques. Nancy Bednar and JoAnne Pugh-Gannon. 336p. Sterling, 2007. $
646.2   TT713

This paperback volume illustrates how to use a sewing machine to its fullest potential. An overview of how to use a machine (any brand) is given as well as generic maintenance tips. The guide on how to select from all the available needles and thread is straightforward. Every presser foot imaginable is detailed with a photograph and then an illustration of the final product the particular foot creates. This is followed by specific tips for each foot. The next section details creative sewing techniques; this is followed by descriptions of indispensable standard techniques. A list of manufacturers and contacts is included. The index is thorough and includes the many tips described.

1089 The Vogue/Butterick step-by-step guide to sewing techniques. 2013 ed. Editors of Vogue and Butterick Patterns.

428p. Sixth & Spring, 2012. $
646.2   TT705
Demonstrates more than 500 of the 2,000 dress-making procedures regularly used in Vogue and Butterick patterns. The alphabetical organization makes this easy to use. The illustrations are well placed. This is a fundamental reference for any sewer. The index is thorough. The vocabulary list is linked to page numbers. The forty-seven sections focus on specific garment pieces or specific techniques (e.g., appliqués, basting, buttonholes, collars, linings, marking, and ruffles).

Woodworking

1090 The complete illustrated guide to furniture and cabinet construction.
Andy Rae. 308p. Taunton Press, 2001. $
684.1   TT195
The complete illustrated guide to joinery. Gary Rogowski. 390p. Taunton Press, 2002. $
684.1   TT185
Setting up shop: The practical guide to designing and building your dream shop. Rev. ed. Sandor Nagyszalanczy. 236p. Taunton Press, 2006. $
684.08   TT152
Taunton's complete illustrated guide to box making. Doug Stowe. 160p. Taunton Press, 2005. $
684.08   TT200
Taunton's complete illustrated guide to choosing and installing hardware. Robert J. Settich. 224p. Taunton Press, 2003. $
684.1   TT186
Taunton's complete illustrated guide to finishing. Jeff Jewitt. 302p. Taunton Press, 2004. $
684.1   TT199
Taunton's complete illustrated guide to sharpening. Thomas Lie-Nielsen. 224p. Taunton Press, 2004. $
684.08   TT186
Taunton's complete illustrated guide to using woodworking tools. Lonnie Bird. 288p. Taunton Press, 2004. $
684.08   TT186

Taunton's complete illustrated guide to working with wood. Andy Rae. 288p. Taunton Press, 2005. $
684.08   TT180
The Taunton Press has provided a truly comprehensive set of reference materials for the woodworker at any level of experience. Each volume is filled with explicit, very high-quality photographs. An easy-to-use visual map at the beginning of each section guides readers to details or essays for specific operations. In addition, each section begins with a thorough overview; the visual guide allows those who want to skip the overview to go directly to specific techniques. The step-by-step instructions are accompanied by illustrations that are mostly photographs but include some drawings. Included are tips, multiple variations on techniques and processes, and safety concerns. Within each essay, or set of instructions, are cross-references to related operations. An extensive index, suggested further readings, suppliers, and organizations complete each volume in this useful set. These titles are also available in electronic format.

1091 Hand tools: Their ways and workings. Aldren A. Watson. 416p. W. W. Norton, 2002. $
684.08   T186
How to identify and use hand woodworking tools. More than 450 drawings detail how each tool is properly used and what it can be used for. Includes suggested workbench plans and hand-tool shop inventories. The text is straightforward with good woodworking hints. Step-by-step instructions are provided. The index is by name of individual tools.

1092 The real wood bible: The complete illustrated guide to choosing and using 100 decorative woods. Nick Gibbs. 256p. Firefly, 2005. $
684.08   TT180
This handy book is a straightforward guide to the woods most commonly used by woodworkers. Also included are woods that are less available but still appropriate for woodworking. The introduction gives an overview of the transformation of trees into boards. Endangered species to be avoided are listed. Various methods of cutting lumber, drying rates, common defects, and storage tips are included. The guide begins with a thumbnail

photograph directing readers to the appropriate page for a detailed description. A clear true-to-size photograph to show grain and figure accompanies each one-page overview. Strengths, weaknesses, key characteristics, and key uses are given for each wood. A small section on special effects of grain, figuring, burls, and identifying quartersawn surfaces precedes the glossary and index.

1093 Taunton's complete illustrated guide to woodworking. Lonnie Bird. 311p. Taunton Press, 2005. $
684.08   TT180

This book is a concise version of the first six volumes of Taunton's Complete Illustrated Guide series. It combines in one volume basic and essential information for any woodworker. The format is the same as for the larger series: high-quality photographs, well-designed step-by-step instructions, and numerous cross-references. The appendix includes further readings, sources for materials, organizations, and a quick guide to wood types. This title is also available in electronic format.

1094 Tool smarts: Workshop dust control. Editors of American Woodworker Magazine. 133p. Fox Chapel, 2010. $
684.08   TT180

This volume addresses the sometimes overlooked hazards of working with wood dust. Everything needed to establish a safe and clean work environment for the home woodworker is contained in this important safety guide. Color photographs accompany extensive discussions of workshop dust issues. The guide offers safety tips from personal respirators to shop-wide air filtration systems that can be built by the woodworker. Sources for materials and a good index are included.

Hobbies

Antiques and Collectibles

1095 Antique trader antiques and collectibles price guide. Krause, 1984–. Annual. $
745.1   NK1125

With more than 1,000 pages, this is the biggest of the antiques and collectibles price guides. There

are more than 4,000 color photographs and more than 18,000 entries in 160 category types. Prices are for items in good condition. Descriptive information accompanies each illustration, which helps to ensure more accurate identification of items. The table of contents lists the categories while the index contains many other entries with cross-references.

1096 Kovels' antiques and collectibles price guide. Terry Kovel and Kim Kovel. Crown Publishers, 1982–. Annual. $
745.1   NK1125

Prices listed are asking prices for the American market: what costs what and when. Listings are by category and then by object, followed by a description. There are more than 45,000 entries in more than 700 categories along with more than 2,500 color photographs in this edition. Product logos as well as tips about care and identification of collectibles are included. A report details items that sold for unusually high prices over the past year. The alphabetical listing is easy to use. The index contains many cross-references.

1097 Warman's antiques and collectibles price guide: The essential field guide to the antiques and collectibles marketplace. Krause, 1994–. Annual. $
745.1   NK1133

Now in full color, this guide includes objects made between 1700 and the present. More than 50,000 objects are listed alphabetically by category, with a capsule history of the object, bibliographic references, periodicals, clubs, museums, photographs, and marks. Within each category, objects that are actively being sold in the antiques market are listed with clear descriptions and asking prices from auctions and dealers. Prices tend to be for items in very good condition. Well indexed.

Coins and Paper Money

1098 The coin atlas: A comprehensive view of the coins of the world throughout history. Joe Cribb et al. 224p. Chartwell Books, 2004. $
737.49   CJ59

This historical atlas of coinage provides a political history of each country's coinage, amply illustrated with more than 400 photographs. More than 100 maps indicate location of mints and general circulation of coins. Includes glossary, selective bibliography, and an index of persons, places, events, metals, and minting processes.

1099 Coins and currency: An historical encyclopedia. Mary Ellen Snodgrass. 562p. McFarland, 2003. $

737.4   CJ59

With more than 250 entries, this volume is an encyclopedia of the use of money throughout history. Included is a timeline of important events in monetary history, from 3,500 BC (Sumerian coin shell money) to AD 2002 (introduction of the Euro). Black-and-white photographs throughout highlight various entries. The entries are listed in the beginning followed by numerous *see* references. A chart lists world currencies by symbol, name of currency, and nation or geographical area for the currency. A glossary lists monetary terms used throughout the encyclopedia and is followed by an extensive bibliography. The index has main entries in bold and illustrations in brackets for easy reference.

1100 Coin world almanac. 8th ed. Beth Deisher et al., eds. 678p. Amos Press, 2011. $

737.4   CJ1

This work contains "the essential facts which form the permanent record of numismatics." Twenty-four chapters record this information through essays, tables, statistics, and directories. Topics covered include coin collecting, investing, paper money, counterfeits, rarities, commemorative coins, and coin design. Highlights from the rare coin market in the last decade are included. Museums, societies, and organizations of interest to coin collectors are listed.

1101 The official blackbook price guide to U.S. paper money. 45th ed. Thomas E. Hudgeons. 400p. House of Collectibles, 2012. $

769.55   HG591

Standard catalog of U.S. paper money. 31st ed. George S. Cuhaj. 480p. Krause, 2012. $

769.5   HG591

Standard catalog of world paper

money, vol. 1: Specialized issues. 11th ed. George S. Cuhaj. 1248p. Krause, 2009. $

769.5   HG353

Standard catalog of world paper money, vol. 2: General issues. 14th ed. George S. Cuhaj. 1296p. Krause, 2012. $

769.5   HG353

Standard catalog of world paper money, vol. 3: Modern issues. 18th ed. George S. Cuhaj. 1160p. Krause, 2012. $

769.5   HG353

These catalogs describe paper money, the use of which dates as far back as the fourteenth century. They provide listings of prices for paper money in various conditions. There is also a variety of supplementary data in each book, depending on the particular specialty that is being covered. Nearly 300 past and current governments are covered in the world volumes. Bank notes issued by states, municipalities, and companies are covered in the U.S. volumes. Each volume also includes general collection care guidelines. All have extensive black-and-white illustrations with pricing information along with currency-grading guidelines adopted by the Grading Committee of the International Bank Note Society.

1102 The official blackbook price guide to U.S. coins. House of Collectibles, 1979–. Annual. $

737.4   CJ1735

Standard catalog of world coins, 1901–present. Krause, 1972–. Annual. $

737.4   CJ1751

Standard catalog of world coins: Seventeenth century, 1601–1700. 5th ed. George S. Cuhaj and Thomas Michael, eds. 1560p. Krause, 2011. $

737.4   CJ1751

Standard catalog of world coins: Eighteenth century, 1701–1800. 5th ed. George S. Cuhaj and Thomas Michael, eds. 1344p. Krause, 2010. $

737.4   CJ1751

Standard directory of world coins: Nineteenth century, 1801–1900. 7th ed. George S. Cuhaj and Thomas Michael, eds. 1344p. Krause, 2012. $

737.4   CJ1751

The purpose of these catalogs is to help collectors identify coins and to list the market prices for coins in various conditions. The world coins volumes contain detailed descriptions of international calendars and dating systems with lengthy explanations for identification. They generally provide a history of each coin, date of minting, size, and identification marks. There is also a variety of supplementary data in each book, depending on the particular specialty that is being covered. Each volume also includes sections on caring for coins.

1103 World encyclopedia of coins and coin collecting. James Mackay. 256p. Lorenz, 2010. $
737.40   CJ67

This is a general and pictorial history of coins of the world. Arranged by continent, with beautiful color photographs, this book is a good introduction to the world of coins and coin collecting. A brief history of coins is given, followed by more specific factors to look for in coins (e.g., denominations and type of metal). This is an introduction to the world and history of coins and coin collecting, not an exhaustive survey.

Stamps

1104 The official blackbook price guide to U.S. postage stamps. House of Collectibles, 1970–. Annual. $
769.56   HE6185

Easy-to-use basic guidebook with valuations of more than 20,000 stamps. How to buy, sell, and care for stamps. Many color photographs.

1105 Specialized catalogue of United States stamps. Scott, 1867–. Annual. $
769   HE6185

Scott's standard postage stamp catalogue. 6v. Scott, 1923–. Annual. $
769.56   HE6226

Scott provides the most comprehensive catalog of stamps printed in the United States. Gives minute details, such as date of issue, design, denomination, color, perforation, and watermark on all stamps issued. Most of the stamps are given a valuation. Volume 1 covers the United States and affiliated territories, the United Nations, Canada, and British America; volumes 2–6 cover the rest of the world. Extensively illustrated.

1106 U.S. first day cover catalogue and checklist. Michael A. Mellone. 300p. Scott, 1984–. Annual. $
769.56   HE6184

First day covers are "commemorative covers with stamps, cancellations, and cachets from the first day that a stamp is issued." Explains the process of producing and the reasons for collecting first day covers. Includes prices. The authoritative guide.

1107 World encyclopedia of stamps and stamp collecting: The ultimate illustrated reference to over 3,000 of the world's best stamps, and a professional guide to starting and perfecting a spectacular collection. James Mackay. 256p. Lorenz, 2005. $
769.56   HE6196

With more than 3,000 color photographs, this is a comprehensive guide for the stamp enthusiast at any level. A history of stamp and postal services from Roman mail coaches to modern air mail is given along with notorious anecdotes from the world of stamp collecting and collectors. Step-by-step instructions are detailed with information on how best to mount and preserve stamps. Additional sources including Internet auction sites are given.

16 *Games and Sports*

MAUREEN BARRY

Many factors have contributed to the increasing popularity of sports and leisure in society. Recently, for example, the popularity of extreme sports has grown dramatically. As a result, sport, recreation, and leisure are growing as academic fields of study, and reference publishing in this area is flourishing. This chapter includes general works, at least one reference work devoted to each of a wide variety of major sports, and reference resources addressing sport's impact on and connection to societies or cultures. Some sports, like bicycling, have been removed since the previous edition because most books published about them are appropriate for circulating collections rather than reference collections. Also, despite the popularity of topics such as women in sport or extreme sports, these subjects do not have separate categories in this chapter because they are often folded into larger, multidisciplinary works such as the third edition of the *Berkshire Encyclopedia of World Sport*.

Small and medium-sized libraries should collect reference works covering the rules and particulars of sports that are locally and regionally popular, like lacrosse.

This consideration, along with limited library budgets, was another factor for excluding certain sports from this chapter. Libraries can purchase the recommended sources as needed. Official rule books have not been listed in previous editions. Since the last edition, national associations for most major sports have begun publishing official rules along with some statistics on the Internet. URLs for these have been listed, giving libraries an economical option of "owning" official rule books. For consistency's sake, some print rule books have been included as needed.

General Sources

Bibliographies and Guides

1108 Sports, exercise, and fitness: A guide to reference and information sources.
Mary Beth Allen. 287p. Libraries Unlimited, 2005. $

Chapters are divided into activity categories, such as Olympic, racquet, precision and accuracy, combat, aquatic, and health and wellness. Most entries contain resources for reference and instruction and Internet sources. Comprehensive guide of sources with annotations.

Dictionaries and Encyclopedias

1109 Berkshire encyclopedia of world sport. 3rd ed. Karen Christensen, David Levinson, and Gertrud Pfister. 3v. Berkshire, 2013. $$$

Entries focus on the culture, history, and business of sport and provide coverage ranging from obscure and ancient sports to popular and emerging sports and everything in between. This title also folds in previous Berkshire reference works on women's sports and extreme sports. The third edition features more than 350 updates, including fan behavior, sports management, fantasy sports, technology, and environmental and economic aspects. The electronic version offers the option for an extended subscription edition that will feature supplemental texts, charts and graphs, regular updates on major sporting events, and much more.

1110 Dictionary of sports and games terminology. Adrian Room. 180p. McFarland, 2010. $

This title provides more than 8,000 definitions for sports and games terminology. Coverage does not include board or card games. The sport or game with which the heading is associated is provided immediately after each entry in brackets. The appendix includes abbreviations of ruling or governing bodies of a wide variety of sports.

1111 A dictionary of sports studies. Alan Tomlinson. 516p. Oxford, 2010. $

This source provides nearly 1,100 concise descriptions of influential figures, concepts, theories, sports, games, organizations, and scientific topics, such as nutrition and anatomy. Each is examined through the lens of studying and understanding sport. The author also includes recommended web links when appropriate.

1112 Encyclopedia of international games. Daniel Bell. 591p. McFarland, 2003. $

International multisport competitions dating back to 1896 and ranging from World Scholar-Athlete Games to X Games are summarized. Most entries include brief contest history and data about year, contest site, sports, dates, and medals awarded. Appendixes include games by year, nation, and host city; largest games by number of participants; and nations and sports.

1113 Encyclopedia of play in today's society. Rodney P. Carlisle, ed. 2v. SAGE, 2009. $$

The coverage of entries ranges from companies (Hasbro) to informal games (jacks, leapfrog, etc.) to concepts such as the sociology of play. Some entries are attributed to specific countries and provide a brief overview of current and/or historic play in their society. A chronology of play dating back to 30,000 BC and play statistics collected by several government agencies are also included.

1114 Encyclopedia of sports in America: A history from foot races to extreme sports. Murry R. Nelson, ed. 573p. Greenwood, 2009. $$

Arranged chronologically by era or by decade starting in the early 1600s, this title highlights perspectives on the role of sport in American history. The most popular sports—baseball, football, basketball, and hockey—are covered in most chapters. Other sports that received societal interest are presented within the appropriate time period.

1115 Sport in American culture: From Ali to X-Games. Joyce Duncan, ed. 479p. ABC-CLIO, 2004. $$

Each entry focuses on the impact of a specific sports figure, sport, event, or idea on American culture. Topics include sports, activities, and athletes and organizations at all levels, including youth, recreational, amateur, and professional. Includes extensive bibliography, helpful cross-references, and an index.

1116 Sports and the physically challenged: An encyclopedia of people, events, and organizations. Linda Mastandrea and Donna Czubernat. 173p. Greenwood, 2006. $

The people, places, sports, concepts, equipment, events, and organizations included in this publication are primarily from the United States. This source also includes a timeline of significant events relating to disability sport.

1117 Sports culture: An A–Z guide. Ellis Cashmore. 482p. Routledge, 2002. $

Topics such as globalization, technological innovations, books with sports themes, and other controversies are covered in this resource. Each of the 174 entries is discussed with regard to their impact on cultures worldwide.

1118 Statistical encyclopedia of North American professional sports: All major league teams and major non-team events year by year, 1876–2006. 2nd ed. K. Michael Gaschnitz. 4v. McFarland, 2008. $$

The bulk of these volumes comprise year-by-year statistics from 1876 to 2006 for baseball, basketball, football, hockey, soccer, and other prominent sports from each year. These include regular season league standings, top-five individual leaders in a variety of categories, award recipients, All-Stars and Hall of Fame inductees. Historic and recent individual team statistics (regular season and play-off records, individual standings in three key statistical categories for each team, and more) are also included for professional teams from each of the major leagues. An appendix provides a list of professional team nicknames.

Directories

1119 Disability sport and recreation resources. 3rd ed. Michael J. Paciorek and Jeffery A. Jones. 312p. Cooper, 2001. $

This title is organized by sport. Includes national and international governing bodies of sport and disability sport organizations. Sport overviews, equipment required, directory of equipment suppliers, and additional resources, including recommended websites. Also has photographs and a bibliography.

1120 Sports museums and halls of fame worldwide. Victor J Danilov. 226p. McFarland, 2005. $

Directory of museums and halls of fame organized by country and sport. Other sections are organized by athletes or sports personnel; high school sports; collegiate sports; local, state, and regional halls of fame; and sports art and media. Facility's contents, history, and contact information are included.

Biographical Sources

1121 African Americans in sports. David Kenneth Wiggins. 2v. Sharpe Reference, 2004. $

Gives brief biographical information about African American athletes. Also covers African American athletes' impact on and participation in major sports. Other entries discuss social issues, institutions and organizations, such key personnel as coaches or sportswriters, and cultural themes. Contains nearly 450 entries, with further reading suggested for each.

1122 Latino athletes. Ian C. Friedman. 278p. Facts on File, 2007. $

Brief biographies and career highlights are outlined for 176 athletes representing twenty-six sports. Each entry concludes with suggested readings. At the end of the A–Z dictionary, lists of entries are organized by sport, birth year, and ethnicity or country of origin.

1123 Native Americans in sports. C. Richard King. 2v. Sharpe Reference, 2004. $$

This title follows the same format as *African Americans in Sports*, with brief biographical information about Native American athletes and social and cultural topics such as mascot controversies. Further reading is suggested for each entry, and a chronology of notable events is presented. Includes bibliography and index.

1124 The Scribner encyclopedia of American lives: Sports figures. Arnie Markoe, ed. 2v. Scribner, 2002. $$

Covers 614 figures, living and dead, important to the history of sport in the United States. Further recommended reading in nearly every entry. Narrative about each athlete offers personal and professional background, influences, and accomplishments. Index sorts athletes alphabetically and by sport.

Auto Racing

1125 NASCAR encyclopedia. 2nd ed. Peter Golenbock and Greg Fielden. 1009p. MBI, 2003. $

The introduction provides a short history of stock car racing. This title is divided into these statistically comprehensive sections: records, year by year (1949–2002), drivers, owners, tracks, and races. Records include the top thirty drivers for categories such as winnings, top ten and top five finishes, laps led, and more. This second edition updates the previous *Stock Car Racing Encyclopedia* and covers every driver who has competed in a race.

Baseball

1126 The All-American Girls Professional Baseball League record book: Comprehensive hitting, fielding, and pitching statistics. W. C. Madden. 294p. McFarland, 1999. $

As the title suggests, this source provides comprehensive hitting, fielding, and pitching statistics. A complete record highlighting stars of the league, individual records, season records, playoff records, players' statistics, pitcher's statistics, league personnel, and playing schedule.

1127 Baseball America's almanac. Baseball America, 1990–. Annual. $

This almanac of American baseball presents a "comprehensive review of the season, featuring statistics and commentary." Provides team statistics and commentary for major leagues, minor leagues, independent leagues, international leagues, and the top college and high school baseball teams. Also contains draft information, such as the top 100 picks and club-by-club selections. The appendix includes the previous year's obituaries.

1128 Baseball America's directory. Baseball America, 1990–. Annual. $

Contact information and broadcast and stadium details are included along with schedules for professional, international, college, amateur. and youth levels. Details associations' information for organizations concerned with scouting, players unions, alumni, umpires, and more. Includes local and national media information as well as driving directions to major league stadiums.

1129 The baseball bibliography. 2nd ed. Myron J. Smith. 4v. McFarland, 2006. $

Completely updates the first edition, which was published in 1986. Includes articles, books, theses, dissertations, yearbooks, programs, fiction, poetry. and government documents.

1130 Baseball desk reference. Lawrence T. Lorimer. 608p. DK, 2002. $

This reference source is arranged by history; big leagues (teams, histories, statistics, business of baseball, manager profiles, records); levels of the game (international, college, youth, women, Negro Leagues); and lore and lingo (media, song, museums, language, film, books, and collectibles). Includes overviews and brief statistics, color illustrations, field dimensions, and an index.

1131 The cultural encyclopedia of baseball. 2nd ed. Jonathan Fraser Light. 1105p. McFarland, 2005. $

This title covers topics from all aspects of the game—for example, night games, grand slams, Hemmingway, and collective-bargaining agreements. Includes entries for every club that played in defunct and present leagues: National Association, National League (NL), American Association, Union Association, Players League, American League (AL), and Federal League. Each NL and AL team has subheadings of origins, first game, key owners, nicknames, key seasons, key players, key managers, ballparks, key broadcasters, and books about the team. Bolded words indicate separate entries. Index includes headings and mentions. Coverage is through 2004 postseason.

1132 Diamonds around the globe: The encyclopedia of international baseball. Peter C. Bjarkman. 607p. Greenwood, 2005. $

Organized by country, this encyclopedia focuses on baseball outside the United States. Each entry includes capsule histories of major and minor league baseball teams, selected statistics, notes and bibliographies, and major players. Appendix A includes greatest moments in world baseball history. Index and annotated bibliography close the book.

1133 The encyclopedia of Negro League baseball. Thom Loverro. 368p. Checkmark Books, 2003. $$

This work covers athletes, owners, managers, and other significant figures and teams from the Negro League. Entries about athletes include position, team, and dates played, along with notable accomplishments for some. Also includes a bibliography and index.

1134 Encyclopedia of women and baseball.
Leslie A. Heaphy and Mel Anthony May, eds. 438p. McFarland, 2006. $

Entries in this source cover past and current athletes and other notable figures involved in women's baseball, along with teams and events. Appendixes cover AAGPBL (All-American Girls Professional Baseball League) rosters, AAGPBL teams, league champions and batting champions, rosters for other U.S. and non-U.S. leagues, women's world series results, women's world series rosters, 2004 world cup rosters, and tournament results. A comprehensive bibliography is also included.

1135 Major League Baseball official rules.
MLB Advanced Media. www.mlb.com/mlb/official_info/official_rules/foreword.jsp. Free

Sections of the official rules include objectives of the game, definition of terms, game preliminaries, starting and ending game, putting the ball in play, the batter, the runner, the pitcher, the umpire, and the official scorer. A useful site on the rules of baseball.

1136 The new Bill James historical baseball abstract. Bill James. 998p. Free Press, 2001. $

The first part of this text highlights the history of baseball decade by decade, starting in the 1870s. Each decade features who played the game, where the game was played, new stadiums, nicknames, and how the game was played. Part 2 includes player ratings and comments organized by position. Part 3 is a reference section that shows win shares of individuals and selected teams and win share team comparisons. The comprehensive historical coverage and index make this a valuable baseball compendium.

1137 The team-by-team encyclopedia of Major League Baseball. Dennis Purdy. 1166p. Workman, 2006. $$

Anecdotal stories are included in each team's coverage, along with records, standings, attendance,

starting lineups, win-loss records versus all opponents, retired uniforms, and awards. Some photographs are included.

1138 Total baseball: The ultimate baseball encyclopedia. 8th ed. John Thorn. 2676p. Sport Media, 2004. $$

This source is a narrative and statistical encyclopedia. Player, pitcher, and postseason registers are presented. Player register is alphabetical by name. Sections include biographies and team histories broken down by the following categories: early days, 1901–1945; golden era, 1946–1968; and modern game, 1969–2003. The international arena is also covered. The appendix gives major league attendance, amateur free-agent draft, evolution of baseball records, all-time leaders (lifetime and single season), manager and umpire rosters, and a glossary of statistical terms.

1139 The women of the All-American Girls Professional Baseball League: A biographical dictionary. Reprint. W. C. Madden. 288p. McFarland, 2005. $

This dictionary is arranged alphabetically by name. Biographical information on more than 600 of the league's players is included. Entries state statistical information (batting, pitching, and fielding) for those players that participated in more than ten games. Contains some photographs and a brief history of the league.

Basketball

1140 Biographical directory of professional basketball coaches. Jeff Marcus. 443p. Scarecrow, 2003. $

Coaches are listed alphabetically. Entries include college attended, birth and death dates, brief paragraphs with career highlights, and regular season and playoff coaching record. Begins with the 1925 American Basketball League and goes through the 2001 National Basketball Association season.

1141 College basketball's national championships: The complete record of every tournament ever played. Morgan G. Brenner. 1036p. Scarecrow, 1999. $

Chronicling major men's and women's association national championship tournaments, this source includes the National Collegiate Athletic Association (NCAA), League of Christian Colleges, and Association for Intercollegiate Athletics for Women tournaments. Lists association national champions, nonassociation national championship tournaments, and school tournament participation history. Appendixes include school information, school names, tournament site and dates, NCAA-vacated tournament teams, and tournament trivia.

1142 ESPN college basketball encyclopedia: The complete history of the men's game. Editors of ESPN. 1213p. Ballantine, 2009. $

This source summarizes each season from 1895–96 to 2008–09 and each NCAA Division I program's history, including best team, player, and coach, greatest game, and season-by-season record. Tournament brackets since 1939 and weekly polls since 1949 are also provided, along with box scores from the sweet sixteen round through the championship game for every NCAA tournament. Defunct programs also receive coverage.

1143 Official NBA encyclopedia. 3rd ed. Jan Hubbard, ed. 911p. Doubleday, 2000. $

Various contributors write essays about modern and early icons of the National Basketball Association (NBA), early professional leagues, NBA pioneers, and expansion teams. Topics also covered include dynasties, rules, coaches, referees, seasons, Women's National Basketball Association, and NBA timeline. Includes index.

1144 Official rules of the National Basketball Association. NBA Media Ventures. www.nba.com/analysis/rules_index.html. Free

In addition to the league's official rules, court dimensions, and referee signals, the site also contains sections explaining the most misunderstood rules and player dress code.

1145 Official rules of the NCAA [basketball]. NCAA Publications. www.ncaapublications.com/p-4227 -2011-2013-mens-womens-basketball -rule-book-2-year-publication.aspx. Free

Complete playing rules of men's and women's National Collegiate Athletic Association basketball in PDF or e-book format.

1146 Official rules of the Women's National Basketball Association. WNBA Enterprises. www.wnba.com/ analysis/wnba_rules_regulations.html. Free

Rulebook can be downloaded in PDF format and includes definitions, official rules, court dimensions, and referee signals.

Billiards and Pool

1147 Billiards: The official rules and records book. Billiard Congress of America. 216p. Billiard Congress of America, 2008. $

Complete playing rules of the Billiard Congress of America. BCA Hall of Fame biographies are also included.

1148 The new illustrated encyclopedia of billiards. Rev. ed. Michael Ian Shamos. 320p. Lyons Press, 2002. $

Entries explain billiards terminology and techniques. Helpful illustrations, diagrams, and figures add value. Appendix A explains important numerical values in billiards. Appendix B lists billiard games. Appendix C gives billiard organizations, and appendix D is an index of names.

Card Games

1149 The A–Z of card games. 2nd ed. David Sidney Parlett. 441p. Oxford, 2004. $

Previous edition was published in 1992 as *A Dictionary of Card Games*. This source is a guide to popular card games like hearts, bridge, and poker.

Chess

1150 U.S. Chess Federation's official rules of chess. 5th ed. Tim Just and Daniel B. Burg, eds. 370p. Random House Puzzles and Games, 2003. $

Comprehensive coverage of the U.S. Chess Federation's official rules. Rules of play, including tournament play, equipment standards, players' rights and responsibilities, code of ethics, rating system, chess notation, Internet chess rules, and conduct. Also has World Chess Federation laws.

Exercise

1151 The encyclopedia of exercise, sport, and health. Peter Brukner, Karim Khan, and John Kron. 501p. Allen & Unwin, 2004. $

This encyclopedia applies to males or females of all ages who are competitive or noncompetitive athletes. More than 1,500 entries covering exercises, sports, health, injuries, anatomy, steroids, supplements, and so forth. Includes helpful diagrams, charts, cross-references, and an index.

Figure Skating

1152 Historical dictionary of figure skating. James R. Hines. 420p. Scarecrow, 2011. $

A chronology and introduction are presented, followed by the dictionary, which features hundreds of entries on athletes, organizations, terminology, and countries where figure skating is popular. Appendixes comprise International Skating Union members and officers, World Figure Skating Hall of Fame members, and world champion medalists.

Fishing

1153 Ken Schultz's concise fishing encyclopedia. Ken Schultz. 473p. Wiley, 2010. $

This title is divided into five fundamental subjects: fish, tools, basic skills, techniques, and practical matters (e.g., safety and etiquette). Helpful color illustrations, diagrams, and photographs supplement the entries.

Football

1154 ESPN college football encyclopedia. Michael MacCambridge, ed. 1629p. ESPN, 2005. $

A sample of the essays includes a history of recruiting, integration of college football, and college football in the movies. Division 1-A schools are listed alphabetically, with profiles of best coaches, games, and players, biggest upsets, key data about university and football history, distinguished alumni, and fight-song lyrics. Bar charts also illustrate schools' winning percentages. The annual review gives history of polls and ratings. Year-by-year overviews from 1869 to 2004, present leading rushers, Heisman Trophy vote counts, and more. Also includes a history of current and defunct bowl games.

1155 NFL rulebook. NFL Enterprises. www .nfl.com/rulebook. Free

Complete official rulebook of the National Football League. Also provided are official signals and penalty summaries and a case book. Users can view by section or download the entire book in PDF format. A rules digest is also available at www.nfl .com/rulebook/digestofrules.

1156 Total football II: The official encyclopedia of the National Football League. Bob Carroll et al., eds. 1812p. HarperCollins, 1999. $

More than 18,000 athletes ranging from those who played only one game in the league to the game's greatest players receive attention in this encyclopedia. The text is divided into six major sections that provide comprehensive coverage of game and league history and evolution: history, men who made the game (players and coaches), annual awards, strategy, the game off the field (influences on society), and other leagues.

1157 The ultimate Super Bowl book: A complete reference to the stats, stars, and stories behind football's biggest game—and why the best team won. Bob McGinn. 384p. MVP Books, 2009. $

Arranged chronologically, this title covers each Super Bowl since the first, in 1967. A narrative is included for each game, along with team and individual statistics. Charts and tables outlining scoring summary, starting lineups, substitutions, and coaching staff are also included. Interspersed throughout the text are top-ten lists such as: ten best running plays, ten best performances by a quarterback, ten hardest hits, top ten coaches, and so forth.

1158 The USA Today college football encyclopedia, 2010–2011. Bob Boyles and Paul Guido. 1415p. Skyhorse, 2010. $
This comprehensive encyclopedia summarizes each season since 1953 for seventy of the most prominent college football programs. For each year, a narrative commentary, milestones, summaries of the top ten to fifteen matchups for each week, bowl game summaries, individual statistical leaders, important personalities, and award winners are provided. The second section details team information for each of the seventy top schools. Career, season, and game statistical leaders, greatest coach, greatest fifty-five players, top ten best seasons, and win-loss records, polls, conference standings, coaching, and bowl game charts are included for each team.

Gambling

1159 Gambling in America: An encyclopedia of history, issues, and society. William Norman Thompson. 509p. ABC-CLIO, 2001. $
Entries cover gambling behaviors, issues relating to gambling, economics, games, individuals associated with gambling, and associations. Chronology of gambling events provided. Appendixes consist of articles and major cases. Includes a glossary and an index.

Games

1160 Sports and games of the ancients. Reprint. Steve Craig. 271p. Greenwood Press, 2005. $
Offers a history of traditional, indigenous games worldwide. With each continent or region, there is an introduction, an explanation, and a history of sports

played and developed, with suggestions for modern play and sources listed for further consultation.

1161 Unique games and sports around the world: A reference guide. Doris Corbett, John Cheffers, and Eileen Crowley Sullivan, eds. 407p. Greenwood, 2001. $
Organized geographically, this source lists characteristics of players (age, sex); object of game; number of players; apparel or equipment required; venue required; length of game; symbolism of game; and rules of play, including scoring. Also, it offers a sociological and anthropological perspective. The appendix features a guide for educators in selecting appropriate games. Includes index and bibliography.

Golf

1162 Golf Digest's best places to play. 7th ed. Golf Digest. 849p. Fodor's Travel, 2006. $
Directory of the best courses to play throughout the United States, Canada, Mexico, and the Caribbean. Includes a geographical directory by town or city. Entries are listed alphabetically by course name, and there is a metro area index by town. Entries include opening date, architect, yards, par, course rating, slope, green fee, cart fee, discounts, walkability, and other notes. Includes star ratings, with explanation, and brief lists featuring "best new courses" and "best service courses."

1163 The historical dictionary of golf. Bill Mallon and Randon Jerris. 797p. Scarecrow, 2011. $
A chronology and an extensive introduction provide history, current trends and problems, technology, and other important developments. The dictionary contains terminology, biographies, events, courses, and organizations. Appendixes list hall of fame players, champions, and major award recipients.

1164 The illustrated golf rules dictionary. Rev. ed. Hadyn Rutter. Triumph Books, 2004. $
Explains rules or techniques with definitions, basic rules, procedures, penalties, and exceptions. Includes many color photos and diagrams.

1165 USGA rules. U.S. Golf Association. www.usga.org/Rules.aspx?id=7788. Free
This site contains rule book, including etiquette and definitions, frequently asked questions, competition guidelines, and an interactive quiz. Also includes rules of amateur status.

Hockey

1166 Official NHL rulebook. National Hockey League. www.nhl.com/ice/page.htm?id=27011. Free
The National Hockey League provides descriptions of fouls, penalties, officials' duties, and game flow. The source also lists teams, equipment, and includes helpful diagrams.

1167 Total hockey: The official encyclopedia of the National Hockey League. 2nd ed. Dan Diamond. 1974p. Total Sports, 2000. $
This encyclopedia discusses everything hockey. Data include National Hockey League attendance, 1960–2000; Canadian, American, European, and women's hockey; Stanley Cup winners, 1917–2000; and a short history of the league broken down by year. International coverage includes the 2002 Olympics, World and European championships, and World Junior championships. Other facets of the game covered include the hall of fame, equipment, safety, hockey and TV, and hockey video games and the Internet. Also contains statistical and biographical registers.

Martial Arts

1168 Martial arts of the world: An encyclopedia of history and innovation. Thomas A. Green and Joseph R. Svinth, eds. 2v. ABC-CLIO, 2010. $$
Topically arranged, this source covers regions and individual arts in the first volume and the philosophical and social themes related to martial arts and combat in the second volume. Nearly all entries conclude with substantial bibliographies.

1169 The practical encyclopedia of martial arts. Fay Goodman. 256p. Lorenz, 2004. $

The introductions to tae kwon do, karate, aikido, ju-jitsu, judo, kung fu, tai chi chuan, kendo, iaido, and Shinto ryu are enhanced with illustrations. Each chapter includes history and philosophy, apparel, equipment, etiquette, exercises, and techniques. Contains brief biographies of best martial artists for each discipline.

Olympics

1170 Encyclopedia of the modern Olympic movement. John E. Findling and Kimberly D. Pelle, eds. 602p. Greenwood Press, 2004. $
This source presents a history of each Olympic Game (summer and winter) and includes information about the then forthcoming 2004, 2006, 2008, and 2010 games. It also includes bibliographical essays. Appendixes highlight International Olympic Committee members, the U.S. Olympic Committee, Olympic Games and television, Olympic feature films, and Internet sources on Olympism. Although increasingly dated, this title can be useful for Olympic history.

1171 Historical dictionary of the Olympic movement. 4th ed. Bill Mallon and Jeroen Heijmans. 507p. Scarecrow, 2011. $$
The introduction provides the highlights from each of the modern games. A–Z entries feature competitive events and their histories, selected athlete biographies, administrator biographies, and participating and host countries. History and politics are covered, as are the differences between the modern and ancient games. Appendixes list number of medals won by country and torch bearers, among other statistics.

Outdoors

1172 Encyclopedia of outdoor and wilderness skills. Chris Townsend and Annie Aggens. 400p. Rugged Mountain Press, 2003. $
Nearly 450 outdoor and wilderness-related entries. Brief commentary intended to supply knowledge about hiking, backpacking, rock climbing, skiing,

kayaking, and other activities. Contains diagrams and photographs. Includes bibliography and index.

Recreation

1173 Encyclopedia of recreation and leisure in America. Gary S. Cross, ed. 2v. Scribner, 2004. CP$
Topics range from caving or dining out to amusement parks and fashion. Lengthy bibliographies close each entry. Commercialization, popularity, criticism, analysis, and sociological perspective are among the examples covered in the content of each entry.

1174 Fun and games in twentieth-century America: A historical guide to leisure. Ralph G. Giordano. 304p. Greenwood, 2003. $
Organized chronologically by era, each chapter covers public interest, lifestyles, entertainment, music and theater, sports and games, transportation, and vacation. Bibliography and index are included.

Running

1175 Running encyclopedia. Richard Benyo and Joe Henderson. 417p. Human Kinetics, 2002. $
This encyclopedia highlights records, races, record setters, well-known figures, and important running resources. Supplemental index includes names of those who do not have separate entries and cross-references. Jargon and technique are also covered.

Rules

1176 NCAA playing rules and officiating. National Collegiate Athletic Association. www.ncaa.org/wps/wcm/connect/public/NCAA/Playing+Rules+Administration/. Free
Rulebooks for sixteen varsity intercollegiate sports. Many are retrospectively archived to 2000 or 2001.

1177 The sports rules book. 3rd ed. Thomas Hanlon. 328p. Human Kinetics, 2009. $
This reference source provides fundamental rules for fifty-four sports. Arranged alphabetically by sport, each entry includes an overview, procedures, terms, playing area, competitors, equipment, officials, rules, modifications (for age or physical disability), scoring, and organizations that govern professional and amateur levels.

Sailing

1178 Complete sailing manual. Rev. ed. Steve Sleight. 448p. DK, 2012. $
This title is divided into the following categories: introduction, first principles, small-boat sailing, advanced small-boat sailing, cruiser sailing, navigation, weather, practical boat care, and staying safe. It simultaneously serves as a basic manual and a thorough reference source. Helpful color illustrations, diagrams, and photographs enhance the entries.

1179 The language of sailing. Richard Mayne. 369p. Fitzroy Dearborn, 2000. $
Comprehensive dictionary of sailing, with nautical and boating terms, including etymology and evolution.

Soccer

1180 The encyclopedia of American soccer history. Roger Allaway, Colin Jose, and David Litterer. 454p. Scarecrow, 2001. $
Entries focus on individuals, countries, associations, coaches, and stadiums important to the history of all levels of soccer in the United States. Appendixes include statistics and records, memorable games, and a bibliography. Covers U.S. soccer at all levels.

1181 Historical dictionary of soccer. Tom Dunmore. 313p. Scarecrow, 2011. $
The majority of coverage in this title is about professional soccer around the globe, including, but not limited to, athletes, teams, nations, coaches, organizations, events, and venues. Appendixes detail presidents of the Fédération Internationale de Football Association (FIFA) and tournament dates, hosts, and results (winners and runners-up) by year.

1182 The ultimate encyclopedia of soccer: The definitive illustrated guide to world soccer. 10th ed. Keir Radnedge, ed. 256p. Carlton Books, 2004. $

This source has good international coverage. It covers early and modern games, major competitions, and great soccer moments by country, great clubs, legends, great players, great matches, stadiums, business, rules and tactics, equipment, soccer culture, scandals, soccer chronology, and major soccer awards. Also includes a chapter about "football" in Great Britain and Ireland and many photos.

1183 U.S. Soccer laws of the game (2012– 2013). U.S. Soccer Federation. www. ussoccer.com/referees/laws-of-the-game. aspx. Free

Interested readers can download the PDF of the "laws" of the game. According to the website, these laws are authorized annually by the International Football Association Board (IFAB) and provided by the Fédération Internationale de Football Association (FIFA).

Swimming

1184 Historical dictionary of competitive swimming. John Lohn. 299p. Scarecrow, 2010. $

The introduction and chronologies in this source present narrative summaries of swimming's history and the history of FINA (International Swimming Federation) championships. Notable swimmers from the past century-plus, strokes, and organizations are featured in the dictionary portion. Appendixes highlight the FINA presidents, FINA men's and women's world champions, and Olympic medal winners in both swimming and diving events.

Tennis

1185 The Bud Collins history of tennis: An authoritative encyclopedia and record book. 2nd ed. Bud Collins. 795p. New Chapter Press, 2010. $

The five major sections of this encyclopedia detail tennis year by year, from 1919 to 2007 (providing a narrative summary and a chart of champions and leaders for each year), major championships (majors and grand slam—Australian championships, Roland Garros, Wimbledon, and U.S. championships); international play (Davis Cup, Fed Cup, Olympics, Wightman Cup); biographies (hall of famers, current elite, and other significant athletes); and tours, rankings, and other championships.

1186 USTA rules. U.S. Tennis Association. www.usta.com/Improve-Your-Game/ Rules/. Free

This page lists code for unofficiated matches. USTA rules follow International Tennis Federation (ITF) rules, which can be found at www.itftennis.com/ officiating/rulebooks/rules-of-tennis.aspx.

Literature

CAROLYN M. MULAC

In updating this chapter, the renewed interest in readers' advisory sources has been taken into account. Particular attention has been paid to expanding the "Specific Genres" section: new genres have been added (graphic novels, Jewish American literature, and urban literature), and other genres have been expanded. In the "National and Regional Literatures" section, several new categories were added (Greek, Southeast Asian, and Spanish literatures). As literature reference sources continue to be produced, many of the print titles we have come to rely on are now available electronically either individually or as part of a literature database. EBSCO's MagillOnLiterature Plus and Literary Reference Center and Gale Cengage's Dictionary of Literary Biography Complete Online, Literature Criticism Online, and Literature Resource Center are some of the most well known of these products.

General Sources

Bibliographies and Guides

1187 The Cambridge guide to literature in English. 3rd ed. Dominic Head, ed. 1208p. Cambridge, 2006. $
820.90   PR85
This title is a one-volume reference guide covering the literature of Great Britain and the United States as well as the English-language literature of Canada, Africa, Australia, New Zealand, Ireland, India, and the Caribbean. Includes authors, titles, characters, literary terms, genres, movements, and critical concepts.

1188 Literary research guide: An annotated listing of reference sources in English literary studies. 5th ed. James L. Harner. 826p. Modern Language Association, 2009. $
016.82   Z2011
Available to the general public in a paperback edition and to libraries in an electronic edition, this annotated guide lists thousands of entries for reference works on English and American literature and related literary topics. The electronic edition links to WorldCat, Google Books, and your institution's online catalog and is regularly revised and updated.

Biographical Sources

1189 Contemporary authors. Gale Cengage, 1962–. $$
810.9   PN51

This long-running series provides bio-bibliographical information for more than 120,000 writers in a variety of fields, including literature, journalism, television, and film. Libraries may want to subscribe to this title online as Contemporary Authors Online, published by Gale Cengage. "Included are author-provided updates, expanded entries, bibliographies, awards, and recent update information."

1190 Cyclopedia of world authors. 4th rev. ed. Frank N. Magill and Tracy Irons-Georges, eds. 5v. Salem Press, 2003. $$

809   PN451

Most of the 2,408 authors included here are represented in various *Masterplots* series. The alphabetically arranged articles include a biographical sketch, a brief critical essay, and a bibliography.

1191 Dictionary of literary biography. Gale Cengage, 1978–. $$

810.9   PS21

This award-winning series provides critical and biographical essays on the most influential writers past and present. Also available as a database, Gale Cengage's Dictionary of Literary Biography Complete Online.

1192 Encyclopedia of world writers: Beginnings to the 20th century. Thierry Boucquey and Marie Josephine Diamond, eds. 3v. Facts on File, 2005. $$

809   PN451

Alphabetically arranged entries of an array of authors not always represented in standard reference sources. Volume 1 covers ancient writers up to the thirteenth century. Volume 2 covers the fourteenth through the eighteenth centuries, and volume 3 deals with the nineteenth and twentieth centuries.

Databases and Indexes

1193 MLA international bibliography of books and articles on modern language and literature. Modern Language Association of America, 1921–. Annual. CP$

016.8   Z7006

Now available only in an electronic format, this classic reference work provides access to more than 2 million citations to books, journal articles, dissertations, and websites covering literature, language, folklore, literary criticism and theory, and much more, from 1921 to the present. Subscriptions are available through EBSCO, Gale Cengage, and ProQuest.

Dictionaries and Encyclopedias

1194 Benet's reader's encyclopedia. 5th ed. Bruce Murphy. 1232p. HarperCollins, 2008. $

809   PN41

The latest revision of a basic literature reference book supplies more than 10,000 entries on authors, titles, plots, characters, allusions, literary terms and movements, historical events, and other related topics.

1195 Encyclopedia of medieval literature. Jay Ruud. 752p. Facts on File, 2006. $

809.02   PN669

Covers the authors and literary works, terms, and concepts of Western Europe, Indian, China, Japan, and the Islamic world from 500 to 1500 CE in concise articles that often include bibliographies.

1196 Encyclopedia of Renaissance literature. James Wyatt Cook. 624p. Facts on File, 2006. $

809   PN721

This source contains articles, many including bibliographies, on the literature of England, France, Germany, Spain, China, India, the Islamic world, and the Jewish diaspora from 1500 to 1660 CE.

1197 Magill's literary annual. John D. Wilson and Steven G. Kellman, eds. 2v. Salem Press, 1977–. Annual. $$

803   PN44

Two annual volumes supply reviews of 200 fiction and nonfiction books published the previous year. Complimentary electronic access to the thirty-six-year archive is included with the purchase of each edition.

1198 Masterplots. 4th ed. Laurence W. Mazzeno, ed. 12v. Salem Press, 2010.

$$$$

808.8	PN44

Consists of 2,220 plot synopses and critical evaluations followed by ready-reference data on the author, type of work, setting, and principal characters. Purchase of this standard print reference work includes electronic access through Salem's online platform, Salem Literature.

Handbooks

1199 Brewer's dictionary of modern phrase and fable. 2nd ed. John Ayto and Ian Crofton, eds. 864p. Chambers, 2010. $

423.1	PE1460

Words, phrases, acronyms, slogans, slang expressions, fictional characters, and the titles of songs, books, films, television programs, and more are explained in this companion to *Brewer's Dictionary of Phrase and Fable.*

1200 Brewer's dictionary of phrase and fable. 19th ed. Susie Dent, ed. 1480p. Hodder Education Publishers, 2012. $

803	PN43

The latest edition of one of the longest-lived reference books (it was first published in 1870) includes hundreds of new and updated entries that explain the meaning and origin of thousands of proper names and curious words and phrases from history, fiction, myth, and folklore. As Dent observes in the foreword, *Brewer's* "is not a straightforward dictionary, nor is it an encyclopaedia. It is, in fact, unlike any other reference book that exists, anywhere."

1201 A glossary of literary terms. 10th ed. M. H. Abrams and Geoffrey G. Harpham. 448p. Cengage Learning, 2011. $

803	PN41

Contains essay-length entries on the terms used in the study of American, British, foreign, and comparative literature. The latest edition of this excellent guide will be useful for students of literature.

1202 A handbook to literature. 12th ed. William Harmon. 672p. Longman, 2011. $

803	PN41

The latest edition of a standard reference work provides more than 2,000 definitions of literary terms and topics and much more.

1203 The Johns Hopkins guide to literary theory and criticism. Michael Groden, Martin Kreiswirth, and Imre Szeman, eds. Johns Hopkins. http://litguide.press.jhu.edu. Free

801.95	PN81

This second edition of a comprehensive survey of ideas and persons who have made their mark in the world of literary theory is now available as a free website.

Literary Characters

1204 Cyclopedia of literary characters. Rev. ed. A. J. Sobczak, Frank N. Magill, and Janet Long, eds. 5v. Salem Press, 1998. $$

809	PN44

This source describes and identifies more than 29,000 characters from more than 3,294 works of literature. Arrangement is alphabetical by the title of the work in which the characters appear. Ready-reference use is facilitated by title, author, and character indexes and a pronunciation guide.

1205 Dictionary of fictional characters. Rev. ed. Martin Seymour-Smith. 598p. Kalmbach Publishing, 1992. $

Seymour-Smith has revised and expanded an earlier edition of this reader's guide to thousands of characters from novels, short stories, plays, and poems by American and British authors.

Literary Prizes

1206 Early word: The publisher–librarian connection. Nora Rawlinson. www.earlyword.com. Free

This is *the* website for the latest news from the world of publishing and a host of special features, including links to the major literary awards.

1207 National Book Foundation. National Book Foundation. www.nationalbook.org. Free

The National Book Foundation is the presenter of the National Book Awards, and on this website you will find a list of current winners by genre as well as lists of previous award winners and finalists and an explanation of the award process.

1208 The Pulitzer prizes. Pulitzer Prize, Columbia University. www.pulitzer.org. Free

The Pulitzer Prize was founded in 1917 and is administered by Columbia University to honor "excellence in journalism and the arts." This site includes a searchable archive of winners and nominated finalists, a history of the awards, and guidelines and entry forms.

Multivolume Criticism

1209 Literature Criticism Online. Gale Cengage. CP$

This online product brings together ten series on literary criticism. Content includes *Contemporary Literary Criticism*, *Literature Criticism from 1400 to 1800*, *Nineteenth-Century Literary Criticism*, and *Twentieth-Century Literary Criticism*. The broad coverage across regions, genre, and times allow students access to a wide range of literary criticism.

Proverbs

1210 Dictionary of American proverbs. Wolfgang Mieder, Stewart A. Kingsbury, and Kelsie B. Harder, eds. 736p. Oxford, 1991. $

398.9   PN6426

The result of many years of scholarship, this dictionary includes 15,000 proverbs currently in use in the United States and Canada. Arrangement is alphabetical by key word.

1211 The Macmillan book of proverbs, maxims, and famous phrases. Burton Egbert Stevenson. 2976p. Simon & Schuster Academic, 1987. $

082   PN6405

Formerly titled *The Home Book of Proverbs, Maxims, and Familiar Phrases*, this work follows the pattern of the author's *Home Book of Quotations*. Contains more than 73,000 sayings arranged by subject and indexed in great detail. Also includes English translations of foreign phrases.

1212 The multicultural dictionary of proverbs: Over 20,000 adages from more than 120 languages, nationalities, and ethnic groups. Harold V. Cordry. 416p. McFarland, 2005. $

082   PN6405

A collection of more than 20,000 proverbs derived from the traditions of more than 120 languages, nationalities, and ethnic groups. Includes subject and keyword indexes and a bibliography.

Quotations

1213 Bartlett's familiar quotations. 18th ed. John Bartlett; Geoffrey O'Brien, ed. 1472p. Little, Brown, 2012. $

808.88   PN6081

The latest edition of the gold standard for quotation collections has been completely revised and updated. Among the new authors included are Warren Buffett, Bill Gates, Jon Stewart, and Barack Obama. Now also available as an app for iPhone, Android, and Nook. Since each new edition omits some older material in order to make room for the new, it's a good idea to retain every edition, if space in the library permits.

1214 Contemporary quotations in black. Anita King, ed. 312p. Greenwood, 1997. $

081   E184

Taking her *Quotations in Black* (Greenwood, 1981) into the 1980s and 1990s, King includes more than 1,000 quotations from notable African Americans and black Africans. Entries are arranged alphabetically by author and then chronologically for each person quoted.

1215 The home book of quotations, classical and modern. 10th ed. Burton Egbert Stevenson. 2816p. Dodd, Mead, 1967. OP

808.88   PN6081

Unfortunately out of print, this is still one of the most comprehensive and useful collections of quotations. More than 50,000 quotations are arranged by subject, and there is a very detailed index. For libraries that own this title, it is recommended to retain it in either reference, circulation, or perhaps storage.

1216 The Oxford dictionary of American quotations. 2nd ed. Hugh Rawson and Margaret Miner, ed. 912p. Oxford, 2005. $
081.03   PN6081
This compilation includes nearly 6,000 quotations categorized under more than 500 topics arranged chronologically within each topic.

1217 Oxford dictionary of modern quotations. 3rd ed. Elizabeth Knowles, ed. 496p. Oxford, 2008. $
080   PN6080
More than 5,000 quotations illustrating popular culture and modern history are arranged by author and indexed by keyword and theme.

1218 Oxford dictionary of quotations. 7th ed. Elizabeth Knowles, ed. 1184p. Oxford, 2009. $
082   PN6080
The latest edition of a reliable reference work summarizes the wit and wisdom of the ages in more than 20,000 quotations arranged by author and indexed by theme and keyword.

1219 The quotable woman. Rev. ed. Elaine Bernstein Partnow, ed. 1056p. Facts on File, 2010. $
305.4   PN6081.5
This edition contains nearly 20,000 quotations from more than 5,000 women throughout history arranged in chronological order by the speaker's year of birth. Indexes by name, occupation, and nationality or ethnicity are included.

1220 Yale book of quotations. Fred R. Shapiro, ed. 1104p. Yale, 2006. $
082   PN6081
More than 12,000 quotations are arranged alphabetically by the name of the author and traced to their earliest possible usage in this carefully compiled collection. A mobile app is now available.

Special Interest

African American Literature

1221 African American dramatists: An A to Z guide. Emmanuel S. Nelson, ed. 544p. Greenwood, 2004. $
812   PS338
Playwrights from the last 150 years are profiled in signed articles that include biographical information, an overview of the entrant's most important works, a bibliography, and more.
The Cambridge companion to African American women's literature, see **1248.**

1222 The Cambridge history of African American literature. Maryemma Graham and Jerry W. Ward Jr., eds. 860p. Cambridge, 2011. $$
810.9   PS153
An overview of 400 years of oral and written African American literary tradition in twenty-eight signed essays. Includes an extensive bibliography.

1223 The Columbia guide to contemporary African American fiction. Darryl Dickson-Carr. 280p. Columbia, 2005. $
813.5   PS374
Provides an overview of the subject, an alphabetical listing of contemporary African American fiction writers, and a selected bibliography.

1224 Contemporary black American playwrights and their plays: A biographical directory and dramatic index. Bernard L. Peterson Jr. 651p. Greenwood, 1998. $$
812.5   PS153
Entries on more than 700 contemporary dramatists, screenwriters, and scriptwriters include brief biographies and annotated lists of dramatic works. Includes a title index and a selective general index to names, organizations, and awards.

1225 The Greenwood encyclopedia of African American literature. Hans Ostrom and J. David Macey, eds. 5v. Greenwood, 2005. $$
810.9   PS153

A comprehensive work that includes writers from colonial times to the present and literary genres from folktales and slave narratives to prison literature and blues poetry. This title also includes a ten-page bibliography and a ten-page chronology.

1226 Notable African American writers. 3v. Salem Press, 2006. $$

810.9   PS153

Eighty essays on important African American poets, playwrights, novelists, and other writers are presented in this title. It also includes four overview essays that discuss specific literary genres, a bibliography, a chronological list of authors, and four indexes.

Asian American Literature

1227 Asian American short story writers: An A-to-Z guide. Guiyou Huang, ed. 359p. Greenwood, 2003. $$

813   PS153

Forty-nine Asian American short story writers are profiled in entries that include a biography, a critical discussion, and bibliographies of primary and secondary sources. There is also an introductory essay on the Asian American short story.

1228 The Columbia guide to Asian American literature since 1945. Guiyou Huang. 272p. Columbia, 2006. $

813.5   PS153

Examines the work of more than 100 U.S. and Canadian writers with origins in Asia and South and Southeast Asia in entries that include a brief biography, a discussion of major works, and a short bibliography of criticism.

1229 Encyclopedia of Asian-American literature. Seiwoong Oh. 400p. Facts on File, 2007. $

810.9   PS153

More than 200 North American authors of Asian descent are discussed in signed articles. Includes a bibliography of major works by Asian American writers and one of secondary sources.

1230 Greenwood encyclopedia of Asian American literature. Guiyou Huang,

ed. 3v. Greenwood, 2008. $$

810.9   PS153

Offers in-depth coverage of Asian American writers from the late nineteenth century to 2007. Title also includes articles on individual authors as well as essays on related topics and key historical events.

Gay and Lesbian Literature

1231 Contemporary gay American novelists: A bio-bibliographical critical sourcebook. Emmanuel S. Nelson, ed. 456p. Greenwood, 1993. $$

813.5   PS374

Fifty-seven writers are discussed in entries that include biographical information, a summary of major works and their critical reception, and bibliographies of primary and secondary sources. This older title presents useful information for a previous generation of gay writers.

1232 Contemporary gay American poets and playwrights: An A-to-Z guide. Emmanuel S. Nelson, ed. 496p. Greenwood, 2003. $$

812.5   PS325

Entries cover sixty-two writers and include biographical information, a summary of major works and their critical reception, and bibliographies of primary and secondary sources.

1233 Contemporary lesbian writers of the United States: A bio-bibliographical critical sourcebook. Sandra Pollock and Denise D. Knight, eds. 688p. Greenwood, 1993. $$

810.9   PS153

One hundred writers from the 1990s and earlier are profiled in articles that include a biography, an analysis of major works and their critical reception, and bibliographies of primary and secondary sources. Includes an introductory essay and an extensive general bibliography.

1234 Encyclopedia of contemporary LGBTQ literature of the United States. Emmanuel S. Nelson, ed. 2v. Greenwood, 2009. $$

810.9   PS153

This is a two-volume survey that provides biographical and critical articles on authors and their works and commentary on related literary movements and social issues in the lesbian, gay, bisexual, transsexual, and queer communities.

1235 Gay and lesbian literary heritage: A reader's companion to the writers and their works, from antiquity to the present. 2nd ed. Claude J. Summers, ed. 864p. Routledge, 2002. $$
809.8   PN56

This revised edition of the 1995 work includes some 400 alphabetically arranged essays by 175 scholars. In addition to articles on individual authors, there are essays on literary topics such as autobiography and comedy of manners. All entries conclude with bibliographic information.

Jewish American Literature

1236 The Cambridge companion to Jewish American literature. Hana Wirth-Nesher and Michael P. Kramer, eds. 316p. Cambridge, 2003. $
810.9   PS153

This volume of Cambridge's *Companion* series covers the contributions of Jewish American writers in popular culture, poetry, literary criticism, and more. It includes a chronology and suggestions for further reading.

1237 Encyclopedia of Jewish-American literature. Gloria L. Cronin and Alan L. Berger, eds. 416p. Facts on File, 2009. $
810.9   PS153

Signed articles discuss Jewish American authors and their works. This source includes a bibliography of major works by Jewish American writers and one of secondary sources.

Latino Literature

1238 Encyclopedia of Hispanic-American literature. Luz Elena Ramirez, ed. 448p. Facts on File, 2008. $
810.9   PS153

Nearly 300 authors and their works are discussed

in signed entries. Includes a bibliography of the works of major Hispanic American writers and one of secondary sources.

1239 Greenwood encyclopedia of Latino writers. Nicolás Kanellos, ed. 3v. Greenwood, 2008. $$
810.9   PS153

More than 700 alphabetically arranged entries by some sixty contributors cover writers, historical topics, literary movements, and more. Also includes a selected bibliography.

1240 Latino and Latina writers. Alan West-Duran, ed. 2v. Scribner, 2003. $$
810.9   PS153

Provides signed articles about Chicano and Chicana authors, Cuban and Cuban American authors, and Dominican and Puerto Rican authors. Includes several essays, such as "Chicana Feminist Criticism" and "Historical Origins of U.S. Latino Literature."

1241 Latino literature: A guide to reading interests. Sara E. Martínez, ed. 364p. Libraries Unlimited, 2009. $
016.86   Z1229

A guide to Latino literature that describes approximately 750 titles by theme, genre, and subgenre. Each entry includes a plot summary, a brief excerpt, and complete bibliographic information. Other features include selection guidelines, an introduction to Latino literature, and several indexes.

1242 Routledge companion to Latino/a Literature. Suzanne Bost and Frances Aparicio, eds. 568p. Routledge, 2012. $$
810.9   PS153

This title offers more than forty signed essays that discuss a variety of critical issues, including regional, cultural, and sexual identities in Latino/a literature and the impact of different literary forms.

1243 Routledge concise history of Latino/a literature. Frederick Luis Aldama. 208p. Routledge, 2012. $$
810.9   PS153

This title presents a comprehensive overview of Latino/a literature that explores key literary themes, current and emerging literary trends, and Latino/a literature by geographic area.

Native American Literature

1244 The Cambridge companion to Native American literature. Kenneth M. Roemer and Joy Porters, eds. 368p. Cambridge, 2005. $
810.9   PS153
This volume of the Cambridge *Companion* series examines the work of Native America writers from 1770 to the present. Includes essays on literary genres and their historical and cultural contexts.

1245 Dictionary of Native American literature. Andrew Wiget, ed. 616p. Garland, 1994. $$
897   PM155
Discusses the oral traditions of individual tribes as well as a number of cultural and historical topics. Includes biocritical essays on more than forty Native American writers.

1246 Encyclopedia of American Indian literature. Jennifer McClinton-Temple and Alan Velie. 480p. Facts on File, 2007. $
810.9   PS135
Signed articles discuss Native American authors and their works. Includes a bibliography of major works by Native American writers and one of secondary sources.

Women's Literature

1247 American women writers: From colonial times to the present; A critical reference guide. 2nd ed. Taryn Benbow-Pfalzgraf, ed. 3v. St. James Press, 1999. $$$
810.9   PS147
Some 1,300 articles about women writing in the fields of anthropology, psychology, history, and religion as well as literature. Each entry includes a biography and a bibliography.

1248 The Cambridge companion to African American women's literature. Angelyn Mitchell and Danille K. Taylor, eds. 336p. Cambridge, 2009. $
810.9   PS153

This volume of the Cambridge *Companion* series offers fourteen specially commissioned essays about the contributions of African American women writers from the eighteenth century to the present day. Includes extensive bibliographies.

1249 Encyclopedia of feminist literary theory. Elizabeth Kowaleski Wallace, ed. 473p. Routledge, 1996. $
801.9   PN98
Provides definitions of critical terms, summaries of the work of feminist literary critics, and descriptions of the development of the feminist perspective over time. Entries emphasize American and British views since 1970.

1250 Encyclopedia of feminist literature. Kathy J. Whitson. 300p. Greenwood, 2004. $
809   PN471
Although primarily focused on English and American authors, some of the writers included are from other countries, and all those included span the centuries from 1400 to the present. Entries include biographical and critical information and suggestions for further reading.

1251 Feminist writers. Pamela Kester-Shelton. 641p. St. James Press, 1996. $$
809   PN451
Alphabetically arranged entries provide biographical, bio-bibliographical, and critical information on more than 300 feminist writers. Indexed by author, title, nationality, genre, and subject.

1252 Irish women writers: An A-to-Z guide. Alexander G. Gonzalez, ed. 360p. Greenwood, 2005. $
820.9   PR8733
Each of the seventy-five articles consist of a short biography, a discussion of major works and their critical reception, and bibliographies of primary and secondary sources. Includes a selected general bibliography.

1253 Modern British women writers: An A-to-Z guide. Vicki Janik and Del Ivan Janik, eds. 448p. Greenwood, 2003. $$
820.9   PR116
Biographical information, critical analyses, and

bibliographies of primary and secondary sources covering fifty-eight British women authors of the twentieth century. Includes a selected general bibliography.

1254 Nineteenth-century British women writers: A bio-bibliographical critical sourcebook. Abigail Burnham Bloom, ed. 472p. Greenwood, 2000. $$

820.9   PR115

Profiles of more than ninety British women writers of the nineteenth century include biographical information and critical analysis supplemented by bibliographies of primary and secondary sources. Concludes with a selected bibliography of anthologies and critical studies.

Specific Genres

Children's Literature

1255 A to zoo: Subject access to children's picture books. 8th ed. Carolyn W. Lima and Rebecca L. Thomas. 1165p. Libraries Unlimited, 2010. $

011   Z1037

The latest edition of a standard reference work on fiction and nonfiction books for children lists thousands of titles. Although it focuses on books published from 2000 to 2009, older classics, award winners, and popular titles are included. Title and illustrator indexes and subject and bibliographic guides are provided.

1256 Best books for children: Preschool through grade 6. 9th ed. Catherine Barr and John T. Gillespie. 1901p. Libraries Unlimited, 2010. $

011.62   Z1037

Best books for children: Preschool through grade 6. Supplement to the 9th ed. Catherine Barr. 450p. Libraries Unlimited, 2012. $

011.62   Z1037

Best books for middle school and junior high readers, grades 6–9. 2nd ed. Catherine Barr and John T. Gillespie. 1242p. Libraries Unlimited, 2009. $

011.62   Z1037

Best books for middle school and junior high readers, grades 6–9. Supplement to the 2nd ed. Catherine Barr. 350p. Libraries Unlimited, 2011. $

011.62   Z1037

Best books for high school readers, grades 9–12. 2nd ed. Catherine Barr and John T. Gillespie. 1075p. Libraries Unlimited, 2009. $

011.62   Z1037

Best books for high school readers, grades 9–12. Supplement to the 2nd ed. Catherine Barr. 350p. Libraries Unlimited, 2011. $

011.62   Z1037

These titles can be used for collection development as well as readers' advisory tools. They help librarians identify the best recreational and educational books for young people recommended by professional reviewing sources. Each volume in the series addresses a particular range of grade levels, and the later editions also indicate the availability of audio and e-book versions.

1257 The children's and young adult literature handbook: A research and reference guide. John T. Gillespie. 404p. Libraries Unlimited, 2005. $

011.62   Z1037

Evaluates more than 1,000 publications, from general background sources, current and retrospective bibliographies, reviewing tools, and author and illustrator biographies to special collections and resources, Internet sites, and other nonprint sources.

1258 Children's core collection. EBSCO. www.ebscohost.com/academic/childrens-core-collection. CP$

Formerly H. W. Wilson's print *Children's Catalog*, this resource is an annotated bibliography of more than 30,000 titles for children from preschool through fifth grade. Fiction and nonfiction, picture books, graphic novels, and more are included. Entries provide full bibliographic information, book review citations, and excerpts. It is updated monthly.

1259 Children's literature review. Gale Cengage, 1976–. $$

028.52   PN1009

This continuing series provides excerpts from criticism on more than 750 authors and illustrators of books for children and young adults. Each volume examines three to five authors in entries consisting of listings of major works and awards and excerpts from reviews and criticism. Also available in Literature Criticism Online.

1260 Companion to American children's picture books. Connie Ann Kirk. 440p. Greenwood, 2005. $

011.62   Z1033

Includes essays discussing the definition and evaluation of a picture book and some 400 entries covering authors and illustrators and their works as well as special topics.

1261 Dictionary of American children's fiction, 1859–1959: Books of recognized merit. Alethea K. Helbig and Agnes R. Perkins. 666p. Greenwood, 1985. $$

813   PS374

Dictionary of American children's fiction, 1960–1984: Recent books of recognized merit. Alethea K. Helbig and Agnes R. Perkins. 930p. Greenwood, 1986. $$

813.5   PS374

Dictionary of American children's fiction, 1985–1989: Books of recognized merit. Alethea K. Helbig and Agnes R. Perkins. 320p. Greenwood, 1993. $$

813.5   PS374

Dictionary of American children's fiction, 1990–1994: Books of recognized merit. Alethea K. Helbig and Agnes R. Perkins. 490p. Greenwood, 1996. $$

813.5   PS490

Dictionary of American children's fiction, 1995–1999: Books of recognized merit. Alethea K. Helbig and Agnes R. Perkins. 632p. Greenwood, 2001. $$

813.5   PS374

Dictionary of American young adult fiction, 1997–2001: Books of recognized merit. Alethea K. Helbig and Agnes R. Perkins. 584p. Greenwood, 2004. $$

813.5   PS374

Brief biographical and bibliographical information as well as plot summaries for American children's fiction written between 1859 and 1999 and for American young adult fiction written between 1997 and 2001. Entries include titles, authors, characters, significant settings, and other elements.

1262 The essential guide to children's books and their creators. Anita Silvey, ed. 560p. Houghton Mifflin, 2002. $

810.9   Z1232

An overview of the best in children's literature from the last 100 years with more than 475 entries on a variety of topics that include genres, multicultural themes and perspectives, personal reflections by authors and illustrators, and more.

1263 Index to fairy tales, myths, and legends. 2nd ed. Mary H. Eastman. 610p. Faxon, 1926. OP

398.2   GR550

Index to fairy tales, myths, and legends: Supplement. Mary H. Eastman. 566p. Faxon, 1937. OP

398.2   GR550

Index to fairy tales, myths, and legends: 2nd Supplement. Mary H. Eastman. 370p. Faxon, 1952. OP

398.2   GR550

Index to fairy tales, 1949–1972, 3rd supplement: Including folklore, legends, and myths in collections. Norma O. Ireland, comp. 741p. Scarecrow, 1988. $$

398.2   GR550

Index to fairy tales, 1973–1977, 4th supplement: Including folklore, legends, and myths in collections. Norma O. Ireland, comp. 259p. Scarecrow, 1986. $$

398.2   GR550

Index to fairy tales, 1978–1986, 5th supplement: Including folklore, legends, and myths in collections. Norma O. Ireland and Joseph W. Sprug, comps. 575p. Scarecrow, 1989. $$

398.2   GR550

Index to fairy tales, 1987–1992, 6th supplement: Including 310 collections of fairy tales, folktales, myths,

and legends with significant pre-1987 titles not previously indexed. Joseph W. Sprug, ed. 602p. Scarecrow, 1994. $$
398.3   GR550

A valuable source for the location of folklore and fairy tale material. Indicates versions of material suitable for small children. Later supplements include folklore, legends, and myths in collections and subject indexes to stories. Libraries short on space in the reference collection may wish to place older editions in storage, if room is available.

1264 Junior book of authors. 2nd ed. 309p. H. W. Wilson, 1951. OP
809.89   PN1009
More junior authors. 235p. H. W. Wilson, 1963. OP
808.89   PN1009
Third book of junior authors. H. W. Wilson, 1972. OP
808.89   PN1009
Fourth book of junior authors and illustrators. 370p. H. W. Wilson, 1978. OP
809.89   PN1009
Fifth book of junior authors and illustrators. 375p. H. W. Wilson, 1983. OP
808.89   PN1009
Sixth book of junior authors and illustrators. 356p. Salem Press, 1989. $$
809.89   PN1009
Seventh book of junior authors and illustrators. 371p. Salem Press, 1996. $$
809.89   PN1009
Eighth book of junior authors and illustrators. Connie C. Rockman, ed. 592p. Salem Press, 2000. $$
809.89   PN1009
Ninth book of junior authors and illustrators. Connie C. Rockman, ed. 600p. Salem Press, 2005. $$
Tenth book of junior authors and illustrators. Connie C. Rockman, ed. 850p. Salem Press, 2008. $$

A standard work in children's literature collections since 1951, this series continues to provide author and illustrator profiles, portraits, bibliographies, lists of major awards and citations, and a comprehensive index to all volumes. As with the previous listing, libraries may want to retain the older editions, even if they are not housed in reference.

1265 The Norton anthology of children's literature: The traditions in English. Lissa Paul et al., eds. 2200p. W. W. Norton, 2006. $
820.8   PZ5

A comprehensive collection drawn from 340 years of literature for children. Features numerous excerpts and the full texts of approximately eighty works. Sixty of the 400 illustrations are reproduced in color.

1266 The Oxford companion to children's literature. Humphrey Carpenter and Mari Prichard. 600p. Oxford, 1999. $
809.8   PN1008.5

This one-volume handbook contains nearly 2,000 entries for authors, titles, characters, literary terms and genres, and a variety of topics associated with the study of children's literature. Emphasis is on British and American literature, with brief summaries of the state of children's literature in other countries.

1267 The Oxford dictionary of nursery rhymes. 2nd ed. Iona Opie and Peter Opie, eds. 592p. Oxford, 1998. $
398.8   PZ8.3

A scholarly collection of nursery rhymes, songs, nonsense jingles, and lullabies with notes and explanations concerning history, literary associations, social uses, and possible portrayals of real people.

1268 The Oxford encyclopedia of children's literature. Jack Zipes, ed. 4v. Oxford, 2006. $$
809   PN1008.5

More than 3,000 signed entries cover authors, illustrators, genres, titles, countries, regions, organizations, trends, awards and award winners, research collections, and more. Many of the articles include short bibliographies, and there is a larger selected bibliography in the fourth volume.

1269 The Oxford handbook of children's literature. Julia Mickenberg and Lynne

Vallone, eds. 656p. Oxford, 2011. $$
820.9 PR990
A comprehensive and scholarly work featuring twenty-six essays that analyze several types of children's literature, including picture books, comics and graphic novels, classic novels, and modern classics from a variety of perspectives.

1270 Picturing the world: Information picture books for children. Kathleen T. Isaacs. 216p. American Library Association, 2012. $
011.62 Z1033
An annotated survey of the best informational titles for children ages three to ten. Useful for collection development as well as readers' advisory.

1271 Primary genreflecting: A guide to picture books and easy readers. Susan Fichtelberg and Bridget Dealy Volz. 493p. Libraries Unlimited, 2010. $
011.62 Z1033
A readers' advisory guide to contemporary books for children ages three to eight ranging from ABC books to fairy tales, animal stories, and more. Arrangement is by genre, subgenre, and theme. Indicates bilingual editions and titles available in Spanish.

1272 Something about the author: Facts and pictures about contemporary authors and illustrators of books for young people. Gale Cengage, 1971–. $$
028.5 PN451
Each volume in this continuing series provides approximately seventy-five illustrated biographical sketches of authors and illustrators of children's books. The entire series is also available online.

PRIZES AND AWARDS

1273 Awards and prizes online. Children's Book Council. http://awardsandprizes .harvestsolutions.ca. $$
A subscription database based on the CBC's *Children's Books: Awards and Prizes* with information on 326 awards and thousands of authors and books. Updated monthly.

1274 The Coretta Scott King Awards, 1970–2009. 4th ed. Henrietta M. Smith,

ed. 232p. American Library Association, 2009. $
016.81 Z1037
Published to commemorate the fortieth anniversary of the award for the best in African American children's literature, this work provides a complete listing of the winning titles as well as profiles of their authors and illustrators.

1275 The Newbery and Caldecott awards: A guide to the medal and honor books. Association for Library Service to Children. 184p. American Library Association, 2012. $
011.62 Z1037
An annual guide to all the medal and honor books since the inception of the awards. Includes indexing by author, illustrator, and title, an explanation of award criteria, and an essay about the importance of the awards in promoting children's literature.

Classical

1276 The classic epic: An annotated bibliography. Thomas J. Sienkewicz. 265p. Scarecrow, 1995. $
883 PA3022
A bibliography "directed toward the first-time reader of the classical epics in English translation." Targets easily accessible materials that discuss social conditions, geographical conditions, composition techniques, characters, and more.

1277 Classical Greek and Roman drama: An annotated bibliography. Robert J. Forman. 239p. Scarecrow, 1995. $
882.01 PA3024
An annotated bibliography of translations, commentaries, and criticism of works by Aeschylus, Aristophanes, Ennius, Euripides, Menander, Plautus, Seneca, Sophocles, and Terence.

1278 Classical studies: A guide to the reference literature. 2nd ed. Fred W. Jenkins. 424p. Libraries Unlimited, 2006. $
016.48 PA91
More than 1,000 reference works on classical studies, including bibliographies, dictionaries,

handbooks, biographical and geographical sources, and Internet resources, are arranged by subject in this useful guide.

1279 The Facts on File companion to classical drama. John E. Thorburn Jr. 688p. Facts on File, 2005. $
880.09   PA3024
Features some 400 alphabetically arranged entries on authors, characters, dramas, settings, historical figures, themes, concepts, genres, and theatrical terms. It covers the major authors of the period.

1280 The Oxford companion to classical literature. 3rd ed. M. C. Howatson, ed. 640p. Oxford, 2011. $
880.9   PA31
The latest edition of a work first published in 1937 offering more than 3,100 entries covering classical literary figures, styles, character and plot summaries, and topics such as aesthetics, love and sexuality, the soul, and universal and natural law.

Drama

1281 Inter-play: An online index to plays in collections, anthologies, and periodicals. Portland State University. www.lib.pdx.edu/systems/interplay/. Free
Maintained by librarians from Portland State University, this site provides citations to thousands of plays and is searchable by author or title.

1282 Notable playwrights. Carl E. Rollyson, ed. 1131p. Salem Press, 2004. $$
809.2   PN1625
More than 100 alphabetically arranged entries drawn from the *Critical Survey of Drama* (rev. ed., Salem Press, 2003) and consisting of articles approximately twelve pages in length that include a bibliography and an illustration of the playwright.

1283 The Oxford dictionary of plays. Michael Patterson. 544p. Oxford, 2005. $
809.2   PN1625
One thousand of the most notable plays in the history of the theater are described in entries that include the dates of writing, first performance, and

first publication as well as a synopsis, commentary, and more. There is also an index of characters and a selected bibliography.

1284 Playdatabase.com. Alora Cheek and Jim Sabo. www.playdatabase.com. Free
This free database offers 12,498 plays by 5,638 authors as well as 356 monologues. Searchable by author, title, cast size, synopsis, length, and more.

Fantasy

1285 The encyclopedia of fantasy. John Clute and John Grant, eds. 1049p. St. Martin's, 1997. $
809.3   PN3435
This survey covers of fantasy in all its forms, including texts, film, art, opera, myth, comic books, authors, characters, and places up until the late twentieth century. Among the authors included are E. T. A. Hoffmann, Edgar Allan Poe, J. R. R. Tolkien, C. S. Lewis, and the Brothers Grimm.

1286 Encyclopedia of fantasy and horror fiction. Don D'Ammassa. 488p. Facts on File, 2006. $
809.38   PR830
Offers comprehensive coverage of the major fantasy and horror authors and their books, from H. P. Lovecraft and Stephen King to R. L. Stine and J. K. Rowling and many more. Entries include a brief biography and complete bibliography as well as a critical analysis.

1287 Fang-tastic fiction: Twenty-first century paranormal reads. Patricia O'Brien Mathews. 272p. American Library Association, 2011. $
016.81   Z1231
This is a guide to the popular series that feature vampires, werewolves, superheroes, and other characters of urban fantasy. It also provides chronological lists of series titles called "read-alikes" and ratings for humor, violence, and sensuality.
Greenwood encyclopedia of science fiction and fantasy: Themes, works, and wonders, **see 1327.**
Reference guide to science fiction, fantasy, and horror, **see 1328.**

1288 Supernatural literature of the world: An encyclopedia. S. T. Joshi and Stefan Dziemianowicz, eds. 3v. Greenwood, 2005. $$

809.93   PN56.58

Nearly 1,000 signed entries on authors, themes, and topics from ancient times to the present provide comprehensive coverage of the subject. Includes indexes to characters and motifs and a general bibliography.

Fiction

1289 Contemporary world fiction: A guide to literature in translation. Juris Dilevko, Keren Dali, and Glenda Garbutt. 526p. Libraries Unlimited, 2011. $

016.8   Z5917

This is an overview of approximately 1,000 fiction titles from many nations. It includes essays about classic world fiction titles and the fiction traditions of other countries. Contains indexes for annotated authors, annotated titles, translators, nations, and subjects/keywords.

1290 Fiction core collection. EBSCO. www.ebscohost.com/academic/fiction-core-collection. CP$

Formerly H. W. Wilson's print *Fiction Catalog*, this title is an annotated bibliography of more than 11,000 works of classic and contemporary fiction. Romance, westerns, mysteries, fantasy, and science fiction are included. Entries provide full bibliographic information, book review citations, and excerpts. Updated monthly.

1291 Genreflecting: A guide to popular reading interests. 6th ed. Diana Tixier Herald; Wayne A. Wiegand, ed. 584p. Libraries Unlimited, 2005. $

016.81   PS374

A reliable readers' advisory tool that supplies reading recommendations for a variety of genres and subgenres. More than 5,000 titles are represented.

1292 The readers' advisory guide to genre fiction. 2nd ed. Joyce G. Saricks. 352p. American Library Association, 2009. $

025.5   Z711.5

Readers' advisor guru Saricks imparts solid and practical advice for those seeking to understand fifteen different genres of fiction, including westerns, suspense, romance, mysteries, and more, and how best to recommend them to library patrons.

Gothic

1293 Encyclopedia of gothic literature. Mary Ellen Snodgrass. 496p. Facts on File, 2004. $

809.9   PN3435

An A–Z guide that offers more than 400 entries on genres, literary terms, characters, people, places, books, stories, and more. Each entry includes a brief bibliography.

1294 Routledge companion to Gothic. Catherine Spooner and Emma McEvoy, eds. 304p. Routledge, 2007. $$

823   PR830

Features scholarly essays on the history of this literary genre throughout the English-speaking world; also covers a variety of related topics, including contemporary gothic and gothic culture, media, and music.

Graphic Novels

1295 Critical survey of graphic novels: Heroes and superheroes. Bart H. Beaty and Stephen Weiner, eds. 2v. Salem Press, 2012. $$

741.5   PN6725

Critical survey of graphic novels: History, theme, and technique. Bart H. Beaty and Stephen Weiner, eds. 440p. Salem Press, 2012. $$

741.5   PN6725

Critical survey of graphic novels: Independent and underground classics. Bart H. Beaty and Stephen Weiner, eds. 3v. Salem Press, 2012. $$

741.5   PN6725

Critical survey of graphic novels: Manga. Bart H. Beaty and Stephen Weiner, eds. 400p. Salem Press, 2012. $$

741.5   PN6725

This series offers detailed studies of various types of graphic novels that include analyses of themes and artistic and production styles as well as descriptions of plots and characters. Suggestions for further reading are included with each essay. All the volumes in the series are also available as e-books.

1296 Mostly manga: A genre guide to popular manga, manhwa, manhua, and anime. Elizabeth F. S. Kalen. 164p. Libraries Unlimited, 2012. $
016.7   Z5956
A readers' advisory guide to Japanese manga and anime, Korean manhwa, and Chinese manhua from the early 1990s to the present that explains the characteristics of each genre, highlights major titles, and discusses terminology, content, and ratings.

1297 Readers' advisory guide to graphic novels. Francisca Goldsmith. 136p. American Library Association, 2010. $
025.2   Z692
A concise and thorough overview of the genre that includes reading lists, practical advice for librarians, and a short course in graphic novels.

Historical

1298 Dickinson's American historical fiction. 5th ed. Virginia B. Gerhardstein. 368p. Scarecrow, 1986. $
016.8   PS374
First published in 1956, this work chronologically classifies thousands of historical novels published between 1917 and 1984. Brief annotations are provided for these titles as well as for selected classics of historical fiction. Author-title and subject indexes are included.

1299 Historical fiction: A guide to the genre. Sarah L. Johnston. 836p. Libraries Unlimited, 2005. $
813.8   PS374
Covers sagas, western historical novels, literary historical novels, Christian historical fiction, and other subgenres. There are reading lists by plot, pattern, or theme as well as a list of award-winning historical novels.

1300 The readers' advisory guide to historical fiction. Jennifer S. Baker. 176p. American Library Association, 2013. $
016.8   PS374
The latest guidebook to historical fiction offers an overview of the genre along with reading lists and discussions of classic and contemporary titles. Helpful lists of print and web-based resources are also included.

Horror

Encyclopedia of fantasy and horror fiction, see **1286.**

1301 Hooked on horror: A guide to reading interests in horror fiction. 2nd ed. Anthony J. Fonseca and June Michele Pulliam. 400p. Libraries Unlimited, 2003. $
016.8   Z5917
Hooked on horror III: A guide to reading interests. Anthony J. Fonseca and June Michele Pulliam. 513p. Libraries Unlimited, 2009. $
016.8   Z5917
These two volumes provide annotations for hundreds of new as well as classic horror titles in thirteen subgenres including techno horror, ghosts and haunted houses, vampires and werewolves, and small-town horror. Other helpful features include lists of resources and indications of availability in large print, audio, and e-book formats. Libraries that own the first edition should retain it because each volume supplements the others.
Reference guide to science fiction, fantasy, and horror, see **1328.**

1302 Readers' advisory guide to horror. 2nd ed. Becky Siegel Spratford. 176p. American Library Association, 2012. $
026.8   Z711.5
The second edition of a helpful guide to this popular genre features lists of recommended authors

and titles, practical tips for readers' advisory, and an extensive list of resources.

Mystery

1303 A catalogue of crime. Rev. ed. Jacques Barzun and Wendell H. Taylor. 864p. HarperCollins, 1989. OP
016.8   Z5917
Although out of print, this is still a useful bibliography of crime and detective fiction. Entries include plot summaries and bibliographic information. There are indexes to authors, titles, and names. Libraries that own this title should retain it, either in the circulating or reference collection.

1304 Crime writers: A research guide. Elizabeth Haynes. 204p. Libraries Unlimited, 2011. $
813   PS374
Provides a wealth of resources about fifty of the top writers in the crime genre. Entries include brief biographies, lists of major works and awards, websites, criticism, and more. In addition, there is a comprehensive bibliography and an overview of crime fiction and its subgenres.
Latin American mystery writers: An A-to-Z guide, **see 1389.**

1305 Make mine a mystery: A reader's guide to mystery and detective fiction. Gary Warren Niebuhr. 624p. Libraries Unlimited, 2003. $
813   PN3448
Make mine a mystery II: A reader's guide to mystery and detective fiction. Gary Warren Niebuhr. 292p. Libraries Unlimited, 2011. $
016.8   Z5917
Nearly 3,000 mystery titles are included in these two volumes along with a variety of useful special features. The novels are presented in sections according to detective type (amateur, public, or private) and further characterized by the personality of the protagonist (e.g., eccentric, hardboiled, or lone wolf). There are indexes by author, title, character, setting, and location.

1306 The readers' advisory guide to mystery. 2nd ed. John Charles, Candace Clark, Joanne Hamilton-Selway, and Joanna Morrison. 224p. American Library Association, 2012. $
025.2   Z711.5
This helpful guide covers some of the most popular subcategories of this genre, including amateur sleuths, private investigators, and historical sleuths. This source also includes chapters on mystery resources and collection development, lists of mystery movies and television series, and a selected bibliography.

1307 Reference and research guide to mystery and detective fiction. 2nd ed. Richard J. Bleiler. 848p. Libraries Unlimited, 2004. $
016.8   Z5917
Provides evaluative reviews and complete bibliographic information for approximately 1,000 reference works on mystery and detective fiction.

Novel

1308 The contemporary novel: A checklist of critical literature on the English language novel since 1945. 2nd ed. Irving Adelman and Rita Dworkin. 696p. Scarecrow, 1997. $$
016.8   Z1231
A selective bibliography of critical literature on the contemporary English-language novel. All of the works of each qualified author are listed, followed by citations to journal articles and books rather than book reviews.

1309 Contemporary novelists. 7th ed. Susan W. Brown, ed. 1166p. St. James Press, 2000. $$
823.9   PR881
This title provides a biographical sketch, an address, a bibliography of works published, and a signed scholarly essay for each of the approximately 650 contemporary English-language novelists included.

1310 Sequels: An annotated guide to novels in series. 4th ed. Janet G. Husband and

Jonathan F. Husband. 792p. American Library Association, 2009. $$

The latest edition of a selective, annotated list of hundreds of series started since 1989 featuring the best, most endearing, and most popular novels in series. Includes indexes by title and subject.

1311 To be continued: An annotated guide to sequels. 2nd ed. Merle L. Jacob and Hope Apple. 488p. Greenwood, 2000. $
016.8   Z6514

English-language fictional sequels and books in series representing a variety of genres, excluding mysteries, are listed by author. Indexed by title, genre, subject, time, and place. Includes a list of additional sources.

Poetry

1312 The Columbia Granger's index to poetry in anthologies. 13th ed. Tessa Kale. 2416p. Columbia, 2007. $$
016.8   PN1022

This title is the standard print reference work for locating poems in anthologies. Some 85,000 poems by 12,000 poets are indexed by title, first and last line, author, and subject. Since some material is dropped from each edition, all previous editions of this title should be retained.

1313 The Columbia Granger's index to poetry in collected and selected works. 2nd ed. Keith Newton. 1152p. Columbia, 2004. $$
016.8   PN1022

Indexes more than 50,000 poems by 251 leading poets that appeared in 315 selected and collected works. Indexing is by author, title, first and last line, and subject. Complements *The Columbia Granger's Index to Poetry in Anthologies*; as is the case with that title, the previous edition should be retained.

1314 The Columbia Granger's world of poetry. Columbia. www.columbia grangers.org. CP$

This subscription database provides the full texts of 250,000 poems as well as a number of books of and about poetry published by Columbia University

Press, including the eighth through the thirteenth editions of *The Columbia Granger's Index to Poetry in Anthologies* and both editions of *The Columbia Granger's Index to Poetry in Collected and Selected Works*. A mobile app is available and updates can be found on Twitter and Facebook. Libraries that subscribe to the electronic product may store or discard the print editions.

1315 Contemporary poets. 7th ed. Thomas Riggs, ed. 1443p. St. James Press, 2000. $$
821.9   PR603

A biographical handbook of contemporary poets with alphabetically arranged entries consisting of a short biography, full bibliography, comments by many of the poets, and a signed critical essay.

1316 Last lines: An index to the last lines of poetry. Victoria Kline. 2v. Facts on File, 1991. $$
016.8   PN1022

Covers more than 174,000 poems written in or translated into English. Indexes each poem by title, last line, author, and keyword.

1317 New Princeton encyclopedia of poetry and poetics. 3rd ed. Alex Preminger. 1434p. Princeton, 1993. $
808.1   PN1021

This title, *the* authoritative, scholarly encyclopedia of poetics and poetry, provides surveys of the poetry of 106 nations, descriptions of poetic forms and genres, explanations of prosody and rhetoric, discussions of major schools and movements, and more.

1318 Poetry criticism. Gale Cengage, 1991–. $$
809.1   PN1010

Each volume in this series provides biographical and critical information on three to five major poets from various countries and time periods. Cumulative indexes by author and nationality and volume-specific title indexes are included. Also available in Gale Cengage's Literature Criticism Online.

1319 Poetry handbook: A dictionary of terms. 4th ed. Babette Deutsch. 224p. Harper Perennial, 2009. $

Definitions are clear and concise and cover terminology and poetic forms as well as broader topics such as romanticism and nonsense verse. Includes cross-references and index of poets cited in the definitions.

Rhetoric

1320 Encyclopedia of rhetoric and composition: Communication from ancient times to the information age. Theresa Enos, ed. 802p. Routledge, 2010. $$

808   PN172

Provides an overview of rhetoric and its role in contemporary life and discusses its application and practical benefits. Signed articles discuss major rhetoricians from all time periods.

1321 Encyclopedia of the essay. Tracy Chevalier, ed. 1024p. Fitzroy Dearborn, 1997. $$

809.4   PN4500

Articles include biographical essays on some 400 noted essayists, including Montaigne, Addison, Hazlitt, and Sontag, and geographic and historical surveys of the essay. Suggestions for further reading and critical bibliographies are included for the articles on individual writers.

Romance

1322 Romance authors: A research guide. Sarah E. Sheehan. 193p. Libraries Unlimited, 2010. $

813   PS374

Offers an overview of the genre, an extensive bibliography, author profiles that include chronological lists of works and bibliographies, and a glossary of romance genre terms.

1323 Romance fiction: A guide to the genre. 2nd ed. Kristin Ramsdell. 719p. Libraries Unlimited, 2012. $

016.8   Z1231

A comprehensive guide that provides an exhaustive list of romance titles and a core collection list in addition to chapters on various genres of contemporary romance fiction, an extensive bibliography of research materials, and indexes by author, title, and subject.

1324 Romance today: An A-to-Z guide to contemporary American romance writers. John Charles and Shelley Mosley. 424p. Greenwood, 2006. $

813   PS374

One hundred contemporary American romance writers are profiled in entries that comprise biographical information and critical analysis as well as a complete list of works. A general bibliography of print and electronic resources is included.

Science Fiction

1325 Anatomy of wonder: A critical guide to science fiction. 5th ed. Neil Barron, ed. 1016p. Libraries Unlimited, 2004. $

016.8   Z5917

A selected annotated bibliography featuring 2,100 works of science fiction and citing 800 research aids that highlight science fiction magazines, publications on the history and criticism of the genre, and science fiction on film and television.

1326 Encyclopedia of science fiction. Don D'Ammassa. 544p. Facts on File, 2005. $

813   PS374

Offers 500 detailed entries on major science fiction authors and works. The articles on authors include a discussion of the entrant's life and work, and there is a glossary of science fiction terms as well as a bibliography of the works of all authors cited and one of secondary sources.

1327 Greenwood encyclopedia of science fiction and fantasy: Themes, works, and wonders. Gary Westfahl, ed. 3v. Greenwood, 2005. $$

813   PS374

A comprehensive treatment of these genres that examines 400 science fiction themes and discusses 200 classic works of science fiction and fantasy. *Latin American science fiction writers: An A-to-Z guide*, see **1390**.

1328 Reference guide to science fiction, fantasy, and horror. 2nd ed. Michael Burgess and Lisa R. Bartle. 598p. Libraries Unlimited, 2002. $

016.8   Z5917

Offers 700 detailed annotations on reference sources for these genres, including bibliographies, encyclopedias, dictionaries, fan publications, and periodicals. Also includes recommendations for a core collection.

1329 Science fiction authors. Maura Heaphy. 352p. Libraries Unlimited, 2008. $
016.8   Z2014
Covers 100 science fiction authors in articles that include a brief biographical sketch, a list of major works, print and web sources for further information, and, for selected authors, "read-alike" lists.

Shakespeare

1330 The Columbia dictionary of Shakespeare quotations. Mary Foakes and Reginald Foakes, eds. 528p. Columbia, 1998. $
822.3   PR2892
Shakespearean quotations on some 600 subjects are arranged topically in entries that supply play title, speaker, act, scene, and line number (using *The Riverside Shakespeare*) and place the excerpt in context.

1331 Critical companion to William Shakespeare. Charles Boyce. 2v. Facts on File, 2005. $$
822.3   PR2892
A revised edition of Facts on File's *Shakespeare A to Z* (1990), this set offers biographical information as well as extensive critical discussions, entries on related themes and topics, and more. There is also a complete bibliography of Shakespeare's works and one of secondary sources.

1332 The essential Shakespeare: An annotated bibliography of major modern studies. 2nd ed. Larry S. Champion. 200p. G. K. Hall, 1993. $
822.3   PR2894
An annotated checklist of the most significant Shakespeare scholarship in English since 1900. Some 2,000 entries are arranged under general studies or under individual works.

1333 The Harvard concordance to Shakespeare. Marvin Spevack. 1600p. Georg Olms Verlag AG, 1973. $$
822.3   PR2892

A computer-produced concordance based on volumes 4–6 of the author's *A Complete and Systematic Concordance to Shakespeare* (Georg Olms, 1968–1970). Includes 29,000 words and statistics on the number of times each occurs in verse and prose passages. Although this title is older, libraries will want to keep it in their reference areas.

1334 Internet Shakespeare editions. University of Victoria and the Social Sciences and Humanities Research Council of Canada. http://internetshakespeare.uvic.ca. Free
The Internet Shakespeare Editions (ISE) is a nonprofit corporation affiliated with the University of Victoria in Victoria, British Columbia, Canada. It provides "scholarly, fully annotated texts of Shakespeare's plays, multimedia explorations of the context of Shakespeare's life and works, and records of his plays in performance."

1335 The quotable Shakespeare: A topical dictionary. Charles DeLoach, comp. 568p. McFarland, 1998. $
822.3   PR2892
This source arranges 6,516 quotations from Shakespeare under some 1,000 topics. Includes title, character, and topical indexes.

1336 The reader's encyclopedia of Shakespeare. Reprint. Oscar James Campbell and Edward G. Quinn, eds. 1014p. MJF Books, 1998. $
822.3   PR2892
This title provides criticism and information on all aspects of Shakespeare's works. Appendixes include a chronology of events related to the life and works of Shakespeare, transcripts of documents, genealogical tables of the Houses of York and Lancaster, and a thirty-page selected bibliography.

1337 Shakespearean criticism: Excerpts from the criticism of William Shakespeare's plays and poetry, from the first published appraisals to current evaluations. Gale Cengage, 1984–. $$
822.3   PR2965

An ongoing series that provides comprehensive coverage of Shakespearean critiques through the years. Most of the critical essays included are full text. Also available in Gale Cengage's Literature Criticism Online.

1338 Shakespeare and film: A Norton guide. Samuel Crowl. 272p. W. W. Norton, 2007. $

791.4   PR3093

Concise analyses of film versions of Shakespeare's plays concentrating on major directors, including Kenneth Branagh, Laurence Olivier, Orson Welles, Akira Kurosawa, and Franco Zeffirelli. Includes a selected bibliography and filmography.

1339 A Shakespeare glossary. 3rd ed. Charles T. Onions and Robert D. Eagleson. 360p. Oxford, 1986. $

822.3   PR2892

This source supplies definitions of now-obsolete words as well as explanations for unfamiliar allusions and proper names. Each definition includes illustrative citations from Shakespeare. Although older, this title should be retained by libraries that own it.

1340 Treasures in full: Shakespeare in quarto. British Library. www.bl.uk/treasures/shakespeare/homepage.html. Free

"On this site you will find the British Library's 93 copies of the 21 plays by William Shakespeare printed in quarto before the theatres were closed in 1642."

Short Story

1341 The Columbia companion to the twentieth-century American short story. Blanche H. Gelfant, ed. 2v. Columbia, 2001. $

813   PS374

A collection of biographical essays on individual short story writers as well as essays that examine common themes in short stories. Each entry includes a concise bibliography.

1342 The Facts on File companion to the American short story. 2nd ed. Abby H. P. Werlock. 2v. Facts on File, 2010. $$

813   PS374

This set supplies entries on authors, characters, literary terms and themes, motifs, and more. Analyses and synopses of significant stories, a selected bibliography, and lists of award winners are included.

1343 The Facts on File companion to the British short story. Andrew Maunder. 448p. Facts on File, 2007. $

823   PR829

This title includes some 450 entries on authors born in Great Britain, Ireland, and British Commonwealth countries; literary movements; notable short story collections; and more. It also includes a bibliography.

1344 Short story criticism: Excerpts from criticism of the works of short fiction writers. Gale Cengage, 1988–. $$

809.3   PN3373

Each volume in this series presents critical and biographical overviews of three to five short story writers. Entries include lists of principal works and selected bibliographies. Also available in Gale Cengage's Literature Criticism Online.

1345 Short story index. Salem Press, 1900–. $$

016   Z5917

This standard reference tool for locating short stories is published annually in a single bound volume. Those who subscribe for a five-year cycle also receive a bound cumulation of the *Index*. Contact EBSCO for online availability.

Urban Literature

1346 The readers' advisory guide to street literature. Vanessa Irvin Morris. 168p. American Library Association, 2012. $

016.8   Z1231

Provides an overview of the genre, also known as urban fiction, and addresses its appeal, themes, subgenres, literary motifs, and more. Offers advice on readers' advisory, collection development strategies, and more. It includes a list of primary and secondary works cited and a list of street-literature publishers.

1347 Urban grit: A guide to street lit. Megan Honig. 251p. Libraries Unlimited, 2010. $

016.8   Z1231

Describes some 400 genre titles and classifies them according to subgenres. Provides an overview of the genre and discusses its appeal. Includes a comprehensive bibliography of core collections for public libraries.

National and Regional Literatures

African

1348 The Columbia guide to Central African literature in English since 1945. Adrian Roscoe. 220p. Columbia, 2007. $
820.9   PR9390.5
The Columbia guide to East African literature in English since 1945. Simon Gikandi and Evan Mwangi. 224p. Columbia, 2007. $
820.9   PR9340
The Columbia guide to South African literature in English since 1945. Gareth Cornwell, Dirk Klopper, and Craig MacKenzie. 288p. Columbia, 2010. $
820.9   PR9350.2
The Columbia guide to West African literature in English since 1945. Oyekan Owomoyela. 216p. Columbia, 2008. $
820.9   PR9340.5
These volumes of the Columbia Guide to Literature since 1945 series cover the literary traditions of, respectively, Zimbabwe, Malawi, Zambia; Kenya, Uganda, Tanzania, Somalia, Ethiopia; South Africa; and Gambia, Sierra Leone, Liberia, Ghana, and Nigeria. Each provides essays that supply historical context, entries on major authors and their works, and bibliographies.

1349 The Routledge encyclopedia of African literature. Simon Gikandi, ed. 638p. Routledge, 2009. $$
809.8   PL8010
Hundreds of scholarly articles discuss African authors and their works as well as literary criticism and theory in this area.

1350 Student encyclopedia of African literature. Douglas Killam and Alicia L.

Kerfoot. 368p. Greenwood, 2007. $
820.9   PR9340
Some 600 alphabetically arranged articles discuss writers and their works, literary genres, and more; many include suggestions for further reading. There is also a selected bibliography.

American

1351 American writers. Elizabeth H. Oakes. 448p. Facts on File, 2004. $
810.9   PS129
Profiles more than 250 American writers from colonial times to the present in entries that include a biography, criticism, and a bibliography. There is a general bibliography as well as a list of suggested titles for further reading.

1352 American writers collection. Gale Cengage, 1974–. $$
810.9   PS129
Now also available in e-book format through the Gale Virtual Reference Library, this ongoing series offers biographical and critical articles on American authors from the seventeenth century to the present. Each essay is accompanied by a selected bibliography and a list of studies for further reading.

1353 The Facts on File companion to the American novel. Abby H. P. Werlock, ed. 3v. Facts on File, 2006. $$
813   PS371
More than 900 alphabetically arranged articles cover authors and novels. Selected bibliographies and suggestions for further study are included with the articles on authors, and there are also extended essays on particular types of novels.

1354 The Greenwood encyclopedia of American poets and poetry. Jeffrey Gray, ed. 5v. Greenwood, 2005. $$$
811   PA303
Extensive coverage of nearly 400 years of poetry and more than 800 writers as well as articles on poetic terms, movements, theories, and more. Articles on individual poets include biographical and critical information and suggestions for further reading. There is also a general bibliography.

1355 The Greenwood encyclopedia of multiethnic American literature. Emmanuel S. Nelson, ed. 5v. Greenwood, 2005. $$$

810.9   PS153

Most of the 1,000 signed entries cover individual authors, and the rest discuss topics such as assimilation, bilingualism, immigration, identity, and ethnic stereotypes. Includes a selected general bibliography.

1356 The Oxford companion to American literature. 6th ed. James D. Hart and Phillip W. Leininger. 800p. Oxford, 1995. $

810.9   PS21

This handbook, arranged by subject in dictionary format, includes short biographies of American authors, brief bibliographies, plot summaries of novels and plays, and entries on literary schools and movements. There is a chronological index.

1357 Reference guide to American literature. 4th ed. Thomas Riggs, ed. 1319p. St. James Press, 1999. $$

810.9   PS129

Offers alphabetically arranged articles on writers and relevant topics. Articles on individual authors contain biographical data, a list of published works, citations to critical studies, and a signed scholarly essay. Includes an exhaustive chronology.

1358 Southern writers: A new biographical dictionary. Joseph M. Flora, Amber Vogel, and Bryan Giemza, eds. 616p. Louisiana State, 2006. $

810.9   PS261

More than 600 writers with either personal or literary connections to the South are represented by biographical sketches and lists of published works. Includes poets, playwrights, novelists, and short story writers.

Arabic

1359 The Routledge encyclopedia of Arabic literature. Julie S. Meisami and Paul Starkey, eds. 862p. Routledge, 2010. $

892.7   PJ7510

Thirteen-hundred signed entries cover Arabic literature, from the classical period to the twentieth century. There are articles on authors and their works, literary genres, terms, concepts, and more. Most entries include suggestions for further reading. A comprehensive index and a glossary are included.

Australian

1360 The Cambridge companion to Australian literature. Elizabeth Webby, ed. 348p. Cambridge, 2000. $

820.9   PR0604.3

Covers indigenous narratives, writers from the colonial period, fiction from 1900 to 1970, poetry from the 1890s to 1970, theatre from 1788 to the 1960s, contemporary fiction, poetry, and theatre, and more.

British

1361 British writers collection. Gale Cengage, 1992–. $$

820.9   PR85

Now also available in e-book format through the Gale Virtual Reference Library, this ongoing series offers biographical and critical articles on British authors from the fourteenth century to the present. Each essay is accompanied by a selected bibliography and a list of studies for further reading.

1362 Encyclopedia of British writers, 16th to 20th centuries. Alan Hager et al., eds. 4v. Facts on File, 2005. $$

820.9   PR421

Some 1,400 British novelists, poets, essayists, and playwrights are represented in articles consisting of a concise biography, a list of major works, and a brief bibliography. The first two volumes cover the sixteenth, seventeenth, and eighteenth centuries, and the second two cover 1800 to the present.

Modern British women writers, see **1253**.
Nineteenth-century British women writers: A bio-bibliographical critical sourcebook, see **1254**.

1363 The Oxford companion to English literature. 7th ed. Dinah Birch, ed.

1184p. Oxford, 2009. $$
820.9   PR19

The latest edition of the standard handbook to English literature first compiled by Sir Paul Harvey in 1932. Hundreds of new entries have been added, and coverage has been expanded to include writers from around the world and the latest in literary scholarship.

1364 The Oxford encyclopedia of British literature. David Scott Kastan, ed. 5v. Oxford, 2006. $$$
820.3   PR19

A comprehensive work covering British literature from the seventh century to the present in more than 500 articles that discuss individual writers, historical figures, and topics such as literary criticism, censorship, serialization, and more. Each entry includes selected annotated bibliographies of primary and secondary sources.

Canadian

1365 Canadian fiction: A guide to reading interests. Sharron Smith and Maureen O'Connor. 448p. Libraries Unlimited, 2005. $
016.8   Z1277

Provides an overview of Canadian works published from 1990 to 2004. More than 650 titles are categorized by primary appeal (language, setting, character, and story), and there are appendixes that list Canadian literary awards, websites, and other resources as well as Canadian publishers.

1366 The concise Oxford companion to Canadian literature. 2nd ed. William Toye, ed. 576p. Oxford, 2011.
810.9   PR9180.2

Based on *The Oxford Companion to Canadian Literature* (Oxford, 1998), this work includes entries on major writers, regional literatures, and other aspects of Canadian literary culture. This edition includes books published up to 2010, and among the new author entries are articles on writers such as Yann Martel, Joseph Boyden, and Lisa Moore.

1367 The Routledge concise history of Canadian literature. Richard J. Lane. 252p. Routledge, 2011. $$
810.9   PR9180

A one-volume resource that discusses Canadian fiction, poetry, and drama and its creators in historical, political, and cultural context.

Caribbean

1368 Encyclopedia of Caribbean literature. D. H. Figueredo, ed. 2v. Greenwood, 2005. $$
809.89   PN849

More than 700 alphabetically arranged entries cover a variety of topics, from authors, works, and genres to cultural and historical figures. Among the topics discussed are immigrant literature and feminism in Caribbean literature. An extensive bibliography is provided.

1369 Literature of the Caribbean. Lizabeth Paravisini-Gebert. 256p. Greenwood, 2008. $
809.89   PN849

Brief biographies and critical assessments of sixteen Caribbean authors include analyses of significant literary works.

1370 The Routledge companion to Anglophone Caribbean literature. Michael A. Bucknor and Alison Donnell, eds. 674p. Routledge, 2011. $$
809.89   PN849

Signed scholarly articles discuss the Anglophone Caribbean literary tradition from a variety of perspectives.

East Asian

1371 The Columbia companion to modern East Asian literature. Joshua S. Mostow, ed. 700p. Columbia, 2003. $$
895   PL493

Covers the literature of Japan, China, and Korea in more than 100 entries that include articles on individual authors, works, and schools and thematic essays that provide historical overviews and examinations of persistent themes.

Eastern European

1372 The Columbia guide to the literatures of Eastern Europe since 1945. Harold

B. Segel. 776p. Columbia, 2003. $$
809.89   Z2483
Articles about writers from Albania and Kosovo, Bosnia-Herzegovina, Bulgaria, Croatia, the Czech Republic, the former German Democratic Republic, Hungary, Macedonia, Poland, Romania, Serbia and Montenegro, Slovakia, and Slovenia include biographies, lists of published works, and English translations and citations to criticism.

1373 The Columbia literary history of Eastern Europe since 1945. Harold B. Segel. 424p. Columbia, 2008. $
809.89   Z2483
Essays cover a variety of topics, including Eastern European prison literature from 1945 to 1990, Eastern European women poets of the 1980s and 1990s, and the postcommunist literary scene in Eastern Europe since 1991. The literatures of Albania, Bosnia-Herzegovina, Bulgaria, Croatia, the Czech Republic, former East Germany, Hungary, Lithuania, Macedonia, Poland, Romania, Serbia, Slovakia, Slovenia, and Ukraine are represented.

French

1374 Guide to French literature: 1789 to the present. Anthony Levi, ed. 2v. St. James Press, 1994. $$
840   PQ226
Provides biographical, critical, and scholarly information on the principal figures in French literature and discusses literary topics, schools, and movements. There is a thorough bibliography for each author included.

1375 The new Oxford companion to literature in French. Peter France, ed. 926p. Oxford, 1995. $
840.9   PQ41
Discusses cultural and literary movements and their participants. Includes entries on individual authors and their works, literary terms and movements, and historical events with relevance to French literature.

German

1376 A companion to twentieth-century German literature. 2nd ed. Raymond Furness and Malcolm Humble, eds.

328p. Routledge, 1997. $$
830.9   PT401
More than 400 entries cover authors from Germany, Austria, and Switzerland and explore literary schools, movements, criticism, and more.

1377 The encyclopedia of German literature. Matthias Konzett, ed. 1136p. Routledge, 2000. $$
830.9   PT91
Individual authors and their works and a variety of literary topics are covered in more than 500 entries. Each article includes suggestions for further reading.

1378 The Oxford companion to German literature. 3rd ed. Henry Garland and Mary Garland, eds. 968p. Oxford, 1997. $$
830.3   PT41
This standard work presents entries of varying lengths on authors and their works; literary terms, festivals, and movements; and historical events with relevance to German literature.

Greek

1379 Encyclopedia of modern Greek literature. Bruce Merry. 544p. Greenwood, 2004. $$
889.19   PA5210
More than 800 entries discuss a variety of topics, including authors, texts, literary genres, and themes from the Byzantine period to the present. A selected general bibliography is provided.

Indian

1380 Handbook of twentieth-century literatures of India. Nalini Natarajan, ed. 448p. Greenwood, 1996. $$
891.1   PK5416
A thorough examination of the major regional literatures and literary traditions of twentieth-century India supplemented by extensive bibliographies.

1381 A History of Indian literature in English. Arvind Krishna Mehrotra, ed. 320p. Columbia, 2003. $
820.9   PR9489.6

Surveys 200 years of Indian literature written in English in essays on individual authors, groups of authors, and genres. Among the writers represented are novelists, playwrights, poets, anthropologists, scientists, and social reformers.
See also "South Asian," in this chapter.

Irish

1382 Dictionary of Irish literature. Rev. ed. Robert Hogan, ed. 2v. Greenwood, 1996. $$
820.9   PR8706
Includes more than 500 biocritical sketches about important Irish literary figures that include bibliographies of primary and secondary sources and articles on significant related institutions and subjects. An extensive bibliography is provided.
Irish women writers: An A-to-Z guide, see **1252**.

1383 Modern Irish writers: A bio-critical sourcebook. Alexander G. Gonzalez, ed. 480p. Greenwood, 1997. $$
820.9   PR8727
Alphabetically arranged entries on more than seventy Irish writers from 1885 to the present include biographical information, a critical analysis, and a bibliography of primary and secondary sources.

1384 The Oxford companion to Irish literature. Robert Welch and Bruce Stewart, eds. 648p. Oxford, 1996. $
820.9   PR8706
Covers sixteen centuries of literature from the Emerald Isle. Alphabetically arranged entries provide a comprehensive guide to the evolution and history of Irish literature framed within the context of the unique culture of Ireland.

Italian

1385 Dictionary of Italian literature. 2nd ed. Peter Bonadella, Julia C. Bonadella, and Jody R. Shiffman, eds. 736p. Greenwood, 1996. $$
850   PQ4006

More than 300 articles introduce authors, genres, schools, and movements of Italian literature from the twelfth century to the present. Bibliographies include English translations of primary texts as well as critical studies in various languages.

1386 The Oxford companion to Italian literature. Peter Hainsworth and David Robey, eds. 692p. Oxford, 2002. $$
850.9   PQ4006
More than 2,400 signed entries cover Italian literature from the early thirteenth century to the present and include a number of topics, from individual authors and their works to literary genres, theories, criticism, and more.

Japanese

1387 The Princeton companion to classical Japanese literature. Reprint. Earl Miner, Hiroko Odagiri, and Robert E. Morrell. 296p. Princeton, 1988. $
895.6   PL726
Includes a chronology, a description of major authors and their works, and entries on literary terms and symbols, theaters, reference tools, relevant geographical information, and costumes.

Latin American

1388 Encyclopedia of Latin American literature. Verity Smith, ed. 950p. Fitzroy Dearborn, 1997. $$
860   PQ7081
Some 500 articles supply a guide to authors, works, and issues relevant to the literary culture of Latin America. This title also includes survey articles about the literature of individual countries.

1389 Latin American mystery writers: An A-to-Z guide. Darrell B. Lockhart, ed. 264p. Greenwood, 2004. $
863   PQ7082
Provides biocritical articles on some fifty-four mystery writers, each of which includes bibliographies of primary and secondary sources. Includes authors from countries where Spanish or Portuguese is spoken but omits Latino writers from the United States.

1390 Latin American science fiction writers: An A-to-Z guide. Darrell B. Lockhart, ed. 248p. Greenwood, 2004. $

863   PQ7082

Identical in format to the preceding entry, this title provides biocritical articles on some seventy science fiction writers with bibliographies of primary and secondary sources. Omits Latino writers from the United States but includes authors from countries where Spanish or Portuguese is spoken.

1391 Literature of Latin America. Rafael Ocasio. 256p. Greenwood, 2004. $

860.9   PQ7081

Analyzes a variety of works by popular as well as lesser-known Latin American authors and includes many suggestions for further reading.

Russian

1392 Handbook of Russian literature. Reprint. Victor Terras, ed. 578p. Yale, 2005. $

891.7   PG2940

Covers authors, critics, genres, literary movements, journals, newspapers, institutions, and other topics of literary interest. Most of the articles include bibliographies of secondary studies, and the author entries also provide a list of major works and important translations.

1393 Reference guide to Russian literature. Neil Cornwell, ed. 1012p. Routledge, 1998. $$

891.7   PG2940

A rich sourcebook on the subject that includes more than a dozen introductory essays and hundreds of articles on authors and their works, each of which includes a bibliography. There is also an extensive general bibliography. A new edition is planned for late 2013.

1394 The Routledge companion to Russian literature. Neil Cornwell, ed. 288p. Routledge, 2001. $$

891.7   PG2951

Covers a thousand years of Russian poetry, drama,

and novels in articles that discuss literary theory, women's writing, socialist realism, émigré writing, and more. Includes suggestions for further reading and a general bibliography.

South Asian

1395 Modern South Asian literature in English. Paul Brians. 264p. Greenwood, 2003. $

820.9   PR9484

Fifteen chapters introduce writers from India, Pakistan, and Sri Lanka. There are discussions of works from 1915 to the present, background information, and a selective bibliography.

1396 South Asian literature in English: An encyclopedia. Jaina C. Sanga, ed. 392p. Greenwood, 2004. $

820.9   PR9570

Includes writers from India, Pakistan, Sri Lanka, and Bangladesh and covers a variety of literary topics, including literary theorists and film adaptations of novels. Entries include suggestions for further reading, and there is also a general selected bibliography.

1397 South Asian novelists in English: An A-to-Z guide. Jaina C. Sanga, ed. 328p. Greenwood, 2003. $

820.9   PR9496

More than fifty writers from Bangladesh, India, Pakistan, and Sri Lanka are discussed in articles that include biographies, a critical analysis, and a bibliography of primary and secondary sources. There is also a general selected bibliography.
See also **"Indian," in this chapter.**

Southeast Asian

1398 The Routledge concise history of Southeast Asian writing in English. Rajeev S. Patke and Philip Holden. 276p. Routledge, 2009. $$

895.9   PR9570

Surveys the literary traditions of the Philippines, Malaysia, Singapore, and Hong Kong and includes an extensive guide to further reading.

Spanish

1399 World literature in Spanish: An encyclopedia. Maureen Ihrie and Salvador A. Oropesa, eds. 3v. ABC-CLIO, 2011. $$
860.9   PQ6006

More than 800 alphabetically arranged entries discuss Spanish-language literature around the world, from the Middle Ages to today. It includes extensive bibliographies and a glossary of cultural and literary terms.

18 *History*

BARRY TROTT

In both public and academic libraries, interest in history remains high. Patrons want to explore the roots of current events and learn about the new scholarship applied to this discipline. This edition includes more coverage of China, Africa, and Latin America. Printed historical atlases remain popular. As in the previous edition, primary sources have continued their importance to historical scholarship.

Bibliographies and Guides

1400 CIA world factbook: Flags of the world. Central Intelligence Agency. www.cia.gov/library/publications/the-world-factbook/docs/flagsoftheworld.html. Free
This subset of the larger CIA Factbook is an excellent resource for images of country and territorial flags. The images are listed alphabetically and include a description and explanation of the flag's iconography. A country link takes the user to the complete set of information on the country in the CIA World Factbook, including articles and data on geography, people, government, economy, energy, communications, transportation, military, and transnational issues. Each country or territory entry also includes a map and small set of photographs.

1401 State names, seals, flags, and symbols: A historical guide. 3rd ed. Benjamin F. Shearer and Barbara S. Shearer. 544p. Greenwood, 2002. $
929.2   E155
The Shearers' work remains an essential source for small and medium-sized libraries. In addition to the information outlined in the title, this guide provides lists of state and territory mottoes, capitals, legal holidays, license plates, postage stamps, fairs and festivals, and universities. It is well illustrated, and has a select bibliography of state and territory histories as well as a general index. This edition is also available as an e-book from the publisher at a slightly higher price ($$).

Chronologies

1402 HyperHistory online. Andreas Nothiger. www.hyperhistory.com/online_n2/History_n2/a.html. Free
Growing out of Nothiger's World History Chart project, HyperHistory Online presents "3,000 years of world history with an interactive combination of synchronoptic lifelines, timelines, and maps." Three separate timelines cover people, major civilizations, and events. Many of the timeline entries are linked to brief annotations, which often include links to other resources on the topic. The charts use colors to indicate the topic's or subject's field

of interest—science, culture, religion, or politics. A useful place to start putting historical persons, places, and events in context.

1403 Smithsonian timelines of history.
Dorling Kindersley and Smithsonian Institution. 512p. DK, 2011. $
902   D11
This very affordable chronology would be a useful resource in almost any library. The work is divided into broad chapters covering human origins, early civilizations, the classical age, the age of trade and invention, the age of reformation, the age of revolution, and the age of technology and superpowers. There is a running chronology at the bottom of each page, and the main entries include short descriptions and are heavily illustrated. The book concludes with a directory that lists rulers and leaders, wars, inventions, and disasters, among other things. There is a comprehensive index of people, places, themes, and subjects as well as a glossary.

1404 This day in American history. 4th ed.
Ernie Gross and Roland H. Worth Jr. 398p. McFarland, 2012. $
973   E174.5
Although not a strict chronology, this work gives a list of all the significant events that occurred on each day of the year. Events for each day are listed in chronological order and give the year of the event and a brief description. The fourth edition includes more than 1,400 new entries that list "notable births, government actions, tragedies, disasters, and accomplishments for each day of the year."

1405 The timetables of history: A horizontal linkage of people and events. 4th ed. rev. Bernard Grun. 835p. Simon & Schuster, 2005. $
902   D11
Based on a translation of Werner Stein's *Kulturfahrplan*, this work remains a reliable and authoritative world chronology of human events over the past 7,000 years. Information is listed by year and is categorized and presented in seven columns—history/politics, literature/theater, religion/philosophy/learning, visual arts, music, science/technology/growth, and daily life. The subject-column format makes it easy to follow trends over the years or to

place events in context. The entries are short but complete, offering useful starting points, and the comprehensive index makes for easy access.

Databases and Indexes

1406 America: History and life with full text. EBSCO. www.ebscohost.com/public/america-history-and-life-with-full-text. CP$
A useful and comprehensive online resource for history bibliography, this database includes selective indexing for more than 1,800 journals published since 1955. Full-text coverage is included for more than 340 journals and monograph titles. Coverage focuses on U.S. and Canadian history and culture and includes abstracts in English for articles published in more than forty languages.

1407 American history. ABC-CLIO. www.abc-clio.com/productaspx?id=2147483682. CP$
Aimed at elementary and secondary students, ABC-CLIO's American History database offers a chronological survey of American history from 1350 to the present, access to "nearly 15,000 primary and secondary sources, including overview essays, biographies, government and court documents, photos, maps, audio/video clips, [and] statistics," and more than 3,000 biographical sketches of political, military, and cultural icons. Users can browse eras—with access to articles, primary source materials, and visuals—or analyze specific topics. An advanced search tool allows users to limit searches by content type and era. A useful and comprehensive resource for public libraries.

1408 Best of history websites. Tom Daccord and Justin Reich. www.besthistorysites.net. Free
This award-winning collection of links to more than 1,200 history-related web resources is a useful tool for students, teachers, and librarians. The browsable lists of sites are arranged by time period or geographic area, often with additional subdivisions to make browsing easier. There are some topical lists (e.g., "2012 Presidential Election"). Other lists offer links to resources on military history, art history, oral history, and the major world

religions. A "Resources" section offers links to maps, lesson plans, and information on doing history research. Links are heavily annotated, making them easy to use.

1409 Pop culture universe. ABC-CLIO.
www.abc-clio.com/product.aspx?isbn =9781598845488. CP$

With a user interface similar to its American History database, ABC-CLIO's Pop Culture Universe allows users to explore specific decades, with an overview, as well as fact and figures, visuals and media, articles, and a glossary of terms. Users can also use the "Analyze" tool to explore key questions in American pop culture. The advanced search tool allows users to limit searches by content type, decade, or broad subject. Content comes from "over 3,500 entries adapted, updated, and reedited from award-winning content from Greenwood Press, Praeger Publishers, and ABC-CLIO." This resource will be of interest to both students and the general public. Pop Culture Universe was the winner of the 2009 Dartmouth Medal from ALA's Reference and User Services Association (RUSA).

Dictionaries and Encyclopedias

1410 China: From the foundation of the empire to the Ming Dynasty. Alexandra Wetzel. 384p. University of California, 2009. $
951   DS 735

An excellent introduction to the history of China, Wetzel's book offers readers a wealth of well-annotated illustrations, lists of important terms, and carefully crafted short descriptions (one page at most) of important people, places, and concepts in the first 2000 years of Chinese history. Chapters cover people, power and public life, religion and philosophy, daily life, the world of the dead, capitals, and Buddhist cave temples. There is a map of China, a brief chronology, a list of museums with important collections of Chinese materials, and a somewhat disappointingly short index. Despite the shortcomings of the index, the breadth of the individual entries, the lavish illustrations, and the price make this an appealing book for small libraries.

1411 A concise companion to history.
Ulinka Rublack, ed. 451. Oxford, 2011. $
907.2   D13

An affordable introduction to the study of history, Rublack's work features essays from sixteen noted scholars on the state of current historical scholarship. The essays are arranged by theme—commerce, power, communication, population, gender, culture, ethnicity, science, environmental history, religion, emotions, and the power of ideas. Four additional essays look at various aspects of the history of history. The essays, while scholarly, are also accessible to the general reader and offer an excellent introduction to contemporary theory on important historical topics.

1412 Dictionary of American history. 3rd ed. Stanley I. Kutler, ed. 10v. Thomson Gale, 2002. $$$$
973   E174

Still a classic work of scholarship, the third edition of the *Dictionary of American History* reflects historical interest in social and cultural diversity in addition to the traditional emphasis on political, military, and economic themes. The articles are extensively cross-referenced and well illustrated. The ninth volume contains an archive of historical maps along with explanatory text and historical documents. The tenth volume has a learning guide and a comprehensive index. Note that there are no biographies. *Dictionary of American History* is an authoritative starting point for both scholarly and general inquiries.

1413 A dictionary of British history. John Cannon, ed. 720p. Oxford, 2009. $
941   DA34

Part of Oxford's highly regarded Paperback Reference series, Cannon's book is an excellent one-volume introduction to the history of England from 55 BC to the present. There are more than 3,800 entries arranged in dictionary format, from the Abbey theatre to Zutphen, battle of. The entries include both subjects and people and range from short paragraphs (Newcastle upon Tyne, diocese of, 53 words) to more substantive pieces (Henry VIII, 1,187 words). Also available as an e-book, the digital version offers useful links to related content and related overviews. A companion website offers access to a regularly updated set of links to websites on English history.

1414 Dictionary of historic documents. Rev. ed. George Childs Kohn, ed. 646p. Facts on File, 2003. $

016.9   D9

Kohn presents a list of historically significant documents in Western civilization from ancient times to the late twentieth century. Each entry includes a description of the document that covers its origins, content, and impact. The actual text of the document is not included. A timetable puts the documents in their historical context. Kohn includes a useful bibliography and index.

1415 Encyclopedia of Africa. Kwame Anthony Appiah and Henry Louis Gates Jr., eds. 2v. Oxford, 2010. $$

960.03   DT3

This work is a comprehensive tool for studying African history. The signed articles range from one or two paragraphs to multiple pages and cover persons, movements, subjects, concepts, themes, places, and more. Articles are supplemented with illustrations and maps when appropriate. The set begins with a chronology of important events and closes with a comprehensive index. This would be a useful book in most libraries.

1416 Encyclopedia of American history. 2nd ed. Peter C. Mancall and Gary B. Nash, eds. 11v. Facts on File, 2010. $$$$

973.03   E174

A comprehensive reference source for all aspects of American history, Mancall and Nash's work begins its presentation of American history with the volume *Three Worlds Meet: Beginnings to 1607* and moves from there through nine more volumes, ending with *Contemporary United States: 1969 to the Present*. Each volume has authoritative entries arranged in alphabetical order. The entries cover people, places, subjects, and broad themes and range from short (one to two paragraphs) to more substantial (Sir Francis Drake gets three pages, including a map). There are numerous useful illustrations, and the signed entries include short bibliographies. Each volume ends with an additional bibliography and a volume index. A further index volume offers increased access to articles. Though expensive, this is a one-stop resource for students, researchers, and the general public. Also available as a digital version.

1417 Encyclopedia of Latin America. Thomas M. Leonard, ed. 4v. Facts on File, 2010. $$

980   F1406

The set is arranged into four volumes: *The Amerindians through Foreign Colonization (Prehistory to 1560)*; *From Colonies to Independent Nations (1550s to 1820s)*; *Search for National Identity (1820s to 1900)*; and *The Age of Globalization (1900 to the Present)*. Within each volume, entries are arranged alphabetically, range from a few paragraphs to several pages, and cover people, places, and subjects. Each volume begins with a timeline and contains suggested further readings and a glossary as well as numerous illustrations. Each volume ends with a brief list of primary source documents. Because of the chronological arrangement of the volumes, it will be necessary for a user studying the broad history of a country or a topic such as art, music, or the Catholic Church to check all four volumes.

1418 Encyclopedia of Native American history. Peter C. Mancall, ed. 3v. Facts on File, 2011. $$

970   E77

Mancall's encyclopedia covers the people, places, events, and themes in the history of Native American peoples from the pre-Columbian period to the present. The three volumes are arranged alphabetically, and the main entries are followed by a list of Indian tribes recognized by the U.S. government, a selected bibliography, a comprehensive index, and a series of maps. The signed entries vary from a couple of paragraphs to a couple of pages and include suggested further readings. There are some illustrations throughout the book. The strength of the set is as an introduction to the broad topics and the important events and people in the history of Native Americans.

1419 Encyclopedia of society and culture in the Ancient World. Peter Bogucki, ed. 4v. Facts on File 2007. $$

930.1   CB311

Bogucki's four-volume set, while not inexpensive, is an excellent one-stop source for information on the ancient world, from prehistoric times to the fall of Rome. The body of the work is sixty-nine entries on cultural or societal topics discussed in terms of the following population centers: Africa, Egypt, the Middle East, Asia and the Pacific, Europe, Greece, Rome, and the Americas. Topics range from the broad and theoretical (gender, economy, social organization) to the more specific (roads and bridges, weights and measures, calendars and clocks). Illustrations, maps, and primary source documents add to the discussions. The back matter includes a glossary, a chronology arranged by region, a general bibliography, and a comprehensive index.

1420 The encyclopedia of war. Gordon Martel, ed. 5v. Wiley-Blackwell, 2012. $$$

355   U27

This ambitious five-volume set covers warfare from ancient times through medieval, early modern, modern, and contemporary conflicts. It has a global perspective. So, for example, contemporary African conflicts and ancient Chinese wars are included. Biographies of significant figures and types of weapons and tactics are also included. This title is appropriate for historians, students, and general readers.

1421 Historical dictionary of the Civil War and Reconstruction. 2nd ed. William L. Richter. 1032p. Scarecrow, 2011. $

973.7   E468

An excellent one-volume introduction to the Civil War and Reconstruction periods, the *Historical Dictionary of the Civil War and Reconstruction* defines and explains the political, judicial, economic, social, and military events and figures that shaped these two eras. There are more than 800 entries, covering the years 1844–1877. The dictionary contains a select chronology and a substantive bibliography.

1422 National Geographic visual history of the world. Douglas Brinkley. 656p. National Geographic, 2005. $

902.22   D21

Students and researchers looking for images related to historical events will find much of value in this useful compilation. The book consists of eight chapters, arranged chronologically from "Prehistory" to "The Contemporary Period." Following an introduction, the chapters are then divided into topical sections covering important events or countries in that period. The book contains more than 4,000 illustrations. A timeline across the bottom of the pages ties together the events illustrated. Sidebars expand on key topics and persons, and a useful index allows easy access to specific topics.

1423 The Oxford classical dictionary. 4th ed. Simon Hornblower, Antony Spawforth, and Esther Eidinow, eds. 1792p. Oxford, 2012. $$

938   DE5

The Oxford Classical Dictionary covers all aspects of the Greco-Roman world. It provides authoritative information on the literature, art, philosophy, mythology, science, daily life, and history of the people, places, and events of the classical period. The more than 6,000 entries in the fourth edition are arranged in an A–Z list and range from a few sentences to a page or more, depending on the subject. There is no index or illustrations. This is an indispensable resource for students and general readers interested in the Greek and Roman worlds.

1424 The Oxford companion to United States history. Paul S. Boyer, ed. 940p. Oxford, 2001. $

973   E174

This single volume offers more than 1,400 entries on the people, events, and ideas that have shaped U.S. history. The entries are arranged alphabetically, and each is followed by a short set of suggested readings. There are numerous cross-references and a comprehensive index. This is an excellent starting point for information on the history of the United States. Titles on the histories of other countries in the Oxford *Companion* series should be purchased as interest warrants.

1425 The Oxford companion to world exploration. David Buisseret, ed. 2v. Oxford, 2007. $$

910.92   G80

Another valuable title in the Oxford *Companion* series, this work compiles more than 700 entries related to world exploration, including people, events, places, and special topics such as navigation. Included in the set, and making it even more useful, are more than 300 images—maps and illustrations—from the Newberry Library collection, many in full color. The articles have reading lists, and a comprehensive index allows for quick access. This is a valuable tool for students and the general reader.

1426 The Oxford encyclopedia of the Civil War. William L. Barney. 384p. Oxford, 2011. $

973.70   E468

The alphabetically arranged entries here cover the major events, topics, and people of the Civil War era. The entries generally run to a page or more and include illustrations, cross-references, and suggested readings. A comprehensive index allows easy location of particular topics. This is an affordable and highly readable introduction to the American Civil War and will be of interest to both students and general readers.

Handbooks, Yearbooks, and Almanacs

1427 Current value of old money. Roy Davies. http://projects.exeter.ac.uk/ RDavies/arian/current/howmuch.html. Free

Davies has compiled a useful collection of links to articles, tables, databases, and calculators that allow users to begin to explore the concept of "the changes in the value of money over time." Sections of the site include "Tools and Online Sources" (arranged by country), "Historical Exchange Rates," "Prices in the Ancient World," "Treasure and Prices in Spain 1505–1650," "Financial Cost of the World Wars," and "Changes in World GDP."

1428 Famous first facts. 6th ed. Joseph Nathan Kane, Steven Anzovin, and Janet Podell, eds. 1307p. H. W. Wilson, 2007. $$

031.02   AG5

The editors arrange important first facts from American history by subject categories in chronological order of their occurrence. There are five indexes—subject, year, day, name, and geographical—making for easy access. The entries are indicated by a four-digit index number. Each fact has a brief annotation giving the details. The sixth edition adds about 1,000 new entries, along

with illustrations and sidebars highlighting select events.

1429 National Geographic almanac of American history. James Miller and John Thompson. 384p. National Geographic, 2006. $

973   E178

Unsurprisingly, this survey of American history begins with the geology of the United States and its effect on the country's history and development. This section is followed by twelve essays on topics crucial to the shaping of American society. The body of the work is divided into eleven historical eras covering the major themes and people of each era. These chapters conclude with a "World Survey" that places the period and its events in the broader context of the world. The outstanding illustrations add value to the text. Important primary source documents are presented in an appendix, and the index makes for easy access to specific topics.

1430 Notable last facts: A compendium of endings, conclusions, terminations, and final events throughout history. William B. Brahms, comp. 848p. Reference Desk Press, 2005. $$

031.02   AG105

Brahms covers more than 16,000 facts about the ends of historically important persons, events, places, or things. Entries, arranged by subject, are easily accessible through an expanded table of contents and a comprehensive index. Each entry has a brief annotation providing significant details. A useful bibliography is included.

1431 The value of a dollar: Colonial era to the Civil War, 1600–1865. Scott Derks and Tony Smith. 436p. Grey House, 2005. $$

338.5   HB235

Each chapter in this useful compendium covers a historical era by providing snapshots of key economic and historical data, selected incomes, services and fees, financial rates and exchanges, the slave trade, commodity prices, and so forth. Each chapter provides a currency conversion table listing approximate price equivalents in today's dollars. The work includes an index and bibliography.

1432 The value of a dollar: Prices and incomes in the United States, 1860–2009. 4th ed. Scott Derks. 690p. Grey House, 2009. $$

338.5   HB235

Like its companion volume, this title tracks the costs of everyday items and income in historical dollars with updated conversion charts for comparisons to modern costs. This new edition also includes expanded data on pricing trends.

Historical Atlases

1433 Atlas of American history. Gary B. Nash and Carter Smith. 346p. Facts on File, 2006. $

911   E179.5

Nash and Smith present more than 200 color maps as well as photographs and charts covering important events in American history. Coverage includes Native America, European and African heritages, colonization, westward expansion, and the twentieth century to the present. Typically the illustrations are quarter- or half-page. This is a useful collection for all libraries.

1434 Atlas of the North American Indian. 3rd ed. Carl Waldman. 450p. Checkmark Books, 2009. $

970.00   G1106

The third edition of Waldman's useful atlas contains more than 120 maps detailing "migrations, tribal locations, historical landmarks, reservations, and other important settings related to American Indians." The book is arranged by topic areas, covering ancient native peoples, ancient civilizations, native lifeways, native peoples and explorers, Indian wars, native land cessions, and contemporary native North Americans. Each chapter is further subdivided into major topics or chronological periods, making it easy for the user to locate items of interest. The text accompanying the maps is accessible to the student or general reader and offers substantive details to complement the full-color maps. Additional illustrations increase the utility of the book. The book includes a useful glossary and comprehensive index. Several appendixes offer additional information, including a chronology of Native American history, a list of the Native Nations of the United States and Canada, and a list of museums and historical and archaeological sites pertaining to Native Americans.

1435 Concise historical atlas of the U.S. Civil War. Aaron Sheehan-Dean. 128p. Oxford, 2008. $

973.70   G1201

Looking at geographic features often adds to our understanding of the political, military, and cultural events that took place in a particular time or place. The *Concise Historical Atlas of the U.S. Civil War* offers fifty maps that not only cover the important military campaigns of the war but also use data to explore the political and cultural issues that led up to and followed the conflict. Maps such as "Industrial Establishments in the United States (1860)" and "Agricultural Productivity in the United States (1860)" help to clarify the importance of existing infrastructure to the outcome of the war. The maps all have a brief introduction to set the context. A set of suggested readings and an index contribute to making this an excellent addition to most library collections.

1436 The historical atlas of the American Revolution. Ian Barnes. 223p. Routledge, 2000. $$

973.3   E208

The history of the American colonies, the American Revolution, and the early days of the American Republic is detailed here in text, full-color maps, and supporting illustrations. The atlas includes a chronology of American history from 1584 to 1820. There are also short biographical sketches of the main participants in the American Revolution. A useful bibliography and a comprehensive index round out the value of the book.

1437 Historical atlas of the United States: With original maps. Derek Hayes. 280p. University of California, 2006. $

911   G1201

Hayes uses more than 500 historical maps to present American history from the age of discovery through the early twenty-first century. In fifty-eight chapters, arranged chronologically, Hayes uses original maps to cover eras and topics such as "The First Peoples"; "Conceptions of a Continent"; "Cities of Gold, Cities of Mud"; "A Trail of Tears";

"Populating a Heartland"; "Remember the Alamo"; "A World Safe for Democracy"; "Boom, Bust, and a New Deal"; and "Good Roads Everywhere"; among others. These sections are introduced with an essay, and each map included in the section has an explanatory narrative.

1438 The new atlas of world history: Global events at a glance. John Haywood. 252p. Princeton, 2011. $

911   G1030

Haywood's atlas is made up of "49 chronologically organized political maps, each followed by a timeline, together with six more specialized maps displaying world religions, writing systems, trade routes or migrations at a particular date." The earliest map covers the period spanning 100,000–11,000 years ago, and the latest map covers 2010: "The Shifting Balance of Global Power." Each map includes a short essay setting the context for the visual display of information. A "How to Use This Book" key in the front makes for easy access to understanding how to read the maps. Each map is followed by a timeline that covers "specific events and developments in the world's cultural evolution during the years, decades or centuries leading up to the highlighted year in question." A glossary explains important concepts and terms. This is a valuable book for any collection.

1439 Perry-Castañeda Library map collection: Historical maps. University of Texas Libraries. www.lib.utexas.edu/maps/historical/. Free

The Perry-Castañeda Library Map Collection at the University of Texas at Austin has more than 250,000 maps, of which more than 11,000 have been digitized and are available through the library's website. This is a superb resource for students, researchers, and anyone interested in maps. The historical map collection linked to here is arranged first by geographic region and then alphabetically by the map subject. In addition to single maps, there are also several fully digitized historical atlases. Links to other map collections round out each list of maps in the Perry-Castañeda collection. The site's frequently-asked-questions section offers useful information on viewing and printing the maps.

1440 Routledge historical atlas of religion in America. Bret E. Carroll. 144p. Routledge, 2000. $

200.9   G1201

This source traces the history of religion in America from the indigenous peoples to modern times. It uses full-color maps as well as charts, illustrations, and text to track the diversity of the American religious experience and its relationship to the development of the country. A short list of further readings and an index support the maps.

Primary Sources

1441 Africa and the West: A documentary history. William H. Worger, Nancy L. Clark, and Edward A. Alpers, eds. 2v. Oxford, 2010. $

303.48   DT353.5

Students, researchers, and general readers interested in the interactions between Africans and the West will find much of interest here. The editors have compiled a valuable collection of primary source material covering the history of Africa and the West from the 1440s to 2008. The collection is arranged chronologically and divided into historic periods. Each chapter has an introduction that sets the stage for the documents, and each entry has a brief annotation giving important details. A comprehensive index enables quick access to specific topics or persons.

1442 American decades, primary sources. Cynthia Rose, ed. 10v. Gale, 2004. $$$$

973.91   E169.1

American Decades covers the twentieth century decade by decade in its ten volumes. Each volume includes approximately 200 full or excerpted primary source documents of importance in that period. Chapters in each volume cover the arts, medicine and health, media, education, world events, religion, business and economy, and sports. This highly useful though costly set is also available in a digital version from Gale.

1443 American memory: Historical collections. Library of Congress. http://memory.loc.gov/ammem/. Free

The digital collections at the Library of Congress

offer students, researchers, and the general public access to a wealth of material, including photographs, illustrations, sound files, and more. Users can browse by topic, time period, format, or place. The whole collection can also be searched. Each of the topical collections can also be browsed by subcollection. This is an invaluable resource for all libraries.

1444 The Avalon project: Documents in law, history, and diplomacy. Lillian Goldman Law Library, Yale University. http://avalon.law.yale.edu. Free

The Avalon Project, as defined in its "Statement of Purpose," provides "digital documents relevant to the fields of Law, History, Economics, Politics, Diplomacy and Government." This collection of primary source materials can be browsed by collection—for example, "The American Constitution—A Documentary Record," "Colonial Charters, Grants and Related Documents," or "Native Americans: Treaties with the United States"—or browsed by time period. A fascinating and wide-ranging collection of resources for students, researchers, and the general public.

1445 Daily life through American history in primary documents. Randall M. Miller, ed. 4v. Greenwood, 2011. $$
973   E161
The four volumes in the set are arranged chronologically, each presenting from about 80 to 140 important primary source documents from the time period covered. Each volume has an introduction that "offers a panoramic view of the time period." Then, separate chapters present the documents arranged in the categories of domestic life, economic and material life, intellectual life, political life, recreational life, and religious life. Each primary source document has a brief introduction. An index provides quick access to specific periods, individuals, or topics.

1446 Milestone documents in American history. Paul Finkelman, ed. 4v. Schlager Group, 2008. $$
973   E173
This set presents 133 of the most important documents in the development of the United States. The volumes are arranged chronologically, and the entries in each volume are also arranged by year. Each entry begins with an overview, an essay, and a timeline placing the document in its historical context. These are followed by a brief narrative about the author(s) of the piece followed by an explanation and analysis. Additional text looks at the audience and the impact of the document. This is followed by related documents and a bibliography. The introductory section concludes with questions for further study and a glossary, followed by the full text of the document. The final volume has a useful subject index. Other titles in this excellent series from Schlager include *Milestone Documents in World History* (2010), *Milestone Documents in African American History* (2010), and *Milestone Documents of World Religions* (2010).

19 Geography, Area Studies, and Travel

JACK O'GORMAN

The Internet is a boon to travelers. Instant information about exotic destinations, how to get there, and where to eat or stay has changed the way people travel. On the other hand, libraries may want to retain the print resources mentioned here. In the travel section, the intent is to highlight classic print sources and include a few niche titles.

Atlases
World Atlases

1447 AAA Europe road atlas. Automobile Association, 1995–. $
912   G1797.21
This atlas covers forty European countries and includes thirty district maps. Maps include cities, highways, toll roads (booth shown), tunnels, and distances in kilometers. Additional points of interest, such as castles, ruins, caves, and panoramic views, are shown. The index, including more than 30,000 towns, indicates the city, country, page, and grid location. A distance chart, in kilometers, is available for nearly sixty major European cities.

1448 Atlas of world history. Concise ed. Patrick K. O'Brien, ed. 312p. Oxford, 2007. $
911   G1030
This work reflects how the "demand for an unbiased overview of world history has steadily grown in schools, colleges, and universities, and among the general reading public." It covers not just traditional military or political topics but also ecological concerns, health and welfare of populations, and other issues. It includes coverage of the ancient world, medieval and early modern times, the age of revolution, and the twentieth century, including the status of states of the former Soviet Union. It is a valuable addition to reference collections.

1449 Goode's world atlas. 22nd ed. Howard Veregin, ed. 400p. Rand McNally, 2010. $
912   G1019
Updated and republished on a regular schedule, Goode's is an excellent small desk atlas at a reasonable price. Popular with students, it is frequently used to illustrate reports. A large variety of thematic and regional maps are included. Newer ones include HIV infection, military power, women's rights, food aid, and telecommunications. An extensive pronunciation index includes page references as well as latitude and longitude.

1450 Google maps. http://maps.google.com. Free
A cool feature from Google, Google Maps is an atlas for the Internet age. It uses maps, satellite imagery,

and street views of cities all over the Earth. Everybody flies to his or her own home, but it can also be used to locate landmarks, schools, or parks. Google Earth (www.google.com/earth/) offers yet another way to see the planet.

1451 MapQuest. MapQuest. www.mapquest.com. Free

This site allows you to get directions and a map to places within the United States and Canada. Includes general world coverage. The company began by producing free road maps for gas stations, launched its website in 1996, and is now a well-known and popular site for directions.

1452 National Geographic atlas of the world. 9th ed. National Geographic Society. National Geographic Society, 2011. $$

912   G1021

A total of seventy-two maps of the world and physical, political, thematic, and city maps are illustrated in this world atlas. Maps of space, ocean floors, and the poles are also included. Additionally, 192 nations and territories are summarized with brief statistics, flag, location on globe, and a description. An index includes the plate and grid locations. Those who purchase also receive access to the online interactive version of the plate maps.

1453 Oxford atlas of the world. 19th ed. Keith Lye. 448p. Oxford, 2012. $

912   G1021

An excellent resource, this work features sections on the universe and solar system, climate, geology, landscape, environment, demography, agriculture, and manufacturing and trade. A selection of sixty-six city maps is also included.

North American Atlases

1454 The atlas of Canada. Natural Resources Canada. http://atlas.nrcan.gc.ca/site/english/. Free

This online atlas includes maps of people, environment, climate, health, and the economy of Canada. An archive on the site includes previous editions

of this atlas in addition to elections, geology, and other features of Canada. Zoom, download, and printing features are available. A new version of this atlas is being developed by Natural Resources Canada to comply with the Web Standards for the Government of Canada.

1455 Atlas of the United States. H. J. de Blij, ed. 208p. Oxford, 2006. $

912.73   G1200

This precise and beautifully illustrated atlas includes U.S. and North American statistics; thematic maps, charts, and diagrams on North American geography; maps of the fifty U.S. states; thirty-four U.S. city maps; and summaries of each of the fifty states, with photos, maps, flags, and statistics. An index of 30,000 place-names includes letter/figure grid references and latitude and longitude. New digital cartographic map techniques make the maps appear three-dimensional.

1456 The Canadian atlas online. Canadian Geographic Enterprises. www.canadiangeographic.ca/atlas/. Free

Produced by the Royal Canadian Geographical Society, this online atlas "brings cartography to life with exciting graphics and animation." Maps zoom in to a range of twenty kilometers. Includes themes, games, and a learning center. Available in English or French.

1457 National atlas of the United States of America. U.S. Geological Survey. www.nationalatlas.gov. Free

912   GA1200

This first appeared in 1970 as *The National Atlas of the United States*, published by the U.S. Geological Survey. In addition to demographic, economic, and sociocultural maps that equal in cartographic skill those of any other atlas, this resource contains a unique section of "administrative" maps reflecting changing configurations of governmental districts, functions, and regions. Subject and place-name indexes.

1458 Rand McNally commercial atlas and marketing guide. Rand McNally, 1876–. Annual. $$

912   G1019

Primarily an atlas of the United States, with large, detailed, clear maps. Includes many statistical tables of population, business and manufacturers, agriculture, and other commercial features, such as indicators of market potential.

1459 The road atlas: United States, Canada, and Mexico. Rand McNally, 1924–. Annual. $

912.7   G1201

A classic road atlas for libraries and automobiles alike, the Rand McNally atlas offers road maps of each state in the United States and each province in Canada and a general map of Mexico. Cities, highways, toll roads, airports, points of interest, hospitals, rest areas, and service areas are included. An index of place-names and mileage/minute charts are included. Large-print version is available.

Dictionaries, Encyclopedias, and Gazetteers

1460 The Cambridge gazetteer of the United States and Canada: A dictionary of places. 1st paperback ed. Archie Hobson, ed. 743p. Cambridge, 2011. $

917.3   E154

This title is a paperback reprint of the 1995 edition. It includes all incorporated municipalities of more than 10,000 (United States) or 8,000 (Canada) people. This work was, in the words of the preface, "written to be read." After locating each place, the entries give qualitative information that might be of interest. It also includes extensive cross-referencing.

1461 The Columbia gazetteer of the world. 2nd ed. Saul B. Cohen, ed. 3v. Columbia, 2008. $$$

910.3   G103.5

This three-volume set continues the classic *Columbia Lippincott Gazetteer of the World* (1952), long a standard in many ready-reference collections. It includes more than 160,000 entries, 30,000 of which are new to this edition. Entries include a pronunciation guide and

latitude and longitude. The source should retain its place on a reference shelf in libraries of all sizes.

1462 The concise dictionary of world place-names. 2nd ed. John Everett-Heath. Oxford, 2010. CP$

910   G103.5

The second edition of this source is available only as an online book from Oxford University Press. More than 8,000 names from around the world, including countries, regions, deserts, bodies of water, islands, and ruins, are included. Names are followed by the location—country, state, region—and include alternate spellings and a brief description of the history and origin of the place. Place-names with multiple locations, like Victoria, are numerically listed within the entry. There is a glossary but no pronunciation guide.

1463 The concise geography encyclopedia. Clive Gifford. 320p. Kingfisher, 2005. $

910   G63

Written and illustrated with children in mind, this encyclopedia is beautifully illustrated with color photographs, flags, and maps of the countries of the world. It is arranged by world regions and then by country. Each highlighted geographic area receives one page, which includes basic geographic, population, and government information; a description of the area; and color illustrations. An index, world map, and Earth statistics are also included.

1464 A dictionary of geography. 4th ed. Susan Mayhew. 551p. Oxford, 2009. $

910   G63

More than 6,400 definitions for human and physical geography terms are included, many unique to this dictionary. Black-and-white illustrations and a country fact finder with basic demographic data for forty countries are included. Cross-references are noted with an asterisk within entries. Available online as part of the Oxford Reference package.

1465 Encyclopedia of world geography. R. W. McColl, ed. 3v. Checkmark Books, 2005. $$

910   G63

This encyclopedia takes a global view on geographic

and geopolitical topics. Locations, like the Mekong River; topics, like desertification; and concepts, like human geography, are covered. Suitable for public, school, and university libraries.

1466 Historical gazetteer of the United States. Paul T. Hellmann. 865p. Routledge, 2005. $$

911 E154

This source states its goal to be "aggregating American history by place." Entries are arranged alphabetically by state and then by location within a state. Covers historical events that happened in towns and cities, including every county seat in the United States. Consideration for inclusion is based on a town's historical value rather than its population.

1467 Merriam-Webster's geographical dictionary. 3rd ed. 1361p. Merriam-Webster, 2007. $

910 G103.5

This inexpensive dictionary is perfect for the small reference collection. Covers 54,000 entries with 250 maps. Includes continents, countries, and regions and a pronunciation guide. Libraries that own the 1997 edition may not need to upgrade to the 2007 edition.

1468 Nicknames and sobriquets of U.S. cities, states, and counties. 3rd ed. Joseph Nathan Kane and Gerard L. Alexander. 429p. Scarecrow, 2003. $

917.3 E155

This fun source lists nicknames of cities, counties, and states. Indexed geographically by city and state and alphabetically by nickname. Just where is the Gem of the Cascades, or the Desert Babylon?

1469 The Penguin dictionary of geography. 3rd ed. Audrey N. Clark. 467p. Penguin, 2003. $

910 G63

Thousands of definitions for terms used by geographers, including physical and human geography, are included. Cross-references appear in all caps within entries, and several black-and-white illustrations are included. There are many distinctive entries compared to other geography dictionaries.

Handbooks, Yearbooks, and Almanacs

1470 Background notes. U.S. Department of State, Bureau of Public Affairs. www.state .gov/r/pa/ei/bgn/. Free

This searchable and A–Z list provides information on the people, history, government, economy, and tourism of more than 200 countries. Statistical data on geography, people, government, and the economy are listed first, followed by short narratives about the people, culture, political conditions, and foreign relations. Travel information is also included. Hyperlinks to other economic, government, and travel information sites make this resource even more useful.

1471 Country study series. Library of Congress. http://lcweb2.loc.gov/frd/cs/. Free

Formerly *Area Handbooks*, this classic series includes books on individual countries with basic facts about social, economic, political, and military conditions. They include extensive bibliographies and contain a wealth of information at a very affordable price. Although many print titles are dated and should be weeded from reference collections, updated versions are available online via the Federal Research Division of the Library of Congress.

1472 Europa world year book. 2v. Europa, 1959–. Annual. $$$$

391.18 JN1

This title is the best annual directory of information on the nations of the world. For each country it includes demographic and economic statistics and facts about constitution and government, political parties, press, trade and industry, publishers, and so forth. Also incorporates a substantive section with listings and information about international organizations.

Travel Guides

1473 The complete guide to bed and breakfasts, inns, and guesthouses in the United States, Canada, and

worldwide. Pamela Lanier. Ten Speed Press, 1997–. Annual. $

917.3   TX907.2

More than 4,500 bed-and-breakfasts in the United States and Canada are included in this inexpensive annual compilation. Arranged by state, each entry contains name and contact information; room information (including children, pets, smoking, and accessible conditions); and a description of the breakfast and other amenities. Special accommodations like hot tubs, weddings, themed dinners, games, community areas, and other events are included.

1474 Expedia. Expedia. www.expedia.com. Free

The Internet has been a boon to travelers looking for discounts. Places to stay and ways to get there are available through this site. Build your trip, plan your trip, and, of course, go shopping on your trip. Other travel sites include Travelocity (www.travelocity.com), Orbitz (www.orbitz.com), and Priceline (www.priceline.com).

1475 Gay travel A to Z. Ferrari International, 1996–. Annual. $

306.766   HQ75.25

A world travel guide featuring tour companies, cruises, hotels, restaurants, bars, dance clubs, and other destinations that cater to gays and lesbians. A trip and events calendar highlights international gay and lesbian events with dates and locations. *See also* "LGBT Studies," in chapter 4.

1476 Globetrotting pets: An international travel guide. David J. Forsythe. 413p. Island, 2003. $

636.08   SF415.45

Compiled in one location are the international regulations for importing pets into the countries of the world. Forsythe includes the regulations, contact information, and useful websites for each country. Additional information includes pet travel supplies, forms and health information, and exotic pet travel. *See also* "Pets," in chapter 11.

1477 Parks directory of the United States. 6th ed. Julia Leeper, Pearline Jaikumar, and Arty Tosh, eds. 1137p. Rich's Business Directories, 2012. $$

917.3   E160

State parks can be hidden jewels. But how can your readers find them? This directory lists national parks, wildlife refuges, and recreational areas, including state parks and parks in Canada. Entries include facilities, activities, and accommodations. Contact information and websites are included.

1478 Roadfood: The coast-to-coast guide to 800 of the best barbecue joints, lobster shacks, ice cream parlors, highway diners, and much, much more. 8th ed. Jane Stern and Michael Stern. 569p. Clarkson Potter, 2011. $

If a great local restaurant is what you're seeking, then this title can serve as your guide. Entries are arranged geographically and include a review of the author's dining experience. I recommend driving out of your way to find a place listed here. You won't be disappointed. Great for either circulating or reference collections.

1479 Traveling with your pet: The AAA pet book. AAA. Annual. $

917.3   SF415.45

More than 14,000 pet-friendly AAA-rated lodgings and campgrounds in the United States and Canada are listed alphabetically by state and city in this pet travel guide. Entries include the name and contact information, AAA star rating, and amenity icons. A section on additional pet-friendly places includes information on dog parks, animal clinics, service-animal policies, attractions with pet amenities, and national public lands.

1480 Ultimate guide to the world's best wedding and honeymoon destinations: A comprehensive guide designed to assist you in choosing the perfect destination, whether it be for the most romantic wedding ceremony, or for an unforgettable honeymoon. Elizabeth Lluch and Alex Lluch. 300p. Wedding Solutions, 2004. $

910.20   GT2798

The title says it all for this guide, which provides a description and color photographs of more than 150 wedding and honeymoon resorts around the world. The resort information includes contact information, room rates, romantic features, attractions, facilities, and wedding services offered.

Additional travel tips including entry requirements and marriage licenses are discussed.

1481 Woodall's North America campground directory: The complete guide to campgrounds, RV parks, service centers, and attractions. Woodall, 1967–. Annual. $

917.59   GV198.56

This comprehensive directory is divided geographically into eastern and western sections that include Canada and Mexico. Road maps of each state and province show location of each site listed. Brief descriptions are accompanied by evaluative ratings of facilities and recreation. Alphabetical index of sites. Also available in eastern, western, and other regional editions.

ABOUT THE CONTRIBUTORS
TO THE EIGHTH EDITION

Jack O'Gorman is a Reference and Instruction Librarian and Associate Professor at the University of Dayton's Roesch Library, where he is also responsible for collection development and liaison work in engineering, physics, math, and geology. With more than thirty years' experience in university, government, and business libraries, Jack has an in-depth knowledge of reference sources. He has a bachelor's degree in mathematics from Walsh University and an MLS from St. John's University. He chaired the editorial board of *Reference Books Bulletin* from 2001 to 2004 and continues as a member of that board. He has served on the award committees for Outstanding Reference Sources and the Dartmouth Medal, both of which are offered by the Reference and User Services Association of ALA. He is coeditor of the third edition of *Recommended Reference Books in Paperback* and has contributed to the fifth through eighth editions of *Reference Sources for Small and Medium-Sized Libraries*, the last two as editor.

Drew Alfgren has been a Reference and Instruction Librarian at University of Maryland, Baltimore County (UMBC), since 1999 and responsible for reference collection management since 2006. He received his MSLIS from Drexel University in 1994 and an MA in Historical Studies from UMBC in 2004. Prior to coming to the Kuhn Library, he worked in public, private, and academic libraries both large and small, getting a variety of experience in reference, circulation, serials, and cataloging. He is a member of the American Library Association, the History of Science Society, and the History of Earth Sciences Society and is currently serving on the award committee for the ALA Dartmouth Medal.

Donald Altschiller is a librarian at Boston University and has also worked at Harvard and Brandeis. A contributor to the seventh edition of *Reference Sources for Small and Medium-Sized Libraries*, he has also written articles for almost a dozen subject encyclopedias. The research for his book *Animal-Assisted Therapy* (ABC-CLIO/Greenwood, 2011) was partially supported by an ALA Carnegie-Whitney Award.

Maureen Barry became a Social Sciences Librarian at Wright State University in Dayton, Ohio, after earning her MLS at the University of North Carolina at Chapel Hill in 2005. In early 2007, Maureen took on a new role at WSU as First Year Experience Librarian. She majored in Sport Management at Bowling Green State University, where she earned her BS in Education in 1999. Maureen blogs at www.libraries.wright.edu/servicelearning.

Barbara M. Bibel has a BA in French from UCLA, an MA in Romance Languages from Johns Hopkins, and an MLS from UC Berkeley. She is certified as a Consumer Health Information Specialist by the Medical Library Association. She is an active book reviewer and former chair of the *Reference Books Bulletin* Editorial Board and of ALA's Collection Development and Evaluation Section (CODES). She received the Isidore Gilbert Mudge Award in 2007. She contributed to the sixth and seventh editions of *Reference Sources for Small and Medium-Sized Libraries*. Currently, she is Reference Librarian/Consumer Health Information Specialist at Oakland Public Library in Oakland, California.

Erica Coe is head of Instruction Services at University of Washington Tacoma. Her subject areas include Business, Criminal Justice, Nursing, and Social Work. She was a contributor to the seventh edition of *Reference Sources for Small and Medium-Sized Libraries*. She serves as a contributing editor for the "Economics and Business" section of ALA's *Guide to Reference* and authors the "Music Reviews" section of *Magazines for Libraries*. She received her MLS degree from Indiana University in 1999.

Terese DeSimio is a Science / Web Services Librarian in the Reference and Instruction Department at the Wright State University Libraries. She has an MLIS from Kent State University and a BS in Biomedical Engineering from Wright State University. Her prior publications include a chapter in *E-Reference Context and Discoverability in Libraries: Issues and Concepts* (2012), and an article for *Booklist* titled "Reference on the Web: Common Health Concerns." She was also a contributor to the seventh edition of *Reference Sources for Small and Medium-Sized Libraries*.

Carole Dyal is the Conservator for the University of Connecticut Libraries. She has been an active member of the American Institute for Conservation since the 1980s and an active member of the American Library Association since the 1990s. Her BA is from the University of Illinois and her MLS from the University of Rhode Island. Carole is coauthor of *Conservation Treatment Procedures: A Manual of Step-by-Step Procedures for the Maintenance and Repair of Library Materials*. She contributed to both the sixth and seventh editions of *Reference Sources for Small and Medium-Sized Libraries*.

Joanna Gadsby is a Reference and Instruction Librarian at the University of Maryland, Baltimore County. She holds a BA in Human Development from St. Mary's College of Maryland, an MEd in Curriculum and Instruction from Loyola College in Maryland, and an MLIS from the University of Maryland, College Park. She worked as an elementary educator for ten years prior to becoming a reference librarian.

Emily A. Hicks is Associate Professor and Director of Information Acquisition and Organization at the University of Dayton. She is the subject selector and liaison for music. She was a contributor to the seventh edition of *Reference Sources for Small and Medium-Sized Libraries*. She earned her MLS from the University of Kentucky and BA from Transylvania University.

Carolyn M. Mulac was formerly Division Chief, General Information Services, at the Chicago Public Library and has more than thirty years' experience in reference work. An active member of ALA's Reference and User Services Association (RUSA), she has served on a number of committees and chaired the *Reference Books Bulletin* Editorial Board, the Dartmouth Medal Committee, and the Wilson Indexes Committee. Mulac received an AM from the Graduate Library School of the University of Chicago and a BA in English and Philosophy from Calumet College of St. Joseph. She reviews books on the performing arts for *Library Journal* and reference books for *Booklist* and contributed to the sixth and seventh editions of *Reference Sources for Small and Medium-Sized Libraries*. In 2008, she received the Illinois Library Association's Reference Services Award. She is the author of *Fundamentals of Reference* (ALA, 2012).

Sheila Nash is the Senior Librarian in the Art, Music, Recreation, and Rare Books Department at the Los Angeles Public Library's Central Library. She has been in this position since 1986, soon after the two devastating fires at the Central Library. Her career at the Los Angeles Public Library began in 1984 in what is now called Access Services, and she then worked for more than two years with the "Save the Books" campaign. She contributed to the seventh edition of *Reference Sources for Small and Medium-Sized Libraries*.

Mary Ellen Quinn was the editor of the *Reference Books Bulletin* section of *Booklist* for fifteen years, as well as being the managing editor of Booklist Online for five years. Prior to that, she worked for nineteen years at the Chicago Public Library, where she had positions in collection development, branch management, and acquisitions, as well as at the reference desks of several branches and departments. From 1985 to 1989, she was a member of the *Reference Books Bulletin* Editorial Board, which she chaired from 1989 to 1991. She also served on the RUSA CODES Executive Board, the RQ Editorial Advisory Board, and the Dartmouth Medal Committee, among others. She has a BA in English from the University of Michigan, an MA in English from the University of Toronto, and an MLS degree from the University of Michigan. She received the Louis Shores-Oryx Press Award in 2001.

Emma Roberts is originally from the United Kingdom, where she gained her BA in Art History and MA in Information and Library Studies. On arrival in the United States, she was a Graduate Intern in Collections Information Planning at the J. Paul Getty Museum, and then went on to work as a consultant for a museums collections management software company. She has held the position of Librarian III/Subject Specialist in the Art, Music, and Recreation and Rare Books Departments at Los Angeles Public Library since 2005. Prior to that, she was at the Studio City Branch Library for three years. Emma is an Editorial Advisory Board Member for the journal *References Services Review* and a peer reviewer for *Art Documentation*.

Kathryn Sullivan has worked as a librarian at the University of Maryland, Baltimore County, since 2002, first as a Reference and Instruction Librarian and currently as Assistant Head of Reference. She received an MLS from the University of Maryland, College Park, in 1998. Prior to working at UMBC, she worked as a Reference Librarian at Towson University. A member of the American Library Association and the Association of College and Research Libraries, she is also an active member of the Maryland Division of the Association of College and Research Libraries.

Barry Trott is the Digital Services Director at the Williamsburg (VA) Regional Library. He oversees all digital collections, the library website and social media, and the technical services department. He earned his MSLS from the Catholic University of America School of Library and Information Science in 1997 and has worked since then at the Williamsburg Regional Library as reference librarian and as readers' services librarian prior to becoming division director. Barry is past president of the American Library Association's Reference and User Services Association (RUSA) and is editor of *Reference and User Services Quarterly*. He writes for the NoveList database and is the series editor for Libraries Unlimited's Read On series and author of *Read On . . . Crime Fiction* (2008). He is also an adjunct faculty member for the library school at the Catholic University of America. In 2007, Barry was awarded both the Public Library Association's Allie Beth Martin Award and the RUSA Margaret E. Monroe Library Adult Services Award in recognition for his work in readers' advisory services.

Sarah Barbara Watstein has worked in academic libraries for more than thirty years, including both public and private institutions on both coasts. She began her career at California State University, Long Beach, and continued at New York University, Hunter College, Virginia Commonwealth University, and UCLA prior to relocating to Wilmington, North Carolina, in May 2010. Watstein currently serves as University Librarian at University of North Carolina Wilmington. Along with Eleanor Mitchell, Watstein coedits *Reference Services Review*. Watstein has published extensively in two broad areas—academic librarianship and HIV/AIDS. She has held and holds a variety of leadership positions within the American Library Association. Her professional service has focused on three areas—publishing, reference and user services, and women's studies. A native New Englander, Watstein received her BA from Northwestern, her MLS from UCLA, and an MPA from New York University.

Index

Numbers in bold refer to entry numbers. Numbers in roman type refer to mentions in annotations of other works.

CPSIA information can be obtained
at www.ICGtesting.com
Printed in the USA
FSOW03n2040310317
32601FS

9 780838 912126